FRENCH DIVORCE FICTION FROM THE
REVOLUTION TO THE FIRST WORLD WAR

LEGENDA

LEGENDA, founded in 1995 by the European Humanities Research Centre of the University of Oxford, is now a joint imprint of the Modern Humanities Research Association and Maney Publishing. Titles range from medieval texts to contemporary cinema and form a widely comparative view of the modern humanities, including works on Arabic, Catalan, English, French, German, Greek, Italian, Portuguese, Russian, Spanish, and Yiddish literature. An Editorial Board of distinguished academic specialists works in collaboration with leading scholarly bodies such as the Society for French Studies and the British Comparative Literature Association.

MHRA

The Modern Humanities Research Association (MHRA) encourages and promotes advanced study and research in the field of the modern humanities, especially modern European languages and literature, including English, and also cinema. It also aims to break down the barriers between scholars working in different disciplines and to maintain the unity of humanistic scholarship in the face of increasing specialization. The Association fulfils this purpose primarily through the publication of journals, bibliographies, monographs and other aids to research.

Maney Publishing is one of the few remaining independent British academic publishers. Founded in 1900 the company has offices both in the UK, in Leeds and London, and in North America, in Philadelphia. Since 1945 Maney Publishing has worked closely with learned societies, their editors, authors, and members, in publishing academic books and journals to the highest traditional standards of materials and production.

French Divorce Fiction from the Revolution to the First World War

❖

Nicholas White

For Holly Christine Woodson

with Love, Nick

March 2013

LEGENDA

Modern Humanities Research Association and Maney Publishing
2013

Published by the
Modern Humanities Research Association and Maney Publishing
1 Carlton House Terrace
London SW1Y 5AF
United Kingdom

LEGENDA is an imprint of the
Modern Humanities Research Association and Maney Publishing

Maney Publishing is the trading name of W. S. Maney & Son Ltd,
whose registered office is at Suite 1C, Joseph's Well, Hanover Walk, Leeds LS3 1AB

ISBN 9-781-907975-47-9

First published 2013

Printed in the UK by Charlesworth Press

Cover: 875 Design

Copy-Editor: Richard Correll

CONTENTS

Acknowledgements   ix

Introduction: Sociology, Epistemology and Modern Marriage   1

1   The History of Divorce from the Revolution to the First World War   25

2   Between Mimesis and Idealism   85

3   Jealousy before Proust   106

4   Famous Fathers and Grumpy Daughters   141

5   Novel Series and Serial Lives   165

    Conclusion   179

    Bibliography   184

    Index   190

FOR NIKOLA

ACKNOWLEDGEMENTS

This book has been roughly a decade in the making, and so the long list of friends and colleagues who have endured conversations with me on the subject of human discontent will have to go unenumerated. As one of them says, 'At least you don't work on commas in Proust,' and it is true that family life seems to be a topic on which we all have opinions to express. Indeed, the more our lives resemble those of characters in the novels I study in this book, the more expert on family life we apparently take ourselves to be.

With the irony demanded by my book's theme, I thank two nuclear families: the one I grew up in, with my brothers and parents; the other I now inhabit, with Nikola and our children, Greta and Jonathan. Elsewhere in Cambridge, I owe debts of an institutional kind to the School of Arts and Humanities, the Faculty of Modern and Medieval Languages, and the Master, Fellows and staff of Emmanuel College. From 2008 to 2011, when much of the work on this project came to fruition, I served as Chair of the Faculty, and so it is with a particular sense of camaraderie that I thank all its academics, administrators and support staff. As I write, I am reminded of the pertinence of the intellectual experience that the College has provided by recollecting the words of the recently deceased Carlos Fuentes in his lecture at his eightieth birthday celebrations in Emmanuel in 2008: 'Even in a matrimonial bed, there is a frontier.' I am very grateful to MML students, past and present, from the College and the Faculty, with whom it has been a delight to work; the undergraduates are now half my age, but still twice as quick-witted. Profound gratitude is offered to three who have shared their doctoral work with me: Andrew Counter, Claire White and Edmund Birch.

I have worked in a range of libraries, but it is with particular affection that I thank the staff of three local ones: the Emmanuel College Library, the Modern and Medieval Languages Faculty Library and the University Library. Parts of Chapter 4 first appeared in *Nineteenth-Century French Studies*, 30 (2001–02) and *Modern Language Review*, 96 (2001); I am grateful to the editors of both journals for permission to reproduce this material. At Legenda, Graham Nelson has been an immensely supportive editor, and Richard Correll's copy-editing has been invaluable.

Finally, I would like to thank wider scholarly communities which have provided me with many opportunities to talk about my research: first, colleagues in France who have listened to me as far north as Cerisy and as far south as Montpellier; second, those in North America whom I have met at the Nineteenth-Century French Studies colloquium since 1995 and whose friendship is much appreciated; third, my home from home, the Society of Dix-Neuviémistes, based in the UK and Ireland, and not least its past presidents, Susan Harrow, Tim Unwin, and Robert

Lethbridge. The latter's friendship and mentorship, dating back to the mid-1980s, have lasted longer than many of the marriages I describe in this book. I have co-edited the Society's journal, *Dix-Neuf*, since its very first number in 2003, and have gained immeasurably from such close engagement with the work of literally scores of colleagues in the field. Indeed, the NCFS and SDN communities have provided metaphorical homes and families much more happy and fulfilling than the fictional ones to be found in the chapters of this book.

N.J.W., Cambridge, July 2012

INTRODUCTION

Sociology, Epistemology and Modern Marriage

Critical interest in the connection between narrative and desire is, of course, much older than Freud, and is still manifest in the work of numerous modern critics such as Peter Brooks and Catherine Belsey. More particularly, in recent decades critics have stressed how nineteenth-century European fiction exhibits a specific fascination with adultery.[1] In different permutations of narratological, ideological, feminist and psychoanalytical reading, these accounts stress the problematic nature of the adulterous wife, alongside male fears of uncertain paternity and fantasies of seduction. All stress the significance of the French fictional tradition too, and in particular Flaubert. Traditionally adultery had provided an outlet for discontent within the marriage structure; with the advent of the Loi Naquet in 1884, divorce provided a means of disposing of that very structure. It is the argument of this book that the divorce question offered French fiction a radically novel way of breaking the mould of the traditional family and recasting the limits of its narratives.

The aim of this book is to analyse the ways in which divorce informed the development of French fiction until the First World War. Except for one or two specific periods, such as the revolutionary years in France, divorces were extremely rare in Western society until the late nineteenth century. Indeed, I will argue that in France the divorce question was intimately related to the rhythm of revolution. The initial divorce law of 1792 provided a remarkably radical reflection of the ideal of *liberté*, only to be curtailed by the Napoleonic Code and quashed by the Restoration in 1816. This 'return to family values' received the intellectual support of social theorists such as Bonald, but in 1830, 1848 and 1871 the question of divorce was raised again and again, only to be lost in the maelstrom of the moment, not least because it was often proposed by feminist activists and associated with marginal interests in the minds of decision-makers and opinion-formers. During the 1860s the development of the modern feminist movement in France provided a political context in which the issue could be repositioned.

The Commune failed to realize many of its aspirations, but its residual radicalism was not forgotten by politicians of the Third Republic such as Alfred Naquet, Jewish deputy for Vaucluse. Though the divorce project was only one aspect of this remarkable polymath's career in science as well as politics, Naquet's reformist zeal was particularly energetic in this domain. He prepared the ground for his legislative proposals not only by making parliamentary addresses but also by touring the country. The written word was adopted, too, in newspaper articles and in book form. Of particular interest to this present book is the relation Naquet fostered with the field of literary production. The debate leading to the new law had explicitly engaged creative writers on both sides: for example, Alexandre Dumas *fils* supporting the 'éléphant indien' of divorce whose shoulders were broad enough to bear the brunt of the social problems it addressed; Paul Féval, author of the popular *Le Bossu*, exclaiming in another title *Pas de divorce!* Only in 1884 did Naquet succeed in pushing through a compromise bill, reformed by fresh legislation in 1886 which, amongst other things, forbade press reporting of divorce cases. Indeed, one of the most provocative aspects of divorce was the way in which it threatened to expose to the public gaze the supposedly private matters of family life. Fiction, however, knew no such boundaries, and much of the literary response to the new laws reflected doubts on the part of progressives about the viability of Naquet's compromises as well as a conservative critique of divorce *per se*.

Social and legal historians have long displayed a fascination with the topic of divorce.[2] Given the commonplace that the novel has provided a vital space in which modern societies have analysed marriage and love, one would expect the debate surrounding the advent of divorce in the nineteenth century to have influenced the plot shapes of family fiction. Yet it is only in recent years that we have observed a mushrooming of critical interest in the literature of divorce in the English-speaking world.[3] But there is simply no book, in English or in French, on the considerable corpus of French divorce fiction which surrounds the Loi Naquet.

In the words of Phillips, 'One of the paradoxes of modern Western society is the simultaneous popularity of marriage and divorce,' and French culture still exerts an ambivalent fascination, as a country where both traditional Catholic family values and the sexual alternatives implicit in the values of the secular Republic have vied for supremacy.[4] Rarely was this more acute than in the French debate on divorce in the final decades of the nineteenth century, which acted as a prelude to the conflict between Church and State that boiled over at the turn of the century in the wake of the Dreyfus Affair. And nowhere was this tension articulated more precisely than in the literary life of the national culture.

It is my argument that the late nineteenth-century French divorce debates which led to the Loi Naquet of 1884 crystallize an epistemological tension in European thought between, on the one hand, an association of truth with origins and, on the other, the nascent sense that the truth of the self might be created rather than discovered. The important tension here lies in the fact that these quests for truth travel in contrary directions. The truth of origins takes us back to a past which can be excavated, back to where (in a double sense) truth lies. According to this model, it is not so much that 'the truth is out there' but rather that the truth lies underneath! The truth of self-creation, however, is concerned not with stripping away the palimpsestic layers of personal, urban or archaeological histories, but instead with the manufacture of a future truth, the self that one might become. Along this future-oriented road lie such wildly diverse twentieth-century phenomena as the philosophy of existentialism, gender's troubling of sex as chronicled by Judith Butler, and, most significantly for the question of divorce, two sociological concepts: first, Anthony Giddens's notion of life politics as a reflexive project of self-actualization, and second, Zygmunt Bauman's notion of liquid modernity. All of these dream of a space for resistance to what New Historicism calls self-fashioning (in which identity and behaviour are constructed in accordance with the accepted standards of the social doxa). The utopian end of this second paradigm of self-reinvention might even dream of the 'a-paradigmatic' state of perpetual paradox. Such utopias seem distant, however, in the divorce fiction we shall study, where heterosexual desire not only needs but wants its own staging posts, *points de repère* and cartographical legibility. In other words, divorce not only undoes marriage but promises the possibility of further marriage. The temporal framework of this tension between paradigms which move backwards or forwards speaks eloquently to the temporality of the romance plot, which, in the divorce narratives I shall explore, permutes the traditional sense of where married love begins and ends.

It is hard to resist the notion that it is in the reordering of the family that the shapes of plots and the shapes of lives meet. Comedies of the Molière variety we expect to culminate in the consummation, or at least promise, of marriage. Novels of adultery unfold in the wake of a wedding, either in the plot's pre-history (Julien Sorel entering the Rênal family in media res) or in the early stages of the plot (Emma Bovary's wedding cake almost collapsing under the weight of its burdensome symbolism). In either event, the adultery plot interrogates the origins of such a marriage, and habitually associates wifely adultery with the curtailment of female choice in traditional society. Marriage may be arranged; happiness, it seems, cannot. The tragic path of such classic fiction often leads to that other archetypal ending, the death of the protagonist (wanton women such as Emma Bovary and Anna Karenina punished by narratives which critique the stuffiness of their marital context but refuse to indulge unambivalently their heroine's desire for air). In both the marriage and the death ending, the family is redefined in emotional and financial arenas.[5] The family (and its story) are defined by the very patterns of perpetuation and rupture which they determine.

Divorce, of course, provides a third moment at which the family is redefined in affective and pecuniary contexts. Feelings and funds are redirected all at once. The Third Republic novels which we shall examine in greater detail in subsequent chapters argue for or against divorce in manifest fashions. Modest and sometimes immodest proposals for marriage reform infuse the novel of adultery more generally. This often entails a redefinition of how marriages should begin: namely, an interrogation of dowries and marriage contracts, and a critique of the father's right to impose on his daughter the groom of his choosing. In their more radical variants, such novels ask — if only by implication — the following question: how should marriages end? By death alone? Or also, in extremis, by divorce, before 'death do us part'?

Indeed, marriage has often been understood in terms of beginnings and endings. As a complement to the marital expression *faire une fin*, we might quote the opening lines of the finale (in other words, the beginning of the end) of *Middlemarch* (1871–72) by George Eliot:

> Every limit is a beginning as well as an ending. Who can quit young lives after being long in company with them, and not desire to know what befell them in their after-years? For the fragment of a life, however typical, is not

> the sample of an even web: promises may not be kept, and an ardent outset
> may be followed by declension; latent-powers may find their long-awaited
> opportunity; a past error may urge a grand retrieval. Marriage, which has
> been the bourne of so many narratives, is still a great beginning, as it was to
> Adam and Eve, who kept their honeymoon in Eden, but had their first little
> one among the thorns and thistles of the wilderness. It is still the beginning of
> the home epic — the gradual conquest or irremediable loss of that complete
> union which makes the advancing years a climax, and age the harvest of sweet
> memories in common.[6]

The very notions of divorce and pre-marital flirtation were seen to challenge the
traditional life plot (particularly of women) which charted a linear path through
stages of respectability — from innocent girlhood via pre-marital virginity to the
dutiful imperatives of wifely and motherly love. Both divorce and pre-marital
flirtation exposed the possibility not only of sexual transgression during marriage
(as in the novel of adultery) but of sex before or after marriage. In a yet more radical
way than the already problematic figure of the widow, the divorcee provided a new
way of reshaping the feminine plot, as the possibility of remarriage legislated for a
chain of feminine desires rather than a singular love.

Divorce provides a way of precipitating the logic of permutation which has always
characterized love plots. Permutation's metaphors are many: from the deterministic
force of chemical bonding in Goethe's *Elective Affinities* to the common figure of
the dance (where, as in *La Princesse de Clèves*, partners conjoin, separate and swap).
Divorce promises and threatens to impose a public outcome on such shenanigans.
It points towards both the newly found stasis of remarriage and the potential for
mobility in such a new marriage. The literary limitations of the divorce plot are felt
most extremely by Briony in Ian McEwan's novel, *Atonement*:

> She vaguely knew that divorce was an affliction, but she did not regard it as a
> proper subject, and gave it no thought. It was a mundane unravelling that could
> not be reversed, and therefore offered no opportunities to the storyteller: it
> belonged in the realm of disorder. Marriage was the thing, or rather, a wedding
> was, with its formal neatness of virtue rewarded, the thrill of its pageantry
> and banqueting, and dizzy promise of lifelong union. A good wedding was an
> unacknowledged representation of the as yet unthinkable — sexual bliss. In the
> aisles of country churches and grand city cathedrals, her heroines and heroes
> reached their innocent climaxes and needed to go no further. If divorce had
> presented itself as the dastardly antithesis of all this, it could easily have been cast
> onto the other pan of the scales, along with betrayal, illness, thieving, assault
> and mendacity. Instead it showed an unglamorous face of dull complexity
> and incessant wrangling. Like re-armament and the Abyssinia Question and
> gardening, it was simply not a subject.[7]

Briony's is the romance plot, but what she does not understand is that divorce offers
many opportunities for betrayal, illness, thieving, assault and mendacity. Indeed,
divorce may represent a desire for the achievement of glamour and the relin-
quishment of gardening.

The association of divorce in nineteenth-century France with the politics of
laïcité brought with it a wider order of philosophical contemplation which may seem

in turns broadly ethical or vaguely existential. These concerns meet the issue of fictional plotting in the arena of the 'life narrative'. What does it mean to imagine a life to be a singular thread whose two ends might be drawn together in the assertion of circular completeness? Is it possible to imagine how a life might begin again? This posed a particular problem for women within polite society. For a widow to remarry was one thing, but for a wife to divorce and remarry was quite another. Against the libertarian tradition of the Revolution which argued that marriage should be the site of individual fulfilment ran a conservative vision of gender order which demanded that women be the subject to the master narratives of men, passed as virginal brides from fathers to grooms. The thread of bourgeois women's sexual narrative was in theory supposed to begin with marriage, where the 'knot' at one end of the thread was first tied. Divorce and remarriage eroded the association of weddings with the idealizing imagery of the virgin. In the words of Onézime Seure's anti-reform poem 'Le Divorce' (1848):

> A qui l'a mérité nous renvoyons le blâme:
> Un mariage impie est un meurtre de l'âme.
> Mais le tombeau n'a point deux portes ici-bas,
> Et la virginité ne se répare pas.[8]

To the conservative mind the marriage vow (like virginity) could not be taken back. To unhappy spouses Seure dictates silent tears:

> Vous donc qui languissez dans des nœuds abhorrés,
> Vous les avez voulus: taisez-vous et pleurez.
> Ce qu'on donne une fois on ne peut le reprendre,
> On ne réclame pas une victime en cendre.
> On peut mentir à Dieu ; mais d'un vœu solennel
> Le seul regret permis, c'est un deuil éternel!

Divorce invited serial plots consonant with the serial lives it permits, as we shall see in the case of Camille Pert in Chapter 5. Alongside Marcel Prévost's notion of the sexually flirtatious adolescent girl which undermined the mythology of feminine purity before marriage, the stereotype of the divorcee eroded the 'once-and-forever' ideology of sexual partnership imposed upon women. Indeed, as we shall see in Chapter 3, the moral debate over the concept of retrospective jealousy was evoked, inter alia, in the fiction of Anatole France and Marie-Anne de Bovet, as well as in the novels of Paul Bourget and Marcelle Tinayre, all of whom considered whether a 'new man' — in both senses — could ever fully accept the sexual past of a divorcee. Hence such fiction explored the narrative possibilities of a law which, for all of its compromises and hypocrisy, promised to offer women a second chance, as we shall see in the cases of André Léo and Claire Vautier in Chapter 2.

Divorce emerges as a potential means of escaping the received plots of social history and classic fiction. The reader is led to inquire whether, by serializing one's desires (serializing in what we might call a bio-narratological sense), by moving from one passion to another, one can avoid duplicity. Or, as Édouard Rod asks in his Michel Teissier novels, is a life led by the passions (in Teissier's case both amorous and political) ultimately misguided, not least in the case of couples with children (as in Rod's fiction and Alphonse Daudet's *Rose et Ninette*)? To both of these novelists

I shall turn in Chapter 4. To divorce and remarry is to double doubleness, or in some sense to give up the idea of uniqueness in the very search for the unique elsewhere. As such, the new legal possibility of divorce after 1884 raised a number of ethical and philosophical questions. Most fundamentally, is it possible to start again? This problem of beginning again ensues from the difficulty in stumbling across an ending in the middle of the thing. Furthermore, can one redeem the fault of a repudiated marriage by forging a coherent second life, by committing oneself to second marriage? Rather than seeing in what has been called 'the culture of divorce' a cynical take on marriage, one could see in divorce a kind of romantic idealism, a hope that marital bliss may be locatable elsewhere, given that divorce (unlike separation) permits remarriage.

Much hangs on whether we would choose individually to put scare-quotes around that notion of divorce as failure. However resistant to judgement modern liberal sentiment may make us, even those brave, desperate or radical enough to use the new divorce law at the end of the nineteenth century would almost certainly have felt that their life had in some sense failed. The question was what to do with that conjugal failure — to bear it, to flee it, to repair it, to risk it again?[9] In truth, nineteenth-century divorcees would rarely have shared a euphoric philosophy of mistakes celebrated and narratives rewritten and relived. Few were the genuine radicals of intimacy who would in all honesty merely chalk such disappointments down to experience in authentically phlegmatic fashion. Divorcees were, in general though, set at odds with the notion that to have failed once was to have failed for good.[10] To rigid moralists, divorce was little short of bigamy. However nineteenth-century progressives cut the cake, such a re-scripting of the life narrative (this second existence) would be associated with a dual life, or in ethical terms with a life of duplicity.

But back to origins... Two key critical voices that have in recent decades explored the first of these cognitive paradigms are Carlo Ginzburg and Malcolm Bowie.[11] Ginzburg uncovers 'the silent emergence of an epistemological model (a paradigm, if you prefer) towards the end of the nineteenth century, in the humanities' (96), to which he connects the art historian, Giovanni Morelli, the fictional detective, Sherlock Holmes, and the father of psychoanalysis, Sigmund Freud. This is known as the conjectural or evidential paradigm. Morelli argues that in order to distinguish original art works from copies, it is vital to focus not 'on the most conspicuous characteristics of a painting, which are the easiest to imitate' but on 'the most trivial details that would have been influenced least by the mannerisms of the artist's school' (96–97). Conan Doyle's hero detects the identity of the criminal 'on the basis of evidence that is imperceptible to most people', clues such as footprints, cigarette ashes, and the like (98). Freud himself identified Morelli's influence on psychoanalytical technique in his 1914 essay 'The Moses of Michelangelo'. Ginzburg glosses that influence thus:

> It was the idea of a method of interpretation based on discarded information, on marginal data, considered in some way significant. By this method, details usually considered of little importance, even trivial or 'minor,' provided the key for approaching higher aspects of the human spirit. [...] In each case, infinitesimal

> traces permit the comprehension of a deeper, otherwise unattainable reality:
> traces — more precisely, symptoms (in the case of Freud), clues (in the case of
> Sherlock Holmes), pictorial marks (in the case of Morelli). (101)

Malcolm Bowie explores the question of Freud's fascination with archaeology ('this predilection for "deep" and "buried" meaning', 24) in the second sub-section of Chapter 1 ('Freud's dreams of knowledge') of *Freud, Proust and Lacan*. In Bowie's words:

> Psychoanalysis, like archaeology, is the quest for, and the systematic study of, anterior states: for Freud *that which came before*, whether in the life of a civilisation or in the life of the mind, has a peculiar and unparalleled capacity to organise our perception of *that which is*. 'Le thème de l'antérieur,' Paul Ricoeur has said of the Freudian theoretical corpus, 'est sa propre hantise'. (18)

To archaeology, Bowie appends Freud's interest in geology and palaeontology. Bowie reads Freud's archaeological passion as 'a dream of unitary and unidirectional knowledge' (25), 'the dream of an alternative logic to the threatening and insidious logic of dreams' (26), in other words, as a kind of anti-oneiric dream. These disciplinary references open a route to Ginzburg's analysis. As well as identifying the ancient origins of the conjectural paradigm (not least in the semiotics of hunting), Ginzburg identifies the constellation of modern disciplines in which it emerges. He cites the French naturalist and zoologist Georges Cuvier (1769–1832) in order to highlight the connection between the detective story and palaeontology.

This constellation takes on a yet richer pattern in Ginzburg's reference to the English evolutionary biologist Thomas Huxley (1825–95) and his methodological reliance on Voltaire's *Zadig* (1747):

> The name 'Zadig' had taken on such symbolic value that in 1880 Thomas Huxley, on a lecture tour to publicize Darwin's discoveries, defined as 'Zadig's method' that procedure which combined history, archaeology, geology, physical astronomy, and palaeontology: namely, the ability to forecast retrospectively. Disciplines such as these, profoundly diachronic, could not avoid turning to the conjectural or divinatory paradigm [...]. When causes cannot be reproduced, there is nothing to do but to deduce them from their effects. (117)

In Chapter 3 of *Zadig*, 'Le Chien et le Cheval', Voltaire's hero manages to describe minutely these two animals which have gone missing, and he does so by deciphering their tracks on the ground. But how could he possibly know them so well if they were not already in his possession? When he is accused of stealing them, he defends himself by inventorying the mental processes which allowed him to sketch the portrait of two animals he had never seen.

For our purposes, it is worth recalling that the key chapter in Voltaire's tale begins with the collapse of Zadig's short-lived marriage. The opening chapter of the tale shows how his plan to marry the lovely Sémire, to whom he seems so well suited socially and amorously, is thwarted when he defends her against the brigands of his jealous rival, Orcan. When Zadig recovers from the wound to his left eye, he learns that 'celle [...] pour qui seule il voulait avoir des yeux' has in fact married Orcan, of all people, citing her insurmountable aversion for one-eyed men as the cause of her change in inclination — hence the reference to 'le borgne' in the title of this opening chapter.[12] In fact, the abscess over his eye clears and sight from his left eye returns, in spite of the public prediction of his incompetent but much fêted physician, le grand Hermès, that unlike an affliction of the right eye, such an affliction of the left eye could not be healed. In a brilliant satire on the incorrect use of conjectural method, and what Ginzburg calls its retrospective forecast, Hermès writes the most useless of books 'où il lui prouva qu'il n'avait pas dû guérir. Zadig ne le lut point.' Reacting against the courtly intrigue of Orcan and Sémire, he marries 'une citoyenne' (to be understood in mid-eighteenth-century terms as a *bourgeoise*). Although Azora appears to be 'la plus sage et la mieux née de la ville' and their first month of wedlock offers 'les douceurs de l'union la plus tendre' (5), he notices her eye for 'les jeunes gens les mieux faits'.

In Chapter 2 Zadig tests her loyalty by pretending to have died and have one of his friends, Cador (one of those young men in whom Azora finds such 'mérite'), offer her a shoulder to cry on. When Cador claims to have inherited Zadig's wealth and offers to share it with Azore, she is all ears — and this only one day after Zadig's apparent demise. But Cador, it seems, suffers from a spleen problem, which can only be treated, he claims, by the application of a nose removed from a fresh corpse. When Azora approaches Zadig's 'corpse', blade in hand, he suddenly rises from 'le tombeau de ses pères', at the bottom of the garden! This episode emblematizes in a forceful manner the homosocial policing of heterosexual love. Key to this test is that it cannot be defined, strictly speaking, as a test of adultery, if one accepts that marriage ends with the death of one spouse (and that a widow is free to start a second life). The problem seems more to lie in the lack of a respectable period of mourning, and what matters most here is not so much the existence of serial love as the negotiation and transmission between the episodes of a serial life. In this sense, a widow's mourning (which will come to loom so large in the collective nineteenth-century vision of the roles of the *bourgeoise*) provides society with a way of negotiating the transmission of women, not between father and husband (as patriarchy initially prescribes), but between husband and husband. And structurally (and thus cynically rather than sympathetically) widowhood can, of course, be seen as a way of having two husbands (one after the other, unlike bigamy), without being divorced. And so Chapter 3 opens with Zadig, not once but twice the victim of disappointed love, turning from marriage to nature. In reference to the writings on marriage offered by Zoroastrianism (in which he sought a rational form of Deism), Voltaire begins:

> Zadig éprouva que le premier mois du mariage, comme il est écrit dans le livre de *Zend*, est la lune du miel, et que le second est la lune de l'absinthe. Il fut quelque temps après obligé de répudier Azora, qui était devenue trop difficile à vivre, et il chercha son bonheur dans l'étude de la nature. (6–7)

Ginzburg locates this Enlightenment form of the *venatic* model of conjecture (literally hunting for clues) within a longer tradition. It points forward by direct influence to Poe, Gaboriau, and 'the mystery novel'.[13] Its distant origins in the hunter's reading of clues is transmitted via the oriental folkloric tale, circulated among Kirghiz, Tartars, Jews, Turks and others, of three brothers who are accused of stealing a camel (or in some versions, a horse) which they describe with immediate and brilliant clarity: it is white, blinded in one eye, and carries two goat-skins on its back, one full of wine, the other of oil. In the face of an accusation of theft, they triumph by showing how myriad small clues have helped them to reconstruct the appearance of an animal they have never actually seen (in other words, 'the ability to construct from apparently insignificant experimental data a complex reality that could not be experienced directly' (103)). Ginzburg can thus even suggest that 'the actual idea of narration (as distinct from charms, exorcisms, or invocation) may have originated in a hunting society, relating the experience of deciphering tracks.'

The venatic tale was first collected in the West by one of Boccaccio's imitators, Giovanni Sercambi of Lucca (1348–1424). It reappeared as the centrepiece of a mid-sixteenth-century Venetian anthology, presented as translations from Persian into Italian by one Cristoforo the Armenian. *Peregrinaggio di tre giovani figliuoli del re Serendippo* was translated into different languages, in particular during the eighteenth-century fascination with things oriental. It is in this context that Horace Walpole coined the neologism *serendipity*, the way in which one accidentally discovers something fortunate, especially while looking for something else entirely. One might well argue, though, that the brothers' achievements are not merely what the French would call *heureux hasard*. In fact, Walpole's letter of 28 January 1754 to Horace Mann offers the following gloss on the story: 'as their highnesses travelled, they were always making discoveries, by accidents and sagacity, of things which they were not in quest of'. Though the term *serendipity* stresses the accidents (in Walpole's emphasis, '*no* discovery of a thing you *are* looking for, comes under this description'), the conjectural paradigm stresses the other means, namely sagacity, though this too means foreseeing that which cannot be seen. In the scopophilic culture of late-nineteenth-century Europe, both the accidents of serendipity and the sagacity of conjecture represent what we might call paradoxes of the gaze, as we ultimately see what we cannot see in front of us, or were not even looking for.

As we have seen, Freud is one of Ginzburg's high priests of conjecture. Bowie, of course, connects Freud to Proust, and at various moments the latter novelist will haunt our close readings of fiction which in many cases shares a similar social context for cultural production (broadly, the *mondain* salon society of *fin de siècle* and *belle époque* Paris), and even some of the thematic concerns which Proust will alchemically transmute (hence our chapter on retrospective jealousy in Anatole France's *Le Lys rouge*), but remains in its aesthetic vision resolutely pre-Proustian and pre-Modernist (in spite of its philosophical anticipations of the life politics of liquid modernity). It is the section on 'Plots and paranoia' in the final chapter of Christopher Prendergast's *The Order of Mimesis* which connects Ginzburg's conjectural paradigm to the classic French novel.[14] Prendergast explains how

> [the paradigm] can, at certain moments, penetrate into the established intel-
> lectual and institutional culture, where it is appropriated and refined as a
> means of social monitoring and control. Such is the case, argues Ginzburg,
> in the late nineteenth century, especially in connection with the growth
> of those human sciences — such as medicine and criminology — that are
> institutionally harnessed to the *policing* of an increasingly complex and mobile
> urban population.

Critically, Prendergast connects this paradigm to a chain of associations which lie at the heart of the narrative project: Aristotelian *anagnorisis*; Freud's theory of the Family Romance and the 'implicit knowledge that the *pater semper incertus est*'; Barthes' connection between narrative order and the law of the father; and Tony Tanner's analysis of the classic novel of adultery and 'the loss of social cohesion when the juridical rights of the institution of the *pater familias* are infringed by the transgressing adulterous woman'. Narratives of disorder, motivated in no small part by a desire for the order which the conjectural paradigm promises and pursues, take class-and-gender-specific forms, as Prendergast explains:

> Adultery and crime are recurring themes of nineteenth-century fiction. If one of the main concerns of the serious 'bourgeois' novel is with the disorder caused by female adultery, the major preoccupation of the 'popular' novel is with avenging disorder caused by the criminal transgressor.

To this comparison between adultery and crime in fiction, one might add Michael Riffaterre's Proudhonian basis for the interpretation of *Madame Bovary*:

> I will apply this moral pronouncement of Proudhon (entered under *adultère* in the first volume of Larousse, published in 1866, nine years after the novel): *L'adultère est un crime qui contient en soi tous les autres* [...]. No phrasing could be apter for generating the descriptive system in question here; the whole novel can be shown to derive from that system.[15]

The divorce fiction which we shall study belongs, in one way or another, to this same bourgeois tradition. And if the novel of wifely adultery takes us back to an original disorder which traumatizes patriarchy (namely, the uncertainty of paternal origins), the novel of divorce compels us forward to a latter-day disorder (namely, the failure of conjugal desire to adhere to the name of the father). Not only do we not know where we come from; it seems that we do not where we are going either. Like the novel of wifely adultery, the novel of divorce unseats the rights and privileges of the first man. It is also significant that the arch-criminal of classic French fiction is Balzac's Vautrin, because in his capacity for self-refashioning we see the seeds of self-manufacture which will be glossed positively in the late twentieth and early twenty-first centuries' model of self-reinvention. For all the avowed conservatism in Balzac's critique of modernity, we can nevertheless see in the sheer glee and energy of Vautrin's own particular 'comédie' an anticipation of this positive gloss. And Vautrin's plot, like the divorce plots at the end of the century, explores the vulnerability of the *état civil* to changes of name.

Rather than turning without reflection to recent French sociology for conceptual models, I would suggest that Anthony Giddens and Zygmunt Bauman provide us with a model of contemporary identity which speaks most persuasively to our question of divorce. Of particular relevance are their accounts of self-reinvention in the 'liquid modern' or 'late modern' age. Few sociologists can claim to have been more prolific than Giddens in their production not only of books but also of paradigms, and we shall make use of his work in the early 1990s on the reflexivity of modern identity and sexuality.[16]

In the introduction to *Modernity and Self-Identity* Giddens applies the notion of reflexive narrative to social experience in ways which speak to, but not of the literary meanings of narrative reflexivity:

> In the post-traditional order of modernity [...] self-identity becomes a reflexively organised endeavour. The reflexive project of the self, which consists in the sustaining of coherent, yet continuously revised, biographical narratives, takes place in the context of multiple choice as filtered through abstract systems. (5)

Such lifestyle choices generate a new 'life politics — concerned with human self-actualization, both on the level of the individual and collectively' (9). Again, in terms which literary critics cannot ignore, Giddens identifies the internally referential order of modern love:

> At one pole of the interaction between the local and the global stands what I call the 'transformation of intimacy'. Intimacy has its own reflexivity and its own form of internally referential order. Of key importance here is the emergence of the 'pure relationship' as prototypical of the new spheres of personal life. A pure relationship is one in which external criteria have become dissolved: the relationship exists solely for whatever rewards that relationship as such can deliver.[...] Trust, in other words, can by definition no longer be anchored in criteria outside the relationship itself — such as criteria of kinship, social duty or traditional obligation. (6)

In the opening pages of the study which follows (Chapter 1, 'The Contours of High Modernity'), divorce plays an exemplary role in the life-politics of contemporary self-identity, as Giddens turns, somewhat self-consciously, to 'a specific sociological study, plucked rather arbitrarily from a particular area of research', *Second Chances* by Wallerstein and Blakeslee (10).[17] To find a second chance, they argue, we need to mourn, to come to terms with 'death' within life, or the end of a certain life before another begins; and claiming the future depends on a reclaiming the past. A divorcee must 'reach back into his or her early experiences and find other images and roots for independence' (11). Self-reinvention depends, then, on a mastery of origins after all, and these Janus-like demands of divorce emblematize modern experience as such: 'The "new sense of identity" which Wallerstein and Blakeslee mention as required following divorce is an acute version of a process of "finding oneself" which the social conditions of modernity enforce on all of us' (12). Furthermore, writings on divorce such as these do not only reflect, but construct 'the *reflexivity* of modernity':

> They serve routinely to organise, and alter, the aspects of social life they report on or analyse. Anyone who contemplates marriage today, or who faces a situation of the break-up of a marriage or a long-term intimate relationship, knows a great deal (not always on the level of discursive awareness) about 'what is going on' in the social arena of marriage and divorce. Such knowledge is not incidental to what is actually going on, but constitutive of it — as it true of all contexts of social life in conditions of modernity. Not only this: everyone is in some sense aware of the reflexive constitution of modern social activity and the implications it has for her or his life. (14)

If this particular book, *Second Chances*, has been plucked out arbitrarily, the question of divorce clearly has not. And it will be our task to ask whether such reflexivity can be found in the late-nineteenth-century discourse on divorce which clearly predates the high modernity to which Giddens refers.

Giddens returns to the issue of divorce in Chapter 3 on 'The Trajectory of the Self'. First, divorce is presented within a fresh order of time and narrative:

> Personal calendars are timing devices for significant events within the life of the individual, inserting such events within a personalised chronology. Like life plans, personal calendars are typically revised and reconstructed in terms of alterations in an individual's circumstances or frame of mind. 'When I got married,' as a basic date within a life-plan calendar [...] may be largely ousted by 'when the marriage broke up' as a more important psychological marker. (85)

In the terms we inherit from the Ancient Greeks, we might say that the modern search for *kairos* (the opportune moment in which something special happens, the time between times) demands a refashioning of *chronos* (sequential time), and such refashioning of time speaks to the refashioning of narrative.

In true sociological fashion, Giddens then lists the seven traits which characterize the 'pure relationship' of contemporary days:

(1) 'In contrast to close personal ties in traditional contexts, the pure relationship is **not anchored in external conditions** of social or economic life [...]. The tendency is towards the eradication of these pre-existing external involvements — a phenomenon originally accompanied by the rise of romantic love as a basic motive for marriage' (89).

(2) 'The pure relationship is sought only for what the relationship can bring to the partners involved [...] and it is precisely in this sense that the relationship is "pure". [...] In relationships which only **exist for their own sake**, anything that goes wrong between the partners intrinsically threatens the relationship itself. Consequently, it is very difficult to "coast along" in the way in which one can in a social relation dominated by external criteria' (90).

(3) 'The pure relationship is **reflexively organised**, in an open fashion, and on a continuous basis. [...] The more a relationship depends upon itself, the more such a reflexive questioning comes to be its core — and contributes to the tensions noted in (2)' (92).

(4) '**Commitment**, within the pure relationship, is essentially what replaces the external anchors that close personal connections used to have in pre-modern situations. [...] Commitment can to some extent be regularised by the force of love, but sentiments of love do not in and of themselves generate commitment, nor do they in any sense authorise it. A person only becomes committed to another when, for whatever reason, she or he decides to be so. [...] Commitment [...] stands in uneasy connection with the reflexivity that is equally central to how the relationship is ordered. The committed person is prepared to accept the risks which the sacrificing of other potential options entails' (92–93).

(5) 'The pure relationship is focused on **intimacy**, which is a major condition of any long-term stability the partners might achieve. [...]. Intimacy is the other face of privacy, or at least only becomes possible (or desired) given substantial privacy. [...] Privacy makes possible the psychic satisfactions that the achievement of intimacy has to offer' (94)

(6) 'The pure relationship depends on **mutual trust** between partners, which in turn is closely related to the achievement of intimacy. In the pure relationship, trust is not and cannot be taken as "given": like other aspects of the relationship, it has to be worked

at — the trust of the other has to be won. [...] This is one reason why **authenticity** has such an important place in self-actualisation' (96).

(7) 'Self-identity is negotiated through linked processes of self-exploration and the development of intimacy with the other. Such processes help create "**shared histories**" of a kind potentially more tightly bound than those characteristic of individuals who share experiences by virtue of a common social position. Such shared histories may be quite divergent from the orderings of time and space that prevail in the wider social world. Yet it is important to emphasise [...] that they are characteristically interpolated within that wider world rather than cut off from it.' (97).

My subsequent analyses of fictional love stories will, in effect, explore their position between such 'purity' and the 'impurity' of tradition.

Giddens returns to the question of divorce in Chapter 5, 'The Sequestration of Experience', where he interrogates the critiques of modern narcissism offered by Richard Sennett and Christopher Lasch. This he does by reference to Judith Stacey's work on modern marriage.[18] Against the vision of pathological narcissism, Giddens glosses Stacey's account:

> In experiencing the unravelling of traditional family patterns, with all the threats and risks which these changes entail, individuals are actively pioneering new social territory and constructing innovative forms of familial relation. [...] 'Recombinant families', no longer organised in terms of pre-established gender divisions, are being created; rather than forming a chasm between a previous and a future mode of existence, divorce is being mobilised as a resource to create networks drawing together new partners and former ones, biological children and stepchildren, friends and other relatives. (176–77)

It is this positive gloss on the potential of divorce which, as we shall see below, Bauman will question.

Giddens focuses fully on the question of modern love in his next book, *The Transformation of Intimacy*, and in particular on the pure relationship, 'a relationship of sexual and emotional equality, which is explosive in its connotations for pre-existing forms of gender power' (2). It relates crucially to his notion of plastic sexuality, 'freed from the needs of reproduction', but also bears witness to a link between nineteenth-century and contemporary ways of loving: 'Romantic love presumes that a durable emotional tie can be established with the other on the basis of qualities intrinsic to that tie itself. It is the harbinger of the pure relationship, although it stands in tension with it' (8).

Before French scholars have the chance to pose the question, Giddens then responds to Foucault. In Foucauldian fashion we learn of biopower's definition of family norms:

> The study of sex and the creation of discourses about it led in the nineteenth century to the development of various contexts of power-knowledge. One concerned [...] marriage and the family. Sex in marriage was to be responsible and self-regulated; not just confined to marriage, but ordered in distinct and specific ways. Contraception was discouraged. Control of family size was supposed to emerge spontaneously from the disciplined pursuit of pleasure. Finally, a catalogue of perversions was introduced and modes of treatment for them described. (21–22)

But, Giddens argues, Foucault 'is silent about the connections of sexuality with romantic love, a phenomenon closely bound up with changes in the family' (24). By 'turn[ing] to what Foucault specifically neglects: the nature of love and, in particular, the rise of the ideals of romantic love,' Giddens sets sail, in Chapters 3 and 4, for the twin ports of the relationship between late nineteenth-century fictional love and our early-twenty-first century reading of it: namely, romantic love and the pure relationship (34). For 'the transmutation of love is as much a phenomenon of modernity as is the emergence of sexuality'.

Chapter 3 offers the kind of broad brush of which we are trained to be suspicious yet very often need. It traces the rise of romantic love, and in this, it provides us with a context for understanding nineteenth-century fictional love. The 'culturally specific' notion of romantic love, which imposes itself 'from the late eighteenth century onwards', is distinct from, but bears a residue of the 'more or less universal phenomenon' of *amour passion* (38–39). In a wonderfully capacious footnote, Giddens explains how he has borrowed this French term from Stendhal, only to recast its meaning. This then allows Giddens to point towards a pre-Durkheimian French tradition (from Destutt de Tracy via Comte and Clothilde de Vaux) in which 'social science was closely intertwined with speculation about the nature of love' (47). *Amour passion* expresses 'a generic connection between love and sexual attachment [...] marked,' as it is, 'by an urgency which sets it apart from the routines of everyday life with which, indeed, it tends to come into conflict' (37). The socially dangerous potential of such passion has habitually made it an insecure basis for marriage (with its duties and obligations), and 'most civilisations seem to have created stories and myths which drive home the message that those who seek to create permanent attachments through passionate love are doomed' — not least, we might add, the adulterous heroine of classic fiction (39). Giddens the sociologist privileges the relationship between romantic love and the rise of the novel, both of which share a fixation with the narrative of the individual: 'Romantic love introduced the idea of a narrative into an individual's life — a formula which radically extended the reflexivity of sublime love.' This quest for narrative closure establishes 'ties between freedom and self-realisation' in the search for 'someone who can make one's life, as it is said, "complete"' (40). And in this, romantic love tends toward both the sublime and the secular. First:

> In romantic love attachments, the element of sublime love tends to predominate over that of sexual ardour. [...] Love breaks with sexuality while embracing it; 'virtue' begins to take on a new sense for both sexes, no longer meaning only innocence but qualities of character which pick out the other person as 'special'.

But then:

> A romance was no longer, as it generally had been before, a specifically unreal conjuring of possibilities in a realm of fiction. Instead, it became a potential avenue for controlling the future, as well as a form of psychological security (in principle) for those whose lives were touched by it. (41)

Romantic love (and its literature) was, it seems, 'essentially feminised love' (43). The question we shall ask is where precisely our divorce corpus should be positioned between romantic love and the so-called pure relationship.

One of the most renowned responses to Giddens's model of confluent love is that of fellow sociologist Zygmunt Bauman. Since the turn of the millennium, Bauman has produced a remarkable array of books (seven, at the time of writing) on the topic of 'liquid modernity', and of particular relevance to our concerns is his notion of 'liquid love'.[19] Though conceived as the conclusion to a trilogy, *Liquid Modernity* sets out the stall of Bauman's new project by focusing on the topics of emancipation, individuality, time, space, work and community, in order to describe a shift from 'heavy' to 'light' modernity. The present study is prefaced (or, in properly chronological terms, one might say postfaced) by Bauman's contention that divorce is emblematic of contemporary living, characterized as it is by 'the mind-boggling speed of circulation or recycling, ageing, dumping and replacement which brings profit today — not the durability and lasting reliability of the product' and 'the falling apart, the friability, the brittleness, the transience, the until-further-noticeness of human bonds and networks' (14).

In its first chapter, on emancipation, *Liquid Modernity* maps out a contemporary conflict between routine (to which the world of marriage belongs) and what Durkheim terms anomie ('a perpetual agony of indecision linked to a state of uncertainty about the intentions and moves of others around', 20), and it is telling that Bauman should return to this *fin de siècle* reference. Norms, habits, and routines may appear stultifying from the perspective of Denis Diderot's adversary Adam Smith, but, according to the tradition which Richard Sennett traces from the Enlightenment to 'Diderot's greatest modern heir, the sociologist Anthony Giddens': 'To imagine a life of momentary impulses, of short-term action, devoid of sustainable routines, a life without habits, is to imagine a mindless existence.'[20] Bauman suggests that the contemporary world has yielded in no small degree to this mindless impulse, such that, in the words of Deleuze and Guattari,

> We no longer believe in the myth of the existence of fragments that, like pieces of an antique statue, are merely waiting for the last one to be turned up, so that they may be all glued back together to create a unity that is precisely the same as the original unity. We no longer believe in a primordial totality that once existed, or in a final totality that awaits us at some future date.[21]

In tension with the truth of origins and 'primordial totality' (which Ginzburg and Bowie diagnose), the culture of divorce also interrogates the existential possibility of a 'final totality', of a wholeness which we can find through the construction of our own lives. The classic critical theory of Adorno and Horkheimer, 'informed by and targeted on the *telos* of emancipation', was critical of a modernity 'endemically pregnant with the tendency towards totalitarianism' and 'the sworn enemy of contingency, variety, ambiguity, waywardness and idiosyncrasy' (24–25). Confluent and liquid love, however, make a virtue (or at least a vehicle) of wayward affections. But in this opening chapter, Bauman also criticizes the rhetoric of liberation he perceives in Giddens's notion of reflexive life-politics: 'We are perhaps more "critically predisposed", much bolder and intransigent in our criticism than our ancestors managed to be in their daily lives, but our critique, so to speak, is "toothless", unable to affect the agenda set for our "life-political" choices' (23). This difference between Giddens and Bauman will inform their different stances on liquid or confluent love. As Bauman puts it:

> The modernity addressed by classic critical theory appears quite different from the one which frames the lives of present-day generations. It appears 'heavy' (as against the contemporary 'light' modernity); better still, 'solid' (as distinct from 'fluid', 'liquid', or 'liquified'); condensed (as against diffuse or 'capillary'); finally, systemic (as distinct from network-like). (25)

For our purposes, it is indicative that Bauman should use the classic romance plot as a metaphor to explain the engagement of classic critical theory with heavy modernity:

> In the likeness of the early Hollywood melodramas, which presumed that the moment when the lovers found each other again and took their marriage vows signalled the end of the drama and the beginning of blissful 'living happily ever after', early critical theory saw the wrenching of individual liberty from the iron grip of routine or letting the individual out of the steely casing of a society afflicted with insatiable totalitarian, homogenizing and uniformizing appetites as the ultimate point of emancipation. (26)

We shall ask whether that metaphor is in fact an emblem. Indeed, a key staging post between the turn-of-the-century world described in my close readings and the reflexive, liquid modernity described by Giddens and Bauman can be found in Stanley Cavell's landmark account of Hollywood remarriage comedies of the 1930s and 1940s, *Pursuits of Happiness* (1981). In Chapter 4, on work, Bauman depends again on the metaphorical power of marriage and divorce. He compares the contemporary workplace to 'a camping site which one visits for just a few days' rather than 'a shared domicile where one is inclined to take trouble and patiently work out the acceptable rules of cohabitation', such that:

> The advent of light, free-floating capitalism [...] replicated the passage from marriage to 'living together' with all its corollary attitudes [...], including the assumption of the temporariness of cohabitation and of the possibility that the association may be broken at any moment and for any reason, once the need or desire dries out. (149)

The more insistent the metaphor, the greater its emblematic potential.

Bauman suggests in his opening chapter that 'there is not much to distinguish between the plight of our grandfathers and our own', to the extent that

> Whatever is man-made, men can un-make. Being modern came to mean [...] being unable to stop and ever less able to stand still [...]. The finishing line of effort and the moment of restful self-congratulation move faster than the fastest of the runners. Fulfilment is always in the future. [...] Being modern means being perpetually ahead of oneself, in a state of constant transgression. (28–29)

Still, Bauman can identify differences between our grandparents' modernity and our own: first, the decline of the illusion that there is an attainable *telos* of historical change (some sort of conflict-free and just society); second, the shift of emphasis from the idea of improvement through the legislative action of society as a whole towards the self-assertion of the individual (hence the shift from the ethical discourse of the 'just society' to that of 'human rights'). Divorce law, we might argue, represents an attempt on the part of the state to legislate for individual happiness — or rather to admit, in a figurative as well as literal sense, that one cannot *legislate for* such happiness (in the case of France, to release the Napoleonic grip on the idea of the Family). The law drags the family into the 'agora', the ancient Greek market place defined by Bauman as

> that intermediary, public/private site where life-politics meets Politics with the capital 'P', where private problems are translated into the language of public issues and public solutions are sought, negotiated and agreed for private troubles. (39)

The law defamiliarizes the familiar, renders the homely public and thus in Freud's sense uncanny (unhomely in the etymological sense of *unheimlich*); and in this, the divorce debate has contributed to 'the colonization of the public sphere by the private', though thinkers such as Habermas have lived in fear of the very opposite (51). In this imbrication of private and public, divorce bespeaks the liquid modern experience:

> Many, perhaps most, are nomads without leaving their caves. They may still seek shelter in their homes, but they would hardly find seclusion there and however hard they may try they would never be truly *chez soi*: the shelters have porous walls, pierced all over by countless wires and easily penetrated by ubiquitous airwaves. (155)

The second chapter of *Liquid Modernity* focuses on the question of individuality, and in particular the commercial context in which identity is shaped by desire:

> That work of art which we want to mould out of the friable stuff of life is called 'identity'. Whenever we speak of identity, there is at the back of our minds a faint image of harmony, logic, consistency: all those things which the flow of our experience seems — to our perpetual despair — so grossly and abominably to lack. The search for identity is the ongoing struggle to arrest or slow down the flow, to solidify the fluid, to give form to the formless. We struggle to deny or at least to cover up the awesome fluidity just below the thin wrapping of the form. (82–83)

Divorce, we might note, is not anti-form, but de-forms as a prelude to re-form (not least in that it makes a second marriage possible). It represents an attempt on the part of social and legal form to accommodate flow and desire. Bauman concludes by criticizing the commercialization of amorous desire and, with a particular directness, Giddens's embrace of post-modern love. This *tour de force* is worthy of citation for its display of the stakes raised, then as well as now, by the divorce question:

> 'Plastic sex', 'confluent love' and 'pure relationships', the aspects of commodification or consumerization of human partnerships, were portrayed by Anthony Giddens as the vehicles of emancipation and a warrant of a new happiness that comes in its wake — the new, unprecedented scale of individual autonomy and freedom to choose. Whether this is indeed true, and nothing but true, for the mobile elite of the rich and mighty is debatable. Even in their case one can

support Giddens's assertion whole-heartedly only if one focuses on the stronger
and more resourceful members of partnerships, which necessarily include also
the weaker, not so lavishly endowed with the resources needed to follow freely
their desires (not to mention the children — these involuntary, though lasting
consequences of partnerships, who hardly ever view the breakdown of marriage
as a manifestation of their own freedom). Changing identity may be a private
affair, but it always includes cutting off certain bonds and cancelling certain
obligations; those on the receiving side are seldom consulted, let alone given
the chance to exercise free choice. (89–90)

Divorce, for Bauman, is then the site of conflict between generational interests.
Moreover, 'happy divorce' is class-specific:

Even if one takes into account such 'secondary effects' of 'pure relationships',
one can still argue that in the case of the high and mighty the customary
divorce settlements and financial provisions for children go some way towards
alleviating the insecurity endemic to until-further-notice relationships, and that
whatever insecurity remains is not an excessive price to pay for the right to 'cut
one's losses' and avoid the need for an eternal repentance for once-committed
sins or errors. But there is little doubt that when 'trickled down' to the poor
and powerless, the new-style partnership with its fragility of marital contract
and the 'purification' of the union of all but the 'mutual satisfaction' function
spawns much misery, agony and human suffering and an ever-growing volume
of broken, loveless and prospectless lives. (90)

The relation between class and our experience of desire's narrative, and, in
particular, the commodification of love in contemporary society suggest that
Bauman's metaphorical use of divorce is not merely an effect of rhetoric. In Chapter
4 he associates liquid modernity with Bourdieu's use of the term *précarité*:

Precarious economic and social conditions train men and women (or make
them learn the hard way) to perceive the world as a container full of *disposable*
objects, objects for *one-off* use; the whole world — including other human
beings. (162)

In *Liquid Love* Bauman identifies 'the ambient sense of *précarité*' as the core of the
tussle for the French presidency in 2002 between Chirac and Jospin (120). In the
2012 presidential contest between Nicolas Sarkozy and François Hollande, it was
the *précarité* of their personal lives which became the subject of a media scrutiny
hitherto unknown in France. Sarkozy was the first president to divorce in office
and then remarry. Hollande's long-term partnership with Ségolène Royal, the
mother of their four children, had come to an end in 2007, and in that same year
Royal had stood as the socialist candidate for the presidency, but been defeated by
Sarkozy. Hollande's new partner Valérie Trierweiler, a divorcee, is the first *première
dame de France* not to be married to the president. At the time of writing, Hollande
is the only president never to have married (Louis-Napoléon did so once the Second
Empire had displaced the Second Republic). It may be that the traditional French
distinction between private lives and public roles has finally succumbed to liquid
modernity.

Bauman describes how love has become a matter of solitary consumption:

Commitments of the 'till death do us part' type become contracts 'until satisfaction lasts', temporal and transient by definition, by design and by pragmatic impact — and so prone to be broken unilaterally, whenever one of the partners sniffs out more opportunity and better value in opting out of the partnership rather than trying to save it at any — incalculable — cost. In other words, bonds and partnerships tend to be viewed as things meant to be *consumed*, not produced [...]. It is no longer the task of both partners to 'make the relationship work' — to see it work through thick and thin, 'for richer for poorer', in sickness and in health, to help each other through good and bad patches, to trim if need be one's own preferences, to compromise and make sacrifices for the sake of a lasting union. It is instead a matter of obtaining satisfaction from a ready-to-consume product; if the pleasure derived is not up to the standard promised and expected, or if the novelty wears off together with the joy, one can sue for divorce, quoting consumer rights and the Trade Descriptions Act. One can think of no reason to stick to an inferior or aged product rather than look for a 'new and improved' one in the shops. [...] Unlike production, consumption is a lonely activity, endemically and irredeemably lonely, even at such moments as it is conducted in the company of others. (163–65)

In this context, Zola's Octave Mouret novels, *Pot-Bouille* and *Au Bonheur des dames*, can be seen to teeter on the brink. The commodification of love, which the novel of adultery has displayed, is underscored by the novel of shopping, which fuels the decadent sense that sex and shopping are becoming one; but this tale of serial desires is confronted by the romance ending in which the shop assistant Denise tames the sexually and financially voracious Mouret (and thus also brings the diptych to an end). As Claire White explains, 'The romantic union of capitalist and worker, Octave and Denise, is symptomatic of the latter's pervasive humanizing impulse in the workplace.'[22]

Bauman then develops this general idea of *Liquid Modernity* in his specific study of *Liquid Love*. Love, he suggests, is unlikely to fare well

in a consumer culture like ours, which favours products ready for instant use, quick fixes, instantaneous satisfaction, results calling for no protracted effort, foolproof recipes, all-risk insurance and money-back guarantees. The promise to learn the art of loving is a (false, deceitful, yet keenly wished to be true) promise to make 'love experience' in the likeness of other commodities, that allure and seduce by brandishing all such features and promise to take the waiting out of wanting, sweat out of effort and effort out of results. (7)

In the present context, it is worth noting that the historical shift from heavy to liquid modernity is measured in novelistic terms: '*Der Mann ohne Eigenschaften* — the man without qualities — of early modernity has matured into (or has he been crowded out by?) *der Mann ohne Verwandtschaften* — the man without bonds' (69). Musil is displaced by a post-modern anti-Goethe. Given the temptation to compare modern soap operas with the episodic form and dissemination of nineteenth-century fiction, it is also worth noting Bauman's analysis of the British soap opera *Eastenders*: 'A viewer with a long memory would see the Square as a graveyard of human relationships [...], and wedding days are not new beginnings ushering the couple into "something completely different" — they are just short breaks in a drama without scenario and scripted lines. Partnership is but a coalition of "confluent interests" [in reference to Giddens], and in the fluid world of *Eastenders* people come and go' (24–25). But Bauman retains his scepticism toward the liquid modernity he describes, once again by reference to children, 'an open-ended and irrevocable commitment with no "until further notice" clause attached; the kind of obligation that goes against the grain of liquid modern life politics' (43), and that will be foregrounded by those novelists who are suspicious of divorce (not least Alphonse Daudet, Paul Bourget and Camille Pert). Against the pure relationship, Bauman contends:

> Intimate connections of sex with love, security, permanence, immortality-through-continuation-of-kin were not after all as useless and constraining as they were thought and felt and charged to be.[...] Perhaps those ['strings attached'] were feats of cultural ingenuity rather than tokens of cultural misconception or failure. (47)

It is this form of 'impure' attachment that the idealized nineteenth-century French family wished to produce (or fabricate) rather than consume:

> Love 'till death us do part', building bridges to eternity, [...] consent to 'giving hostages to fate' and to no-going-back commitments [...] used to be the 'natural instincts' of the *homo faber*, just as they go now against the equally 'natural' instincts of the *homo consumens*. [...] Love and willingness to procreate were indispensable companions to *homo faber*'s sex, just as the lasting unions they helped to create were 'main products' — not 'side-effects', let alone the rejects or wastage, of sexual acts. [...] When deployed on the building site of human bonds, sexual need/desire prodded *homo sexualis* to stay on the job and see it through once started. The builders wished the outcome of their efforts, like one wishes all buildings, to be solidly constructed, durable and (ideally forever) reliable. (48–49)

Returning in other terms to the tension between routine and anomie, Bauman promotes their necessary imbrication:

> *Communitas* [which Bauman associated with spontaneity and experimentation] is, for better or worse, a lining of every *societas* cloud — and in its absence (were such absence conceivable) that cloud would disperse — *societas* would fall apart at its seams. It is *societas* with its routine and *communitas* with its anarchy that *together*, in their reluctant and conflict-ridden cooperation, make the difference between order and chaos. [...] The survival and well-being of *communitas* (and so, indirectly, of *societas* as well) depend on human imagination, inventiveness and courage in *breaking* the routine and trying the *untried* ways. They depend, in other words, on the human ability to live with risk and accept responsibility for the consequences. It is these abilities that are the supports for the 'moral economy' — mutual care and help, living *for* the other, weaving the tissue of human commitments, fastening and servicing interhuman bonds, translating rights into obligations, sharing responsibility for everyone's fortune and welfare. (73–74)

Divorce can thus be viewed as a way for *societas* to assimilate *communitas*, for routine to listen to anomie's potential for reform without yielding to its demand for revolution. To connect love to society in this way (as Bauman does in the second half of *Liquid Love*, in his analysis of relations between classes, citizens and nations) is to rewrite the scene of metonymy on which conservative ideologies have traditionally depended (in a series of reciprocal relationships between our place in the world, the socio-economic order of the nation and the generational and gender hierarchy of the family). It is to the collective, national and self-consciously political end of that metonymical spectrum post-9/11 that Bauman turns in the fourth and fifth books of the series, *Liquid Times* and *Liquid Fear*.

To conclude this account of Bauman, we turn now to the third book in the series, *Liquid Life*, which begins by questioning the pleasure in new beginnings (and, we might say, new relationships):

> Liquid life is a succession of new beginnings — yet precisely for that reason it is the swift and painless endings, without which new beginnings would be unthinkable, that tend to be its most challenging moments and most upsetting headaches. Among the arts of liquid modern living and the skills needed to practise them, getting rid of things takes precedence over their acquisition. (2)

What price conjugal love, we might ask, in an age of waste-disposal, of 'creative destruction', where 'speed, not duration, matters', where 'loyalty is a cause of shame, not pride (3, 7, 9)? The logical (but unattainable as well as undesirable) conclusion might be the Eutropia of Italo Calvino's *Invisible Cities* (1972) whose inhabitants, once they 'feel the grip of weariness and can no longer bear job, relatives, house and life', 'move to the next city' where 'each will take a new job, a different wife' (4)? Such liquidity presents itself as an answer to death, such that 'one can go on squeezing into the timespan of mortal life ever more lives' (8). But in truth, it 'feeds on the self's dissatisfaction with *itself*' (11). Bauman questions the glamour of the globe-trotting liquid modern hero, mobile phone in hand, by offering a different gloss on this 'war of liberation that is never ultimately victorious: a day-in, day-out battle with no respite allowed, to *get rid of*, to *put paid to*, to *forget*', like a cyclist who risks falling over if he stops pedalling (32–33). Thus we may conclude that in the private arena of love, as in the national and international arenas of politics, modern identity is being forged in the tension between freedom and security.

In Chapter 5 Bauman addresses, from yet another perspective, the consumerization of love and the rise of divorce. He cites Phil Hogan's observation that 'you can hardly expect a nation that has been encouraged to embrace the endless novelty of the flexible job market to spend too long working at a relationship' (87). Indeed:

> Gradually, yet relentlessly, [the consumer syndrome] takes hold of interhuman relationships and bonds. Why should partnerships be an exception to the rest of life's rules? [...] But this may present problems of its own: for most of us, telling a partner to go away because he or she no longer delivers the goods or because the goods the partner delivers are no longer exciting might after all prove more harrowing than getting rid of an old-style car or an outdated computer.

The fusing of commercial and affective plots leads then to a subsequent bifurcation, in which individuals conjoining and separating must face the difference at the heart of metaphor (love is but is also not like shopping), and the stubborn resistance of the sentimental life to banalization. In *Liquid Life* Bauman cites the following emblem of such banalization: 'It is hardly astonishing [...] that one of the leading supermarket

chains now offers its customers DIY "divorce kits" at a discount price of £7.49' (87).
And from this difference and resistance, the modern plot emerges. As we return to
the issue of beginnings and endings, we see that the endings of relationships and of
plots are not as clear-cut as the concept of the pure relationship might hope:

> Every encounter leaves behind a sediment of a human bond, and that thick
> sediment thickens in time as it becomes enriched by memories of togetherness.
> Every encounter is both a winding-up moment and a new beginning —
> interaction has no 'natural end' [not even in death, but especially in a culture
> where the end of relationships often precedes death]. The end can only be
> artificially contrived, and it is far from obvious who is to decide when that end
> has arrived, since (to apply consumerist concepts) in human interaction both
> sides are, simultaneously, consumers and the objects of consumption and the
> 'sovereignty of the consumer' can be claimed by both. The established bond
> may be broken, further interaction refused — but not without a bitter aftertaste
> and a feeling of guilt. It is difficult to double-cross moral conscience. (107)

It is with these epistemological, philosophical and sociological tools in mind that
we turn now to the novels in question. Indeed, most striking from our perspective
is the extent to which Bauman and Giddens turn to fictional plots in order to
exemplify and animate their arguments, and indeed to kick-start these arguments.
Chapter 1 of *The Transformation of Intimacy*, for instance, begins with an account
of Julian Barnes's *Before She Met Me* whose hero, Graham Hendrick, divorces
and remarries, only to become obsessed with his new wife's sexual past; and the
Foreword to *Liquid Love* begins, as we have seen, by evoking Ulrich, the hero of *Der
Mann ohne Eigenschaften*, as the man without bonds. It is a lesson of what Giddens
would call high modern reflexivity, moreover, that a cultural example is never just
a passive, mimetic instance.

What I wish to explore is the extent to which we might find signs of what
one might call pre-liquidity within the fiction of heavy modernity (to which
the culture of pre-First World War France might be said to belong, given that
the icons Bauman associates with such modernity include the Fordist factory,
bureaucracy and the Panopticon). A key question (in spite of — and, it should be
admitted, because of — all of its teleological temptations) is whether the French
divorce debates of the nineteenth century (and, more generally, European and
American responses to the Enlightenment discourse on the individual) anticipate
liquid modernity. In particular, we should ask whether (in however circuitous or
subterranean a fashion) divorce marks an ideological turn away from the truth of
origins, which Ginzburg and Bowie diagnose. All of this must take place in the
context of a social order in which the family, in western Europe and elsewhere, is
manifestly not moribund (as an idea or a social fact), but is — equally clearly —
subject to vast social and cultural pressures which mean that it cannot remain static.
This tenacious but fluctuating investment in the family is particularly significant in
the context of an institution which tends ideologically to define its own virtues as
ones of transmission, continuity and permanence. It is in this context that Ulrich
Beck can ask whether the contemporary family is a 'zombie institution', which is
'dead and still alive':

Ask yourself what actually is a family nowadays? What does it mean? Of course there are children, my children, our children. But even parenthood, the core of family life, is beginning to disintegrate under conditions of divorce. [...] Grandmothers and grandfathers get included and excluded without any means of participation in the decisions of their sons and daughters. From the point of view of their grandchildren the meaning of the grandparents has to be determined by individual decisions and choices.[23]

Such contemporary sociologists ask how and why the family is alive, however many times it has received its last rites; we in turn shall ask how and why the late-nineteenth-century family, though manifestly still alive and kicking, already spoke of itself, and was spoken of, in ways which foregrounded its own mortality. It is to this history that we shall turn in Chapter 1, before engaging, in subsequent chapters, with novels themselves.

Notes to the Introduction

1. See Michael Black, *The Literature of Fidelity* (London: Chatto & Windus, 1975), Judith Armstrong, *The Novel of Adultery* (Basingstoke: Macmillan, 1976), Tony Tanner, *Adultery in the Novel* (Baltimore, MD: Johns Hopkins University Press, 1979), Naomi Segal, *The Adulteress's Child* (Cambridge: Polity, 1992), Alison Sinclair, *The Deceived Husband* (Oxford: Oxford University Press, 1993), Bill Overton, *The Novel of Female Adultery* (Basingstoke: Macmillan, 1996), Nicholas White, *The Family in Crisis in Late Nineteenth-Century French Fiction* (Cambridge: Cambridge University Press, 1999), and *Scarlet Letters: Fictions of Adultery from Antiquity to the 1990s*, ed. by Nicholas White and Naomi Segal (Basingstoke: Macmillan, 1997). For a wide-ranging account of the family in nineteenth-century French literature, see *State of the Union: Marriage in Nineteenth-Century France*, ed. by Rachel Mesch and Masha Belenky, special issue of *Dix-Neuf*, 11.1 (2008).
2. See Lawrence Stone, *The Family, Sex and Marriage in England, 1500–1800* (London: Weidenfeld and Nicolson, 1977) and *Road to Divorce* (Oxford: Oxford University Press, 1990); also Roderick Phillips, *Family Breakdown in Late Eighteenth-Century France* (Oxford: Oxford University Press, 1980), *Putting Asunder* (Cambridge: Cambridge University Press, 1988), and *Untying the Knot* (Cambridge: Cambridge University Press, 1991). The dominant voice in the writing of the history of French divorce has been Francis Ronsin: *Le Contrat sentimental* (Paris; Aubier, 1990) and *Les Divorciaires* (Paris: Aubier, 1992).
3. See Barbara Leckie, *Culture and Adultery: The Novel, the Newspaper, and the Law* (Philadelphia: University of Pennsylvania Press, 1999), Janice Hubbard Harris, *Edwardian Stories of Divorce* (New Brunswick, NJ: Rutgers University Press, 1996), Debra Ann MacComb, *Tales of Liberation/ Strategies of Containment: Divorce and the Representation of Womanhood in American Fiction, 1880–1920* (New York: Garland, 2000), Karl Leydecker, *Marriage and Divorce in the Plays of Hermann Sudermann* (Frankfurt am Main: Lang, 1996), and *After Intimacy: The Culture of Divorce in the West since 1789*, ed. by Karl Leydecker and Nicholas White (Oxford: Lang, 2007).
4. Phillips, *Untying the Knot*, p. ix.
5. The prevalence of these two endings is famously stressed in E. M. Forster, *Aspects of the Novel* (London: Edward Arnold, 1927), p. 128.
6. George Eliot, *Middlemarch* (London: Everyman, 1991), pp. 881–82.
7. Ian McEwan, *Atonement* (London: Jonathan Cape, 2001), pp. 8–9.
8. Onézime Seure, *Le Divorce, précédé d'une lettre de Victor Hugo* (Paris: Chaumerot, 1848), pp. 10–11.
9. Roderick Phillips expresses the modern liberal view when he asserts that 'the notion that divorce is pathological is objectionable.' *Divorce in New Zealand: A Social History* (Auckland: Oxford University Press, 1981), p. 16.
10. Again, there is an admirable modern rhetoric which refuses to see a divorce as a failure.

However, this is a long way from the vast majority of nineteenth-century writing on the subject (even of the pro-divorce variety).

11. Carlo Ginzburg, 'Clues: Roots of an Evidential Paradigm', in his *Myths, Emblems, Clues*, trans. by. J. and A. C. Tedeschi (London: Hutchinson, 1990), pp. 96–125; Malcolm Bowie, *Freud, Proust and Lacan: Theory as Fiction* (Cambridge: Cambridge University Press, 1987), pp. 18–27.

12. Voltaire, 'Zadig', in *Romans et contes* (Paris: Garnier, 1953), p. 4.

13. Ginzburg, p. 116. Perhaps a more precise term is to be found in Ginzburg's reference here to R. Méssac's 1929 study of *le 'detective novel'*. Ginzburg suggests that Conan Doyle is subject to indirect Voltairean influence.

14. Christopher Prendergast, *The Order of Mimesis* (Cambridge: Cambridge University Press, 1986), pp. 220–26.

15. Michael Riffaterre, 'Flaubert's Presuppositions', *Diacritics*, 11 (1981), 2–11 (p. 5).

16. The general paradigm is laid out in Anthony Giddens, *Modernity and Self-Identity* (Cambridge: Polity, 1991) and its particular purchase for matters of the heart is explored in *The Transformation of Intimacy* (Cambridge: Polity, 1992).

17. See Judith Wallerstein and Sandra Blakeslee, *Second Chances* (London: Bantam, 1989).

18. See Judith Stacey, *Brave New Families* (New York: Basic Books, 1990).

19. The following books by Zygmunt Bauman have all been published in Cambridge by Polity: *Liquid Modernity* (2000), *Liquid Love* (2003), *Liquid Life* (2005), *Liquid Fear* (2006), *Liquid Times: Living in an Age of Uncertainty* (2007), *44 Letters from the Liquid Modern World* (2010), *Culture in a Liquid Modern World* (2011).

20. Richard Sennett, *The Corrosion of Character* (New York: Norton, 1998), p. 44.

21. Gilles Deleuze and Félix Guattari, *Anti-Oedipus*, trans. by Robert Hurley (New York: Viking, 1977), p. 42.

22. Claire White, 'Rewriting Work and Leisure in Émile Zola's *Travail*', *Dix-Neuf*, 13 (2009) 55–70 (p. 63).

23. Ulrich Beck interviewed by Jonathan Rutherford on 3 February 1999, cited in *Liquid Modernity*, p. 6.

The History of Divorce from the Revolution to the First World War

Statute and Song

The first period of French divorce ran from 1792 to 1816, and the political armature of revolutionary divorce had a grand ring to it. As a 'conséquence de l'établissement de la société civile', divorce embodied 'la liberté comme principe fondamental de la morale'.[1] Indeed, the divorce law of 20 September 1792, voted by the Legislative Assembly, instituted remarkably liberal possibilities at the heart of family life, allowing divorce not only by mutual consent but also at the behest of one spouse alone on the grounds of temperamental incompatibility. The oft-cited term was 'incompatibilité d'humeur', though Naquet reminds us in his 1881 edition of *Le Divorce* that this incompatibility was 'd'humeur ou de caractère'.[2] The destructive force of 'humeurs' is translated in Zola's *Thérèse Raquin* from its medieval origins into the modern language of physiology and temperament. Contrary to this melodramatic connection between 'humeur' and murder, the notion of 'humeur' might also suggest a mood rather than a drama, a state of mind rather than a set of actions and turning-points. One of the main arguments in the ensuing century against these grounds for divorce would be that they would not lend themselves to verification in a forensic narrative (hence in narrative terms its resistance to emplotment), whereas physical acts (such as adultery and beating) might. In Ginette André's terms, the new law represented 'le Divorce intégral, le Divorce Maximum, le Démariage'.[3]

Le Moniteur Universel of 1792 asserted the revolutionary credentials of divorce: 'L'Assemblée Nationale, considérant combien il importe de faire jouir les Français de la faculté du divorce, qui résulte de la liberté individuelle dont un engagement indissoluble serait la perte [...] décrète ce qui suit.'[4] Article 1 stated with unerring simplicity: 'Le mariage se dissout par le divorce.' The chemical analogy with dissolving a solid structure will be echoed in the debates of the following century. In the 'solution' — in a double sense — which divorce offers, individual elements, freed of their bonds, can move around in relative liberty. In the distance we can intuit Bauman's language of liquid modernity. Article 2 to 4 detailed the grounds for divorce: mutual consent; the mere allegation of temperamental incompatibility; insanity; the sentencing of a spouse to 'peines afflictives ou infamantes'; crimes, 'sévices' or grave injury against a spouse; notorious *dérèglement de mœurs*; abandonment of either spouse for at least two years; absence of a spouse without any news for at least five years; emigration dictated by the law, in particular the decree of 8 April 1792. Once existing separations were cleared up (Articles 5 & 6), *séparation de corps* was abolished by article 7. Significantly, divorce did not require the intervention of a judge; the officier d'État-Civil alone could pronounce it. The names of future divorcees would be advertised at the town hall just as one would advertise the names of those to be married. Of the 'Effets du divorce par rapport aux époux', the primary effect was to permit a new marriage (Article 1). They could remarry each other or, after one year, someone else (Article 2). Article 8 made provision for alimony ('une pension alimentaire' for an 'époux divorcé qui se trouvera dans le besoin'), to be stipulated by 'arbitres de famille', but 'autant néanmoins que les biens de l'autre époux pourront la supporter, déduction faite de ses propres besoins'. This arrangement would be dissolved if the recipient married again (Article 9). In the section on 'Effets du divorce par rapport aux enfants', Article 1 on temperamental incompatibility conveyed to mothers those sons under the age of seven and all daughters. Older sons would be put into the hands of fathers. Divorcing parents on these grounds were, however, free to make their own arrangements. Article 2 gave the responsibility of settling such matters in the case of *causes déterminées* to an 'assemblée de famille'. Whatever the arrangement, even if a third party cared for the children, parents were still required to contribute financially (Article 5). In a bid to tie up the narrative denouements of real families, Article 7 maintained that the children of divorced parents should retain their rights of succession. Children from different marriages should inherit 'en concurrence' and in equal portions.

Subsequently, divorce was largely an urban phenomenon. Between 1792 and 1803 there was, according to Phillips, in Nantes one divorce to every twenty-six marriages, in Lyons one to every eleven, in Rouen one to every eight, and in Paris a staggering one divorce to every four marriages (12,431 to 51,827).[5] The reasons for this urban focus were not just ideological or 'ideational'; in rural communities the family economy was more interdependent (people needed each other just to survive). In Phillips's object of study, Rouen, the mean age of marrying men was 29.6 and women 26.8, whilst the mean age of divorcing men was 39.1 and women 35.6. In spite of the distinction between divorce and mere separation, it is worth noting that rates of remarriage were far lower for divorcees in this period than modern remarriage after divorce, and lower than remarriage after widowing in the eighteenth century.

Beyond the law, we can already see in formation the discursive tropes of divorce, which will in turn shape the fictional treatments we will encounter in the literary chapters which will follow this historical account. From the beginning, divorce was associated with women's rights, as the Convention nationale heard on 18 brumaire Year II (30 October 1793):

> La citoyenne Gavot, femme libre, vient solennellement rendre hommage à la loi sainte du divorce. Hier, gémissante sous l'empire d'un mari despote, la liberté n'était qu'un vain titre pour elle. Aujourd'hui rendue à la dignité de femme indépendante, elle adore cette loi bienfaisante qui rompt les nœuds mal assortis, qui rend les cœurs à eux-mêmes, à la nature, enfin à la divine liberté.[6]

From the opposite, conservative perspective, women's very access to divorce turned them into the guardians of family order:

> Et si le Ciel du nom de mère
> Vous fit don, ah! gardez-vous bien,
> Entre vos enfants et leur père
> D'élever ce mur mitoyen!..[7]

As one would imagine, the question of children loomed large in anti-divorce rhetoric throughout the period with which this book is concerned. In 'Le Divorce' (1848), Onézime Seure intones:

> Vous, qui contre un remords cherchez ce vil refuge,
> Entre l'épouse et vous prenez l'enfant pour juge:
> Demandez-lui tous deux, en lui tendant la main,
> De quel côté du cœur il veut être orphelin,
> [...]
> Car, inaliénable et vivant héritage,
> Ce n'est qu'avec le fer qu'un enfant se partage![8]

In flesh, unlike money, partibility was impossible. As well as redistributing judicial roles and turning the child into the judge, Seure invokes the long-standing analogy between divorce and widowhood to which we shall return at various points.

To reconstruct popular opinion on such subjects is notoriously difficult. But, certainly, songs about divorce became a key site of popular cultural warfare in the revolutionary period. The royalist pamphleteer François Marchant was particularly keen to satirize the libertarian excesses of the Revolution, 'collecting' *chansons des dames de la Halle*. 'Les droits de la femme', to be sung on the air of 'Je connais un berger discret', ridicules the potential dilution by multiplication of marriage's significance:

> Bientôt on verra parmi nous
> Une volage dame,
> Vingt fois par an changer d'époux
> Grâce aux droits de la femme.[9]

The liberal perception of divorce as one of the processes necessary to maintain individual liberty was undermined by a conservative caricature of the dizzying merry-go-round of spouse exchange which divorce might produce. The traditional idealization of the unique couple produced a mathematical basis for much satire. In 'Rabâchage du père Lubon' we hear:

> Je n'avions qu'un'femme, et queuqu'fois
> C'était trop dans l'ménage;
> J'en aurons deux, j'en aurons trois,
> Queu délic! Queu ramage!
> Maintenant qu'on peut divorcer,
> Queu plaisir tous les ans de se remarier![10]

As 'Explication de la loi du divorce' suggests, the irony of the merry-go-round is that what goes around comes around:

> On pourra
> Troquer sa
> Citoyenne,
> Et ce qui bien pis sera
> Parfois on reprendra
> La sienne.[11]

The libertarian fantasy of the sequential life is checked by this conservative image of the ineffaceable power of the first union. There is no escape from the past one thinks one has left behind. The series becomes a cycle.

Satire, of course, quotes the discourse it abhors, including the anti-papist gallicanism in this Rousseauist echo of freedom beyond chains, 'Le Divorce: Dialogue entre Madame Engueule et Madame Saumon, et M. Mannequin':

> D'ailleurs que croient les droits de l'homme
> Sans le divorce point de liberté
> Leur indissolubricité
> Est une chaîne elle vient de Rome,
> J'lavons traînée assez long-temps;
> Plus de chaîne, et qu'les français soient francs.[12]

The traditional assertion of the indissolubility of marriage is tainted by neologistic portmanteau contact with 'lubricité'. Indeed, Ronsin notes the widespread reference to divorce as 'la satisfaction populaire s'exprime en chanson', not least in 'Bénissons nos législateurs' which concludes with an invocation of classical, pre-Christian Rome (and of the model republic):

> Aux Romains, qui nous valaient bien,
> On doit cette loi sage;
> Que le Français, bon citoyen,
> En fasse un juste usage.[13]

Naquet would later stress the durability of the new divorce law amidst the turmoil of the 1790s and in particular the Directorate:

> Malgré toute l'agitation qui fut faite contre le divorce pendant la période directoriale, la loi du 20 septembre 1792 demeura intacte et, pour la restreindre, pour faire disparaître le divorce provoqué par la volonté d'un seul sans allégation de motifs déterminés, il ne fallut rien moins que le 18 brumaire et la réaction consulaire et impériale.[14]

Theatrical responses were also swift: *Le Divorce* by François-George Fouques dit Desfontaine (18 May 1793); Dupont de l'Ille's *La Double réconciliation* (5 thermidor Year IV); Augustin Prévost's *L'Utilité du divorce* (24 fructidor Year VI); and Nicolas-Julien Fargeot, *Le Double divorce ou le Bienfait de la loi*. At the Comédie française spectators could watch Beaumarchais's satire on divorce as the 'publication of shame', *L'Autre Tartuffe ou la mère coupable*. To the 'perfidious' Bégearss's 'le divorce accrédité chez cette nation hasardeuse vous permettra d'user de ce moyen', the 'admirably kind' Count retorts: 'Moi, publier ma honte! Quelques lâches l'on fait: c'est le dernier degré de l'avilissement du siècle. Que l'opprobre soit le partage de qui donne un pareil scandale, et des fripons qui le provoquent.' In the dictatorial atmosphere of the 1790s, though, censorship could be used to attack conservative scepticism. The author of *L'Homme sans façon*, for example, had to agree to the deletion of four lines about divorce. As the censor wrote, 'to attack a new institution in its effects and to proclaim its abuses is to expose it too easily to its detractors and to slander the institution itself in its principle.'[15] To display the frailty of private life was, it seemed, ignoble. Indeed, one of the paradoxes of the divorce question is its confrontation of private and public spheres. Although it spoke to the emerging association of marriage with romantic and erotic love (and thus to a bourgeois notion of marriage which grew in the eighteenth century), it also contravened the Theory of Separate Spheres often associated with the bourgeoisie of the nineteenth century.

Napoleonic Paternalism

The Revolution's liberal provision for divorce was finally diluted in the Civil Code under Title VI (Articles 229–311), decreed on 21 March 1803 and promulgated on 31 March. In André's terms, 'Rien ne ressemble moins au démariage de 1792 que le divorce de 1803. Celui du Code Civil. Peu libéral, ce divorce établit un déséquilibre entre les époux dont les droits deviennent inégaux.'[16] We should note Napoleon's personal investment in the need to maintain divorce provision in spite of the paternalism of the new code. In Ronsin's terms: 'La liberté du divorce n'est maintenue dans le Code civil, sous une forme extrêmement limitée, que grâce à la détermination de Bonaparte.'[17] In due course, he would make use of this law to dispose of Josephine.

The first Chapter of this new law ('Des causes du divorce') articulated the gender iniquity which the Civil Code institutionalized more generally. Most important for historians looking back is that this gender ideology was not an insidious and implicit value-system which imperial society hid beneath a politically correct veneer; nor was it a kind of collective unconscious. On the contrary, such inequality was proposed explicitly and consciously as a riposte to the excesses of revolutionary *égalité*. Article 229's plain assertion that 'le mari pourra demander le divorce pour cause d'adultère de sa femme' was nuanced in Article 230 which specified that 'la femme pourra demander le divorce pour cause d'adultère de son mari, lorsqu'il aura tenu sa concubine dans la maison commune'. Though forced by repeated failures to shift the grounds for divorce from the terms of 1792 to 1803 as he pushed the case of divorce in the early Third Republic, Naquet could not stomach the disparity enshrined in the subordinate clause of Article 230, which performed grammatically the dissymmetry of gender in Napoleonic France. Other causes provided for in the Civil Code were: 'excès [rather than the 'crimes' of 1792], sévices ou injures graves' against a spouse; sentencing of one's spouse to 'une peine infamante'; and, as a 'cause péremptoire', mutual (and 'persévérant' consent).

Chapter II ('Du divorce pour cause déterminée') focuses on 'Des formes du divorce pour cause déterminée' and defines the role of judges and the courts, by contrast with the DIY element of the 1792 provision. The gravity of divorce was enshrined by Article 234 in the courtroom institutionalization of the process. Only in the case of illness verified by two doctors could the *époux demandeur* avoid presenting their evidence in person to the court. The *demandeur* and judge would sign a *procès-verbal* to be copied to the other spouse, and both parties would be summoned before the judge. Before the case could be sent to the *tribunal*, the judge should make 'les représentations qu'il croira propres à opérer un rapprochement'. Once a list of witnesses and evidence had been drawn up, both parties would sign a further *procès-verbal*, leading to an 'audience publique'. As Article 258 indicated, divorce proceedings must produce a public judgement on private life. Articles 259 and 260 made provision in the case of 'excès, sévices ou injures graves' for judges to postpone divorce for a year in which the wife might leave her husband's company and refuse his visits. Only if this failed would the divorce then be granted. Divorce where one's spouse had been sentenced for 'une peine infamante' was far more straightforward. In all events, including appeals, this section of Chapter II was keen to ensure that proceedings unfolded promptly. Section II stipulated the 'mesures provisoires auxquelles peut donner lieu la demande en divorce pour cause déterminée'. Ordinarily, provisional care of children would now fall to husbands, be they *demandeur* or *défendeur* (Article 267). The wife, *demanderesse* or *défenderesse*, could leave the conjugal home during the proceedings and receive a 'pension alimentaire proportionnée aux facultés du mari' (Article 268). In anticipation of that nineteenth-century drive to name and know the place of the individual in the face of the anonymity and mobility of modernity, the court would need to know and be able to check in which house the wife would be residing (§268 & 269). Articles 270 and 271 were designed to stop spouses exploiting the *régime de la communauté* by secreting the spoils of an imminent divorce. Section III devoted to 'Des fins de non-recevoir contre l'action en divorce pour cause déterminée' deals with the question of reconciliation, which should interrupt divorce proceedings, but leave open the possibility of a future action. These articles emblematize the uneasy relationship between the necessarily stiff and categorical definitions of publically and legally sanctioned relationships and the fluidity of what, in Giddens's terms, we might see as the increasing 'confluence' of desire. The former is forever attempting to catch up with and assimilate the latter, most melodramatically in the connection between divorce and adultery in the opening articles of the Civil Code's provision.

The Civil Code disposed of divorce on the grounds of temperamental incompatibility and reintroduced *séparation de corps*. But Chapter III (Articles 275–94) did provide for divorce by mutual consent, even if it was designed to curtail caprice and *de facto* abandonment by imposing humiliating obstacles. It could not be granted either to husbands under twenty-five or to wives who were under the age of twenty-one or had reached forty-five years of age. It could not be admitted in the first two years of marriage nor after twenty. In all cases, it would require the authorization of their mothers and fathers (or other living ascendants). Here we see a flashpoint between the rise of the atomized modern couple and the generational ties of the traditional family, the latter sponsored by the state to tame the former. The spouses would have to agree on childcare henceforth, and the wife's residence and maintenance during the proceedings. As in Article 239, Article 282 stressed the judge's role in ensuring that the would-be divorcees understood the gravity of their actions. If the action proceeded, their notaries would draw up a *procès-verbal* which had to be confirmed in the first fortnight of the fourth, seventh and tenth months which followed, with their parents' continued assent proffered 'par acte public'. After a year, the couple would have to represent all four *procès-verbaux* to the court, each in the presence of two friends, 'personnes notables dans l'arrondissement', and at least fifty years of age — tying the 'anti-social' couple into the matrix of social (as well as familial) relationships. Article 289 suggested that the courts might prefer to impede such divorces ('La loi empêche'), even if 'la loi permet' once all the criteria of the process had been met. Only at this point would the officier de l'État-Civil be called upon to register this divorce (by contrast with the speed with which he had entered the process in accordance with the law of 1792).

Chapter IV ('Des effets du divorce') continues in a similar vein, keen to check the whimsicality of desire. Divorced spouses could not under any circumstances get remarried to each other (§295). In the case of 'cause déterminée', the ex-wife could only marry again after ten months, to stop the manipulation of divorce so that an adulterous wife might hope to marry her lover before the birth of their child (§296). Indeed, the Civil Code asserted the primacy of the social father (the wife's husband simply was, *de jure*, the father of children born during their marriage). This very assertion, however, avowed the epistemological uncertainty of biological paternity. In the case of mutual consent, neither spouse could marry again for three years (§297). One form of socially conservative logic might encourage the reintegration of monadic and nomadic divorcees back into the dyadic fabric of a society based on marriage, hence the idea prevalent in England after its law of 1857, that propriety required that a divorcee should repair the social fabric by marrying their lover. However, the socially conservative logic of the French Civil Code wanted to discourage divorce, even if it permitted it. Hence Article 298, which would become notorious, forbad adulterous spouses from marrying their 'accomplice', and in a further display of gender disparity, an adulterous wife would be sentenced to 'réclusion' in a house of correction for three months to two years. Articles 299–301 ensured that in cases other than mutual consent the guilty party could not reap the benefits established by the marriage contract or accrued since, whilst the plaintiff would retain such advantages. If needs be, the court could requisition up to a third of the guilty party's wealth in order to provide a 'pension alimentaire' for the plaintiff. Articles 302–05 made provision for children, custody normally being granted to the wronged spouse, though both parents retained rights ('le droit de surveiller l'entretien et l'éducation de leurs enfants') and financial responsibilities. In the particular case of mutual consent, Article 305 reserved half of each ex-spouse's wealth for the benefit of children born of the marriage, the ex-spouses only retaining authority over these resources until the children reached majority.

Chapter V ('De la séparation de corps') allowed for *séparation de corps* in the case of 'cause déterminée', but not by mutual consent. With *séparation de corps* there would necessarily be *séparation de biens*. An adulterous wife would still be liable to 'réclusion' from three months up to two years in a house of correction, whereas the adulterous husband is not mentioned. In this sense, the errant husband benefited from the notion of the doxa as that which goes without saying, literally as well as figuratively.

The authority of the cuckold, however, demanded legal support. He remained 'le maître' with the power to free his imprisoned wife by consenting to take her back. In order to check the limbo which mere separation might produce, after three years the 'défendeur' could request a divorce if the 'demandeur' did not agree to end their separation. Otherwise separation would hold people in a conjugally nebulous zone between marriage and remarriage, between a first marriage and a second. The only exception to this three-year limit was the adulterous wife — she might suffer in perpetuity, it seemed.

Between Napoleon and Naquet

Following the definitive removal of Napoleon, even this 'divorce minimum'[18] was unacceptable to the Chambre Introuvable of the Restoration by 1816. The brief law of abrogation (only three articles long) was unambiguous: 'Article 1er — Le divorce est aboli.' To clean up cases in progress, Article 2 converted requests for divorce for 'causes déterminées' into requests for *séparation de corps*, and Article 3 cancelled all processes based on mutual consent where divorce had not yet been pronounced. Of 'la loi abolitive du divorce du 8 mai 1816' Naquet would later say that it was 'dictée par l'esprit clérical' and constituted 'une première brèche faite par le passé à l'édifice de la révolution française'.[19] In fact, Naquet argued, it was the desacralization of marriage which had changed everything: 'c'est le mariage civil qui est le vrai principe en opposition avec les prétentions de la cour romaine, et non le divorce *civil* qui n'en est qu'une conséquence'.

To argue over the merits of divorce was to engage in the moral auditing of the Revolution which characterized the long nineteenth century. Such a retrospection began virtually immediately. Indeed, the family values of the counter-revolution were enshrined in Napoleonic France by vicomte Louis-Gabriel-Ambroise de Bonald's *Du divorce: considéré au XIXe siècle, relativement à l'état domestique et à l'état public de société* (1801). Ronsin notes the swiftly developed 'habitude d'inclure, parmi les innombrables et épouvantables méfaits commis au cours de la période précédente, l'établissement d'une législation du divorce outrageusement libérale, véritable attentat au profit de la débauche et au détriment de la famille et de la religion.'[20] The fact that the question of divorce should emerge at each of the revolutionary turning-points of the nineteenth century, without fail, was naturally a reflection of radical opportunism, striking when all manner of values and choices were up for grabs. But such an insistent association of *divorciaire* discourse with political crisis only fuelled the original connection in the conservative imagination which, as Ronsin explains in *Les Divorciaires*, equated divorce with the crimes of the Convention, with anarchy, and with the corruption of mores. As banal as it might seem 'to reduce all politics to the eternal metaphor of the family'[21], whose normativity may threaten to ensnare us, the gesture seems from another perspective to be quite comprehensible. It is in fact hard to imagine a politics without a discourse on the family, however eccentric or radical.

To return to the Civil Code as such would have meant a return to divorce, but as Ronsin notes of the July Revolution: 'Monarchistes libéraux et républicains sont unanimes, en 1830, à considérer le retour au Code civil comme une conséquence logique de la révolution. Voté à quatre reprises par les députés, celui-ci est cependant interdit par la force de l'opposition rencontrée à la Chambre des pairs'.[22] Once again verse was used to polemicize, as in the 'mémoire en forme de requête' which pleaded for 'Divorce entre la demoiselle Françoise L'Éplorée et le sieur Judas son soi-disant mari' after a forced marriage. Its opening critique of the notion of divorce as the 'sacrament of adultery' reveals how the discourse between 1816 and 1884 consistently returned to its own clichés:

> Le divorce, qu'un sot a très-mal défini
>   Le sacrement de l'adultère.
> Du Code à l'avenir ne sera plus banni;
> L'hymen est nul de droit quand il cesse de plaire.
> Puisqu'un grand magistrat, noble appui des vertus,
> En dépit de Bonald nous rend ce cher divorce,
> Les nœuds qui les premiers doivent être rompus.[23]

But the Chamber of Peers refused to allow divorce to return, in 1830 and in subsequent attempts between 1831 and 1834 to rescind the 1816 law. For the nascent feminist movement, the impossibility of divorce meant that women in impossible marriages were driven to whatever alternatives would allow them to survive beyond the realm of polite society, in particular by prostitution. As Flora Tristan argues, 'If you do not expose her to every abuse of power due to the despotism of paternal power and the indissolubility of marriage, she would never be in the position of having to choose between oppression and infamy.'[24] Indeed, divorce became a habitual element in the litany of reformist claims made by the critics of the July Monarchy. Jann Matlock describes how the fan mail generated by the serialization of Eugène Sue's *Les Mystères de Paris* counselled the author on how to save the adolescent Fleur; and 'when she did not survive, they registered the meaning that had been circulated through her body. They demanded social change, prison reform, better wages for women, education for girls, *divorce rights*, and the vote for women'.[25] Much medical opinion focused on the supposed link between continence and hysteria. As Matlock notes, 'If male continence was not dangerous, then all the justifications for prostitution crumbled'. Those concerned about the dangers of continence, such as Antoine de Montègre, J. B. Louyer-Villermay, Hector Landouzy, Émile Mathieu and Auguste Debay, did not, however, hope for the sexual emancipation of women:

> They questioned any reinstitution of divorce, yet acknowledged that the sexual excesses of unsatisfied married women led them to accesses of hysteria as severe as any suffered by unmarried younger women or widows. They would not have granted Emma Bovary a divorce; nor would they have left her to books and adulterous affairs. Rather they would have demanded that Charles Bovary find a way to convince her to like sex with him. And if that had been impossible, they would have simply assumed that she would find some way to contain her displeasure *and* her desire.

It is not surprising that the issue resurfaced in 1848. In spite of Victor Hugo's ambivalence towards Onézime Seure's anti-divorce position, and the distraction of the June Days, Seure's poem 'Le Divorce' of 1848 is prefaced by Hugo's letter, written 'De l'Assemblée, vendredi 23 juin':

> Ce matin, Monsieur, j'avais lu vos beaux vers et j'en avais l'esprit rempli, quand l'émeute est venue m'arracher à la poésie. En ce moment, dans cette heure de trouble, au milieu du tumulte et dans l'approche de l'orage, je songe à vous, Monsieur, aux nobles inspirations qui m'ont ému, et ma pensée se repose sur la vôtre. Votre opinion sur une question bien grave et très délicate me paraît un peu absolue; mais vous l'exprimez avec une telle hauteur de cœur, avec une telle honnêteté d'âme, que toutes mes objections s'évanouissent devant votre talent. Le penseur murmure un peu, mais le poète applaudit.

It seemed for a while as if divorce, like much else, would be possible during the Second Republic, and Crémieux, Ernest Legouvé and Louis Blanc (author of an *Essai sur le divorce*, 1849) were keen to advocate its reintroduction. Even Louis Napoléon promised this, beseeching Louis-Philippe: 'Qu'avez-vous fait? vous n'avez même pas rétabli le divorce, qui était le palladium de l'honneur des familles!'[26] Seure rails against fresh calls for divorce, and Hugo still had some way to go on his journey to radicalism.

Unlike Fourier, who demanded women's right to sexual pleasure, the republican Ernest Legouvé (whose lectures at the Collège de France in spring 1848 were published as *Histoire morale des femmes* in the same year) called for women's rights to be protected from the pleasure-seeking of men. Whereas the Saint-Simonians of the early July Monarchy had embraced liberty, Legouvé warned against the ills of adultery and prostitution in his depiction of 'the free woman'. Such 'abuses of marriage' should be resolved, he argued, by the temporary institution of divorce and an enlargement of the rights of mothers.

However, divorce was largely associated with feminist radicalism. The abolition of the press censorship of the July Monarchy and the end to restrictions on public meetings left the women of 1848 hopeful of radical change. Women's clubs and a new paper, *La Voix des femmes*, called for women's right to vote and a reinstitution of divorce. The 'Opinion de la Mère Duchêne sur le divorce' (1848) recounts the demands for divorce on a multiplicity of grounds that this unhappy old wife proffers to citizen Crémieux.[27] When she arrives in his office, she finds the minister being harangued by 'la crème des bas-bleus parisiens en train de s'émanciper', in an echo of the stereotype of female volubility. When Mère Duchêne expresses her request, the blue-stockings (a radical urban intellectual elite) claim her as one of their own. In a long-standing analogy which politicizes the family, husbands are compared to tyrants: 'Oh! les hommes! les hommes! quelle race! Ce sont tous des tyrans, des despotes, des persécuteurs, des infâmes, des jaloux. N'ont-ils pas la prétention de nous faire rester à la maison, tandis qu'eux sont toujours en route?' The traditional family is seen as very *ancien régime*, and very old hat. A race apart, husbands are caricatured as icons of inequality and domestic despots. The family sanctioned by the Civil Code is seen to be fundamentally counter-revolutionary. In the space of a sentence, political vocabulary is connected syntagmatically with moral ('infâmes') and sentimental ('jaloux') diction. Such feminists (though by no means all) championed divorce as a way of policing a domesticity otherwise hidden away behind the Theory of Separate Spheres. The public discourse of law should be used to challenge this separation between 'maison' and 'route' and allow women access to the latter; women were to use public means to attain public visibility. To pursue a divorce suit was in and of itself a contravention of the theory of gender separation, a challenge to men on their own home ground (which was, precisely, outside the home). This account of the politicization of women bears witness, however, to a perceived gap between Mère Duchêne's everyday experience and elite feminism. When the blue-stockings hear Mère Duchêne's inventory of grounds for divorce, they are amazed that she is so well-informed on the matter of unhappy marriages. Her somewhat typical inventory includes drunkenness and vulgarity; incurable sickness hidden prior to the wedding; madness (even if apparent only after the wedding), for fear that 'the torture of a living person attached to a corpse' would lead to suicide; the notoriously vague term 'sévices', mistreatment so bad as to harm *her* reputation amongst decent folk; to save men from strangling their wives and the latter from poisoning the former (civil law to be used to prevent criminal activity); in the well-worn phrase 'condamnation à des peines afflictives ou infamantes', in order to protect an innocent wife and her unfortunate children from 'un nom qui serait à jamais une marque d'infamie empreinte sur leur front' (to erase the patronym from the visible body, so that to be married would not mean to be brandished); by implicit comparison, cases of 'dérèglement de mœurs chez la femme', so as to save husbands from ridicule; abandonment and long-term absence; and finally, before Crémieux begs her to stop, spending and wasting the family's entire resources. Mère Duchêne then has to return home to face the anger of her obstreperous spouse.

Mère Duchêne's example of poisoning was the much-discussed case of the newly-wed Mme Marie Cappelle-Lafarge, sentenced to death in 1840 for the murder of her husband. Matlock argues that the very impossibility of divorce would have seemed to many to provide Mme Cappelle-Lafarge with a strong motive for murder: 'Marie's case was not helped by the fact that she would have had few alternatives if she had indeed been unable to endure life with this unkempt man in a village distant from her family and friends. Divorce had been outlawed since 1816. A separation would have dishonored all parties. A woman's adultery was even less acceptable in the countryside than in Paris' (250). In short, the law of 1816 made desperate criminality plausible. What other plots were available to Mme Cappelle-Lafarge? As Matlock explains, 'Cappelle-Lafarge's contemporaries could easily imagine her driven to murder because she had no other alternative to regain control over her existence. As a widow, she could have taken her dowry and gone back to Paris, enjoying, for the first time in her life, a kind of self-reliance possible *only* for women whose husbands were dead.'[28] In literary and social terms, the return of divorce in 1884 promised to defuse the marriage plot — a problem for novelists, a boon for social reformers.

The discourse on women's rights was caricatured in the satirical review, *Le Charivari*. 'Les seules chaînes que les femmes se décident à porter volontiers' of 10 January 1848 may imply that the suitor's offering is never a pure gift and, in a common figure, rings and jewellery are associated with the enslavement of chains. But divorce was aligned with the carnivalesque upturning of order, in the words of 'Manifestation des femmes' (31 March 1848): 'Plus de vilains maris... vive le Divorce!...'. Women's self-assertion was subjected to terrified ridicule in depictions of the strict inversion of traditional gender roles, not least in the series 'Les Vésuviennes', curvaceous but armed, and often bearing a military *képi*. One thumbs her nose at a laden husband who beseeches: 'Mâme Coquardeau, j'te défends d'aller au rappel... n'y a pas d'bon sens de me laisser comme ça avec trois enfans sur les bras...... et pas de biberon!......' (1 May 1848). In a logic which modern readers will still recognize, the possibility for the social transformation of stereotypical roles is decried on the grounds that men are not allowed access to traditionally female domains; one rather camp young man is driven out, his hands over his ears, as 'angry young *wo*men' chant 'À bas les modistes mâles!...' (12 May 1848). The nurturing role of radical mothers seemed to threaten the future of the nation too. In one image a child shows her bewildered father a sheet of paper where she has copied out repeatedly the word 'Divorce': 'Tiens, papa, voilà le devoir que maman m'a donné ce matin...' (11 June 1848). The phrase used in these caricatures to signal the entropic potential of divorce was the 'abolition of the family' (in the wetnurse's complaint to Proudhon about the proposed law, 22 August 1848; and in the toast of the Femino-Socialist Banquet, 19 December 1848).

Conservative feminists, yet more visible later in the century, would have agreed that a new divorce law would in fact confront women with more than they bargained for. One wife turns a corner only to be surprised by the sight of her husband adding to the posters on the walls of the revolutionary city: 'Ciel de Dieu! que vois-je! mon mari collant une affiche en faveur du divorce!' (21 May 1848). To some it seemed that the goose was playing into the gander's hands. The mathematics of carnival meant not only inversion but also multiplication, as readers would have seen on that same day, in two more images. In 'Ce qui arriverait par suite du divorce' a desperate town hall official pleads to the groom: 'Citoyen, je vous ai déjà marié onze fois ce mois-ci. Cela devient fatigant, à la fin.' And with a back view of a new wife with the number 14 stuck to her rear, husband quips to male friend: 'C'est ma nouvelle femme. Comme je m'en brouille les noms, je leur donne un numéro.' At odds with the habitual association of divorce with the right to individual determination of the self (from 1792 all the way through to Giddens), here its tendency to multiply the supposedly unique relationship is seen to depersonalize love. In the search for the 'right' relationship, what remains is the structure of relationships, whose nodes can be filled by innumerable different folk.

This anti-divorce strain culminated in a series of caricatures entitled, precisely, 'Les Divorceuses'. To the news that the proposal will not become law, one woman demands from the crowd of *citoyennes* civil disobedience: 'déclarons que la patrie est en danger!...' (4 August 1848). Such women are accused of a perverse distaste for the everyday; one radical comments to her friend on the pictorial cliché and social norm of mother with child: 'Voilà une femme qui, à l'heure solennelle où nous sommes, s'occupe bêtement de ses enfants. Qu'il y a encore en France des êtres abruptes et arriérés!' In a desire to divide and conquer, such radicals are depicted as a hedonistic elite who do not share the interests of most women, hence the 'toast porté à l'émancipation des femmes, par des femmes déjà furieusement émancipées'

(12 October 1848). In a further play on the idea of the revolutionary banquet, like the Femino-Socialist banquet, the toast represents the momentary pause of crystallized aspiration, in other words carnival culminating in ritual.

During the Second Empire, separations were recorded on a regular basis, and calls for divorce persisted in radical discourse.[29] Against this strain persisted a fragile yet assertive vision of marriage as a once-and-forever union, which nevertheless shared an understanding of the high stakes involved in the idealization of marriage:

> Le mariage est tout ou rien. Il n y'a pas de partage possible d'affection et de rapports intimes. Quand une brèche y est faite, si petite qu'elle soit, c'est comme le coussin à air percé par une épingle. Tout fuit par ce point invisible; le fardeau seul reste, et l'on a tiré, à jamais, ce qui rend léger et doux.[30]

From the 1860s there was, as Paul Baquiast explains, a sharp increase in the number of publications devoted to women and their relations with men.[31] In the wake of Michelet's L'Amour (1858) and La Femme (1859) which asks 'pourquoi l'on ne se marie pas', feminists such as Jenny d'Héricourt savaged his unremittingly biological vision of women's dependent state (La Femme affranchie, 1860). Even Michelet's follower, Eugène Pelletan, sketches a more nuanced history of civilization in La Mère (1865). A woman of Ancient Greece, he says, 'entre dans le mariage, non plus à titre de mobilier, mais sur le pied de sociétaire, et à la rupture de l'association, par décès ou par divorce, elle reprend son apport.'[32] The direction of her life narrative could be recast, and divorce was vital in this process. After the misogynistic idealization of women in medieval culture, Pelletan proclaims that the Reformation reintroduced divorce precisely so as to guarantee the value of marriage. This long history culminated in the law of 1792, but was undermined by the Civil Code and the hypocrisy of reciprocal infidelity in modern marriage, in his terms 'le divorce aimable'. Although divorce was of course on the Commune's agenda in 1871, only the Third Republic would be able to assert the long-term possibility of divorce in modern France.

Naquet Comes To Paris

Decisive in the reestablishment of divorce was one Alfred Joseph Naquet.[33] He was born on 6 October 1834 in Carpentras (Vaucluse), with a physical abnormality, in André's words 'la colonne vertébrale tordue, le dos voûté, la tête enfoncée dans les épaules, ce que n'arrangea pas une taille qui resta petite'.[34] As Daniel Mollenhauer explains, he was of above-average intelligence and, amidst this free-thinking family, highly sensitive to political questions, 'with a marked propensity for the politics of the outsider'.[35] 'Israélite de naissance, libre-penseur de conviction',[36] his political life followed 'a complete series of radical changes in direction', always keen to collaborate with new radical projects. Ginette André stresses the rootedness (rather than the rootlessness) of his family and community:

> Naquet [...] appartenait à une vieille famille israélite du Comtat-Venaissin, ou mieux, il descendait de toutes ces familles juives, solidement enracinées dans ce terroir depuis le Moyen-Age, peut-être même venues aux derniers siècles de l'Antiquité — sa mère s'appelait Paméla Vidal.[37]

Semé-David and Paméla (named after Richardson's heroine) married in May 1830 in Nîmes, and managed to integrate themselves into the bourgeois prosperity of the July Monarchy, Semé-David forsaking the bar for the more lucrative activity as *marchand de biens*, in André's phrase 'un gros trafiquant de maisons, de granges et de terres'. In 1843 Alfred's brother, Eliacin, was born. Mother ensured the boys' religious education, whilst father was a free-thinking republican. André argues that Naquet's upbringing was rather fortunate:

> L'enfant Naquet se sentait français et l'égal de n'importe quel autre. [...] Les hommes sont égaux et un juif vaut un chrétien. Ne sont-ils pas tous deux français? On le pensait à Carpentras. [...] L'enfance d'Alfred Naquet s'écoula à une époque heureuse, qui s'était délivré du vieil antisémitisme religieux et qui ne connaissait pas encore l'antisémitisme racial. Il fut un enfant juif sans complexe, aimé par ses parents et lui-même fils affectueux, grandissant dans une ville où voisinent en bonne amitié l'Eglise et la Synagogue. (34–35)

Years later, the Marseille poet Clovis Hugues would quip in *L'Égalité* on 16 August 1876:

> A Carpentras, que l'on gasconne,
> Les socialistes sont gras
> Les curés doux, la bière bonne,
> Tout est bizarre à Carpentras.

Initially drawn to the study of Judaism, 1848 imposed questions of the here and now which Alfred pursued in his political and philosophical reading (not least of Comte and Proudhon). As he was later to recall: 'Je suis arrivé à la vie intellectuelle et morale en 1848. [...] J'ignore absolument ce qui serait advenu de moi si les événements de 1848 n'avaient pas bouleversé le cours de mes idées ...'[38] His philosophy was then fixed: 'Déjà, j'étais positiviste sans m'en douter. [...] Il y a deux points sur lesquels je n'ai jamais varié depuis. Je suis demeuré positiviste et républicain.' But much of his politics, particularly in the context of marriage and the family, can be understood as a response to a Catholic France which had not, of course, undergone the Reformation.

Before entering the public realm of politics, he was a professional scientist. After passing the baccalauréat in Aix in 1851 with the *prix d'excellence*, he was to study in Montpellier, but observed the brutal suppression of the people at the hands of the future Napoléon III which took place across the Midi. In the words of his autobiography he was 'cruellement froissé par le coup d'Etat de décembre'.[39] In 1852 he left to study in Paris at 26, rue de Bréa, with his friend Jules Cazot, future senator and minister of justice. He would remain in the Montparnasse district. In Paris he progressed to the *licence* in physics in 1857. In 1859, at the age of twenty-five, he was awarded his doctorate in medicine for his thesis on the *Application de l'analyse chimique à la toxicologie*, though he would not go on to practice. Following his *thèse de concours* entitled *De l'allotropie et de l'isomérie* (1860), at the second time of asking, he succeeded in 1863 in the *agrégation* in Chemistry (with a thesis on sugars). He also spent two *années de stage* teaching physics and chemistry at the technical institute in Palermo. His *Principes de chimie fondés sur les théories modernes* (Paris, 1865) was translated into English, German and Russian. The clearest evidence of Naquet's position amongst the scientific elite is his appearance in André Brouillet's famous painting of Charcot, *Une leçon clinique à la Salpêtrière* (1887). In this picture of one of Charcot's displays of female hysteria from 1886 (the patient is Blanche Wittmann), reproduced in Abel Lurat's engraving, Naquet sits third from left behind Vigouroux, Brissaud and Gilles de la Tourette. The previous year, the young Sigmund Freud had arrived in Paris to study under Charcot.[40]

His civil union with Estelle Combemale, celebrated on 5 April 1862 in the town hall of the 6th arrondissement, lasted until 1867 and produced three children, all of whom were initially spared a religious upbringing. Though her father's family were Catholic, Estelle's mother's (the Michelons) were known in Privas to be 'rouges', so for Estelle to relinquish the religion of her childhood and adopt her husband's free thought was not such a break with family tradition as we might at first presume. Alfred's family was more exercised by her lack of a fortune, and in the classic mode of the *mal assortis* 'où l'on veut bien unir les cœurs mais non les sacs d'écus'[41], they married under the *régime de la communauté réduite aux acquêts*, so that each would retain the *mobilier* they might individually receive by inheritance or succession in the course of their marriage. After the death of two children (their firstborn buried in Palermo in 1865; the other, Rachel, in Paris in 1867, barely four years old), his wife returned to the Catholic Church. As Naquet explains in his letter of 29 May 1879 to *Le Figaro*, this loss was cited in the Senate in 1868 by Cardinal de Bonnechose (who quoted Naquet's analogy between the soul and a battery). It even became the subject of a press polemic (Naquet responding to *Le Moniteur Universel* of 21 May in *L'Avenir National* on 24 May). The materialist and atheist analogy between soul and battery had been voiced in his *Cours de philosophie chimique*:

> Votre âme est sous la dépendance immédiate de votre corps. Elle se transforme et se renouvelle sans cesse tant qu'il vit, elle disparaît avec lui. Rien ne se perd, il est vrai. Le mouvement qui est en moi et qui constitue ma pensée se transformera en travail d'une autre nature. Les atomes qui composent mon corps iront, après ma mort, et même pendant ma vie, former d'autres corps différents du mien. Mais moi, individu déterminé, défini, ayant une existence séparée de ce qui m'entoure, j'aurai cessé d'exister.[42]

Such demystification of human matter makes it easier to accept Goethe's notion of 'elective affinities', namely that love may recompose in different form, as divorce and remarriage imply. Estelle had their marriage blessed by the Church and had their remaining son, Paul, baptized whilst Naquet was in Mazas prison and raised, as his autobiography puts it, in accordance with 'un catholicisme exagéré'.[43] All this was unacceptable to Naquet who separated from her, though he did not intend to divorce and marry again — as he proclaimed in *Le Figaro* in 1879. After his return from exile in Spain, the estranged couple met up in Nice in 1870, where it became clear that no reconciliation was possible.

In the 1879 letter he claimed that his *divorciaire* propaganda was for the common good, not personal interest. Of any such new law, he stresses, '*je n'ai pas la moindre velléité de me servir*'. Still, when the law did come, Naquet wanted to allow divorce on the grounds of 'les dissentiments religieux survenus après le mariage et prouvés soit par le changement de religion de l'un des époux, soit par la religion imposée aux enfants lors de leur naissance ou plus tard par l'un des époux, malgré la volonté ou à l'insu de l'autre, soit par l'aveu des parties'. His autobiographical letter of 1879 intends to dismiss the significance of such personal details (in a kind of anti-autobiography). Naquet retained with his wife 'les meilleurs rapports' and held her in 'la plus parfaite estime', he declared. Only after the death of his first wife in 1903 did he marry again. The 1879 letter pauses to consider the 'devoirs contradictoires' of the absent father. On the one hand, he feels compelled to withdraw his son from a Catholic education of which he wholly disapproves. On the other and ultimately more significant hand, he considers it an act of injustice and barbarism to rob this already bereaved mother of this once sickly child whom she has brought into the world. In spite of his legal rights, the child belongs morally to its mother, he argues.

Under the Second Empire, Naquet had belonged to the 'revolutionary' opposition of the Latin Quarter. He had visited Blanqui in Belgium and attended several meetings of the *Commune révolutionnaire des ouvriers français* at the home of Chouteau, its agent provocateur.[44] He also collaborated with a young Georges Clémenceau on *La Revue Encyclopédique*, established by the Blanquist Regnard. From 9 to 12 September 1867 he organized in Geneva with his friend, the law professor Émile Acollas, the first congress of the League of Peace and Liberty. The mood deteriorated when, on 11 September, he openly criticized the French Empire and in particular Napoleon I as the father of modern militarism. Of particular notoriety was his much-glossed attack on 'Napoléon Ier, le plus grand malfaiteur du siècle', dismissed by other delegates: 'A la salle de Police! C'est un échappé de Charenton!'[45] He was arrested on 12 November, and sentenced on 23 December in the 6th Chamber of the Seine correctional court to fifteen months in prison, a 500 franc fine and the privation of civil rights for five years. This sentence for covert manoeuvres to disturb public peace and incite anti-government sentiment was spent in convalescence, due to his ill health. He and Acollas were initially transferred to the pavillon Gabrielle at the Hôpital Saint-Louis and then to the maison Duval, rue de Dôme, where he met Lockroy.[46] From these locations he published numerous articles and worked on Pierre Larousse's *Grand Dictionnaire Universel*. His scientific chronicle for *La Tribune* alternated with a literary chronicle penned by a certain Émile Zola. But in one of his letters to the Alsatian industrialist, Scheurer-Kestner, he measures the depths of his situation: 'En sortant de prison, j'aurai perdu mon agrégation, mes leçons qui sont une dépendance de mon agrégation, le Dictionnaire Larousse qui sera épuisé et celui de Würtz qui sera bien près de l'être aussi. Comme c'étaient là mes quatre sources de revenus, j'aurai donc tout perdu.'[47] But his politics continued apace, as in another letter to Scheurer-Kestner: 'L'Empire, nous tuera-t-il? *That is the question.*'[48]

In the final dark days of the Second Empire, Naquet's radicalism reached beyond divorce in the direction of free union. As an elected politician of the Third Republic, he would be more pragmatic. Of his programmatic *Religion, propriété, famille* (1869), written during these long months of incarceration, Ronsin notes:

> A la base de ses vues d'alors se trouvaient la suppression du mariage et l'établissement du matriarcat, le divorce lui apparaissant comme une mesure

sans intérêt, un simple aménagement [...]. Sept ans plus tard, nous le retrouvons
député, auteur d'un projet de loi dont l'objet n'est autre que le rétablissement
du divorce.[49]

In his critique of marriage as the origin of prostitution and abortion, Naquet
imagines a future in which maternity displaces the dominant principle of paternity
— shored up by the Civil Code but wracked by the uncertainty of paternity on
which the genre of the novel of adultery consistently plays:

> La paternité n'est jamais sûre, tandis que la maternité l'est toujours. [...] Il serait
> cent fois plus raisonnable de faire pivoter la famille autour de qui en est une
> origine sûre, qu'autour de qui en est une origine douteuse. Dans l'avenir, le
> pivot de la famille ne sera plus le père, ce sera la mère. Ce sera la mère seule
> qui pourra laisser son nom aux enfants, et qui, pendant leur enfance, aura, sur
> eux, certain droits limités.[50]

Of this 'livre qui a eu un grand retentissement et qui a été très imparfaitement
compris', Naquet's autobiography explains: 'M. Naquet critiquait sévèrement les
doctrines déistes et religieuses, défendait l'institution de la propriété, et attaquait
vigoureusement le mariage et la famille actuelle.'[51] Naquet was threatened with
four months re-imprisonment in March, another 500 franc fine, and the loss of his
civil rights in perpetuity. Freed pending his appeal, he fled to Spain, writing for *Le
Réveil* and taking part in the republican insurrection. He returned after Napoleon
III's amnesty for all political criminals on 14 August 1869, reaching his flat at 42
rue Montparnasse on 1 December.

Naquet would go on writing for papers such as *Le Rappel*. In the plebiscite of
8 May 1870, Naquet joined republicans in encouraging a 'no' vote, at odds with
those like Jules Vallès who favoured abstention, but as expected the republicans lost
the plebiscite to the Emperor. Naquet clearly had friends in the Commune such as
Delescluze and Chouteau. The association of Naquet with Communard radicalism
was reasserted over a decade later, at the height of his divorce notoriety, in Vallès's
L'Insurgé (1886). In the entry for 15 July in Chapter 16, even the perverse anti-
patriotism of Vingtras, condemned by a magistrate for 'excitation à la guerre civile',
hoping for a Prussian victory over the French, is not quite as extreme as Naquet's
radicalism. In his introspection he laments:

> Tu avais été au fond, avoue-le, plus malheureux que content quand on t'avait
> appris que l'Empereur avait un triomphe à son actif. Tu avais souffert quand tu
> croyais la victoire vraie, — presque autant que Naquet, le bossu, qui en pleurait
> de rage![52]

This accusation is all the more striking in a country where the tradition of the
Revolution has associated itself with the patriotism of the flag more easily than the
Left would do on the other side of the Channel. In the fleet-footed narrative of the
pavé, which attempts to capture the language and speed of immediate events from
street level rather than the high view of an omniscient narrator, Vallès manipulates
ironically the stereotypes of everyday discourse. Indeed, the epithetical power of
the apposition 'Naquet, le bossu' reflects his public image; this is how he was often
referred to, not least visually as well as verbally in satire and caricature. Distaste for
his politics was filtered through this image of bodily imperfection.

Appeals to the New Republic

From 4 September 1870 until 1894 Naquet worked in the vanguard of republican politics. After the failed insurrection of 7 August 1870, he wrote to a friend in Carpentras, Dr Cyprien Poujade: 'Dix-huit années d'Empire nous ont terriblement avachis.' Indeed, he took an active part in the fall of the Second Empire. On 4 September 1870, on the pont de la Concorde, he joined those (including Lockroy) invading the Corps législatif. In the centre of the Salle des Délibérations of the Chamber of Deputies a tricolour was unfurled, bearing the year 1792 (vital, of course, in the history of divorce). During the Franco-Prussian War he worked under Gambetta, serving in the Government of National Defence as Chef de cabinet du personnel in the ministry at Place Beauvau. To avoid being trapped in the capital by the Prussian attack on 19 September, Naquet had left for the south two days earlier (hence avoiding the need for a balloon trip like Gambetta). He spent his days until the armistice of 28 January 1871 as secretary of the rather quirky Commission d'Étude des Moyens de Défense in Tours and Bordeaux. But Naquet distanced himself early in 1871 as he saw no further possibility of prosecuting the war successfully. Naquet voted for the constitution of the new Republic so as to 'rendre la parole au pays' and emerged as a speaker at the Union républicaine on the rue de la Soudière, praised by Gambetta who supposedly predicted that he might become 'non seulement un homme utile mais un homme nécessaire'.[53] But by 1875 the 'entente' with Gambetta was over.

On 8 February 1871 he was elected representative of the people of Vaucluse, alongside Gent, Poujade, Pin and Delord. Along with the fellow Vaucluse republicans in the National Assembly (apart from Gent), he kept his promise and voted for peace rather than *la guerre à outrance*. With the election result contested, he and his fellow Vauclusian deputies resigned, preferring the radical republic to the territorial integrity of the nation. From 8 March until 2 July he stayed in Vaucluse and Avignon, whilst the Commune raged and spread to Marseille. Editing the *Démocratie du Midi*, Naquet was keen not to compromise the position of the Left in its entirety. Paris should be supported against Versailles, he felt, but not so aggressively as to invite subsequent reprisals. In particular, Naquet was keen to keep Avignon out of the events in Paris and Marseille. After an inquest into the election, his 4000 majority rose to 9000 on 2 July 1871.[54] Blanquists and radicals might have succeeded in deposing the Emperor and dissolving his court; but they would not dominate a republic which appeared ever more bourgeois, ever less democratic. At the Assemblée nationale in Versailles, Naquet sat amongst the most radical left-wing faction (those who had escaped the shipwreck of the Commune, a group of only 40 out of more than 700, in André's phrase 'cette minorité de la minorité'). Here he made a name for himself through his oratory, though his physical incapacity made him an easy target for the bully-boy tactics of the Chamber. Even in the tiny Union républicaine he maintained an independent position.

Naquet really came to the public's attention for the first time with his speech of 5 September 1871, largely ignored by the Assembly, where he marked the anniversary of the fall of the Empire with a call for the deputies to return to Paris from Versailles.

He would emerge again on 24 January 1872 when he and Millaud tried in vain to pass a law to seize and sell Louis-Napoléon Bonaparte's property in order to pay the war indemnity demanded by the Germans. On 29 July 1872 he and Gambetta, under attack from the Commission des Marchés, had to offer a detailed defence of their role in the Government of National Defence. Their speeches were sold in a 20 centimes brochure, and took up 18 columns of the *Journal officiel*. The fact that the Assembly found Naquet and Gambetta innocent says much for the reconciliation between Thiers and Gambetta — and, *par ricochet*, Naquet too.

Unlike Thiers, when Mac-Mahon became President of the Republic in May 1873, everyone knew that he would be willing to play the straw man, ready to bow before a king. Once more, it seemed that the republic was in danger, and in this context Naquet published his constitutional theory of *La République radicale* which called for universal suffrage at the expense of monarchy: 'On peut prédire à coup sûr que la prochaine assemblée sera, sinon une assemblée radicale, du moins une assemblée républicaine.' Step by dogged step, progressive modernization would follow: 'A chaque législature nouvelle, on verra se constituer une nouvelle minorité proposant de nouvelles réformes que le pays acceptera lorsqu'elles seront suffisamment mûres, ou repoussera lorsque, définitivement, elles lui paraîtront inapplicables ou injustes'.[55] 1873 signalled the era of Ordre Moral, Mac-Mahon in thrall to the duc de Broglie, who proposed that Mac-Mahon's powers be extended for seven years. Although Gambetta voted with Naquet against the *septennat*, this issue provoked their first disagreement. In May 1874 Naquet joined Thiers, Gambetta, Jules Grévy, Jules Ferry, Jules Favre and Jules Simon, in overturning Broglie's ministry. Henceforth the established order could hardly hold.

Ronsin admits that it is impossible to pinpoint the exact date of Naquet's conversion to the pro-divorce position. He was present at the banquet of the radical *L'Avenir des femmes* on 7 July 1872, but his first clear statement in favour of divorce was registered in a discussion of Léon Richer's new bill at a dinner organized by *L'Avenir des femmes* on 11 May 1873. Richer had already presented a divorce bill prefaced with the support of Louis Blanc (*Le Divorce, projet de loi précédé d'un exposé des motifs et suivi des principaux documents officiels se rattachant à la question*, 1874). In 1874 Naquet campaigned in his home departement of Vaucluse for the election of Ledru-Rollin, radical veteran of 1848, 'un homme avec lequel on pourrait battre en brèche la politique de Gambetta'.[56] Naquet had been consistently concerned with constitutional questions, his programme for *La République radicale* bringing to book the compromises of the so-called 'conservative republic'. He demanded

> une forme de gouvernement qui ne permet aucun pouvoir irresponsable, aucun pouvoir irrévocable. C'est une forme de gouvernement sous laquelle la souver-aineté réelle, effective, permanente réside dans le corps électoral et dans le corps électoral seulement.[57]

In his bid for an elected constituent assembly, he recalled Rousseau's distinction between laws and decrees in *Du contrat social* and proposed the introduction of a one-chamber system with a clear preponderance of legislative over executive authority.

By the summer of 1875 Naquet was of the view that the radical faction should clearly position and organize itself at some distance from Gambetta. From August to October he went on several tours of the south, drawing clear red water between Gambetta and the 'élément républicain conservateur' on the one hand, and his own 'groupe d'avant-garde de combat démocratique' on the other. The conservative Marseille newspaper *La Gazette du Midi* named them 'les frères ennemis' (12 September 1875). On 3 September 1875 they reported the speech which sealed their rupture, the gibbous Naquet glaring, as the impatient Gambetta exclaimed: 'Que voulez-vous? Il n'y a rien à faire! C'est un cas de gibbosité cérébrale'. Even if this encounter is apocryphal, Naquet had more substantial reasons to oppose the 'opportunisme' of the leader of the Union républicaine. Feeling betrayed by the republican centre, Naquet moved from a *politique des transactions* to a *politique des principes* which would demand universal suffrage: 'Nous ne pouvons être sauvés que par un de ces grands courants d'opinion auxquels rien ne résiste. Ce courant, il faut le provoquer,' he explained in Arles:

> Or, si nous voulons le provoquer, si nous voulons que le pays se sauve lui-même, il faut lui dire la vérité, il faut lui parler un langage viril, il faut cesser de l'endormir par des espérances et des promesses qui n'ont pas de réalisation possible [...]. Il faut, en un mot, parler, agir, écrire avec énergie, arrêter les découragements produits ou prêts à se produire; il faut crier: 'haut les cœurs'![58]

In response to the dismissive irony of *La Gazette de France* and *La République française*, Naquet intoned in idealistic terms:

> Je comprends que le cri 'Haut les cœurs' n'aille pas à ceux qui, depuis tantôt quatre ans, cherchent à chasser de la politique l'idée de dévouement et de sacrifice, en répétant sans cesse que le cycle héroïque de la démocratie est fermé.[59]

Naquet's strategy was therefore to associate left-wing radicalism with what we might call a political sublime.

Naquet's initial attempts to reinstitute divorce, in 1876 and 1878, harked back explicitly beyond the Civil Code to the radicalism of the Revolution's divorce law. On 6 June 1876, seven years after *Religion, propriété, famille*, his first *proposition* was presented to the deputies. Others had already presented this view — not least in *De la nécessité civile, morale et politique du rétablissement du divorce dans le code civil français: Pétition adressée au Gouvernement et à la Chambre française, le 20 juillet 1871*, by Dr Arsène Drouet and Émile Rénier (1871), reissued by Chaix in 1876. Naquet realized how hard it would be to have the principle of divorce accepted, and he hesitated before proposing it in a radical form (with mutual consent and without *cause déterminée*). In the homosocial discourse of male suffrage, Naquet's manifesto, printed in *Le Temps* on 10 September 1875, prior to the 1876 elections of 20 February and 6 March, made a broad declaration to fellow men:

> Nous voulons que le divorce, établi dans nos lois par la Révolution de 1792 et aboli par la réaction cléricale en 1816, y soit rétabli. Nous voulons que la femme devienne, sinon au point de vue civil, l'égale de l'homme qu'elle puisse gérer ses biens, qu'elle puisse tester en justice, qu'elle reçoive, elle qui élève nos enfants, une éducation égale à celle que nous recevons nous-mêmes.

This policy made the election campaign particularly difficult. In the eulogy of his autobiography:

> On sait quels préjugés enracinés régnaient alors en souverains dans les populations. Pour leur faire comprendre que le divorce était une loi morale, pour les retourner en quelques jours, il fallut une dépense incalculable de force, d'énergie. On a beaucoup loué l'ardeur avec laquelle plus tard il a fait, pour défendre la même cause, des conférences dans la France entière.[60]

Naquet joined other Intransigeants such as Louis Blanc, Charles Loquet and Madier-Montjau in opposing Gambetta.

All in all, the election was a triumph for the republicans. Out of 530 deputies, the block of the Left, Centre-Left and Extreme-Left made up 340 candidates, with Grévy presiding over the Chamber. The devil, though, was indeed in the detail. Beaten by Gambetta in the first round in Marseille, though Louis Blanc won in the 13th arrondissement, Naquet was then elected in Apt (Vaucluse) in the second round and sat on the extreme left in the Chamber of Deputies. Here too, though, 'l'impossible M. Naquet'[61] was isolated, in political quarantine. His was a triple project of 'une loi sur la liberté des réunions publiques, une loi sur la liberté de la presse, et une loi portant rétablissement du divorce'.[62] After long processes of negotiation and compromise, laws were passed in 1881 on the freedoms of public meetings and of the press — both ways of liberalizing the parameters of public discourse. However, the effect of Naquet's first divorce bill on public opinion was, in Ronsin's terms, 'nul, ou quasiment nul!'[63] It was ignored by key newspapers such as Le Temps. It was mentioned by L'Avenir des femmes, though its readers were few, and the other supposedly feminist periodical, La Gazette des femmes, avoided the matter. It was Jean Constans's report which held up progress long enough for the constitutional crisis of 16 May 1877 to intervene, and as Naquet explained in his book on divorce which appeared that year, he himself did not expect the bill to be prise en considération. Once again, in the refrain of his autobiography, 'il attendit'. In 1876 the 'campagne intransigeante' was supported by the establishment of several radical newspapers, including Naquet's own La Révolution (which ran to 30 numbers from 12 November to 13 December). Its politics were clear: 'Si, depuis 85 ans, le peuple lutte pour la République... ce n'est pas pour la satisfaction platonique de remplacer un empereur ou un roi, par un monarque temporaire nommé Président. C'est parce qu'à ses yeux, le mot République résume un ensemble d'améliorations auxquelles il aspire' (13 November 1876).

In his leader articles Naquet compares the conflicts between opportunists and radicals at the key moments of political choice in the nineteenth century: in the Restoration and the July Monarchy, between monarchists and republicans; in the Second Republic, between the 'démoc-soc' and reactionaries; during the Second Empire, between Bonapartists and republicans. In Naquet's radical interpretation, 1848 was not so much the cultural breaking-point identified by Roland Barthes's Le Degré zéro de l'écriture as the most intense articulation of a stubbornly persistent socio-political landscape. As such, Naquet could not allow himself Flaubert's intellectualized response to 1848. He could not afford to laugh at Bouvard and Pécuchet. In his emblematically titled piece 'Poissons variés, même sauce' of 30

November 1876, he concludes:

> Il n'y a en France, il n'y a en Europe que deux partis: le parti des travailleurs et
> le parti bourgeois. Les opportunistes appartiennent, comme les bonapartistes,
> comme les orléanistes, au parti bourgeois, dont on pourrait dire qu'ils sont
> la branche cadette; ils appartiennent à ce parti dont les moyens se modifient
> suivant les circonstances, mais dont le but est malheureusement invariable.

In practical terms, this means that 'il faut constituer le véritable parti de l'avenir:
le parti du travailleur, le parti de l'ouvrier, le parti de la Révolution sociale'. As
Mollenhauer argues, it would be wrong to conflate this position with that of Jules
Guesde's group, whose small weekly *L'Égalité* was the first Marxist paper in France.
In spite of *La Révolution*'s motto 'La terre aux paysans, l'usine aux ouvriers', his
connections with Guesde, his reading of *Das Kapital*, and his take on capital and
private property meant that he was not a collectivist in the sense that this term
would acquire. It is in this context that we can understand his later affiliation with
Boulangism. Only in the twentieth century did he convert to the socialist party.

  We may well be interested in these early efforts at divorce reform because they
contribute to a narrative which culminates in the short term, in the Loi Naquet and
in the long term in the diversified forms of the modern family, not least in France.
However, by analogy with modern Britain, the proposal of 6 June 1876 probably felt
more akin to some apparently eccentric private member's bill, discussed seriously
that morning on BBC Radio 4 but soon dismissed as kite-flying by the political
mainstream in parliament. In Ronsin's sobering judgement on *l'air du temps*, 'La
France profonde est indifférente, voire hostile au rétablissement du divorce, certes'.[64]
As Naquet himself would later explain in his account of the bill of 6 June 1876:

> Naquet y remontait non pas au Code de 1803 mais à la loi révolutionnaire du 22
> septembre 1792, qui est celle de l'avenir. [...] Il fut accueilli par des éclats de rire.
> Et si l'on riait à la Chambre, on allait plus loin dans le pays; on avait horreur,
> dans les masses ignorantes, de la proposition. Les prêtres n'avaient-ils pas fait
> croire aux femmes qu'elle tendait à la destruction de la famille, et que dès le
> jour où elle deviendrait loi elles seraient toutes ou presque toutes abandonnées
> par leurs maris? Un jour Naquet passait à Avignon dans la rue des Infirmières.
> Une femme du peuple était sur sa porte; elle s'écria en provençal en le voyant:
> 'Sé foudrié pas l'espoutira.' '*Ne faudrait-il pas le mettre en pièces!*'[65]

Divorciaire discourse was not the language of the street, even if it had originally
emerged at the end of the eighteenth century in the wake of the barricades. Indeed,
just as the literature of the bourgeoisie (rather than the *roman du peuple*) focused
on adultery, so too was divorce in large part a concern of bourgeois (and indeed
aristocratic) society (and its literature). Perhaps this is why Zola never came to grips
with the subject matter of divorce (even if *Pot-Bouille* contributed to the cynicism
about modern marriage which Naquet exploited in the early 1880s). In the world
of *Germinal*, it does not seem to matter so much whether or not one is married, but
how many other family members share the bedroom. Both the overpopulation of
the bedroom (in the supposedly private realm) and women working at the mine (in
the public domain) meant that the Theory of Separate Spheres holds far less sway
in the working-class society described by Zola.

If at first...

In 1877, Naquet published *Le Divorce*, ultimately one of the key texts in the promotion of reform, although it does not seem to have sparked an immediate publication war. The major political event of the year was Thiers's death on — of all dates — 4 September, seven years after the fall of the Second Empire. Expected as it was that he might return to the presidency in a coalition with Gambetta, this was, in Naquet's phrase, 'un coup de foudre'. That year, Naquet had met several times with Thiers in discussion of an amnesty for the Déportés de la Commune. The task had been given to Naquet by Rochefort in 1875; it would only bear fruit on 14 July 1880. In fact, Naquet lost his mandate as deputy for Vaucluse on 14 October 1877 at the hands of conservative high jinks. As a candidate in Apt, he was hampered by officials such as Bressy who would say at the end of the ceremony to the fiancés he was marrying: 'Vous ne voterez pas, je suppose, pour M. Alfred Naquet, un candidat qui demande le divorce!'[66]

The same lack of response met the appearance in 1878 of *De la dignité dans le mariage par le divorce* by Alexandra Laya. At this point, though, Naquet's second push of lectures, his articles in *Le Voltaire*, and debates in the Chamber of Deputies did spark a vast wave of interest in the subject, and as Naquet himself would later explain, his second bill (1878) was very different from that of two years previous: 'Au lieu d'une loi nouvelle, calquée sur la législation révolutionnaire, je demandais simplement au parlement de revenir [...] à la législation de 1803, au Code civil.' His only major abridgement would have meant that article 230 ('La femme pourra demander le divorce pour cause d'adultère de son mari, lorsqu'il aura tenu sa concubine dans la maison commune') would become 'la femme pourra demander le divorce pour cause d'adultère de son mari'. Naquet's speech of 21 May 1878 argued that a reform of Article 230 would be 'éminemment morale. Non seulement, en effet, il y a dans ces mots l'affirmation d'une inégalité choquante et inutile entre les deux sexes, mais encore il y a un demi-encouragement accordé à l'adultère du mari.' Even this was too much for deputies to stomach.

The end of the decade emerges from the archive as the period in which the French divorce debate was ignited fully. There followed a fresh discussion in the Chamber of Deputies of Naquet's new bill in 1879, and in 1881 a second edition of Naquet's *Le Divorce*. On 30 January 1879 Mac-Mahon resigned and the presidency went to Grévy, whom Naquet saluted as the successor to Thiers. In 1879 Naquet founded a Comité en faveur du divorce, following the Chamber's decision to respond to his proposal by setting up a Commission spéciale loaded with *anti-divorciaires*. His one and a half hour speech on 27 May 1879 was now taken seriously and deputies at least voted in favour of a *prise en considération*. Even if the law itself lay some distance in the future, divorce was on the political agenda.[67] Fearing that his bill would go through the Chamber of Deputies but be halted by the Senate, Naquet called for an assault on prejudice throughout the country. In his circular of 23 July 1879 Naquet invited the committed to a meeting at 8 pm on Tuesday 29th in the lecture hall at 39 boulevard des Capucines.

The Comité's activity and influence appear to have been limited, and the debates were deferred until February 1881, when Naquet was narrowly defeated. This time Naquet found 'un vigoureux compagnon de lutte': 'Un député d'éloquence précise, un républicain conservateur inscrit alors au centre gauche, un ancien préfet de police, un avocat du plus haut mérite, M. Léon Renault s'était fait nommer membre de la commission et avait été désigné comme rapporteur'.[68] And this time the commission's conclusions were indeed open to challenge. Naquet's attack was in his own words, 'une révélation pour la Chambre et pour le pays', and this time they did vote in favour of a *prise en considération*.[69] Naquet was zealous and energetic in his bid to spread his opinion, zigzagging across the country from lecture appointment to lecture appointment. Divorce, he felt, needed to escape its narrowly Parisian associations. In response he received the sackloads of post to which he refers in his pro-divorce publications — even if we might share Ronsin's scepticism with regard to Philibert Audebrand's claim in *Les Divorces de Paris: Scènes de la vie intime* (1881) that Naquet received 500 letters a day 'à l'heure de son chocolat'! On 8 February 1881, after three days of impassioned debate, his bill was rejected by 247 votes to 216. In the terms of his autobiography 'une telle défaite était une certitude de victoire pour le lendemain'.[70] Naquet wrote of 'Une victoire à la Pyrrhus' in *L'Indépendant*, the newspaper he ran at the time. Both sides felt that it was only a matter of time. Alphonse Maynard penned a poem which captures this mood, 'Le Divorce opportunément enseveli, quant à présent pour ressusciter après les élections', and, Canute-like, presents marriage as the touchstone of the monumental State:

> Tel est le mariage, il est pierre angulaire
> De ce vieux monument tant de fois séculaire,
> Basé sur la famille et devenant l'État:
> L'oser vouloir toucher est un grave attentat.[71]

This is the conservative fantasy that the substance of the State might be resistant to historical erosion, or in cultural terms, that it might take shape in architectural or sculptural space, but remain resistant to narrative time. If it is strange to see even poetry address the issue of divorce, this is due in part to the genre's usual distance from plot-based literary forms. The conservative fantasy is haunted by the fear of decadence, and in Maynard's address to 'Orateurs de désordre aux lubriques instincts', women are defined as the barometer of such disorder:

> Vous transformez la femme en un être inconstant,
> Qui d'amours en amours volerait sans vergogne.

The final eighteen-line stanza apostrophizes order ('O douce majesté du lien conjugal! / O premier élément de l'ordre social!') and in its penultimate couplet berates disorder ('Honte à ceux qui manquant de sentiment, de force, / Se laisseraient aller à l'appât du divorce!'), calling finally on the doxa to prevail ('Que le bons sens public, et que l'opinion / Les flétrissent d'un sceau de réprobation.'). He appeals not just to the good sense of the general public, or collective good sense, but the good sense which may emanate from the public realm and discipline private life.

1880 had seen the appearance of pro-divorce books by Louis Fiaux, *La Femme, le mariage et le divorce: Étude de physiologie et de sociologie* and Émile Acollas, *Le Mariage: Son passé, son présent, son avenir*. Born in 1826 and thus able to recall the disappointments of 1848, Acollas had campaigned under the Second Empire, arguing for *la recherche de la paternité* (as Naquet would do) in his *L'Enfant né hors mariage* (1865). In 1871 his *Trois leçons sur les principes philosophiques et juridiques du mariage* appeared. The *divorciaires* penetrated the popular consciousness through the publication of modestly priced little pamphlets, such as Florimond Schoemaeker's or L. Bonneau's, both with the title *Le Divorce*. These were countered by Catholic-inspired *anti-divorciaire* brochures such as *Contre le divorce* by Ph. Lofez and *Mariage et divorce* by Paul Antonini, both from 1879. A further marker of this newly vibrant debate was the re-publication of its great forefathers: on the *divorciaire* side, Cerfvol's *Le Cri d'un honnête homme*, prefaced by Naquet; in the enemy camp, a re-edition of Bonald's *Résumé sur la question du divorce*, Ozanam's *Du divorce*, and in 1881 the re-edition by Lescure of Mme Necker's *Réflexions sur le divorce*.

Of course, the Catholic Church was opposed to the Jew's plans, and in this the divorce question prefigured the tensions which exploded in the Dreyfus Affair. To counter Naquet's lectures, two particular voices spoke out at this point. First, Charles Loyson (known as Père Hyacinthe), a former man of the cloth who had broken with the Church in order to get married and attempted to create a rival church, schismatic, national, democratic and republican.[72] Second, Père Henri Didon's *Indissolubilité et divorce, conférences de Saint-Philippe du Roule, avec préface et épilogue* (1880) went into five editions in its first year. Although Père Didon's theses were rejected out of hand by the pro-divorce lobby, the latter overlooked his desire to allow divorce for those couples who had undergone only a civil marriage. As Ronsin points out, the antithetical dynamic of social policy debate meant that Naquet & Co. failed to credit 'la véritable révolution qui est en train de s'opérer dans certains milieux catholiques'. This 'ideological revolution', 'une donnée majeure qui bouleverse les perspectives de l'affrontement en cours' meant that Didon & Co. 'ouvrent largement la porte à la modification de la législation.'[73] It would be an error to depict Catholicism as a static doxa. The surest sign of Catholic fears was the *entrée en lice* of his holiness Léon XIII, his encyclical on the family and divorce, *Arcanum*, appearing in 1880. At the same time French Catholics spread the word via ten-centimes pamphlets, such as the two anonymous tracts printed in Lyons in 1880 by the Imprimerie générale: *Le Divorce et la loi religieuse, le divorce et la loi morale, le divorce et la famille...* and *Bientôt le Divorce!*

From the legal and political classes, Louis Legrand had long been an advocate of indissolubility, his *anti-divorciaire* law thesis defended in 1865 and his *Le Mariage et les mœurs en France* (1879) honoured by the Académie des sciences morales et politiques. As one biographer explains, though, this 'avocat, homme politique et littérateur français' belonged to the 'gauche républicaine'.[74] 1879 saw the appearance of Eugène-Désiré Glasson's manifesto for indissolubility, *Le Mariage civil et le divorce dans les principaux pays de l'Europe précédé d'un aperçu sur les origines du droit civil moderne*. Glasson stressed the gap between culture-vultures and the mainstream (just as *Le Charivari* of 1848 had attempted to chart clear blue water between feminists and housewives): 'Des littérateurs, des auteurs dramatiques, se sont faits les champions de la cause du divorce dans leurs livres, dans leurs pièces de théâtre, dans leurs conférences; ils ne sont pas parvenus à émouvoir l'opinion publique'.

Abbé Vidieu's *Famille et divorce* (1879), 'réquisitoire assez banal d'un homme d'Eglise'[75], is one of those books noteworthy for the contradiction it inspired, in this case from Alexandre Dumas fils's *La Question du divorce* (1880). A second edition from this vicaire of Saint-Roch appeared with a reply to Dumas that same year. Ronsin notes the particular relationship between the literary field and the divorce question: 'Les plus grands écrivains sont fréquemment intervenus, avec toute l'autorité qu'ils devaient à leur notoriété, sur la question de l'issue judiciaire qu'il convient d'offrir aux crises matrimoniales.'[76] Of particular significance, he notes, was Dumas 'dont les essais retentissants ont fortement concouru à la victoire remportée par Alfred Naquet'. As early as 11 November 1879, in a sketch by Mars in *Le Charivari* of a couple at the theatre, a balding husband muses: 'Dumas là-bas dans cette loge... Il a l'air de me regarder'; to which his *lorgnette*-wielding wife exclaims: 'Dame! On dit qu'il réunit des arguments en faveur du divorce.' *Le Charivari* primed its public further with a sketch by Alfred Le Petit on 27 December 1879 of an interminable line of women ready to offer flowers and kisses: 'Une députation de femmes coupables vient remercier Dumas fils pour avoir bien voulu remplacer son *Tue-la* par le divorce.'

Dumas's project generated swift and robust replies: first in the press (2 February 1880 in *Le Figaro*, and then 16 February in *Le Gaulois*), and second in longer format: Georges Berry, *Moralité du divorce*; abbé Paulin Moniquet, *Les Idées de M. A. Dumas fils à propos du divorce et de l'homme-femme*; anon., *Le Divorce — Réponse à MM. Naquet et Dumas fils*; père Girondon, *Conférence sur le livre de M. A. Dumas fils — La Question du divorce*; and above all Paul Féval: *Pas de divorce! Réponse à M. Alexandre Dumas*.[77] Eight editions of Dumas's polemic appeared in its first year! In the words of Naquet's autobiography, 'les éditions s'enlevèrent avec une rapidité surprenante et qui, pénétrant dans des milieux où ne pénétraient pas les écrits de l'auteur de la proposition de loi, achevèrent l'œuvre de propagande de ce dernier' (20). *Le Voltaire* caricatures a sizeable Dumas pouring a jug of black ink onto a sheet of paper bearing the word 'Divorce' (8 February 1880). To his right, a *théâtre de polichinelle* and to his left, a miniature Naquet, hunchbacked and bewildered. The legend reads: 'Minute, mon garçon, je vais t'éclaircir ton affaire. J'ai ce qu'il faut, de la bonne encre, de mon enncrre à moi, de l'ennncrrrre d'Alexandre! Tu vois comme ça devient clair et amusant; je lâche le point de vue légal, et je pars d'Adam et Ève, en suivant; et tant que tu voudras, mon bon!' The reference to Adam and Eve highlights one of the most humorously blasphemous arguments in Dumas's book. Dumas cites Voltaire's famous observation that 'le divorce est probablement de la même date à peu près que le mariage. Je crois cependant que le mariage est de quelques semaines plus ancien' and offers his own blasphemous gloss on the Adam and Eve story:

> Si Adam n'a pas réclamé le divorce, c'est pour cette raison bien simple qu'il n'y avait pas alors sur la terre d'autre femme que la sienne et qu'il était forcé de s'en tenir à celle-là, malgré les bonnes raisons qu'il avait eues de la quitter et de demander à Dieu de lui en donner une autre. Une compagne qui vous fait perdre le paradis, la vertu, le bonheur et la vie éternelle, mériterait bien qu'on divorçât d'avec elle et qu'on la renvoyât au serpent qui vient si facilement et si vite compromettre et corrompre l'œuvre admirable et primitivement si bien conçue du Créateur.[78]

Before the year was out he produced another *divorciaire* tract, *Les Femmes qui tuent et les femmes qui votent*. A reply was forthcoming from Émile de Girardin, *L'Égale de l'homme, lettre à M. Alexandre Dumas fils*. In 1881 there appeared a second revised and augmented edition of Naquet's *Le Divorce*, and in 1882 Dumas reasserted his position in his *Lettre à M. Naquet* of 22 June. The following year he was enshrined by Jules Clarétie in the sixth volume of the series *Les Célébrités contemporaines* (after luminaries such as Hugo, Grévy, Louis Blanc, and Gambetta), sold for 75 centimes. Clarétie positions him thus:

> Il tient — au-dessus de ce grand craquement social qui nous menace depuis tant d'années — à faire entendre la libre parole d'un homme dépourvu de préjugés et qui pense. Sa brochure 'sensationale' *l'Homme-Femme* n'est rien d'ailleurs qu'un éloquent et curieux plaidoyer en faveur de l'union intime de deux êtres fondus, si je puis dire, par l'amour.[79]

As such, 'M. Dumas réclame deux choses: la sainteté du mariage et la possibilité du divorce. Le foyer purifié parce qu'il n'est plus prison. M. Dumas ne se trompe pas: le salut du monde aux abois est là peut-être'. Ronsin argues that the theatre was more important than Naquet himself in bringing the divorce question back to the collective consciousness, and in this Dumas fils was also significant.[80] The stage polemic on divorce began with Nus and Belot's *Miss Multon* of 1866, closely followed by a number of playwrights: Augier, Legouvé, Bergerat (*Séparés de corps* 1874), Ennès (*Un divorce*, translated in 1878), Kirsch (*Divorce*, 1876), Numès (*Une séparation* 1877), Buguet (*Les Femmes des autres*, 1878), Grangé (*Le Divorce*, 1879), Lopez (*Les Ricochets du divorce*, 1879), Sardou (*Daniel Rochat* 1880; *Divorçons*, 1880 with Émile Najac). Ronsin contends that the widening of divorce law in favour of women can be tracked via theatrical polemic: 'après Dumas fils, à Hervieu, Brieux, Sardou aussi. Bataille récemment.' The first landmark around the time of Naquet's first bill was *Madame Caverlet* by Émile Augier, performed on 1 February 1876 at the Vaudeville. In Ronsin's words, 'On parle du divorce, mais au théâtre et en raison du théâtre.' The second came in December 1877, when the Vaudeville put on *Une séparation* by Ernest Legouvé. In a curious innovation which left the audience in no doubt as to the dominance of 'instruire' over 'plaire', Legouvé demanded a matinée performance preceded by a lecture! That other dramatist of divorce, Noel Coward, would have chuckled at such earnestness. In this climate, Ronsin argues, 'tout va donc dépendre de cette question essentielle, sans cesse posée mais à laquelle personne n'a jamais pu répondre: les députés pleurent-ils au théâtre?'

The press reflected the variety of public opinion. Pro-Naquet were *Le Voltaire* from July 1879 on, *Le Petit Lyonnais* from May 1880, and Naquet's own paper, *L'Indépendant*, from 12 January to 15 June 1881. His articles also appeared in many other papers: *La Petite République française*, *Le Réveil du Midi*, *L'Égalité* (in Marseille), *Le Radical de Marseille*, and *Le Phare du littoral* (in Nice). In the major press, Legouvé's *Une séparation* was published in *Le Temps* in 1874 before being staged. *Le Petit Parisien* fuelled intense republican anti-clerical propaganda in favour of divorce, including Jean Frollo's series of articles on 'La Question des femmes' in 1879. *Le XIXe siècle*'s pro-divorce stance was established. *La Revue des Deux Mondes* was less partisan: Henri Baudrillart's anti-feminist and anti-divorce articles of October 1872 were counterbalanced by Victor Cherbuliez's piece on 'L'Émancipation des femmes' (1 November 1880), signed G. Valbert. Similarly, *La République française* began openly to support divorce in 1879, when Gambetta gave up his political control over it. *Le Rappel* consistently favoured the re-establishment of divorce.

Thirty years had passed since the ferocious satires on 'les divorceuses' by Daumier and Cham, and *Le Charivari* was now strongly republican, free-thinking and pro-divorce, even at the expense of the cuckold. In 'Retour de Versailles' of 31 March 1879 the man of state spies through the window his wife in an adulterous embrace and exclaims: 'Ciel! Et moi qui viens de parler pendant trois heures contre le rétablissment du divorce!' In the representations of this culture of separate spheres, male fears and female retaliation flourished 'when the (tom-)cat was away'; even the mousey could play. And in one of Cham's sketches of 6 April 1879 a speech in favour of divorce is illustrated by a pair of trousers and the explanation: 'Messieurs! Encore un mari qui vient de m'envoyer ce document oublié chez lui par un visiteur.' In the same number the traditional conjugal ideal of the unique relationship is subject to further satire in a conversation between mother and daughter:

> — Ma chère enfant, ce prétendu te convient?
> — Oui, maman, mais il faudra m'en trouver encore un second.
> — Un second?
> — Oui, maman, si nous avons le divorce!

Once more the older generation can barely keep up. There is, however, uniqueness in duplicity. In a sketch by Cham of 14/15 April 1879, a wife looks up at her husband's portrait and replies in the negative to her friend's question about the future possibility of divorce: 'En tromperais-je un autre avec autant de satisfaction?'

A group of sketches in *Le Charivari* highlight the problem in translating the reality of private life into the public discourse of politics. In 'En vacances' the spectacle of a deputy visiting his bellicose constituents is easily explained: 'A l'approche du député, tous les ménages viennent se battre sur le devant de leurs portes pour le rendre favorable au divorce' (24 April 1879). Naquet himself is depicted as the target of opposed opinions: one woman holding a bouquet, the other a stick, both hiding behind trees as the silhouetted Naquet approaches, 'attendant chacune à son point de vue le passage de l'apôtre du divorce' (23 July 1879); and he is the target of enemies who share the same opinion — such as the startled couple in 'le mari et la femme se recontrent tous les deux à la porte de l'Assemblée, y portant chacun un bouquet à M. Naquet' (31 May 1879).[81]

The attitude of the right-wing press was yet more ambiguous, even contradictory. If not provocatively reactionary and Catholic in their views, papers would prefer to appear open-minded and permit the expression of diverse opinion. In September 1879 *Le Gaulois* suggested that Augier write a series of articles to spread his pro-divorce views, but in January 1880 it reprinted the preface to the book based on père Didon's anti-divorce lectures. *Le Figaro* revealed a similar variation of opinion. Most famously, its satire on Naquet of 29 May 1879 (p. 1, cols. 4 & 5), entitled 'L'Apôtre du Divorce' and signed Rénal. Rénal was keen to expose Naquet's supposed personal interest in seeking the recreation of divorce provision:

> Vivant séparé de sa femme il est dans le cas de tous les infortunés que le divorce intéresse. La lune de miel passée, les deux époux s'examinèrent réciproquement sur la question religieuse. Mme Naquet parla de Dieu avec ses accents convaincus. Son mari, plein d'affabilité: 'Pardonnez-moi, dit-il, en lui parlant tout bas, mais je crois, entre nous, que Dieu n'existe pas.' C'est ainsi que les deux intelligences divorcèrent; bientôt les deux cœurs firent de même. [...] Je ne crois pas qu'aucun avoué se soit mêlé de l'affaire; la séparation n'eut rien de judiciaire; elle fut purement philosophique.[82]

Surely, Rénal implies, Naquet will need another wife to do domestic chores such as knitting and darning:

> L'autre semaine, se promenant avec un bonapartiste dans la salle des Pas-Perdus, M. Alfred Naquet tira de sa poche un mouchoir fraichement sorti de l'armoire. Il le déplia et l'ouvrit largement. Ce mouchoir était une véritable guipure, il n'y avait pas une place où le nez de M. Naquet pût se caser et se satisfaire. Ce fut un rire général. Le bonapartiste voulut faire sortir de cette aventure un argument contre le divorce; mais M. Naquet lui répliqua sans hésiter que si le divorce était rétabli, il pourrait se remettre en ménage et avoir ses mouchoirs en meilleur état.

Literally and figuratively, Naquet would need another woman to sew things back together.

Rénal's piece was followed immediately by Naquet's own right of reply, a letter to the editor, to which we have referred above. In this remarkably candid piece, Naquet focuses not on his own politics but on his personal life. The gibbous Naquet accepts that a typically cruel depiction of his 'imperfections physiques' is consonant with the generic rules of the newspaper 'portrait'.[83] In fact, Rénal had stressed the paradoxical appeal of Naquet:

> Malgré le défaut d'harmonie de sa personne et son indépendance à l'égard du mariage, les femmes sont bien loin de tenir M. Naquet pour un monstre; il n'y a pas comme la sienne pour en dire du bien. La vérité est que notre héros est doué de façons aimables et d'une exquise politesse.

Perhaps Naquet was a 'lady's man', but not in the sense that Rénal has in mind. Naquet claims to be motivated to write out of a desire to correct the myth ('une erreur absolue') that he himself was married in the Church. In other words, he cannot accept the slander that his political morality is deformed. Like Jules Ferry, he notes, his was a civil marriage. He concludes with a brief foray into the public realm of politics by embracing the charge of hypocritical friendships across ideological boundaries. Indeed, self-contradiction, he suggests, is the democratic privilege of republicanism (by contrast with the Second Empire at which he takes a swipe): 'Je suis de ceux qui pensent que la France deviendrait inhabitable si l'on devait absolument se fuir parce qu'on ne pense pas de même.' In his *Autobiographie* Naquet looks back on this moment as vital in winning over salon society; he was now in a position to inform informed opinion:

> Les salons, qui l'ignoraient jusque-là, s'ouvraient devant lui, et si sa santé et son goût de l'étude ne l'en avaient empêché, il ne tenait qu'à lui dès ce moment de se répandre dans le monde. L'engouement fut tel qu'un soir dans une réunion

mondaine — où il n'était pas — , un musicien de grande valeur, mort depuis, le regretté Cœdès, chanta sa lettre au piano en improvisant pour elle un récitatif. L'opinion avait été retournée comme un gant: d'hostile, elle était soudain devenue favorable au rétablissement du divorce.[84]

As he explains, he had already seen how difficult it was to persuade provincial deputies to sacrifice their local popularity for the *divorciaire* cause. The effect, he claimed, was to 'empêcher une majorité de se constituer à la Chambre bien qu'elle y existât virtuellement'.

As such, 'il fallait aller porter partout la bonne parole', and hence his lecture series in the summer of 1879: in Lille, Cambrai, Douai, Valenciennes, Amiens, Saint-Quentin, Boulogne, Bourges, Vichy, Moulin, Nevers, Versailles, Saint-Germain, Vincennes, Auxerre, Cherbourg, not to count Paris, where he often spoke. After a few months of recuperation, he set of again, this time for the south: in Nice, Toulon, Marseille, Arles, Tarascon, Alais, Nîmes, Cette, Montpellier, Béziers, Millau, Narbonne, Carcassonne, Toulouse, Saint-Gaudens, Pau, Bayonne, and Bordeaux (twice), Agen, Montauban, Auch, Limoges, Angoulême, Rochefort, La Rochelle, Poitiers, Niort, Tours, Angers, Nantes, Brest, Granville, Le Mans, Chartres and Evreux. The following Easter he began a fresh tour in Avignon, Valence and Grenoble, but scarlet fever drove him back to Paris. Though in general 'là où il avait passé on peut dire que la cause était gagnée', he recalls one incident in Millau (Aveyron).[85] He claims that 'les prêtres avaient excité les femmes contre le conférencier', in the kind of conservative compact between women and the clergy castigated by Zola in *La Conquête de Plassans*. The lecture was set to take place in a great hall separated from the public square by iron grills covered in canvas. At the appointed hour virtually the entire male population was present in this improvised lecture theatre, but — in a striking emblem of the gender divide which this question could fuel — the women amassed in the square were less sympathetic. Naquet and his friends were allowed to pass through the crowd to reach the hall, but once Naquet began to speak, he was drowned out by the formidable cry from the square. Naquet recalls his role in asserting the right of free assembly, 'la liberté de réunion ne pouvant être abandonnée', one of Naquet's innovations underpinning the other. The mayor ordered in the *gendarmerie à cheval*, the women dispersed, and the evening finished — as per usual, Naquet claims — with applause from his audience. In a lecture on 'Un Juif comtadin, Alfred Naquet' before the Cercle d'Études Juives on 16 February 1932, Armand Mossé who, as a child, had known the aged Naquet, would tell another story: 'Son plus grand encouragement lui est donné à Toulouse où, au premier rang des fauteuils, il remarque un jeune couple dont la femme est en toilette de mariée.'[86]

As Naquet's writing in *Le Figaro* gave him entry into salon society, so his compromises lost him the radical support of the *divorciaire* Léon Richer and *L'Avenir des femmes*. By the turn of the decade, the feminist press had grown, but it would be an error to exaggerate women's support for divorce. Even some feminists (of a conservative persuasion) felt that divorce would encourage in husbands a kind of serial promiscuity (even if today we might call this serial monogamy). The logic of this argument was, in its way, not unlike the cynical observation that the sexual liberation of 1960s was *inter alia* a great thing for the male libido. *La Femme*, mademoiselle C. Delpech's protestant feminist newspaper, founded in January 1879, was highly circumspect, but Hubertine Auclert's *La Citoyenne* (founded in February 1881) defended a rather fluid notion of the couple, against both free union and traditional marriage, in favour of 'rational marriage'. Only two feminist newspapers supported Naquet completely: Olympe Audouard's *Le Papillon* and Louise Koppe's *La Femme dans la famille et dans la société*. On 10 June 1884, *La Gazette des femmes*, directed by Jean d'Alensson, expressed ambivalence rather than joy as the new law finally dawned:

> Pour les femmes séparées, pour les femmes mal mariées, c'est autre chose. La loi qu'on vient rétablir est pour elle un événement capital, et M. Naquet doit en ce moment respirer avec délices l'encens que brûle à ses pieds la reconnaissance féminine. Cela veut-il dire qu'en général les femmes aient à se féliciter du rétablissement du divorce? Il est assez difficile de se prononcer là-dessus.

After several imagined scenarios, some in favour of divorce, some warning of its dangers, the paper concluded: 'Madame, laissez-moi me réjouir avec vous de la victoire éclatante de Little-Duck. Deux fois vainqueur, ce brave cheval, et cela malgré vents et marée! L'année a été bonne, et notre cœur de patriote doit être content.'

Most peculiar amongst this small-circulation press was *Le Libérateur*, founded in April 1881 by one commandant Épailly, who had recently formed the Société des amis du divorce. Naquet sent polite apologies when invited to their banquet. Nevertheless, these petits bourgeois, generally separated from their spouses, would meet at the 'Divorce-club' on the rue du Temple every Tuesday evening. Mallarmé would have nothing to fear in this diary clash... The newspaper was supported by several personalities: prince and princesse Bibesco, caught up in a second marriage imbroglio in Belgium; Delaville, journalist with *La Presse*; Laforêt, from *La Presse* and *Le Charivari*; and even Olympe Audouard. A 'matinée artistique' was held by the Society on 1 May 1881 at the Théâtre Déjazet, entry prices ranging from 50 centimes up to 10 francs. The bill included the English singer Georgina Weldon; the violinist Planel; a performance of *Les Petits* by the Cochets; Jacob, 'professeur de prestidigitation'; a lecture on Hugo by Laguerre, a lawyer at the Court of Appeal; and even a 'chansonette comique' entitled 'Divorçons'. Whilst a new law was awaited, Épailly called, on the inauguration of a monument at Crémieux's tomb on 13 March 1881, for malcontents to change nationality and commit to a 'contrat d'association matrimoniale' in front of witnesses (but no mayor). The movement suddenly disappears off the radar at the end of August, perhaps due to a violent quarrel between Épailly and Auclert. Even if he was, in Ronsin's phrase, 'très original, certainement, un peu escroc, peut-être', Épailly certainly caught the flavour of the moment, and particularly of much cosmopolitan and sophisticated opinion.

Naquet's Thesis

In preparation for Naquet's third attempt, as we have noted, a heavily revised edition of *Le Divorce* appeared in 1881, and I shall pause to reflect on its arguments.[87] The reflective opening chapter on 'le chemin parcouru' portrays divorce as vital to 'la grande cause sociale' (3), whereas 'le mariage est un grand aléa' (7). Against 'notre législation draconienne sur le mariage' (8), upheld by the likes of Henri Brisson and Louis Legrand, Naquet was keen to demystify the present state of unhappy couples by asking: who really believes that all those separated couples will choose celibacy in their life apart? In other words, it is not that one can simply prevent the breakdown of marriage *per se*. Without divorce, he claimed, the swapping of 'life'-partners simply disappeared beneath the radar of public discourse: 'le concubinage clandestin est plus facile, nécessite moins de courage civique qu'un procès courageusement et publiquement soutenu' (10). Divorce would force marriage to clean up its act. Another myth to be dispelled was the notion that 'le divorce n'est pas compris dans les campagnes' (11). From his own electoral experience, Naquet argued against the fear that the divorce question might divide the Republic, given that in Weber's terms peasants were barely Frenchmen. In Naquet's view, 'à Paris et dans les grandes villes, on veut le divorce avec passion. Dans les campagnes [...] on en comprend la nécessité, on l'accepte, on le veut aussi' (14). The difference between city and country was, therefore, one of degree, not of orientation.

The affirmation of Chapter 2 that 'le divorce est conforme aux principes généraux de notre droit public' explores the contractual (rather than sacramental) basis of marriage since the Revolution: 'Depuis 1789, le mariage ne peut plus être considéré que comme un contrat résultant de la libre volonté des contractants. Or, il est de la nature de tous les contrats de pouvoir être résiliés' (19). Ironically, both 'indissolubilistes' such as Legrand, Constans and Albert Millet, and the partisans of free union opposed the notion of marriage as a contract.[88] Of the conservatives, he notes, 'ces messieurs n'admettent pas que le mariage soit un contrat par cette raison qu'on ne peut y introduire ni conditions de moralité, ni conditions de durée' (20). Closer to Naquet was Acollas's definition of marriage as an 'association fondée sur le sentiment moral de l'amour, et soumise à la double loi de la liberté et de l'égalité' (19). In fact, despite the setbacks of the 1870s, Naquet still argues that 'le mariage est un contrat personnel [...] il doit pouvoir se résoudre [...] — sauf recours pécuniaire — par la volonté persistante d'un seul des conjoints', in an explicit echo of the provisions of 1792 (21).

Chapter 3 recalls 'les origines du divorce en France. — Ce qu'il a été, ce qu'il doit être'. Naquet is particularly keen here to calm the fears of those who fear that 'le divorce sera quelque peu analogue à l'union libre', i.e. 'un élément de dissolution de la famille' (32). He reminds us that divorce was 'la conséquence des principes qui ont servi de base à la Révolution française, de la sécularisation du mariage proclamée en 1789' (35). However, he consoles the mainstream with the claim that he wishes to turn the clock back only as far as the law of 1803 and not as far as 1792. In particular he notes article 296 of the Code which, in the case of divorce for *cause déterminée*, only allowed wives to marry again ten months after the pronouncement of divorce (so that the adulteress could not remarry before giving birth to the fruit of her transgression).

Chapters 4 to 8 deal with a series of objections to divorce, namely the interests of mores, the interests of women and children, and Catholics' freedom of conscience. In the case of mores, Naquet claims that people do not stay together because of the law and that liberty will not result in the dissolution of family structures (pointing, as he does, to many fine examples of free union, 50–68). Separation without divorce only creates 'une famille adultérine' in spite of the law. Proximate examples are cited for a Gallic audience: the successful divorce law in that 'petite France' known as Belgium; and since the war, the reinstitution of divorce in Alsace-Lorraine: 'il y a moins de familles désunies chez les Alsaciens-Lorrains qui jouissent des bienfaits du divorce, qu'il y en a chez nous qui n'en jouissons pas encore'.

With regard to women, Naquet is keen to confront the ideologically artful suggestion that divorce would punish women, in particular the view exemplified by Montesquieu that indissolubility stops older women who may have lost their charms from being abandoned (69–90). Naquet gallantly retorts: 'je vois chaque jour des femmes séparées et des veuves fort séduisantes.' Less ridiculous to modern ears is Louis Blanc's lecture on the sexual double standard, given in Avignon (October 1879) and cited by Naquet:

> Malheur à une femme coupable, non pas même de corruption, mais d'un moment de défaillance! Vainement donnerait-elle pour excuse de sa conduite son amour trahi, son foyer devenu solitaire, ses caresses brutalement repoussées, ses larmes raillées: elle a succombé; elle portera son châtiment jusqu'au tombeau. En butte à la fois au mépris qui la fuit et au mépris qui la poursuit, où trouverait-elle consolation et asile? En ce qui concerne les femmes, toute une vie de repentir, de larmes, de vertus, ne suffit pas toujours, aux yeux du monde, à faire oublier une heure d'égarement et la défaite d'un cœur troublé.

In other words, marriage does not currently protect women from the 'homme à bonnes fortunes'. Naquet then offers a string of pro-divorce narratives from and about unfortunate wives, many drawn from the correspondence which Naquet had been sent as the standard-bearer of the *divorciaire* movement. One woman from the Côte-d'Or tells of her husband who has left for Brazil in the 1860s and lost touch, thereby abandoning his wife and two daughters. In 1869 she attracts an admirer who offers to help, but her resistance fails after the calamity of 1870 and the onset of ill health:

> Que faire? Elle n'avait que deux issues: tomber ou mourir. Mourir, elle n'en avait pas le droit: Que seraient devenues de ses deux filles? Elle tomba... si l'on doit, suivant le langage consacré, appeler chute l'acte d'une femme qui se donne à celui qu'elle aime, à celui dont elle est aimée, à celui qui élève ses enfants, et à l'égard duquel elle se montre, quoique l'autorité n'ait pas consacré son union, épouse vertueuse et dévouée.

Such women are trapped by the impossibility of divorce and remarriage. Trapped in Hobson's choice between the sin of suicide and the sin of adultery, she is not allowed — in terms relevant to this book — to renarrativize her life.

Given Naquet's later arguments in favour of free union, it is tempting to see strategic compromise with mainstream opinion in Naquet's argument that divorce would actually support the interests of the child by encouraging those who would separate to divorce and then marry again (113–31). Naquet plays on the paradox that divorce both undoes marriage and makes marriage possible. As such, it lends itself to conservative but realistic arguments about the safeguarding of marriage, even if this conceals a more radical agenda. Given that indissolubility does not stop 'les désunions entre époux', divorce would offer greater family security for children. Separate spheres, he argues, mean that both father and mother are necessary for the upbringing of a child, as 'l'homme a une vie extérieure': 'Ce n'est que tout à fait exceptionnellement qu'il est chez lui et qu'il peut veiller sur ses enfants.' Better a stepmother than a governess or a single mother. In any event, the new family units formed by separated parents mean that children will be raised by *de facto* stepparents without the guarantee of the law, not to mention the subsequent children born out of wedlock: 'l'indissolubilité du mariage protège moins les enfants légitimes que le divorce et détermine la naissance de toute une classe d'enfants adultérins auxquels nos lois font une situation qui est un crime social.' And again, Naquet provides six examples (or 'faits'). Throughout the divorce debate, the figure of the widow is cited time and time again, and the position of individuals on the spectrum of opinion could often be measured in the degree to which they accepted the analogy between divorcees and widows. Both divorced and widowed women posed a challenge to the linear sexual narrative imposed on women by patriarchy, for both were sexually knowledgeable but unmarried women. Neither could be (or appear to be) the virgin bride about which patriarchy fantasized, but patriarchy still had an investment in marrying them off again and tying as many people as possible into the dyadic pattern of heteronormativity. Naquet suggested that society could not have it both ways: 'Ou les secondes noces sont préjudiciables aux enfants; et alors pourquoi les permettre aux veufs? Ou les secondes noces sont profitables aux enfants; et alors pourquoi les interdire aux époux séparés?'

These arguments about private life are backed up in Chapter 8 by the rhetoric of 'l'intérêt social'. Without divorce, Naquet argued, separation was producing either celibacy, Malthusian 'concubinat', or illegitimate children. It was socially irresponsible to condemn the latter to live as the fruit of adultery, and the sterility of the first two categories was deemed unpatriotic in the *revanchiste* atmosphere which followed defeat by the Prussians: 'dans l'état d'insolidarité où sont les placées les nations européennes, il ne peut être que nuisible à un pays comme le nôtre de voir sa population devenir stationnaire ou décroître quand celle des pays voisins s'accroît, au contraire, rapidement.' In this further compromise with mainstream opinion, Naquet makes the most of the metonymy between family, fatherland and mother country.

Before Naquet appended to his study the laws of 20 September 1792, 21 March 1803 and 8 May 1816, he considered in Chapter 11 'dans quels cas le divorce doit-il être admis?'. In an argument which we also find in the tongue-in-cheek complaints by Zola and Maupassant that divorce will kill off the literary plot, Naquet's ultimate sop to middling opinion is that divorce will combat adultery:

> De nos jours l'adultère est plus fréquent que les unions libres entre jeunes gens non mariés. En voici la raison: Qu'un homme non marié fasse la cour à une jeune fille; celle-ci lui répond: 'Épousez-moi ou retirez-vous.' Mais qu'un homme marié fasse la cour à une jeune fille, ou un jeune homme à une femme mariée; comme la loi ne leur permet pas le mariage, si l'amour existe, on se livre l'un à l'autre, un adultère est commis. [...] Si le divorce existait, et s'il était très facile à obtenir, l'adultère deviendrait plus rare encore que les unions libres

entre gens non mariés; le nombre des liaisons clandestines irait en diminuant et, avec elles, diminuerait aussi le nombre des enfants que cette clandestinité prive de toute garantie. (262–63)

It says much for his contorted relation to the doxa that this — like his other compromises with the mainstream — should sound like a paradox.

1881 had also seen Naquet contribute successfully to a new law on the freedom of the press and secure an easy re-election as deputy for Apt. In the subtle shifts of anti-monarchist politics, he distanced himself from the 'groupe fermé' of the 'extrême gauche' and attempted to curry favour with both the 'gauche radicale' and the Union républicaine. Renault had been defeated in the election in Seine-et-Oise, though by another supporter of divorce. Marcère, another 'représentant distingué de l'opinion moyenne' (22), took over his role as *rapporteur* at the behest of the Chamber's *commission d'initiative*. Naquet's third divorce bill, harking back to the principle of mutual consent, was presented on 11 November 1881, and from 6 to 8 May 1882, it was discussed. The bill was adopted at first reading by 327 votes to 119, and the second deliberation began on 13 June 1882. Though this was dominated by the virulent speech from Freppel, Bishop of Angers, Ronsin stresses the moderation of the debate.

The mood of the time is captured in Charles Gilbert-Martin's poem, 'L'Ange de la Délivrance', published in *Don Quichotte* on 12 May 1882, and accompanied by a caricature of Naquet in the role of the angel:

> Tout n'est pas rose en mariage
> L'hymen a pour temple une cage
> Où l'amour est souvent martyr
> Le bonheur y fait purgatoire
> Et le plus triste de l'histoire
> C'est que l'on n'en peut plus sortir.
> [...]
> Mais un ange au contour suave,
> Vient délier l'amour esclave,
> Libérer le couple captif
> Et les contrats, grâce au divorce,
> Peut-être offriront moins d'amorce
> Aux donneurs de coups de canif.

The bill adopted by the Chamber was sent to the Senate on 27 June 1882. Their opposition was reflected in the composition of the senatorial commission set up to examine the bill: six hostile (Allou, Eymard-Duvernay, Testelin, Marcel Barthe, Michel and Saint-Vallier), only three in favour (Émile Labiche, Eugène Pelletan and Édouard Millaud). The latter played for time, and when Testelin resigned, he was replaced by Salneuve, another 'partisan du divorce' (to use Naquet's own phrase). The hostile majority of three was reduced to one at a stroke (from six vs. three to five vs. four). Subsequent deaths and departures did not, however, change this ratio. Even though the partisans abandoned the Chamber's position and took up the former titre VI of the Civil Code without modifications, they could not win over the commission. Then, in an odd move, Eymard-Duvernay came up with his own rather eccentric pro-divorce proposal which the partisans managed to accommodate, thus gaining a majority which allowed them to install Labiche as *rapporteur*.

That same year, as if in preparation, the *juriste* Georges Vibert, under the pseudonym Georges de Cavilly, dedicated to Naquet his treatise on *La Séparation de corps et le divorce à l'usage des gens du monde et la manière de s'en servir*, which not only contributes to the discourse on divorce but also its iconography. The scandalous nature of the topic is registered in the red ink used on the front cover to advertise the publisher and the 'D' word... In P. Kauffmann's design Lucifer sits on the capital L at the start of the book's title, and the three stages of the conjugal narrative are depicted. We begin with the romance of the 'Commencement'. In the 'Suite' that follows, as the couple age (the man acquires a beard), they start to argue (the butterfly becomes a scorpion).[89] Coyness is replaced by wifely assertiveness and conflict (she now looks straight back at him), and the circle and trail of flowers have been transformed into chains. In the 'Fin!....' at the bottom of the cover, both parties are struggling to free themselves. Their chains seem to be broken, but their wrists are still cuffed — a fitting analogy for the state of play prior to Naquet's law. Kaufmann's title page displays a larger than life child bursting through a circular drum which is held in place by man and wife. The couple look at each other though not the child. But the display of the child also holds them apart; their fingers above the circular drum do not quite touch.

With the hopes for Naquet's 1882 bill in the background, the book opens with an exchange of open letters between Cavilly and Naquet which suggest that divorce will cure some of the ills of the body social (rather than politic). Indeed, Cavilly praises Naquet for addressing this 'question sociale' at a time when 'les questions politiques tiennent trop de place'. In keeping with this biological metaphor of society, Cavilly mocks healthy people who disdain medicine, and notes that just because medicine may taste unpleasant does not mean that we should stop taking it. Of course, separation and divorce are not perfect, he concedes, but if absolute perfection existed, there would be no need for divorce. Cavilly hopes that the Senate will pass a divorce law as 'le viatique nécessaire aux époux mal assortis qui entreprennent le voyage à longue procédure de la séparation ou du divorce'. Naquet's reply is dated 10 June 1882, just prior to the second reading of his bill, and expresses the confident view that 'l'opinion l'a compris: elle est avec nous', though in the event the Senate will not be. The very notion of divorce admits the dystopian possibilities of marriage, and Naquet continues the metaphor of bodily decline to warn that 'tel est robuste aujourd'hui qui est malade demain' given the contagion of 'les maladies morales'.

Part I deals with forms of marital unhappiness such as violence and adultery; Part II with legal procedure. The vision of marital incompatibility which Cavilly's book proposes casts its net far and wide: 'Cet ouvrage est fait pour les époux mal assortis, il s'adresse donc probablement à un assez grand nombre de personnes'.[90] The text is, however, addressed to men rather than women. Marriage is contrasted with 'toute union de fantaisie' with a 'grisette', a 'cocotte', or a married woman. Still, men are drawn to complete possession: 'Il n'est pas dans notre nature d'aimer le provisoire'. Though spouses share a commonwealth ('un patrimoine des joies et des douleurs partagées'), Cavilly advises that we think long and hard about 'un bail qui vous liera demain et le jour d'ensuite, le mois prochain et le mois suivant et les années qui viendront et toujours, toujours'. Returning to the image of the journey, spouses are compared to travellers who tire of each other's company. The difficulties of the journey are both intellectual and physical. Spouses should be of compatible intelligence. If they cannot share conversation, 'l'état de séparation intellectuelle' will ensue. In spite of the gendering of spheres, wives must be up to the mark, 'avec un mari que son éducation et sa connaissance des choses mettent souvent au-dessus d'elles'. Otherwise, 'ils sont deux et cependant ils se sentent seuls.' Still, she must be not more intelligent than him! 'L'esprit et la bêtise ont toujours fait mauvais ménage.' Cavilly also questions the feasibility of fidelity, citing the cynicism of the comtesse de Champagne and Balzac. Indeed, things may be rotten from the start, from the wedding night itself. The loss of virginity, brutally scripted by the public gesture of marriage, may generate 'antipathies insurmontables pour l'avenir', as Claire Vautier's *Adultère et divorce* will argue in its critique of 'viol légal'.

The book closes with a remarkably detailed eight-page ledger of costs which separation and — Cavilly anticipates — divorce will impose.[91] First, 'Demande en divorce (ou en séparation de corps)' whose 'total général' may come to 'débours' of 805 francs and 21 centimes and 'émoluments' of 308 francs and 50 centimes. In bold, Cavilly notes below these figures: 'Le divorce par défaut coûte la moitié moins.' He also observes that 'on peut compter que la procédure de divorce coûte environ 200 francs de plus que celle de séparation.' Second, 'Défense à la demande en divorce (ou séparation de corps)' is priced at 'débours' of 284 francs and 90 centimes, and 'émoluments' of 222 francs and 36 centimes. The ledger concludes with 'débours' of 226 francs and 66 centimes and 'émoluments' of 66 francs and 25 centimes for 'Demande à fin de séparation de biens', which bears the following explanation: 'Nous ne nous occupons que de la séparation des biens *par défaut*, parce que la séparation contradictoire se présente très rarement, le mari n'y défendant pas ordinairement.' In any event, the lawyers' fees are not to be sniffed at: 'NOTA. — Il faut compter en outre environ 40 francs pour le procès-verbal d'ouverture de liquidation à payer au notaire, et les honoraires de l'avocat, environ 100 francs.'

Meanwhile, other pots boiled — Naquet also promoting in 1882 a bill on the freedom of *transactions à terme* in commerce, and his *Questions constitutionnelles* appearing in 1883. Incensed by the laborious progress of his divorce legislation, Naquet called for a root and branch reform which would give legislative power to a single chamber. Forgetting the imperial despotism of his youth, his desire to do away with the vices of the parliamentary system would ultimately lead to his self-compromise in Boulanger's movement.

Enfin

In order to address this final stumbling block for divorce legislation, Naquet got himself elected to the Senate on 23 July 1883, after the death of Elzéar Pin, senator for Vaucluse. In the parliamentary jargon of the time, 'Naquet, malgré ses prédilections pour la Chambre basse où le retenait l'ardeur de son tempérament, s'était décidé à passer au Luxembourg pour y livrer la lutte suprême.'[92] On 26 May 1884 the Senate's discussions began, with a convert to Naquet, Monsieur le baron Lafond de Saint-Mûr, drawing on aristocratic and Catholic precedents:

> Le prince de Monaco, marié depuis huit ans, ayant eu un enfant de cette union, a bénéficié d'une annulation pontificale qui lui a permis d'épouser lady Hamilton. [...] Le marquis de Groslay de Virville a obtenu, grâce à son avocat, Jules Favre, sa séparation de corps en France. Il a fait annuler son mariage à Rome et a épousé une jeune Florentine dont il a eu trois enfants. Bigame devant la loi française, il a dû adopter la nationalité italienne. Mademoiselle de Haugsbourg a pu faire annuler son mariage avec le fils du maréchal Maisons, légalement, elle reste mariée avec lui. Autant de cas où le Code civil est plus sévère que la justice de l'Eglise.

The debate would last for seven sittings. Naquet himself spoke over two sittings to much applause. The Garde des sceaux, Martin-Feuillée, finally gave the Government's support to the project, explaining on 29 May, in response to Jules Simon's speech of the previous day, that the government was of a mind to permit divorce for *causes déterminées* and in all cases where *séparation de corps* was then possible, but not simply on the basis of mutual consent. For Naquet's opponent, Édouard Allou, the plot potential of divorce was testament to its capacity to generate ridiculously incoherent lives:

> Il y a une chose que je puis bien promettre aux partisans du divorce; c'est que le lendemain du jour où la loi nouvelle aurait été votée, ceux qui s'enrichiraient les premiers de la loi et des conséquences qu'elle produirait, ce seraient à la fois et les romanciers et les auteurs dramatiques et qu'il ne sera pas difficile pour eux de faire sortir, du rétablissement du divorce, et le côté ridicule et le côté dramatique des conditions nouvelles faites à l'union conjugale.

Zola and Maupassant, however, complained that divorce would kill off many of the literary situations of married life: why commit adultery, they quipped, when divorce was an option? On 7 June the first deliberation of the Senate culminated in a majority in favour of 151 to 108. The second deliberation ran from 19 to 24 June and was carried by similar numbers (151 to 116). All of this brought with it high drama not usually associated with the Senate. *Le Voltaire* reports on women bursting into tears when the first article — the suppression of the 1816 law — was voted on; it was adopted by 160 votes to 118.

Once more, even poetry was put to the service of the cause. As the Senate deliberated, one mediocre but well-intentioned poet, Évariste Carrance, used the alexandrines of his poem, 'Le Divorce', to remind jealous husbands that remorse pursues those acquitted by human justice. The poem culminates thus:

> A vous! Les grands faiseurs de lois, dont la morale
> En discours très pompeux de temps en temps s'étale
> Ne vous semble-t-il pas qu'il faudrait, par hasard,
> A l'époux outragé défendre le poignard?
> Eh bien! Pour que le droit puisse arrêter la force
> Il ne faut qu'une loi.
>   Laquelle?
>   Le Divorce![93]

In another instance of that privileged relationship between Naquet and literature, it bore a prefatory letter from Naquet, dated 16 June 1884, thanking Carrance for his attempt to 'achever de déraciner ce qui reste de l'absurde préjugé sur lequel a vécu le régime de 1816'.

Naquet did not have everything his own way, with some of his proposed grounds for divorce being denied. The medical profession was divided as to whether madness could be cited as grounds for divorce. Esprit-Sylvestre Blanche argued against such a move in *La Folie doit-elle être considérée comme cause de divorce?* (1882). Jules Luys, however, quoted two situations in which it might be permitted: dementia concealed at the time of the wedding, and, after five years, dementia caused by alcoholism ('La Folie doit-elle être considérée comme une cause de divorce?', *Encéphale*, June 1882). In the event, Naquet failed in his attempt to establish as grounds for divorce persistent mental illness of one of the spouses for at least two years.

One of the most contentious issues was whether divorce could be granted on the grounds of long-term absence. As noted above, debates on divorce in the nineteenth century often turned on the extent of the analogy between widowhood and divorce. Naquet asked the senators to follow the deputies by modifying the law of 1803 and making absence grounds for divorce. His opponent, Anselme Batbie, warned that this would create terrible problems of inheritance were the absent spouse to return, as if from the dead: 'Il suffit que le retour de l'absent soit possible, et dans le cas où le fait se produira, vous aurez, si le système de la commission était admis, créé une bigamie autorisée par la loi'. The long-standing place of the returning spouse in the literary imagination is clear from the Martin Guerre case, around which so much recent scholarship has revolved in what we might term the postmodern Renaissance. In the nineteenth century this wartime fracturing of the family is witnessed in Balzac's *Le Colonel Chabert*. Indeed, this book will close on the First World War, that period of mass state-induced family separation, after which little would seem the same again. The Commission was asked to study the matter and on 7 June 1884, it declared that absence would not be a peremptory cause of divorce but the courts would be able to pronounce a divorce five years after the declaration of disappearance (this declaration only possible after five years without news of the absentee). Batbie contested this decision:

> Je répète mon dilemme; s'il est mort, vous ne pouvez pas prononcer le divorce, car on ne prononce pas judiciairement le divorce avec une personne décédée; s'il ne reparaît pas parce qu'il ne le veut pas, c'est un cas d'injure grave et la disposition est inutile; si, enfin, il ne reparaît pas parce qu'il ne le peut, on ne doit pas prononcer le divorce contre lui.

A majority of senators sided with him, 146 votes to 81. Naquet's autobiography argues that this setback was graver than the loss of mutual consent.[94]

The Senate returned the bill to the Chamber, who were of a mind to accept the Senate's diluted version in the knowledge that once the principle was accepted, its terms could be subsequently reformed. Bishop Freppel's speech of 19 July 1884 was seared onto the collective memory, not least because of its virulent anti-Semitism:

> Qui donc vous a demandé le divorce? Qui, messieurs? Quelques femmes écervelées..., quelques romanciers qui se font un jeu des mœurs et des lois. [...]

> Et dans cette campagne antifrançaise, anticatholique sur qui se sont-ils appuyés?
> [...] Ils se sont appuyés sur une poignée d'israélites... (Exclamations à gauche.
> — Très bien! très bien! à droite.) [...] Le mouvement qui va aboutir à la loi du
> divorce est, dans le véritable sens du mot, un mouvement sémitique [...] un
> mouvement qui a commencé à M. Crémieux pour finir à M. Naquet... à travers
> toute une série d'israélites fauteurs et promoteurs du divorce. [...] Allez, si vous
> le voulez, du côté d'Israël, allez vers les Juifs! Nous restons, nous, du côté de
> l'Eglise et de la France![95]

But 355 deputies voted for divorce, 115 against, and Naquet had finally reached his
goal. The law was definitively promulgated on 27 July. Even those radicals who had
castigated the concessions made by the Apostle of Divorce were caught up in the
euphoria of victory. In the words of Léon Richer in *L'Avenir des Femmes* on 6 July
1884: 'La société moderne triomphait; l'esprit de justice, l'esprit de la Révolution se
retrouvaient enfin.' In return, Naquet joined the Ligue française pour le Droit des
Femmes.[96] In his autobiography, Naquet counts the days from his first bill on 13
March 1876 to the promulgation of 27 July 1884: it had taken eight years and over
four months to achieve victory.[97]

  The Loi Naquet reproduced the former Titre VI of the 1803 Civil Code, but for
a few details. Naquet had proposed several corrections to the Civil Code of 1803 to
which he wished otherwise to return. The first Article to be recast was the notorious
230 which had only allowed wives to ask for divorce on the grounds of a husband's
adultery 'lorsqu'il aura tenu sa concubine dans la maison commune'. His wish was
to establish equivalent treatment of spouses with regard to adultery by striking out
this sub-clause. As the 'partie officielle' of the *Journal officel de la République française*
on 29 July 1884 reveals, Naquet was less successful in proposing an extension of the
grounds of 'excès, sévices et injures graves' in Article 231 to include imprisonment
'pour vol, escroquerie, abus de confiance, outrage publique à la pudeur, excitation
de mineurs à la débauche'. *Pace* Article 232 the grounds of 'condamnation à une
peine infamante' should not include 'le banissement et la dégradation civique pour
cause politique' (the wounds of the Commune were not yet healed).

  In Chapter III ('Des effets du divorce') the attempt in Article 295 to instil doubt
in would-be divorcees by prohibiting divorcees from remarrying each other was
diluted in its new version which permitted such a marriage if, in the meantime,
neither ex-spouse had married and divorced a second partner. In other words, one
could not divorce a second spouse in order to remarry the first. This was only possible
if the remarried spouse had been widowed (as Senator Bérenger suggested). The fear
that the ceremony of marriage would be submerged by the carnival of divorce is
reflected in the reminder that such a remarriage of divorced spouses would require
'une nouvelle célébration du mariage'. In order to forestall financial shenanigans,
such remarrying couples could not change the terms of their initial marital *régime*.
And once remarried to each other, such couples could only divorce again if one of
them was subsequently sentenced to 'une peine afflictive et infamante'. Article 298
was simplified so as to remove the gender disparity of 1803 whereby an adulterous
wife had been sentenced to 'réclusion' in a house of correction for three months
to two years. However, the new law retained this article's interdiction on culpable
spouses subsequently marrying their accomplice in adultery. This was in keeping

with Naquet's desire for divorce to be a means of defence offered to the innocent spouse so that they could free themselves of a painful union and replace it with one that had equivalent legal status. Article 298 would, however, be rescinded by the law of 15 December 1904.

Unlike 1792, but in keeping with the Civil Code, *séparation de corps* (Chapter IV) was left in place in 1884, in a concession to Catholics repulsed by divorce. Mutual consent and the grounds of temperamental incompatibility were not permitted, by contrast with the permissible grounds: of adultery; 'excès, sévices ou injures graves'; and 'condamnation à une peine afflictive et infamante'. Importantly, the law of 1884 removed the mutual consent clause. The Senate modified the Chamber's article 310 which had intended to make the conversion of *séparation de corps* into divorce optional after three years. Instead, each spouse would have the right to request such a conversion, but it would be left to the courts to grant it or not. Article 2 now asserted that a husband could disown a child born 300 days after the wife had been authorised to live apart from her husband during a separation or divorce trial, and less than 180 days since the definitive rejection of the case or a reconciliation. Such a disavowal would not be permitted if the wife could prove 'réunion de fait entre les époux'.

The term 'excès' was defined to categorize extreme behaviour: 'Les excès sont des actes de violence qui passent toute mesure, et qui peuvent mettre la vie de l'époux en danger'.[98] Proof of such life-threatening behaviour would certainly lead to *séparation de corps* or divorce. The accompanying term 'sévices' was, however, subject to wide interpretation in divorce cases, in spite of attempts at definition: 'Les sévices sont des actes de cruauté, de brutalité ou de méchanceté qui ne portent pas atteinte à la vie de l'époux, mais qui cependant lui rendent la vie commune insupportable'.[99] This gave the courts freedom to expect that such 'sévices' should be grave and repeated if they were to justify the legal dissolution of marriage. Judges would often draw a line between unacceptable 'sévices' and an acceptable severity in the exercising of marital authority. This imprecise law could not generate clear jurisprudence, but instead some rather curious decisions. Those seeking divorce would therefore often add to 'sévices' the yet vaguer accusation of 'injures graves'. This was particularly important in cases based on the husband's adultery, where this did not take place in the conjugal home and where it could not be proven irrefutably. 'Peines afflictives et infamantes' included death, forced labour in perpetuity or for a fixed period, deportation, detention and *réclusion*. Although abandonment was not grounds for divorce, it could be cited as an 'injure grave', and was often used against spouses who might for good reason have refused to return home.

Another frequently invoked 'injure grave' was refusal to fulfil conjugal duties, which would often lead to confusing trials. If the wife's virginity was taken as incontrovertible proof for which the husband would generally be thought culpable, he could defend himself on the ground of his wife's resistance or his own impotence. Equally perplexing were those trials which accused husbands of communicating a venereal disease to their wife. Though not flagged in the law, such a misdeed was often considered to be an 'injure grave' if committed knowingly or even wilfully. Demanding 'caresses contre nature' was one of the many motives not specified in law but recognized in jurisprudence, as was the husband's passivity if a third party insulted his wife. As such, we should not be surprised that the appearance in 1884 of the husband's adultery in any location as grounds for divorce did not produce a mass of such accusations: recourse to 'injures graves' remained much easier. This *fourre-tout* motive also replaced those grounds cited during the Revolutionary period: abandonment, absence, and temperamental incompatibility. Indeed, the abolition of the grounds of temperamental incompatibility invited much fraudulent evidence in the courtroom which would only be combated later by the reestablishment of mutual consent. Another problem was the awkwardness in converting *séparation de corps* into divorce. Naquet's push in 1886 failed, and only in 1908 would this become a matter of course.

The new law was disseminated in a flurry of publications in 1884 and 1885 by lawyers keen to explain the new provisions. Their verbose front covers give a flavour of the discourse. These include A. Baralle, *Loi du divorce avec toutes les formalités à remplir* (Paris: F. de Boyères, 1884); Max Botton and André Lebon, *Code annoté du divorce, contenant le commentaire du Livre I, Titre sixième du Code Civil revisé par la loi de 1884, l'analyse de la discussion devant les Chambres et celle des travaux préparatoires du Code Civil*, prefaced by Senator Naquet (Paris: A. Rousseau, 1884); Paul Vraye and Georges Gode, *Le Divorce et la séparation de corps: commentaire théorique et pratique de la Loi du 29 juillet 1884*; Charles Constant, *Code du divorce: commentaire de la loi du 27 juillet 1884*; Léopold Goirand, *Traité pratique du divorce, suivi d'un formulaire particulier à la procédure du divorce*; Robert Fremont, *Traité pratique du divorce et de la séparation de corps: ouvrage contenant l'analyse complète de la procédure et de la jurisprudence française et étrangère relative au divorce* (Paris: Chevalier-Maresq, 1884–85); Henri Coulon, A. Faivre and E. Jacob, *Manuel formulaire du divorce, contenant le texte de la loi du 19 juillet 1884* (Paris: Marchal & Billard, 1884); Guignot, *Instructions pratiques sur le divorce en forme de questionnaire* (Paris: L. Larose & Forcel, 1884). One can only imagine the fate of such instructive and timely volumes in the unwritten melodrama of private life: purchased discreetly in the bookshops of Paris, secreted perhaps in the very home which their owner wished to escape, or suddenly discovered by a suspicious (or unsuspecting) spouse. Half DIY guides to liberation, half cynical encounters between the legal profession and the general public, these volumes are parodied in the *mode d'emploi* offered by Gyp in the quasi-Vernian title, *Autour du divorce*.

There were already 3715 requests for divorce lined up in 1883, with around 3000 separations per year on average during the 1880s. Requests for divorce grew to 5439 in 1884 and 7550 in 1885. Although, 'the divorce law passed in 1884 was not really taken advantage of till two years later', as Naquet later explained, it still worked 'like a safety valve in a steam engine':

> A law which suddenly establishes divorce finds itself necessarily brought face to face with a mass of cases which have been accumulating for years. The first act is a sort of general liquidation, which produces exaggerated optical effects. But when this clearing of the docket is accomplished, and there come up for decision only the divorce cases belonging to each successive year, then a decrease follows the increase, and the public mind is calmed.[100]

In 1885, 4227 divorces were granted, rising to 6751 in 1895. Requests for *séparations de corps* were still predominantly female (85% of all such requests). For Naquet, the dominant pattern is clear:

> In 1883 [...] there were granted in France 3,010 separations (*a mensâ et thoro*). In 1888 the number of separations and divorces together had risen to 7,166. [...] As there is much divorcing in France, the reestablishment of divorce was a crying necessity.

By contrast with requests for mere separation, there was a considerably smaller gender gap in the number of requests for divorce (60% of requests coming from women, and 40% from men), and the total number of requests for divorce quickly outstripped the total number of such requests for separation (4:1). The usual reasons cited were 'excès, sévices ou injures graves'. Adultery was rarely cited, though not, one imagines, because would-be divorcees rarely committed adultery. Female adultery was cited in, for instance, 11% of cases in 1894. That same year, only 6.4% of cases cited male adultery, though this percentage was increasing.

Ronsin is right to resist the temptation to exaggerate the significance of our subject and to concede that 'dans la grande œuvre de construction d'un état laïc entreprise par les républicains, la réforme de l'enseignement était sans doute le point essentiel, l'action anti-cléricale le plus spectaculaire, le divorce n'était que très accessoire'.[101] Still, the stakes of the Loi Naquet were considerable for its debates crystallized a vital question: to what extent was the Third Republic heir to the principles of the original Revolution? Indeed, we could well argue that in the nineteenth century divorce was more important as an idea than as a fact. The compromises which were forced on Naquet were testament to the conservatism of the regime. The spirit of compromise at large in the early Third Republic produced, and the Loi Naquet in particular reflected, a government and a politics acceptable to the economic, social and moral interests of the middle classes. In the language of 1848, it stopped February turning into June. And it was neither Empire nor Commune.

The Loi Naquet only increased its author's celebrity. Laurent Tailhade describes how he became one of the most visible men of the age, 'quelque chose de plus qu'un homme célèbre, une physionomie à la mode et l'engouement de Paris'.[102] The 'bons poètes' of Rodolphe Salis's cabaret, Le Chat-Noir, deployed their humour to Naquet's advantage. At the Folies-Dramatiques, a spectacular review culminated in the crowning of Naquet's bust by a chorus of divorcees. In 1881 the painter Alphonse Hirsch produced a portrait of Naquet for the Salon.

To tidy up procedure a second divorce law was passed on 18 April 1886, carried through the Senate paradoxically enough under the wing of one of Naquet's adversaries, Brisson, then Garde des sceaux. After a vigorous press campaign, Naquet acquired a favourable commission, of which he was himself *rapporteur*. His particular disappointment was, however, in failing to correct article 310 on the conversion of *séparations de corps* into divorce after three years. The 1886 reform did include a gagging restriction on the press in response to an awareness that the divorce courts could provide unwelcome fodder for the popular press. If divorce necessarily meant the intervention of the public realm into personal matters, it was still considered better not to encourage invasive and prurient transparency. Fiction, however, could not be gagged so easily.

Fin de siècle **Reflections**

As ever, one of the best litmus tests of *fin de siècle* opinion is *La Grande Encyclopédie*, though it is worth noting that the lead author of the entry for 'divorce' was one of Naquet's opponents, Glasson, professor in the Parisian Law Faculty.[103] Its six parts cover 'Antiquité judaïque', 'Droit grec', 'Droit romain', 'Droit canonique et ancien droit français', 'Droit actuel' and 'Législation comparée', all authored by Glasson except the Greek section, by Charles Lécrivain. Most expansive is Part IV which completes the historical survey and associates the prohibition of divorce with Catholic France. The Church, Glasson notes, has always repelled divorce by mutual consent, although in early times the question of wifely adultery was a cause for 'doutes'. Under the residual influence of pre-Christian Rome, barbarian law had often permitted divorce 'avec une extrême facilité'. Around the tenth century Glasson identifies the ecclesiastical origin of 'séparation de corps perpétuelle' (without the right to 'convoler à de nouvelles noces') in the diverse cases of adultery, murder, magic and violation of the sepulchre. Although the Middle Ages offered rare cases of 'divorce déguisé', Glasson makes the warning which all subsequent historians of divorce will recognize that 'ce mot divorce était alors aussi employé comme synonyme de nullité de mariage'. It was the Protestant Reformation, Glasson notes, which re-established divorce, not merely on the grounds of wifely adultery. Against Enlightenment relativism, Glasson and other conservatives extoled innately French Catholic values. Small wonder that Diderot and Rousseau were associated with the corruption of mores. Against the notion of marriage as a private contract which could be ruptured, Glasson cites the case of adoption as an example of the social interest in maintaining that contractual bind. The particular problems he identifies in the law of 1792 are divorce by mutual consent and the ease of divorce 'même pour les motifs les plus futiles'. The removal of divorce was one of the first acts of the Restoration and was, he argues, both reactionary and popular.

The culmination of the entry in *La Grande Encyclopédie* is the analysis of current French law in Part V. Although divorce confirms the eradicable nature of marriage, Glasson stresses the limits in repressing its 'causes déterminées'. In the case of adultery and 'excès, sévices ou injures graves', a divorce action may be halted by reconciliation but 'l'époux qui a renoncé à son action peut cependant l'intenter plus tard, si une nouvelle cause de divorce est survenue depuis la réconciliation.' Moreover, reconciliation is not possible in the case of 'la condamnation à une peine afflictive et infamante': 'car cette condamnation frappe l'époux d'une déchéance qui se perpétue indéfiniment, de sorte qu'à proprement parler la réconciliation ne peut pas être postérieure à cette déchéance'. What this suggests is a particular narrative of married life in which events cannot be buried. Even after a reconciliation, continued mistreatment can take a couple back to the divorce court. 'La condamnation à une peine afflictive et infamante', whose procedure was 'très simple', is the beginning of the end.

Glasson also stresses the need for privacy in this public domain. The court could order 'le huis clos, par exemple dans l'intérêt des bonnes mœurs'. In accordance with 'une disposition très sage de la loi du 18 avril 1886', for fear of 'publicité' and 'scandale' a fine of 100 to 2,000 francs could be imposed on newspapers reproducing the debates of divorce trials. The very privacy of marriage, however, imposed evidential difficulties for the courts. The 'enquête' and witnesses were vital in combatting the faking of evidence for 'un divorce en réalité par consentement mutuel'. Due process in divorce cases required the forensic exposure of private life, and thus its own 'strangers in the house': 'il faut reconnaître que les ascendants et les domestiques seront, le plus souvent, les seuls témoins sérieux dans les demandes en divorce et qu'à leur défaut la preuve serait à peu près impossible.' In other words, paradoxically enough, those junior by age or class may fulfil the demands of Ginzburg's conjectural paradigm. Glasson does not explain how to deal with couples with neither children nor servants. On the other hand, such strangers in the house posed a threat to the discretion of the initial proceedings. In a strikingly modern awareness of the pain of the divorce process, Glasson promotes the acceleration of proceedings as they unfold. Initially, the *président* may attempt reconciliation, perhaps requesting the parties to appear before him twenty days later: 'On aura remarqué que toute cette procédure devant le président est encore parfois assez lente,' whilst the possibility of reconciliation remains considerable. The proceedings themselves tend to drive the wedge between spouses yet further, he argues. The process may follow a slow-slow-quick-quick-slow rhythm if there is an appeal:

> En vertu d'une dérogation au droit commun facile à comprendre, le pourvoi en cassation et même (quoique la loi ne le dise pas) le délai du pourvoi sont suspensifs de l'exécution de l'arrêt qui prononce le divorce. Si l'on appliquait la règle ordinaire, si l'on permettait d'exécuter cet arrêt, les époux pourraient contracter tout de suite un nouveau mariage et si, plus tard, l'arrêt prononçant le divorce de leur premier mariage était cassé, comme le premier mariage revivrait, le second devait disparaître; de là des troubles et des scandales qu'on évite en déclarant suspensif le pourvoi en cassation.

This postponement of the effect of the original divorce ruling is intended to disarm the farcical plot potential of divorce which is witnessed on the turn-of-the-century Parisian stage. The real fear is that the divorce/remarriage life narrative might be reinterpreted by the court of appeal as bigamy. Even for the pro-divorce camp, the *honnêteté* of serial monogamy was a narrative far preferable to the scandal of promiscuous doubling in this crisis of compromised sequentiality. Once confirmed, however, divorce required oral and written affirmation which was 'aussi public que possible': 'dans l'auditoire des tribunaux civils et de commerce'; 'dans les chambres des avoués et des notaires'; and 'dans l'un des journaux qui se publient dans le lieu où siège le tribunal ou, s'il n'y en a pas, dans l'un de ceux publiés dans le département'. The textual relationship between divorce and marriage was quite particular:

> L'exécution du jugement ou de l'arrêt devenu irrévocable consiste dans sa transcription sur les registres de l'état civil du lieu où le mariage a été célébré. En outre, il est fait mention de ce jugement ou arrêt en marge de l'acte du mariage.

Returning to this scene of *célébration*, indeed of *fête*, the sober carnival of divorce undoes the social and sexual reordering of the wedding day. Geographically and rhetorically divorce returns to the topos (or 'lieu') of the wedding day to erase its force. Or at least to undo it, for divorce as ~~marriage~~ is a negation but not an erasure, the halting of the marriage that would otherwise unfold, not the amnesia of the marriage that has been. And children, of course, are the best reminder of that shared past. It is conspicuous that divorce was a marginal annotation of the marriage text.

Glasson's encyclopaedia entry concludes in Part VI with an act of comparison. He categorizes three European models in a manner which positions France at the hybrid interface of old and new Europes. First come those who prohibited divorce, such as Italy, Spain and Portugal. Second come those who permitted it 'pour causes déterminées', notably France. Finally there are those who even permitted divorce by mutual consent. A particular contrast is drawn between Article 298 and the English law of 1857:

> Toutes les fois que le divorce a été prononcé pour cause d'adultère, le conjoint coupable peut épouser son complice; on est même réputé manquer à l'honneur lorsqu'après avoir séduit une femme mariée on ne répare pas sa faute en l'épousant. C'est là une particularité curieuse des mœurs anglaises; dans la plupart des autres législations, il y a, au contraire, empêchement de mariage entre l'époux coupable et son complice, pour que l'adultère ne conduise pas au mariage par le divorce.

The model for a middle way between the Latin and Germanic/Scandinavian model, Glasson concludes, is not in fact France, but the Slavic countries which admit divorce but only under rigorous conditions.

The effects of divorce in the France of the *fin de siècle* were measured by the 'moral sciences' in the atmosphere of statistical zeal characterized by Jacques Bertillon and of sociological exploration spearheaded by Émile Durkheim. The demographer Bertillon's 'Notes pour l'étude statistique du divorce' in the *Annales de démographie internationale* of 1880 were often cited by the *divorciaires* such as Naquet and Marcère. He also provided regular commentaries on divorce statistics for readers of *Le XIXe siècle* and, notably, his 'Étude démographique du divorce et de la séparation de corps dans les différents pays de l'Europe' for the *Annales de démographie internationale* in 1882. Prior to 1884 he was keen to show the relatively high incidence of French requests for legal separation even in the European context of a decade of increasing requests. The frequency of legal separations was in fact related to factors such as religion, 'race', profession, the presence of children, and urban or rural location, and to imagine that law could govern sentiment was, Bertillon argued, an illusion:

> La véritable cause du divorce n'est généralement pas celui qu'on invoque devant le juge. Une femme se sépare de son mari non parce qu'il l'a trompée, ni parce qu'il l'a battue, mais parce que ce mari lui est insupportable et que la vie commune est intolérable. [...] Je ne puis m'empêcher de sourire quand je vois des législateurs se disputer sur les dangers de telle ou telle disposition qu'ils proposent d'ajouter ou de retrancher de la loi. [...] Quand on se décide à divorcer, ce n'est pas pour un seul grief: c'est pour cent! sur le nombre, il s'en trouvera toujours un que votre loi aura visé.

Bertillon thus demystifies the forensic authority of the divorce case. Rather than exposing to the public gaze the *petits faits vrais* of private life, divorce law is depicted as a pragmatic mechanism in the public sphere which facilitates the formal rearrangement of the private realm. In Bertillon's view, the official discourse finds the gnawing discontent and tedium of conjugal life somehow unreadable and thus unnarratable. The melodramatic rhetoric of *excès, sévices, injures*, itself an excessive gloss, amplifies and simplifies incompatibility, which is felt as a mood but told as a drama. Divorce narrates a certain history of marriage, heightened by the peripeteia of 'grounds' for divorce. Indeed, it might be helpful to connect these notions of grounds and grounding to Peter Brooks's brilliant play on narrative plots and plots of land.[104] The irony is that these grounds cannot be *terre à terre*. Divorce, it seems, is not a particularly reliable ledger of discord: 'It is absolutely imperative to retain the distinction between divorce and marital breakdown, and to remember that the rate of divorce is no guide to the extent of marital unhappiness, breakdown or dissolution.'[105]

Bertillon wants the law to leave the door as wide open as possible and to let mores unfold without the law fantasizing that it can halt their development. If the early nineteenth century weaves suicide into the fictions of Romantic yearning emblematized by *Werther*, the *fin de siècle* attempts to rationalize this ultimate rejection of the real. Drawing links between the statistical graphs and maps of divorce and suicide, Bertillon suggests that unbalanced or even suicidal folk will end up making their spouses seek divorce. He also counters the conservative image of divorce as the touchstone for manifold social disorder: 'Il serait tout à fait ridicule de conclure de ce qui précède qu'une loi qui rendrait le divorce facile multiplierait les suicides [...] c'est justement le contraire qui est vrai.'[106]

The 'father of sociology', Émile Durkheim, responded to Bertillon's findings and a general concern at the time for suicide in his 1897 book on the subject, *Le Suicide: Étude de sociologie*. To explain the pan-European connection between divorce and suicide which Bertillon had emphasized, Durkheim argues that 'ce n'est pas dans les prédispositions organiques des sujets, mais dans la nature intrinsèque du divorce qu'il faut aller chercher la cause de cette remarquable relation'.[107] Divorcees committed suicide three to four times more than married folk, and even more than widows and widowers — even though the latter's trauma was considered more painful as it was involuntary, whereas divorcees might feel some sort of deliverance. In reality, Durkheim argued, it was not the break-up which pushed divorcees to suicide: 's'ils ont un si violent penchant au suicide, c'est qu'ils y étaient déjà fortement enclins alors qu'ils vivaient ensemble et par le fait même de leur vie commune.' For Durkheim, the frequency of suicide was not a function of the number of *désaxés* nor a consequence of the number of divorces but, more fundamentally, due to the character of matrimonial structures when they lost their rigidity. Suicide was encouraged by a certain *état de la famille*:

> Le divorce implique un affaiblissement de la réglementation matrimoniale. Là où il est établi, là surtout où le droit et les mœurs en facilitent avec excès la pratique, le mariage n'est plus qu'une forme affaiblie de lui-même; c'est un moindre mariage. [...] C'est [...] l'état d'anomie conjugale, produit par l'institution du divorce, qui explique le développement parallèle des divorces et des suicides. [...] L'anomie matrimoniale peut [...] exister dans l'opinion sans être encore inscrite dans la loi. Mais, d'un autre côté, c'est seulement quand

elle a pris une forme légale, qu'elle peut produire toutes ses conséquences. Tant que le droit matrimonial n'est pas modifié, il sert tout au moins à contenir matériellement les passions; surtout, il s'oppose à ce que le goût de l'anomie gagne du terrain, par cela seul qu'il la réprouve.

Pace Bertillon, Durkheim opposes the liberalization of divorce law as this would, in his view, increase the suicide rate of spouses and this would not be compensated for by the parallel decrease in female suicide. *Inter alia*, Émile Faguet praised Durkheim's position in *La Revue bleue*, 9 April 1898.

The way in which divorce had facilitated the Third Republic's retrospection on the Revolution itself had been apparent in the reissuing of classic anti-divorce literature by the likes of Bonald, Mme Necker, and Cerfvol. The turn-of-the-century discourse on divorce was constituted in no small part by a reflection on the history of divorce, not least by jurists in the campaign for divorce by mutual consent: Pierre Damas's thesis, *Les Origines du divorce en France: Étude historique sur la loi du 20 septembre 1792*(Bordeaux, 1896–97), Olivier Martin, *La Crise du mariage dans la législation intermédiaire* (1901), Marcel Cruppi, *Le Divorce pendant la Révolution, 1792–1804* (1909), and Jean Sourdois, *Le Mariage et le divorce sous la législation intermédiaire (1789–1804)* (Paris: Fontemoing, 1910). Even in 1884 a biographical dictionary asserted that 'M. Naquet a depuis lors [the passing of the new law] plaidé, mais sans succès, la cause de la recherche de la paternité'.[108] Between 1887 (the final year of his autobiography, to be published much later) and 1889 he provided a theorizing voice for Boulangism, publishing tracts and engaging in debates. In his epilogue to the autobiography, Pillias defines this as, 'après la loi du divorce, le deuxième grand événement de sa vie politique'.[109] Naquet saw Boulanger as a vehicle for the triumph of his old plan for a new constitution. Naquet's public image suffered greatly in this shift from the international movement of the radical Left to a movement which absorbed all political colours in the service of national imperatives. As he would recall at the turn of the century, 'On nous a reproché, à Boulanger et à moi, d'avoir lié partie avec la réaction.'[110] In 1897 he was also accused of benefiting from the Panama Scandal, returning from exile in London to appear in court on 2 March 1898, only to be acquitted. In 1898 he sunk back into private life, once the contamination from the Panama Affair had robbed him of any remaining political authority. Still, there appeared *Temps futurs: Socialisme — Anarchie* (Paris, 1900), a preface to the translation of J. C. Spence's *L'Aurore de la civilisation ou l'Angleterre au XXe siècle* (Paris, 1900), *L'Humanité et la patrie* (Paris, 1901), *L'Anarchie et le collectivisme* (Paris, 1904), *Désarmement ou alliance anglaise* (Paris, 1908), and collaborations with G. Hardy on *Néo-Malthusisme et socialisme* (Paris, 1910) and André Lorulot, *Le Socialisme marxiste, l'individualisme anarchique et la révolution* (Paris, 1911). He had returned to the anarchist faith of his youth, earning the title 'Naquet, l'anarchiste' recently awarded to him by Pierre Birnbaum.[111]

But Naquet could never quite escape his pet issue. Internationally, Naquet would remain associated with the divorce question. For an American audience he asks in 1892 whether 'the experiment [of 1884] has produced good or bad results'.[112] Quoting Bertillon once more, he argues that 'what legislation can accomplish [...] is the bringing to light of existing social facts or the checking of the manifestation of these same facts'. And 'it is a well-established fact that to-day in every country, whatever may be the nature of its legislation in respect to the subject now under consideration, the number of separations is continually progressing'. The law did not so much produce social facts as expose and regulate them. Typical of the manner in which science became for Naquet less a field of endeavour and more a source of analogy, is his conclusion that 'the divorce law was a sort of microscope which had enabled the statistician to see [...] what was hitherto beyond his ken'. From this perspective, far from simply fulfilling the avant-garde impulses of individuals, or a purely libertarian agenda, divorce also contributed to the state's policing of intimacy, which D. A. Miller has connected to the voyeurism of the classic novel. In the terms of Carlo Ginzburg's 'conjectural paradigm', which Christopher Prendergast has linked to the epistemophilia of nineteenth-century fiction, divorce — like the discovery of finger-printing and the birth of psychoanalysis — was one more device of 'ken'.

Naquet returned to the fray in *La Loi du divorce* (1903). That same year, on 21 February, Naquet lost his wife, Estelle, who had devoted her remaining years to their son, Paul. Naquet had been separated from her since the Second Empire, without having made use of the law which bore his name. In spite of his famous latter to *Le Figaro* in 1879, Naquet was usually reticent in divulging details of his personal life. Throughout his period of parliamentary activity he had lived with his friends, the Vaucluse deputies Poujade and Saint-Martin, in what André calls 'une sorte de phalanstère'.[113] In 1887 one Mlle Odile Siquoir went into domestic service for Naquet, who was touched by her devotion and fortitude. On 2 May 1903, aged 69, he married Odile, aged 48, in the town hall of the 16th arrondissement (as he lived in Auteuil), witnessed by two Boulangist friends, Georges Laguerre and Alfred Laisant. We may ask why this advocate of free union should remarry so soon after being widowed. The pragmatic reality was that only in this way could he leave the loyal Odile the pension of a parliamentarian's widow. Naquet's marriage seems not to have been the kind of passionate rejuvenation which Zola found with his maid, Jeanne Rozerot.

Vers l'union libre (1908) — whose very title seemed to confirm the fears of his opponents a quarter of a century earlier — begins with an assertion (*pace* Frédéric Stack) that 'le mariage et la famille varient comme varient les formes sociales'. The mathematics of the functional relationship between family and state reprises the rhetoric of metonymy which habitually connected the two. He also uses this opening chapter to satirize the conservative writer, Paul Bourget, who — Naquet claims — has revitalized the divorce debate in a way that Naquet and other marginal radicals could scarcely have dreamed of. He goes on to focus on the evolution of a communitarian notion of familial bonds beyond the solitude of the bourgeois family, an ideal which he calls 'la famille élargie'. But he still feels obliged to return from philosophy ('vers le communisme') to reality (the current need for divorce; 66–68). He invokes his own argument with Elisée Reclus so as to portray the ambivalent status of divorce in radical circles, which reflects an important disagreement as to the nature of historical transformation. Against Naquet's vision of history inching forward in hand-to-hand parliamentary struggle against the Right (implicit in his title's reference to 'vers'), Reclus contends that any attempt simply to improve or modernize marriage (including divorce) serves merely to prop up that defunct and reactionary structure. In a letter of 22 December 1898 Reclus complains: 'Le mariage était devenu aux yeux des hommes intelligents une intolérable nuisance et vous avez tâché de l'accommoder à la sauce du jour. [...] Vous n'avez fait autre chose que *d'assurer au mal une plus grande durée.*' And in another letter which Naquet cites: 'Jamais diligence à chevaux ne se fera locomotive; jamais actes légaux de mariage ou de divorce ne se transformeront en amour libre.' Like the Industrial Revolution, Reclus argues, sexual and social revolution requires a paradigm shift rather than Naquet's syntagmatic inching forwards. Reclus argues that divorce is not in the end a radical social policy, as it attempts to cure marriage rather than kill it off.

Here Naquet is unwilling to resolve this philosophical dilemma about the process of history: 'Et maintenant l'institution du divorce précipite-t-elle en fait la marche vers l'union libre? ou consolide-t-elle pour un temps le mariage comme le croyait Elisée Reclus et comme l'affirmait — en s'en réjouissant — le docteur Toulouse dans un article du *Journal* du 19 janvier 1903? Je l'ignore.' But divorce, he concludes, is the right answer for the present and must aid the ultimate goal of sentimental liberation. Indeed, whilst radical idealists dream, Naquet asserts the need to defend what has already been achieved: 'A l'heure qu'il est la situation est autre. Un parti s'est réformé qui cherche à ameuter l'opinion contre l'institution du divorce elle-même.' He says that the failed arguments of 'la réaction cléricale' must be crushed again, as they were thirty years before. As such, he apologizes for going over old ground in subsequent chapters.

This book also addresses the vexed question of children and divorce. Naquet cites Marcel Prévost on the superiority of divorce over living in an unhappy household:

> C'est le droit de l'écrivain de représenter dans le livre et au théâtre ce qu'une loi humaine peut susciter de misères — le *déchet* d'une loi. Mais le lecteur ni le spectateur ne doivent oublier:
>
> (1). Que le sort des époux divorcés, et des enfants de divorcés, ne doit pas être comparé (pour tirer une juste conclusion) au sort des époux et des enfants, dans un ménage uni 'qui va bien'. Il faut le comparer au sort des époux et des enfants, dans un ménage désuni, impatient, mécontent.
>
> (2). Que nulle conscience n'est en droit de se révolter contre une loi d'usage facultatif dont chacun est libre d'éviter les conséquences plus ou moins fâcheuses tout simplement en n'ayant en aucun point recours.

Even if children sometimes suffer, Naquet asserts pragmatically, the new situation is better than what preceded it: 'Je ne voudrais pas affirmer que les dangers que l'on signale ne se réalisent jamais. Je ne prétends pas que le bien absolu règne en France depuis que le divorce y a été rétabli, ni qu'il y régnera lorsque le divorce aura été élargi jusqu'à la législation de 1792, ou jusqu'à l'union libre.' In his timeworn custom, Naquet verifies his position by citing five cases from letters which he has received.

By 1886 (the year of the *recensement*) the new law had spawned a vast growth in the number of legal break-ups: 10.17 per 10,000 couples, more than twice the rate of separations in 1883. Ronsin describes the spread of divorce from divorce as 'un phénomène de contagion',[114] spreading particularly quickly to the north of the Loire and in those *départements* dominated by a large town. The number of divorces grew steadily in the pre-war years, reaching 14,261 in 1910. In particular, the new law promised and threatened to liberate suffering wives. Still, just as with married women's property law in England, the Loi Naquet required further legislation. Though marriage contracts protected the property women brought to marriage, the wife's right to manage her property was limited. Against this, successive laws were passed: in 1881, permitting women savings accounts, in 1893, granting them absolute control of their property and, in 1907, complete control of their income.

Naquet's argument in *La Loi du divorce* culminates in an assertion of the need to widen divorce provision: 'sans la faculté de divorcer accordée à chaque époux sur sa seule volonté, la loi est absolument boiteuse.'[115] The inevitability of the law of 1904 permitting adulterers subsequently to be joined in marriage was sketched out in hindsight by Charles Morizot-Thibault's piece on 'Comment les juges, en pervertissant la loi, ruinent la moralité publique'.[116] He explains the initial desire in 1884 to protect the 'pudeur' of women against 'un mal qui est le principe de tous les relâchements', namely adultery: 'On ne voulait pas encourager l'adultère en en faisant l'antichambre du mariage légitime.' Morizot-Thibault blamed magistrates for their laxness in applying this law. Often aware of the adulterous accomplices, they would suggest: 'Nous ne désignons pas le complice?', to which the lawyers would respond: 'Parfaitement, Monsieur le Président!' To Morizot-Thibault's question: 'Et pourquoi [...] violer la prescription impérieuse de la loi?', such magistrates would offer the retort: 'Oh! [...] ces gens-là vont vivre ensemble et il faut préférer le mariage légitime au concubinage', which we might term the English solution.

Furthermore, Morizot-Thibault argued that the divorce law had in some cases actually encouraged the violence of husbands who did not have just cause for divorce. Although this 'cause de divorce' was particularly important for battered 'femmes du peuple', others manipulated this dispensation. He notes the case of one official from the higher ranks of Parisian society who, 'dégoûté de sa femme', beat her in order to force her to seek a divorce. Another such wife admitted her reticence:

> Je n'en voulais pas. Je sais bien ce qui m'attend lorsque le salaire marital ne tombera plus dans le ménage. Mais mon mari ne veut plus de moi et comme il ne peut réclamer le divorce, il me bat pour que je le demande. J'ai des enfants, Monsieur, et je ne veux pas qu'on me tue.

Similarly, he notes 'des adultères provoqués ou simulés': prostitutes paid by wives to lure their husbands into the violation of conjugal duty; and the simulation of 'comédies' of adultery so as to procure for spouses the means to divorce. Such farces were not reserved for the *fin de siècle* stage. In other words, divorce did not simply resolve otherwise insufferable problems. In fact, rather than reflecting social facts, it might simply feed personal whim. One easy route to divorce was for the wife, in league with her husband, simply to desert the marital home and to ignore the summons for her to return — thereby giving her husband just cause. Even though the law of 1792 had permitted divorce by mutual consent, Morizot-Thibault argues that it had been hedged in with checks and balances. In the early years of the twentieth century, however, it was forbidden in law, but exercised *de facto*: 'il n'y a d'autre règle que l'arbitraire des époux.'

Although we might note the relative paucity of the divorce rate, contemporaries such as Morizot-Thibault were appalled by the 'conveyor belt' effect of divorce. The hotbed was courtroom (or chambre civile) no. 4 at the tribunal de la Seine, renowned for 'la spécialité de dissoudre les mariages'. He refers to one of its magistrates as 'le grand divorceur', not because of a particular liking for the legislation, but because of his immense industry and efficiency. On Thursday 15 December 1898 he pronounced at one sitting 294 divorces! This only increased the sense of diluted interpersonal ties which perturbed conservatives. Two days later in *Le Figaro* Cornély criticized 'Le Divorce chez le peuple'. With more than one divorce per minute, courtroom 4 was castigated as the polite face of social collapse:

> Tout cela se fait le plus proprement du monde, au moyen de trois messieurs en robe qui marmottent, d'un grincheux monsieur qui est censé requérir et d'un cinquième monsieur qui prend des notes. Ce vestibule de l'enfer social, peuplé d'hommes graves, qui défont la société au moyen de la loi, et sous l'image de Christ, a tout à fait bon air.

The reckoning will be the price of confluent love: 'Seulement cela se paiera, vous pouvez en être sûrs. Tout se paye. Par la faute du législateur, avec la complicité, avec presque l'excitation de la justice, l'union libre remplace peu à peu le mariage. Elle détruit la famille.' In a pattern we cannot help but recognize, the metonymical force of the family allows Cornély's argument its full scope: 'Elle livre sans défense l'homme à l'alcoolisme, la femme à la prostitution et l'enfant aux vices précoces. Des faits semblables projettent des lueurs inquiétantes sur tout un état social.'

The period from 1870 to 1914 was studded with moments of centennial reflection on the Revolution and Napoleon; in particular, 1904 saw the centenary of the Napoleonic Code, which had diluted the divorce provision of 1792. A team of law professors produced a series of essays, *Le Code civil, 1804–1904: Livre du centenaire* to coincide with celebrations in Paris on 27–30 October 1904.[117] In its preface, the 'Comité de rédaction' proclaimed its desire to 'marquer par une manifestation de caractère scientifique l'année du Centenaire du Code civil' and 'recueillir dans un volume jubilaire des études de nature très diverse sur le Code lui-même, son influence dans le passé et ses transformations possibles dans l'avenir'. Albert Sorel's introduction stresses the practicality of the Code: 'Le Code civil est dépourvu de toute transcendance; il ne vise point au sublime; il est fait pour le commun des Français, et le commun de leur vie sociale' (xvi), and this practicality is linked to Napoleon's literary tastes:

> Il n'affecte nullement pour la littérature le dédain des professionnels de la justice abstraite ou de la jurisprudence déductive. Il sait que, de tout temps, la littérature a vécu des profonds litiges et des passions des hommes, que les maximes des moralistes ne sont que de l'observation concrétée, distillée, sublimée. Si un gouvernement de notre temps, mettant à l'étude les lois sur le divorce, y eût appelé, par exemple, selon les époques, un Balzac, un Dumas fils, un Sainte-Beuve, le ton de la discussion n'eût guère différé des propos du Premier Consul. (xxvii–xxviii)

Sorel cites Napoleon's rejoinder in debate with Thibaudeau:

> La vertu des femmes est mise en question depuis le commencement du monde. L'histoire ancienne et moderne, toute notre littérature, notre littérature dramatique ne reposait sur autre chose que sur l'adultère. *Andromaque, Œdipe, Phèdre, Mithridate, Oreste*, qui sont de véritables chefs-d'œuvre, ont pour action principale un adultère et souvent quelque chose de pire, quelque chose de monstrueux, l'inceste! Lisez Beaumarchais, son *Figaro*, l'histoire de France, celle du moyen âge; partout il n'est que question que de femmes aimées à l'encontre des lois. Après cela, comment vouloir que l'adultère n'entre pas comme élément littéraire dans notre littérature, puisque cet élément abonde dans l'histoire et dans la société?... (xxviii)

Indeed, it is conspicuous that in the introduction to such a general volume on nineteenth-century French law Sorel should bother to spend a couple of pages discussing the relationship between divorce and literature (xxxvi–xxxviii). 1830 is pinpointed as the moment when 'la condition, très subordonnée, des femmes dans le Code' starts to generate the literary theme of 'l'émancipation de la femme' in a literature which Margaret Cohen dubs the Great Unread: 'George Sand personnifie, de loin, cette littérature qui ne se lit plus guère.' It is a cliché to observe that the Napoleonic Code has been the basis of modern French law, and in this context Sorel notes that 'on a pu argumenter d'autant plus à l'aise pour et contre le divorce qu'il ne fait point, à proprement parler, partie intégrante du Code civil.' The memory of 1816–84 means that conservatives could easily imagine the hallowed Code without divorce.

The shape of French divorce history emerged from the revolving door of social behaviour and experience rather than open-and-shut legal hypothesis: 'il [le divorce] y [dans le Code] est entré, il en est sorti, il y est rentré beaucoup plus par l'effet des mœurs sociales que par l'œuvre des légistes, sous l'influence de passions, d'émotions, de théories qui souvent se trouvaient en contradiction avec les principes généraux des lois sur la famille et sur le mariage.' On Sorel's historical model, the effect of 1884 — based on the whim of mores rather than solid legal reason — has been to risk a return to the Directory's travesty of marriage:

> Les conséquences, en moins d'un quart de siècle, semblent désastreuses et c'est simplement se montrer prévoyant que de redouter, de ce relâchement de la jurisprudence, un retour au temps du Directoire, 'au scandale de ces divorces continuels dont parle le *Discours préliminaire*, qui ont failli travestir mariage en une sorte de concubinage avoué'.

Sorel notes that the literary product of the Third Republic divorce debate has been considerable: 'Il est sorti de là toute une littérature, qui compte plusieurs chefs-d'œuvre [...]. Le *divorce* est le plus passionnant entre les thèmes de la législation au théâtre et dans le roman.' Prior to 1884: 'douloureuse et tragique, d'abord, dans la réclamation, le cri de révolte, le cri du cœur, l'appel au bonheur et l'appel à l'amour des internés du mauvais mariage, c'est la période illustrée par Dumas fils et Émile Augier'. After 1884: 'très vite, la réaction s'est faite au spectacle des troubles infinis, des misères et déceptions sans nombre des libérés sans foyer, des naufragés, des désemparés en eux-mêmes, en leur famille, en leurs enfants, des victimes enfin, volontaires ou inconscientes du divorce.'

The main body of this commemorative volume falls into four parts: 'Généralités'; 'Études spéciales'; 'Le Code civil à l'étranger'; and 'La Question de la Revision'. Part II includes an analysis of 'La Famille et le Code civil' by Paul Lerebours-Pigeonnière, professeur agrégé at the Faculté de Droit in the Université de Rennes (263–94). It begins by presenting the family as a sociological unit resistant to legislative moulding: 'La famille est, peut-être, de toutes les institutions, celle dont la constitution, l'organisation et le développement ont le moins subi à toute époque l'influence des réglementations légales; elle est plus qu'aucune autre le produit des mœurs.' Nevertheless, 'la famille que les mœurs ont organisée doit obtenir de la loi une consécration nécessaire.' In the Revolution's initial desire to reform the traditional Catholic family, 'on n'avait songé qu'à donner satisfaction à certains mouvements qui s'étaient manifestés jusque dans les mœurs. C'est en se fondant sur l'état des mœurs que l'on réclama d'assez bonne heure la sécularisation du mariage et l'établissement du divorce.' Soon, however, philosophical idealism intensified this empirically grounded project of the 'réformateurs de la Révolution': 'les bases de la société ancienne leur parurent inconciliables avec deux aspirations dont ils voulaient assurer l'épanouissement, l'aspiration à une complète liberté individuelle, l'aspiration à l'égalité.' Lerebours-Pigeonnière cites Oliver Martin's 1901 thesis on *La Crise du mariage* to explain the philosophical basis of the radicalism of the 1792 law (which nineteenth-century divorce law would never reproduce):

> ce qui toucha le plus, semble-t-il, les législateurs, c'est que la possibilité du divorce leur parut une conséquence nécessaire de la liberté individuelle. La preuve, c'est qu'ils admirent le divorce par la volonté d'un seul, pour incompatibilité d'humeur, malgré les raisons morales ou sociales invoquées contre cette extension, parce qu'aucun des époux ne pouvait être maintenu dans les chaînes du mariage malgré lui.

Then followed the Convention's decree of 4–9 floréal, Year II, which gave marriage 'la physionomie d'une véritable union libre, en abrégeant les délais d'épreuve, en débarrassant la procédure des obstacles ou des pratiques gênantes'.

Lerebours-Pigeonnière argues that the Civil Code maintained three innovations in the domain of the family, whilst recognizing the need to compromise with the pragmatic ground on which mores must meet idealism. First, 'le principe de la sécularisation du mariage ne fut pas remis en question.' This separation of civil law and religious marriage had been affirmed as a corollary of the freedom of individual conscience, not as an assertion of the independence of the State. Indeed, the very absence in the State of the Church's moral assertiveness meant that it must reflect mores rather than govern them. Hence the secularization of marriage opened the door, Lerebours-Pigeonnière claims, to 'les variations possibles de la loi civile.' *Autres temps, autres mœurs*, indeed. Second, the Code attempted to iron out differences in inheritance between the eldest child and its siblings.

Third, the maintenance of divorce under the Civil Code, though quashed in 1816, remains 'le signe d'une ère nouvelle, l'ère des variations possibles'. He argues that unlike the Revolution, however, the Code did not wish to deconstruct marriage, merely to nuance it. In Portalis's words, 'Si nous avions affaire à un peuple neuf, je n'établirais pas le divorce.' The very relativism which facilitated divorce meant that it need not be seen as an absolute form of liberty. Presenting the bill to the Legislative

Body, Treilhard noted: 'La question doit recevoir une solution différente, suivant le génie et les mœurs du peuple, l'esprit des siècles et l'influence des idées religieuses sur l'ordre politique.' To pragmatic legislators: 'le mariage leur est apparu, dans les mœurs traditionnelles, comme une union théoriquement indissoluble, mais qui, en fait, était souvent reniée, méconnue, par suite de mésintelligence des époux ou de leurs désordres.' Even article 233 on mutual consent revealed the ambivalence of the Code. Mutual consent 'prouvera insuffisamment que la vie commune est insupportable et qu'il existe [...] une cause péremptoire du divorce'. As such, Lerebours-Pigeonnière explains, this article did not simply sanction the caprice of spouses; rather it still based divorce on 'une cause indépendante et déterminée', even if this could be presumed rather than proven.

Part II of Lerebours-Pigeonnière's chapter questions the influence of the Code on the mores of the masses:

> Les partisans du divorce et ceux de l'union libre ont, après coup, tiré argument de la sécularisation du mariage, argument sans valeur du reste, mais c'est là, dans tous les cas, un argument théorique, qui n'a eu aucune influence sur les faits. D'abord [...] la masse n'a jamais cessé de considérer le mariage comme un acte religieux [...]. Puis, l'idée que le mariage contrat civil serait par nature soumis aux fluctuations de la volonté est une idée de dilettante et sophiste, et la masse, tout au contraire, n'ignore pas que contrat est synonyme de contrainte et de responsabilité.

For Lerebours-Pigeonnière, divorce had not originally been a mainstream matter: 'Le divorce avait surtout servi, à l'époque de la Révolution, l'intérêt ou le caprice de cette partie de la population qui escomptait l'abolition de toute règle; il n'avait pénétré la meilleure partie de la nation.' The influence of the 1884 law in all milieus did not reflect the influence of the Code but the cult of individual freedom, 'cette impatience d'émancipation': 'c'est l'égoïsme individuel qui, en devenant l'un des facteurs prédominants des mœurs, a provoqué l'usage du divorce et plus spécialement dans les milieux ouvriers la pratique de l'union libre.' Indeed, it is this cult of the ego, he argues, rather than divorce itself which has fuelled the 'instabilité relative' of the modern family. In conclusion, he warns against haste in family legislation: 'Les rapports de famille, parce qu'ils touchent à l'intimité même de l'homme et représentent la partie la plus vraiment humaine des institutions juridiques, évoluent *autour* d'un petit nombre d'idées et se transforment lentement.'

Naquet spent the long years of his old age in his quiet house in Auteuil. He would of course suffer from the Dreyfus Affair and then bore witness to Théodore Hertz's subsequent Zionist campaign. He died in Paris on 12 November 1916, aged 82, with Europe in ruins. The 'Chronique de sa vie' appeared in *Le Temps*, as did brief notices in other papers. As with so many others, however, news of Naquet's death was effectively lost from view amongst the millions. And even in death, Naquet seemed bound to connect literature and the law. Pillias's epilogue to Naquet's autobiography reminds us that '*Le Temps* crut devoir publier une chronique ironique sur les ressources apportées à l'art dramatique par la loi du divorce', as if nothing and nobody on the Left could remain sacred, and safe from irony.[118] Naquet's ashes were transferred to the *colombarium* at Père-Lachaise.

Whereas Francis Ronsin reads literature in order to explain social and legal history, this book works in the other direction — whilst constantly trying to recall the pitfalls of such mapping. It is not simply modern-day critics of nineteenth-century mimetic fiction who question its referential force. As we turn to the novels of Léo, Vautier, Bovet, France, Alphonse Daudet, Rod and Pert, we might recall the caution of an account written for an anglophone audience by Albert Léon Guérard during the First World War, where this book will end:

> One of the essential facts in French life is the so-called 'marriage of convenience'. Many irregularities which take place in real life are acts of rebellion, at times almost excusable, against a heartless and sordid system which disposes of human beings with scant regard for their sentiments. Those intrigues, so far as we can judge, are the exception, and no more prevalent than in other leading countries. French novels seem to give a different impression. The fondness of irreproachable husbands and wives for a literature which to us appears unduly spicy represents the craving for adventure, for romance, which they were denied in their own youth, and which they satisfy, innocently enough, in this vicarious way. Be it said without paradox, the heroes of fiction are scapegoats which take away the sins of Israel. Literature is a distorting mirror; it gives caricatural prominence to one aspect of French life — the love affairs of the Parisian smart set. [...] The student of French civilization should beware of conclusions hastily based on such one-sided documents.[119]

Notes to Chapter 1

1. Francis Ronsin, 'Du divorce et de la séparation de corps en France au XIX siècle' (unpublished doctoral thesis, Université Paris 7, 1988), pp. 23, 102. Henceforth, Ronsin, 'Du divorce'.
2. Alfred Naquet, *Le Divorce*, revised, 'très augmentée' (Paris: Dentu, 1881), p. 188.
3. Ginette André, 'Alfred Naquet, adversaire de l'Empire et défenseur de la République radicale, 1867–1884', 5 vols (unpublished doctoral thesis, Université d'Aix-Marseille, 1972), IV, 211.
4. *Le Moniteur Universel*, 1.284 (1792), p. 1202.
5. See Phillips, *Family Breakdown in Late Eighteenth-Century France*.
6. Cited in Ronsin, 'Du divorce', p. 153.
7. Barié and Bourgueil, *Le Mur mitoyen* at the théâtre du Vaudeville (from 3 ventôse Year IV/22 February 1796). Cited in Ronsin, 'Du divorce', p. 189.
8. Seure, *Le Divorce, précédé d'une lettre de Victor Hugo*, pp. 9–10.
9. François Marchant, *La Constitution en vaudeville, suivie des droits de l'homme, de la femme, et de plusieurs vaudevilles constitutionnels* (Paris: Chez les libraires royalistes, 1792).
10. Cited in in Ronsin, 'Du divorce', pp. 188–89.
11. François Marchant, *La République en vaudeville* (Paris: Chez les marchands de nouveautés, 1793).
12. Cited in Ronsin, 'Du divorce', p. 137.
13. Ronsin, 'Du divorce', p. 152. Legal theses also highlighted the Roman exemplum. This association of divorce with Rome fitted only too well into the conservative discourse of those who feared decadence.
14. Naquet, *Le Divorce*, p. 194.
15. Cited in F. W. J. Hemmings, *Theatre and State in France, 1760–1905* (Cambridge: Cambridge University Press, 1994), p. 99.
16. André, IV, 212.
17. Ronsin, 'Du divorce', p. 3.
18. André, IV, 213.
19. Naquet, *Le Divorce*, p. 13.

20. Ronsin, 'Du divorce', p. 10.
21. Edward Berenson, *The Trial of Madame Caillaux* (Berkeley: University of California Press, 1992), p. 159.
22. Ronsin, 'Du divorce', p. 3.
23. Cited in Ronsin, 'Du divorce', p. 370.
24. Cited in Jann Matlock, *Scenes of Seduction* (New York: Columbia University Press, 1994), pp. 58–59. For an important intervention on the representability of divorce, see also Matlock, 'The Limits of Reformism: The Novel, Censorship, and the Politics of Adultery in Nineteenth-Century France', in *Cultural Institutions of the Novel*, ed. by Deirdre Lynch and William B. Warner (Durham, NC: Duke University Press, 1996), pp. 335–68.
25. Matlock, *Scenes of Seduction*, pp. 103 (my emphasis), 156–57.
26. Cited in Naquet, *Le Divorce*, p. 12.
27. Reprinted in Ronsin, 'Du divorce', pp. 456–60.
28. Matlock, *Scenes of Seduction*, pp. 365–66, n. 48.
29. In *The Fall of Paris* (London: Macmillan, 1965), Alistair Horne gleans from Parisian police records that in one month in 1866 2,344 wives left their husbands, and 4,427 husbands left their wives (p. 18).
30. Louis-Désiré Véron, *Mémoires d'un bourgeois de Paris*, 6 vols (Paris: Gabriel de Gonet, 1853–55), V, 211–12.
31. Paul Baquiast, *Une dynastie de la bourgeoisie républicaine: Les Pelletan* (Paris: L'Harmattan, 1996), pp. 125, 134.
32. Eugène Pelletan, *La Mère* (Paris & Brussels: Pagnerre, Lacroix & Verboeckhoven, 1866), p. 66.
33. Though we may read it with the proverbial pinch of salt, much is to be gleaned from his third-person *Autobiographie* (Paris: Sirye, 1939). Émile Pillias explains how he acquired it in 1934, in the sale of the papers left by Georges Moreau, former associate of the Librairie Larousse. Moreau's own explanation is then cited: 'M. Alfred Naquet, à qui j'avais demandé de rectifier et de compléter l'article qui lui fut consacré au Larousse répondit copieusement à mon appel en me retournant l'autobiographie que voici: c'est un document humain des plus curieux' (p. 1). Though it stops in 1887, its coverage of the divorce debate is considerable, even if — as Pillias claims — Naquet's hubris is conspicuous. Also published by Émile Pillias in *Revue d'histoire politique et constitutionnelle*, 3 (1939), 63–91.
34. André, I, 6, 43, 34–35.
35. Daniel Mollenhauer, *Auf der Suche nach der 'wahren Republik': Die französischen 'radicaux' in der frühen Dritten Republik (1870–1890)* (Bonn: Bouvier, 1997), p. 70.
36. Naquet, *Autobiographie*, p. 17.
37. André, I, 22.
38. Alfred Naquet, *Temps futurs, Socialisme, Anarchie* (Paris: Stock, 1900), pp. ii–iv.
39. Naquet, *Autobiographie*, p. 4.
40. Naquet's scientific past informs the caricature in *La Nouvelle Lune* of 21 May 1882 where Naquet, dressed as a doctor, dispenses to the new sitting of the Chamber of Deputies his Elixir of Divorce.
41. André, I, 92.
42. Alfred Naquet, *Cours de philosophie chimique* (Paris: Savy, 1866), p. 15.
43. Naquet, *Autobiographie*, p. 17.
44. Naquet is categorized as a 'militant blanquiste, puis sénateur' by the *Dictionnaire biographique du mouvement ouvrier français*, vol. XIV (Paris: Les Éditions ouvrières, 1976), p. 168. In its abridged bibliography, none of Naquet's divorce writing is listed, whereas his later socialist theory is. Perhaps the issue of divorce was still a little too bourgeois — as it had been, nearly a century earlier, for Zola, who was largely uninterested in the topic.
45. *Le Journal des Débats*, 14 September 1867, p. 1, col. 4.
46. Lockroy married Alice, the widow of Charles Hugo and mother of George and Jeanne, the poet's grandchildren. As such he would figure over a quarter of a century later in the Hugo–Daudet divorce anticipated in Daudet's *Rose et Ninette*. See below, Chapter 4. Naquet would sometimes take his vacations with Lockroy in Montreux, rather than Nice where his parents had moved. Indeed, he befriended Hugo too, as his father notes in a letter from Nice dated

11 September 1883: 'Alfred est chez Victor Hugo.' Laurent Tailhade recalls Naquet's flattering answer to Hugo's question about the eternal soul: 'De la nôtre, Maître, cela est malaisé à croire mais quand la nature enfante un esprit comme le vôtre, il est certain qu'elle doit tout mettre en œuvre pour le conserver à jamais.' *Quelques fantômes de jadis* (Paris: Messein, 1913).

47. Cited in André, I, 156.
48. Cited in André, I, 161, who calculates its date as late May 1868.
49. Ronsin, 'Du divorce', p. 522.
50. Alfred Naquet, *Religion, propriété, famille* (Paris: Chez tous les libraires, 1869), pp. 290–99.
51. Naquet, *Autobiographie*, p. 5.
52. Jules Vallès, *L'Insurgé* (Paris: Charpentier, 1908), pp. 173–74.
53. Naquet, *Autobiographie*, p. 7.
54. Two days later *La Démocratie du Midi* would turn on him: 'Naquet est un singe.'
55. Alfred Naquet, *La République radicale* (Paris: Germer Baillière), pp. 58–59.
56. Naquet to Sheurer-Kestner, 2 October 1875 (BN Nafr. 24409, Nr. 122).
57. Naquet, *La République radicale*, p. 9.
58. Alfred Naquet, 'Lettre à mes commettants: Discours prononcé le dimanche, 22 août 1875 à Arles', in *L'Evénement*, 26 August 1875.
59. *L'Evénement*, 30 August 1875. Such an outlet for Naquet was provided by this newspaper due to a taste for melodrama and sensation rather than genuine radical sentiment.
60. Naquet, *Autobiographie*, p. 8. It is worth comparing this account of rural conservatism with the contrary argument in *Le Divorce* (1881) that the divorce debate would not cleave the Republic into the urban avant-garde and rural reaction.
61. *Le Comtat*, 5 March 1876.
62. Naquet, *Autobiographie*, pp. 10–11.
63. Ronsin, 'Du divorce', p. 528.
64. Ronsin, 'Du divorce', p. 538.
65. Naquet, *Autobiographie*, pp. 14–15.
66. From *L'Égalité*, cited in André, IV, 222–23.
67. André pinpoints the high age of the divorce question: 'A partir de 1879 — vote de prise en considération par la Chambre — et jusqu'à 1884 — vote définitif du Sénat — la question du divorce passionne l'opinion publique. On est pour, on est contre, on n'est que rarement indifférent' (IV, 226).
68. Naquet, *Autobiographie*, p. 20.
69. Ibid., p. 16.
70. Ibid., p. 20.
71. Quoted in Ronsin, 'Du divorce', pp. 601–02.
72. Charles Loyson, *Lettre sur le mariage* (Paris: Sandoz & Fichbacher, 1872) followed by *Ni cléricaux ni athées, discours et lettres sur la Troisième République* (Paris: Marpon & Flammarion, 1890).
73. Ronsin, 'Du divorce', pp. 549–50.
74. Adolphe Bitard, *Dictionnaire général de biographie contemporaine* (Paris: A. Lévy, 1878), pp. 549–50.
75. Ronsin, 'Du divorce', p. 553.
76. Ronsin, 'Du divorce', p. 5.
77. Paul Féval was well known for his popular swashbuckling novel, *Le Bossu* (1857), resurrected by Daniel Auteuil in the film of 1997. *Pas de divorce!* went into nine editions in 1880. Associated with the Catholic militancy of the early Third Republic, he was a 'fervent producteur de brochures pieuses de circonstance', *Dictionnaires des littératures de langue française*, ed. by J.-P. Beaumarchais (Paris: Bordas, 1994), II, 870.
78. Alexandre Dumas fils, *La Question du divorce* (Paris: Calmann Lévy, 1880), pp. 20–21.
79. Jules Clarétie, *Les Célébrités contemporaine: Alexandre Dumas fils* (Paris: Quantin, 1883), pp. 21–22.
80. Ronsin, 'Du divorce', pp. 527–32. See the wealth of data and analysis in Jean Elisabeth Pedersen's excellent study *Legislating the French Family: Feminism, Theater and Republican Politics, 1870–1920* (New Brunswick, NJ: Rutgers University Press, 2003).
81. At exactly the same location on 27 August 1879, in another sketch by Cham, one woman complains to another: 'Qu'est-ce que je trouve là-haut? Mon mari qui venait aussi demander l'adresse de M. Naquet.'

82. This clash between private interest and public role would reappear in literary representations of other stock types such as the divorce lawyer.
83. Many contemporary caricatures stress Naquet's hunchback. Some would invert his physical impoverishment in a skit on his heroic struggle. *La Jeune Garde* of 6 April 1879 shows him as a fairground Hercules, rolling up his sleeves, about to lift an enormous weight called 'le divorce'.
84. Naquet, *Autobiographie*, p. 19.
85. Ibid., p. 20.
86. Cited in André, IV, 222.
87. Naquet, *Le Divorce* (1881), to which interpolated references will be made in the remainder of this chapter.
88. Naquet's self-distancing from free union needs to be understood in the context of attacks such as the caricature in *La Jeune Garde*, 21 December 1879, which show him and Émile de Girardin astride the same wooden (hobby...) horse, bearing the words 'Divorce — Union Libre'.
89. The scorpion is associated with various legends, not least the scorpion's suicide evoked in Vigny's *Chatterton* as his 'dernière nuit de travail'. The scorpion-marriage, Kauffmann implies, destroys itself.
90. Georges de Cavilly, *La Séparation de corps et le divorce à l'usage des gens du monde, et la manière de s'en servir: manuel des époux mal assortis* (Paris: Jouvet, 1882), pp. i–11.
91. Cavilly, pp. 189–96.
92. *Autobiographie*, p. 23.
93. Évariste Carrance, *Le Divorce*, monologue en vers (Agen: Librairie du Comité Poétique et de la Revue française, 1884).
94. *Autobiographie*, p. 24.
95. Naquet's autobiography deals with Freppel by simply noting that the report was accepted 'presque sans discussion' (p. 23).
96. Naquet's autobiography echoed Richer's refrain: 'Grâce à la courageuse initiative de Naquet et à son inépuisable ardeur, la honte du 8 mai 1816 était effacée, et l'œuvre de la Révolution était rétablie' (p. 23). The centenary of the Revolution was now only 5 years away. For an account of how divorce played in the commemorative discourse of 1889, see the interpretation of Claire Vautier's *Adultère et divorce* in the next chapter.
97. The terms of the new law were reported two days later in the *Journal Officiel de la République française*, 16. 206 (1884), 4041. In *La Grande Encyclopédie*, Glasson dates the law from 29 July 1884.
98. Dalloz, 'Séparation de corps' in his *Répertoire de législation* (Paris: Bureau de la Jurisprudence Générale, 1858).
99. Dalloz, 'Divorce' in his *Jurisprudence générale* (Paris, 1890).
100. Alfred Naquet, 'Divorce: From a French Point of View', *The North American Review*, 155 (November 1892), 721–30 (pp. 722–23). An excellent account of such cases is to be found in Chapter 3 of Andrea Mansker, *Sex, Honor and Citizenship in Early Third Republic France* (Basingstoke: Palgrave Macmillan, 2011).
101. Ronsin, 'Du divorce', p. 603.
102. Tailhade, p. 155.
103. *La Grande Encyclopédie* (Paris: Lamirault, 1885–1902), XIV, 754–62.
104. Peter Brooks, *Reading for the Plot* (Cambridge, MA: Harvard University Press, 1992), pp. 11–12
105. Phillips, *Divorce in New Zealand*, p. 14.
106. Ronsin notes the ideological ambivalence of Bertillon's position: 'la liberté, la très large liberté du divorce est une bonne chose, le divorce en lui-même, comme le suicide, en sont de mauvaises' (Ronsin, 'Du divorce', p. 713).
107. Émile Durkheim, *Le Suicide: Étude de sociologie* (Paris: Alcan, 1897), pp. 293, 305–07.
108. Jules Lermina, *Dictionnaire universel illustré de la France contemporaine* (Paris: Boulanger, 1884), p. 1060.
109. Naquet, *Autobiographie*, p. 27.
110. Naquet, *Temps futurs, socialisme, anarchie*, p. 8.
111. Pierre Birnbaum, *Les Fous de la République* (Paris: Fayard, 1993), pp. 316–33.

112. Alfred Naquet, 'Divorce: From a French Point of View', pp. 721.
113. André, IV, 299.
114. Ronsin, 'Du divorce', p. 832.
115. Naquet, *La Loi du divorce*, p. 248.
116. Reprinted in Ronsin, *Les Divorciaires*, pp. 312–15.
117. *Le Code civil, 1804–1904: Livre du centenaire*, publ. for La Société d'études législatives (Paris: Arthur Rousseau, 1904). Interpolated references are made to this edition.
118. Naquet, *Autobiographie*, p. 30.
119. Albert Léon Guérard, *Five Masters of French Romance: Anatole France, Pierre Loti, Paul Bourget, Maurice Barrès, Romain Rolland* (London: T. Fisher Unwin, 1916), pp. 17–19.

CHAPTER 2

Between Mimesis and Idealism

We turn now from the historical and philosophical contexts which frame our analysis of French divorce fiction to these novels themselves. Beyond general identifications of literature with the exploration of love and its discontents, the rise of the novel from the eighteenth century is often linked to the rise of the middle classes, not least in Western Europe, and their association of family life not just with convenient economic union but also affective fulfilment. The genre of the novel allowed for densely contextualized accounts of, first, the quest for marital love and, second, the fragility of such union. It is not just Jane Austen who is capable of the first kind of plot; even Zola provides such a happy ending in *Au Bonheur des dames*. It is the second type of plot, however, which looms large in classic European fiction, and comes to emblematize a dystopian worldview in post-1848 fiction.

In this regard, the dominant continental tradition, first excavated by Tony Tanner and subsequently glossed by a range of critics is, of course, the novel of adultery, particularly wifely adultery. Indeed, it is the novel of adultery which offers the most corrosive critique of bourgeois marriage. The novels of divorce which we will introduce in the remainder of this book are, then, closely related to but significantly different from this tradition. The novel of adultery lays out the context in which nineteenth-century debates about marriage raged: in liberal terms, dramatizing the flaws of bourgeois marriage in a manner pursued by the *divorciaire* camp and, in particular, French feminists; in conservative terms, voicing male paranoia about female sexuality and the need to police pernicious influence. Much turned, of course, on whether adultery was depicted as a cause or an effect of marital breakdown. Between 1816 and 1884, adultery could not lead to divorce in France, and to depict divorce, and its *pour et contre*, novelists would have to look elsewhere, as in André Léo's *Un divorce* (1866), to which we will turn first. After 1884, divorce added to the range of family plots available both to mainstream writers such as Maupassant and to virtually forgotten authors such as Claire Vautier, whose *Adultère et divorce* (1889) will provide the focus for the conclusion of this chapter. One of the most perverse responses to the new law of 1884 was Zola's claim that it would rob authors of their traditional plots, as adulterous deception and crimes of passion would supposedly no longer be necessary once people had access to the divorce courts. Imagine writing *Thérèse Raquin* if there were really no need for the crime! The reality was that divorce created a new range of plot permutations, not least because it offered another ending to the traditional ones of marriage and death. The first striking example of this is Maupassant's *Bel-Ami* of 1885. It responds immediately to the new law by narrating in two parts the Bildungsroman of a modern-day Don Giovanni who marries an influential widow, only to arrange for himself to be caught *in flagrante delicto* with another woman, in order to take advantage of the new divorce law and exchange her, by the end, for a younger wife.[1]

The dystopian potential in depictions of marital breakdown is clear; but for a number of women writers divorce was not simply a symptom of, but also a potential solution to such crises. Of particular interest is the way in which such novels borrow and reshape the tropes of adultery in fiction. Canonical male writers of the first half of the century probed the issue of divorce, torn between its assertion of individual will and its interrogation of the traditional family (in particular Constant, who made personal use of the early divorce law, and Balzac in *La Maison du chat-qui-pelote* and *La Paix du ménage*). All of this is set against the backdrop of Napoleon's own strategic use of the divorce law to replace Josephine with a dynastic marriage to Marie-Louise of Austria. Women-authored fiction invoked divorce as a polemical or utopian motif. Mme de Staël and George Sand examine divorce as a response to the legal and hence fictional limitations on women's behaviour. The 'failure' of such romance fiction to fulfil the descriptive demands of realism might often be re-read as articulating sotto voce the prescriptions of radical thought, be it feminist or socialist.[2]

But the late eighteenth-century model for fictionalizing the potential virtues of divorce was Louvet de Couvray's, *Émilie de Varmont; ou, le divorce nécessaire, et les amours du curé Sévin* (1791), a complex plot set in the *ancien régime* of 1782 (hence the reference to Laclos in the play on Varmont/Valmont), which anticipates the new law of 1792, not least in its address to the reader on the final page:

> Quand l'assemblée nationale aura décrété le MARIAGE DES PRÊTRES et le DIVORCE il me sera permis de vous donner dans une très courte brochure, que vous appellerez un supplément, si bon vous semble, les détails peut-être intéressans d'un triple mariage: celui de Bovile et d'Éléonore, celui de Dolerval et d'Émilie, celui de M. Sévin et... Je vous le dirai; je vous dirai quelle femme, assez charmante pour ressembler beaucoup à sa Juliette, a pu rendre au bon curé la raison et le bonheur.[3]

Without recounting all the plot's manifold details, an exposition of its shape explains this concatenation of unfulfilled loves which could only be resolved by the legalization of divorce and of marriage for priests. Émilie's sister has had to enter a convent against her will, and their widowed mother wishes the same fate on Émilie, so that she can channel funds towards her favoured but ne'er-do-well son. Although in love with another, a friend of Émilie's deceased father, Bovile, agrees to marry her so as to save her from this fate, signing a fictitious note saying that he has received a considerable dowry. Surviving an attack from her avaricious brother, Émilie takes refuge with a poor priest, who falls in love with her, as does his friend, Dolerval. Émilie and Bovile each believe the other to be dead. Thus Bovile decides to marry his true beloved, Madame Éléonore d'Étioles, now a widow (and thus available for remarriage, unlike the bigamists and the priest). How, the novel asks, might Émilie,

Bovile and Sévin be similarly liberated? Malcolm Cook is right to highlight the particular twinning of subject matter in the novel: 'Le roman nous surprend par son titre car il semble relier deux sujets différents. Peut-on dire que Louvet a su choisir les deux sujets politico-religieux qui étaient susceptibles d'intéresser le plus les lecteurs de l'époque?'[4] What Louvet's treatment of both subjects, divorce and the marriage of priests, did share was the desire to allow marriage between those whose love was otherwise proscribed.

Divorce, then, was the plot that remained to be written, *scriptible* but not yet possible; and it is this possibility which we will address in this book. Louvet has been remembered since for his libertine fiction, *Les Amours du chevalier de Faublas* (1787–90), whose nevertheless sombre ending is echoed in the switch to sentimentality which we find in *Émilie de Varmont*, the other novel with which his contemporaries were well acquainted. The novel advertises both the personal and social urgency of the subject and the aesthetic dangers of *engagé* thesis fiction, in a way that looks forward to the stakes in the later novels we shall analyse at length. Louvet joined the Girondins and attacked Robespierre, and as such was that rare commodity at the end of the century, a novelist at the political heart of the Revolution. John Rivers, a contemporary of many of the authors we will soon turn to, describes the book as 'a failure' in spite of the 'abundant evidence of careful workmanship'.[5] But its ideological position in proposing divorce reform enjoys more nuance than we might at first imagine. Rivers identifies

> a plea for more liberal views and a greater facility of divorce. The fact that Madame Cholet had for years past vainly sought a legal separation from her husband in order to marry Louvet had probably not a little to do with his choice of a subject.

Kathryn Norberg fleshes out this position:

> Divorce is so important to Louvet because it renders an ancient, traditional institution — marriage — modern and republican. Like all Jacobins, Louvet argues that man is not bound by his past, that he cannot alienate his own freedom by a promise or a vow.[6]

But as she concludes:

> 'Republican' marriage [...] revealed the contradictions at the heart of republican liberal ideology. [...] There was no doubt in anyone's mind, including Louvet's, that marriage meant the subordination of women and the containment of their dangerous sexuality. Divorce, he believed, would compel women to abide by their marriage vows, that is, their promise to obey.

As Norbert implies, the push for divorce brought into play forms of gender ideology that it would be very tempting to read anachronistically, at the end of the eighteenth century but also at the end of the nineteenth.

As we have seen, the plea for divorce was one of the many forms of idealism dashed by the failure of the 1848 Revolution. Divorce, Flaubert recalls from the depths of the Second Empire, had become one of the clichés of radicalism, hence Frédéric's pontificating at the Dambreuse party:

> Les dames formaient un demi-cercle en l'écoutant, et, afin de briller, il se

prononça pour le rétablissement du divorce, qui devait être facile jusqu'à pouvoir se quitter et se reprendre indéfiniment, tant qu'on voudrait. Elles se récrièrent; d'autres chuchotaient; il y avait de petits éclats de voix dans l'ombre [...]. C'était comme un caquetage de poules en gaieté; et il développait sa théorie, avec cet aplomb que la conscience du succès procure.[7]

The sexual politics of the Second Empire, presided over by Napoleon III, saw a reaffirmation of conservative family values. The policy of strict literary censorship meant that novelists could best attack the status quo through code, analogy and inference rather than outright polemic. The best example of women's exploration of the divorce question during these decades was *Un divorce* by André Léo, the pseudonym of Léodile Béra (1824–1900), also known as Mme de Champseix.[8]

Rather than focusing on the lack of divorce in France since the Restoration, Léo's novel explores the marriage (and eventual divorce) of Claire and Ferdinand Desfayes in Lausanne. Léo employs Switzerland to depict a form of Frenchness which is not French. Between 1816 and 1884 mimesis would forbid the depiction of French divorce as it was impossible. Indeed, in a rather strange version of the mimetic question which usually asks how fiction should assimilate events which are possible but implausible, Léo's representation of such a proximate Francophone society allows divorce to appear impossible (according to French law) and yet plausible — or certainly imaginable, given its existence in broadly analogous circumstances, notwithstanding the issue of Swiss Protestantism which the novel raises. Of course, there were many novels which had addressed the problems of modern marriage by depicting the impossibility of divorce, not least women novelists of the July Monarchy such as George Sand and the Great Unread examined by Margaret Cohen. Léo's novel is significant as the major divorce novel by a Frenchwoman to coincide with that key stage in the organization of French feminism in the 1860s. The mimetic possibilities in the local exoticism offered by Switzerland suggest, though, that the existence of a divorce law, however desirable, provides insufficient solace to the cause of women in the face of unbowed patriarchy, and in this Léo seems to suggest that divorce must be tethered to other forms of social liberation (not least equality across classes and the redefinition of masculinity itself).

The honeymoon period of the marriage at the centre of the novel is brief, as Ferdinand is drawn back to male friendship and his ongoing affair with the dressmaker Herminie who is, ironically, employed to make Claire's wedding dress. In a manner consistent with the age, homosociality is seen to underpin hetero-normativity. The separation of male and female spheres appears to be particularly acute in the Protestant Swiss culture of the novel, their only common spaces being the dining table and the marriage bed, each assigned to their own sphere (him to the town, her to the home). This shapes their characters, the man rough, severe, and given to drunkenness, the woman dried-up and melancholic. The mismatch of the spouses' values is evident as early as their boat trip back to Lausanne from their honeymoon in Oberland. Claire simply wants to live in a white house she spies up on the terraces of the Alps, whereas he also wants to keep a flat in Lausanne, arguing that people cannot live exclusively in coupledom throughout their lives, as they have their own affairs and other relationships to develop. In social terms at least, men's access to the public sphere renders their lives 'promiscuous', whereas women such as Claire cling on to the ideal of love as a refuge against the world. According to his stereotype, 'Les femmes sont toutes comme cela [...]. Elles ne comprennent au monde aucune affaire, aucun intérêt que l'amour.'[9] This scene provides an ideological complement to that most famous of boat journeys in French fiction, the opening scene of *L'Éducation sentimentale*. In Léo's version, published earlier in the decade, female isolation within marriage is viewed from the wife's perspective and not through the rose-tinted lens of the admiring young hero. As we have noted, historians have often commented on the rising association of marriage with romantic love in the eighteenth and nineteenth centuries, but Léo's point seems to be that love may define female identity but does not define the limits of male agency. Once Claire realizes that her marriage is less intimate than she had hoped, she starts to feel like a twin, walking hand in hand with a brother:

> Mais que ferait-elle alors de sa vie, mon Dieu! Est-ce qu'on peut trouver en dehors de l'amour du bonheur ou de l'intérêt à quelque chose? Elle a beau regarder en cherchant, elle ne voit pas. Les femmes sont nées pour aimer et n'ont point d'autre destinée: on le lui a dit. Elle n'a rien à faire au monde que d'être la femme de Ferdinand. (93)

The association of femininity and love fuels the nineteenth-century discourse on wifely adultery. If, by definition, women require love, what else are they to do in a loveless marriage?

Male homosociality is fostered by access to the public sphere, whereas Claire feels isolated when Ferdinand hooks up with his old friend, the worldly Monadier who boards at Clarens. Once abandoned by her homosocially engaged husband, Claire suddenly looks to the new passengers who board at Vevey like a woman of loose virtue rather than a respectable wife. Why else would she be alone, they wonder. And to cap it all, the newly married Herminie happens to saunter by with her husband in tow. Either repudiated or triumphant, women do not seem to be able to find an equilibrium within the marital couple, perhaps because traditional marriage will not explore the egalitarian possibilities of the radical heterosocial ethos championed by Claire's cousin, Mathilde.

Traditional marriage, it seems, suffers from a smug lack of reflexivity, which, as Giddens argues, will be challenged by the development of modernity. As the guests scrutinize the arrival at supper of the betrothed Claire and Ferdinand in Chapter 2, the narrator quips: 'S'il y a peu de choses moins réfléchies que le mariage au sein des familles, il n'y en a guère de plus discutées aux entours' (39). It is precisely this problem of linguistic reflexivity, of how to fill a marriage with unplatitudinous language, which Flaubert airs in *Madame Bovary*. Though the transparent sphere of the marital 'goldfish bowl' allows Claire to look out (like Emma Bovary through the window), she does not have access to the homosocial discourse of the public realm as she seems to inhabit a different medium. She cannot imagine what Ferdinand and Monadier have to talk about. Very quickly she will renounce her own friends whereas Ferdinand follows Monadier back to café life: 'Elle se demanda une centième fois quel plaisir les hommes pouvaient trouver ensemble, à causer de choses si ennuyeuses et à boire en fumant, accoudés. Quel attrait pouvait attacher

Ferdinand à cet homme vulgaire?' (92). Mathilde encourages Claire to learn more of the world if only so that she can discuss its matters with her husband, but Claire finds solace in the soirées of a small circle of women whose men go to the café every evening. The problem, however, is that patriarchy's association of femininity and love alienates women's homosocial relations, leaving only jealousy.

In fact, the long-suffering Claire is interpellated by radically divergent models of feminine identity. On the one hand, her mother and father initially counsel patience. On the other hand, radical commentary on this marriage is offered by Claire's cousin, the young feminist intellectual Mathilde Sargeaz, and Ferdinand's acquaintance, the French painter Camille, who falls in love with Claire, though neither becomes aware of this passion until Claire has already married and suffered at the hands of Ferdinand. Mathilde views traditional marriage as a maelstrom of discontent and mutual incomprehension. The narrator is keen to stress that Claire herself is no shrinking violet, always keen to give her opinion on their domestic plans for the future: 'Construire un nid, quelle occupation plus grave et plus chère pour la plus sérieuse des femmes, aussi bien que pour la plus gaie des fauvettes?' (37). Mathilde's arguments with Sir John Schirling over Kant's *Critique of Pure Reason* (1781) reveal the philosophical cornerstones of the marriage debate; he privileges fate, she subjective will. But just as intimacy cannot escape philosophy, so philosophy is compromised by intimacy; for it is only in the final pages of the novel that Sir John reveals that he is in fact Mathilde's biological father. This biological connection seems in fact to fulfil the heteronormative demand that men and women simply could not enjoy each other's intellect and conversation without thinking of sexual difference, and should thus otherwise be kept apart. Like so many French feminists of the nineteenth century, Léo does not dream of a purely female utopia, or gynaecium; instead she dreams of genuine heterosociality (relations between men and women which are not ultimately dependent on sex).

Once the pregnant Claire realizes that her husband is still having an affair with Mme Fonjallaz, Mathilde encourages her to practice a kind of inner exile. She ends up criticizing women such as Claire and in fact displays some admiration for a woman such as Herminie Fonjallaz who at least has a resolute personality. However ethically reprehensible Herminie may appear, she represents a kind of feminine assertiveness which both controls men and appeals to them. Hers is a kind of active feminine agency which, paradoxically enough, fulfils a political agenda for Mathilde's feminism whilst playing to the myth-making which fuels male desire. It is this, we are told, which makes Herminie more desirable than Cleopatra!

Although the title of the novel is unambiguously direct in its focus, divorce is only addressed directly in Chapter 13 (of this twenty-chapter novel). Hitherto this title hangs over the plot, voiced paratextually then repressed *in medias res*. When Claire finally confronts her husband, she learns that, in the eyes of society, her accusation is itself guilty on grounds of etiquette and form, which allows Ferdinand to turn the tables and focus in court on her relationship with Camille. For the feminist Mathilde, divorce is important because it transforms staccato moments of dissent into a sustained narrative of defiance. Mathilde explains that she should leave the family home, thus bringing Claire to feminine (if not yet feminist) consciousness when the latter exclaims: 'Un divorce!' (302). As far as Mathilde is concerned, divorce would formalize the new status quo: 'N'existe-t-il pas déjà entre vous? Et que pourrais-tu gagner à poursuivre désormais une série de discussions et de scandales domestiques?'

One of the provocative implications of divorce was that it suggested that women might enjoy agency and identity (and in particular, civil status) without depending on relations with a father or a husband. And this definition of womanhood in terms of relations rather than identities was enforced by the infamous theory of separate spheres which means that Claire courts scandal when, in Chapter 14, she decides to go out to look for Ferdinand in the evening (as she first did when abandoned in the public location of the boat). As elsewhere in the novel, Switzerland allows Léo to explore the vicissitudes of divorce in a society that, like Second Empire France, still takes an essentially conservative view of gender relations. The analogy with the task facing French progressives was unmistakable: divorce law in and of itself would be insufficient for liberation. To reach the café, Claire must cross the notorious Grand-Pont where she is harassed as a prostitute by a series of men, one of whom defends his approach on the grounds of plausibility and a relational definition of womanhood. He argues that she must be there to meet someone, as if a woman could not be alone, as if she had to be partnered off, respectably (by marriage) or scandalously (in prostitution or adultery). And so we might say that compulsory heterosexuality offered no safe space for women between compliant wifehood and moral decadence, in part because of the gender apartheid which prohibited heterosociality.

When Camille realizes that it would not be customary to keep visiting Claire, even if only to offer moral support, he laments: 'c'est un des plus tristes usages de ce pays que les hommes et les femmes y vivent à part, comme s'ils étaient de race différente' (329). Once Claire has found Ferdinand and Herminie Fonjallaz hand in hand, she allows Camille to express his affection in code. He expresses dismay at the gap between sublime nature and human imperfection, and concludes that women are of two kinds, those would-be romantic heroines who know how to live and suffer, and all the rest. The ideological problem, Léo implies, is that even the sympathetic Camille reproduces in his very affection for Claire the oft-observed double standard of the nineteenth century which opposes 'Madonnas' and 'whores'. His is a simplistic analysis at odds with the nuance in Mathilde's view that Herminie is more desirable then Cleopatra. And in accordance with this idealization, Claire resists Camille. When M. Grandvaux declares his support for the idea of divorce, Claire is racked by doubt:

> L'idée du divorce, sans qu'elle la rejetât absolument, la terrifiait. [...] Ce qui la troublait le plus, c'est que la pensée de Camille s'associait en elle à l'idée en elle de sa liberté retrouvée. Elle ne comprenait plus vraiment ce qui était coupable et ce qui était permis. (340)

During the divorce proceedings, Ferdinand manipulates the judicial rhetoric of marital guilt so as to impugn Claire's character, proposing that she has been having an affair with Camille. Even prior to the trial, the local gossip Mme Rovère had accused Claire of abandoning her husband. It is only when Claire's father employs a spy to catch Ferdinand and la Fonjallaz in the act that the former agrees to leave their son, Fernand, in Claire's safe keeping.

In fact, Claire's relationship with Camille is rather more tortuous than Ferdinand proposes. Once divorce proceedings have begun, Camille declares his love, but Claire retorts with the claim that she intends to defend her decency. The sublime solution to this bourgeois problem lies in a rare abstinence, Claire accepting his 'pact' that they exchange merely their hearts and minds, but not their bodies. Theirs is a vow of fidelity without mutual satisfaction, but crucially he persuades her to agree to resist sexual relations with her husband, and thereby becomes her 'lover'. Theirs is a relationship of adulterous love, but not sex.

The end of Léo's novel offers conclusions but not solutions. As so often in divorce fiction of the nineteenth century, children represent an insuperable obstacle to the idea of divorce as liberation, as we shall see in Chapter 4. It is telling that Claire and Ferdinand produce children who bear the onomastic imprint of their parents (named Clara and Fernand). Oedipal and adulterous triangles meet in the rival compensations of sexual and maternal love. It is when Claire's sister, Anna, sees her stop Ferdinand strike their son that she conjures up the image of marriage as a godless temple:

> elle se demandait naïvement pourquoi le mariage, parmi les hommes, est chose si universellement acceptée, et si peu goûtée, à la fois; pourquoi l'on se marie tant, quand il est rare de s'unir? Elle entrevit cette force des choses morales qui mène l'homme, bien que non comprise par lui. Le monde est plein de temples, bâtis pour des dieux qui n'y résident pas. (267)

Even after divorce proceedings begin, Claire is reminded of the heterosexual similarities within their nuclear family matrix: her daughter resembles her father; Fernand resembles Claire. The insertion of children into a new narrative pattern under the aegis of divorce is symbolized by the folktale of the cricket (a traditional symbol of future happiness when found in the family home) who is only happy enough to sing when he is free but whose voice attracts the boy who imprisons him.[10] Having often told this tale before, Anna has to change the ending so as to stop her nephew, Fernand, from crying. In response to a tale of freedom, happiness and imprisonment whose resonance is unmistakeable in this context, Fernand appears disorientated by Anna's narrative refashioning of a happy ending. This, Léo implies (quite accurately), is the future which awaits France, in which divorce may well be legalized, but the socio-cultural response to the new dispensation will be one of considerable disorientation. Once divorce becomes possible in France after 1884, the parameters of the mimetic contract shift, as we shall now see in the case of Vautier's *Adultère et divorce*.

Few can claim to offer a better 'thick description' of Third Republic discourses than the historian Marc Angenot. The centenary of the Revolution, on which he has focused, brings back into focus the awkward relationship between the compromises of the modern Republic and its radical late eighteenth-century origins. The divorce legislation of the 1880s offers one such compromise, and as Angenot indicates, *Adultère et divorce* dramatizes the failings of such a compromise.[11] In one review of *Le Cru et le Faisandé*, Nicole Ward Jouve underscores indignantly the contrary ideology of Vautier's novel:

> La littérature soi-disant innovatrice, en particulier les romanciers naturalistes, ne sortent à aucun moment du réseau des représentations et des idéologies dominantes: sexe-rigolade ou sexe-abjection. [...] Et — lisez si vous ne me croyez pas — un seul roman de femme, *Adultère et divorce*, de Claire Vautier, aborde de front l'oppression sexuelle de la femme.[12]

Oddly, Angenot does not pause to reflect on a novel he takes to be so conspicuous and does not offer a close reading of it.

This tripartite novel tells the story of Marcelle de Morange (née Heurteaux) whose marriage of convenience exposes the heroine to the perversity of her husband, M. le baron Abel de Morange (in Part I, 'Un viol légal'). Separated *de facto* but not *de jure*, Marcelle returns to the family home, only to fall in love with the artist Jacques Lenormand (in Part II, 'Un adultère'). The novel concludes with the termination of Marcelle's marriage to Morange, which nevertheless leaves her and Jacques in a melancholy state of romantic limbo (in Part III, 'Un divorce'). In historical terms, the novel charts the shift from the 1870s, when Naquet is striving to pass a divorce law, to the advent of the new law in the mid-1880s, with all the flaws which Vautier sees in its provisions.

The oxymoronic title of Part I, 'Un viol légal', contests the morality of that 'Victorian' logic which demands of the bride a radical change of state from innocence to knowledge. As such, the melodrama of the novel's title is suddenly politicized by the lexis of violence. The five chapters of Part I begin with the engagement and conclude with the separation. From the very first chapter, Marcelle's mother incarnates the language of official morality: 'Il faut de la rectitude dans la vie, et surtout dans la vie d'une femme. Souviens-toi de cela toujours, ma fille, et que tous tes actes, quels qu'ils soient dans l'avenir, se basent là-dessus.'[13] So over-determined and over-reactive are her responses to her daughter's interest in love, so akin to the linguistic violence of, say, Ionesco's characters, that the reader is left wondering where to place the novel on the spectrum between mimesis and caricature (or between would-be objective reflection and exaggerated critique). Marcelle notices that Morange has arrived early but is dawdling before ringing the doorbell: 'Ne voilà-t-il pas, pour moi, un exemple admirable, et une touchante preuve d'amour, n'est-il pas vrai maman?' at which she explodes: 'cette dernière remarque est absolument choquante', in her defence of the social codes of 'les usages' rather than the romantic code of love.

The violence against this virgin-bride on her wedding night discolours the flower symbolism in this opening chapter, set at a dinner party in the Heurteaux household. When Marcelle thanks Morange for her daily bouquet of flowers, he replies: 'C'est un usage, mademoiselle, un simple usage auquel, en ma qualité de fiancé, il est de mon devoir de me conformer' (3). Any inkling of romantic idiolect is suppressed by the sociolect of 'usages'. He is furious at the florist's 'bévue' of not delivering orange blossom: 'Je suis confus, désespéré' (4). The epithets of romantic despair are thus transferred to the banal rote of social convention. Indeed, from an anthropological perspective, we might well wish to interpret marriage in general as an attempt to tether desire to decorum, or the *surprise des sens* to the predictability of social roles. In a novel which turns on the narrative path which awaits the virgin, it is hard to over-interpret this matter of delivering the right flowers at the right time. As *Le Petit Robert* has it, orange blossom is a 'symbole de la virginité et du mariage', and cites as its example the performance of *Lucia di Lammermoor* in Part II Chapter 15 of *Madame Bovary*, which triggers Emma's daydream about her own wedding day and her realization of the tawdry 'désillusion de l'adultère' which follows.

It is irony which separates the engaged couple from the very beginning, Marcelle feigning shock at 'quelle grave infraction à l'étiquette' and promising to hide the bouquet from the other guests (5). As she informs her stern tutor and godfather, M. le comte de la Vertpillère, and the more sympathetic prelate ('Monseigneur') of this 'dérogation à l'usage', she pretends to hide the flowers, 'très rieuse, bien qu'une certaine ironie perçât dans sa gaieté'. The alternative romantic lead is, in the first instance, her cousin, Georges Dupont, 'un jeune homme de vingt-deux ans à peine, grand et élancé' (9). When she tells la Vertpillère that she loves another, her request to abandon wedding plans is met by laughter: 'Ce rire, elle le connaissait bien' (14), and as he leaves and the opening chapter closes, 'ce petit rire s'entendait toujours, jetant sa note ironique et discordante sur la douleur et la désespérance qui devaient être désormais toute la vie de Marcelle' (15). Ironic laughter, it seems, can be the expression of youthful gaiety or senescent stricture. Who, the reader wonders, will have the last laugh?

In keeping with the principle of a rapid departure on honeymoon, the novel skips the wedding itself. Chapter 2 focuses on that honeymoon, which involves a trip to London via Paris, and gives Part I its morally arresting subtitle. The language of violation which foregrounds the body politics of the novel is introduced in bathetic vein on the train to Paris. In an anticipation of his impatience in their hotel suite in Paris, Morange complains angrily to his wife for opening a window, but then apologizes. She admonishes him: 'Vous avez violé l'étiquette,' which she corrects to 'la galanterie' (26–27). They have adjoining rooms in the hôtel du Louvre, but in prefiguration of the feminist language of 'a room of one's own', the reader may note that he has the key to her room (and thus to her body), neither of which she cannot lock from the inside. She waits in her room for 'l'arrivée de son mari, ou plutôt de l'ennemi' (30). At first he retreats, but only to return to enjoy his husbandly rights, imposing on her the judgement which the sympathetic reader will turn against him: 'que tout cela est de mauvais goût' (32). Rape is presented as feminine submission to a collective law, rather than simply an individual act: 'toutes les lois divines et humaines l'avaient livrée à cet homme [...]. Sa mère et son tuteur l'avaient voulu ainsi; il fallait obéir. Et dans le viol qu'elle subissait, défaillante et brisée, elle leur obéissait encore' (33). When the couple return early to Orleans from their honeymoon, Mme Heurteaux suggests that her daughter might be pregnant; 'la maternité étant la conséquence du mariage' (p. 51), she is taken aback by her daughter's horror at the idea. Chapter 3 amplifies the ideological cleavage between la Vertpillère and 'Monseigneur' and maps this onto two class-specific Catholic camps, 'les rétrogrades' ('de la vieille aristocratie et de l'ancienne bourgeoisie') and 'les avancés' ('les petits bourgeois', 43).[14]

When la Vertpillère visits Marcelle in Paris, after eighteen months of marriage, she asks him to take her away, as Morange has infringed the Civil Code by introducing into the family home 'des concubines' (the biblical and legal term which saves la Vertpillère from having to pronounce 'des maîtresses, mot bas et vulgaire' (62)). In fact, these rivals turn out to be men, vicomte Hasth and M. Paul Bonnin, her husband accusing her of 'bégueulerie' when she refuses the advances of the latter (who, like Morange, is bisexual). La Vertpillère is horrified when she shows him photographs 'de la Sodome biblique et des flammes qui la dévorèrent' (64), and only then agrees that 'dans ce cas, [les Pères de l'Église] autorisent l'épouse à se séparer de l'époux indigne de ce titre sacré,' and takes her away (65). As such, radical feminism is underpinned here by intense heteronormativity. In order to secure 'une séparation aimable' from Morange (70), la Vertpillère warns the latter against 'une action judiciaire qui aboutirait fatalement à un effroyable scandale' (68) and confronts him with the letters Morange has sent to Bonnin which la Vertpillère has purchased. Part I closes with Morange about to leave for Russia, but promising himself revenge.

The 'adultère' which gives Part II its subtitle is the love affair between Marcelle and the sculptor Jacques Lenormand, following her retreat to the family seat, the château de Savenay. This culminates in Marcelle, still only twenty, setting off to Paris to set up home with him illicitly. Divorce fiction is well placed to nuance that traditional notion of marriage itself as a moment of separation from the family in which one has grown up, as Marcelle has explained to Morange on their honeymoon: 'si raisonnable que l'on soit, on éprouve toujours une grande tristesse au moment de telles séparations' (18). The irony which bedecks the opening to Part II is that conjugal separation seems to undo that initial separation (habitually from parents and siblings). But as la Vertpillère explains to Mme Heurteaux in offering Marcelle the best of rooms rather than her childhood bedroom, things have changed. By contrast with Gide's protean ethos and the mobile possibilities of liquid modernity, la Vertpillère is symbolized by the mythological figure of Medusa, who is, in a double sense, petrifying. In the final chapter of Part I, Morange finds him 'semblable à l'hydre fabuleuse ou à l'impitoyable Méduse' (68) and his subsequent display of the compromising letters to Bonnin leave Morange 'complètement médusé' (71). It is ironic that it should be a sculptor who offers Marcelle the chance to embrace liquidity.

Separation ruptures the linear logic of the well-made life narrative, of course, and Marcelle reflects on this sequential confusion: 'quelle doit être ma vie? Finie sans avoir commencé, et je n'ai pas vingt ans!' (82). La Vertpillère comments on 'ta vie, que, dès à présent, je le déplore, mais il le faut, tu dois considérer comme terminée' (83). But he is shocked that she should fantasize about Morange's death (which would allow her to love again with official blessing). As in other texts of the period, much turns on the limits of the analogy between failed marriages and widowhood. In one sense, this might suggest the possibility of remarriage, but in la Vertpillère's conservative vision, it suggests only mourning and confinement: 'Les veuves [...] lorsqu'elles demeurent sans enfants, font en effet sagement en se condamnant à la solitude' (190). The management of death is vital to the question of separation (and, after 1884, divorce), and Marcelle accepts la Vertpillère's decision to cut her out of his will, so that Morange will not be able to get his hands on any of his estate and 'dénaturer ma fortune', given the rights he maintains over her possessions and person (85). La Vertpillère encourages her towards charity work and diagnoses 'hérésie' in her new plan for life at Savenay, which will include riding, walking and painting: 'Ce que je veux à tout prix, c'est le libre arbitre de mon moi' (87). And without specifying the source of this theory of free self-determination, she simply tells la Vertpillère: 'J'ai lu.' The opening chapter of Part II closes with la Vertpillère warning Marcelle of Georges's return home and Morange's accusation, not unfounded, that she once loved him.

Georges has returned from Africa with a scantily clad slave girl, Marouna, who undresses him and sleeps on a tigerskin in his bedroom. No longer the adolescent, but 'un vigoureux soldat, bronzé au soleil d'Afrique,' Georges impresses Marcelle with his 'beauté mâle et énergique' (93). He calls his slave princess Kaleb [sic], in reference to Byron's poem 'Lara' (1814). Marcelle persuades Georges to give her Marouna/Kaleb, who falls immediately at her feet. The narrator explains that 'la race noire est née esclave,' and Georges's mother happily compares her with an orang-utan in the Jardin des Plantes (105). Black people, it seems, are excluded from the social contract which Rousseau bequeaths to the revolutionary tradition; in a parallel movement on which divorce depended, the Catholic sacrament of marriage was transmuted after 1789 into a civil contract. Indeed, perhaps the marriage contract is to private life as the social contract is to public citizenship. The implicit ideological question in the novel runs thus: to what extent are the positions of women and black people analogous? In the archetypal role of romantically compromised matchmaker, Marcelle accepts the task of persuading Georges to marry Marie Blanchard (whose surname suggests a distancing from his African adventure). Marcelle only persuades Georges once she herself has resisted his advances.

Chapter 5 introduces Marcelle and the reader to the handsome artist, Jacques Lenormand, who has served in the same regiment in Africa as Georges. Though of bourgeois origin, he belongs to one of the oldest families in Poitou. His father played a role in the events of 1830 and his family is monarchist, even if Jacques himself displays worrying liberal-utopian tendencies. The range of her reading is suggested by the fact that she realizes that he is the sculptor of the much-admired statue of a female slave which was overlooked by the Salon jury the year before last. The chapter concludes with la Vertpillère praising the manners of their guest but vowing not to allow scandal to befall Marcelle.

In the very next chapter, however, Jacques and Marcelle discuss her separation. He glosses her life as one of accelerated exhaustion in which the sequence of events has unfolded too quickly: 'Vous avez une vie un peu triste pour une si jeune personne. [...] Cette monotonie, ce silence et ce calme, ne conviennent guère qu'à ceux qui, ayant longtemps vécu, aspirent au repos et à l'oubli' (144). Art becomes the alibi for their passion, Jacques persuading her to visit him as he works on the statue for the tomb of the deceased Marouna/Kaleb (which, the reader may conclude, must be in some sense a reworking of his spurned Salon work). He then borrows the scientific language of Goethe to convince Marcelle of the inevitability of their rapid infatuation: 'C'est ce qui s'appelle s'obéir aux affinités attractives' (148). Chapter

6 ends with their pact metaphorically signed and sealed, in the exchange of her heart for his friendship and esteem. He defines the figure of the artist as 'une sorte d'androgyne, mis, par sa dualité, en dehors de toutes les lois sociales.' But jealous of her feelings for Georges, he excuses himself from the commission to paint Mme Heurteaux's portrait, confesses his romantic desire to Marcelle, which is more than the mere friendship they have professed, and threatens to run off back to Paris. The heterosocial fantasy sheltered by art (which recasts the forces of beauty, pleasure and desire) has been shattered.

In the meantime, Georges's marriage, which Marcelle has engineered, has turned within three months to acrimony and insolence. We learn at the unveiling of Marouna's sepulchral sculpture, that he now dubs his wife cuttlefish, or 'seiche', a homonym of *sèche* (166)... Marcelle persists with her heterosocial fantasy: 'l'amitié, entre un homme et une femme qui se respectent et s'estiment, est-elle donc une utopie?' (170). But her defences are only weakened by Jacques's cold rebuff of this question. He clinches his prey by comparing her as abused wife and himself as suffering artist in a lexicon that immediately recalls Flora Tristan:

> Nous voici deux parias [...]; toi, pour avoir été sacrifiée aux convenances, à l'usage ou à d'indignes calculs d'intérêt; moi, pour m'être engagé dans cette voie infernale et divine où l'artiste est vaincu s'il ne sait pas combattre, non plus avec les armes de l'athlète antique, le travail et le génie, mais avec celles que fournit l'astuce, que fait triompher l'intrigue. Nous pouvons nous unir, et frappés tous les deux par une société dont nous méprisons les lois tyranniques et infâmes, nous donner une fête sans fin. (172–73)

In Vautier's one-sentence paragraph which distils the sublime, we read: 'La fête de l'amour consacré par la fidelité.' This sublime connection is fostered by the death of the outsider (Marouna), and Chapter 9 closes with the consecration of her tomb serving as an alibi for Marcelle who returns home late.

Jacques encourages Marcelle to embrace the counter-cultural position which her failed marriage has imposed on her. If a failed marriage means social 'death', and hence, as we have seen, the undoing of a well-made life narrative, then rebirth becomes the only possible path:

> il faut mourir, vois-tu; renaître dans un autre; renoncer à l'autrefois; à ceux que, par un préjugé que rien ne justifie, tu nommes encore 'ta famille'; oublier tout; surtout nom et fortune. Si je te prends, ce sera pauvre et seule, comme un autre moi-même.

The only way out he perceives lies in the renunciation of social relations, by dropping out of the bottom of the class system to a place where only the idea of the couple remains, where people fuse into the smallest possible community, the community of two.

Chapter 10 introduces a figure who will haunt and undermine this love affair. Jacques is called back to Paris by a long-standing friend, who signs his name Marc Ω, and dates his letter 4 September 1877, which the narrator glosses as the 'septième et glorieux anniversaire de l'austère République' (178). Jacques, addressed as Oublieux Alpha, explains to Marcelle their respective Greek associations with origins and endings: 'ce qui m'attrayait le plus, c'était le début, la nouveauté,' whereas Marc was interested only in 'la solution qu'il résolvait de cinquante manières différentes' (180). And thus the question of how the beginning and end of loving relationships should be managed is transposed to the aesthetic sphere. In a melodramatic *coup de théâtre* Jacques returns under the cloak of darkness and climbs a ladder to her room to persuade her to follow him. A pair of metaphorical threads (widowhood and petrification) are drawn together in the confrontational scene in Chapter 11 where Marcelle, still only twenty, tells her mother and godfather that she will begin again: 'Les veuves ont le droit de se marier [...]. Je suis donc venue vous dire [...] que j'use de mon droit et que je me marie [...]. Vous m'avez faite veuve, et je me suis donné un époux' (198, 202). In this ongoing sentimental education, Marcelle can now resist la Vertpillère's 'regard terne [...] qui si souvent avait médusé la jeune femme' (198). Part II of the novel closes with Marc warning Jacques about Marcelle:

> Pour contracter une union comme celle qui te tente, il faut d'irréfutables preuves d'amour, une foi robuste, basée sur des actes et qui puisse ainsi garantir la fidélité. Celle-là seule, souviens-t'en, sera votre raison vis-à-vis de vous-même, et votre excuse dans l'avenir si la loi, représentée par le mari, vient un jour réclamer contre vous. (207)

Only the most naive of readers would forget the bisexuality of Marcelle's first husband, indeed this 'feminist' novel (as Angenot dubs it) presents relations between men as a major obstacle to women's satisfaction in love. Jealous as Marc is of her arrival in Paris and the fact that he cannot therefore spend the evening with Jacques, it seems that even avant-garde male homosociality cannot accept such transgressive heterosexuality. Indeed, it is hard to resist the playful notion that he fears that her femininity represents a supplement rather than a lack, in other words that Marcelle = Marc + elle.

In a pattern repeated elsewhere, *Adultère et divorce* concludes inconclusively, with Marcelle and Jacques together, yet not quite one, even though Part III ('Un divorce') carries us over the threshold that is 1884. Chapter 1 opens with 'M. & madame Jacques Normand', as they are bigamously known, having lived together for a year in a fifth-floor flat on rue Mansart (in the 9th arrondissement). Before his friends Jacques refers to Marcelle as 'ma femme' (211), and all but Marc, who lives in the neighbouring flat, accept her. She is visited by M. J. James, the *chargé d'affaires* of Morange, who has returned to Paris from Russia, in need of capital. As they were married under the 'régime de la communauté', Morange needs Marcelle's signature in order to sell their farm in Sologne, which belonged to her 'apport de la communauté' (213). James threatens Marcelle with the possibility of Morange calling on his rights 'en vous obligeant à réintégrer le domicile conjugal, afin de faire cesser le scandale de votre situation actuelle' (214). One of the problems for women whose marriage had clearly failed was the way in which it exposed the intimate details of their private life to public comment, hence Marcelle's shock when James asserts his knowledge that she has been living with Jacques for a year 'maritalement' (212). And for nineteenth-century Frenchwomen to inhabit the public realm was of course very awkward. Unlike the covert ruses of adultery (which involves a displacement of the heart), Marcelle's visible displacement of her person from the marital home foregrounds her choice of sexual partner and renders her vulnerable to disrespect. For her sexual life is thereby exposed to misappropriation by gossip.

Marcelle's notary, Mesnard, warns her against signing the document proposed by James and foresees blackmail. He suggests instead that she take her own apartment and secretly continue to see Jacques, making it very difficult to prove in law her adultery. Meanwhile, she should file for a 'séparation de corps et de biens' so that Morange cannot demand her return 'home' (216). Idealistically, Marcelle refuses with the claim that she is 'en un mot' Jacques's wife, though in law, she is not (217). Meanwhile, Marc succeeds in seducing Jacques though his art. He argues that 'les tracas de la vie matérielle' which accompany heterosexual coupling are at odds with the creative androgyny of artists: 'L'amour a des ailes. Seulement le mariage les lui rase' (226). The sight of Marc's masterful canvas overcomes Jacques's resistance, and 'comme un enfant vaincu par le dévouement et l'amour maternel' he throws himself into Marc's arms (228).

A year on since the sale of the domaine des Bordes, James returns in Chapter 4 to press for the need to sell Savenay as well. The avuncular Mesnard, who has enjoyed over the decades 'le loisir d'approfondir bien des choses' (240), again advises her in vain to cease cohabitation. Nor will Marcelle approach la Vertpillère for the letters compromising the disreputable Morange. Mesnard persuades the Bishop to buy Savenay as if to create a hospice, but really to guard it for Marcelle so that she might profit from it, given the atmosphere of the divorce debate at the end of the 1870s:

> J'ai la conviction que, tôt ou tard, la loi sur le divorce obtiendra la sanction des Chambres et même du Sénat, si chauve et si sénile qu'il soit. Or, Marcelle [...] pourra bénéficier d'une loi devenue si nécessaire en ce temps de mauvais ménages [...]. Nous devons donc manœuvrer de telle sorte qu'un chacun la croit dépouillée. (248–49)

Mesnard is therefore furious when Mme Heurteaux explains that la Vertpillère has persuaded her to disinherit Marcelle by ploughing money into good works for the Church. Unlike Marcelle's *régime de la communauté*, her widowed mother was married under the *régime dotal*, and this, Mesnard argues, means that morally she is but a conduit between father and daughter:

> Vous avez commis un vol, madame. [...] Vous n'aviez donc aucun droit à la fortune acquise pendant la communauté, et la part que votre mari vous attribue par son testament, ne devait être considérée par vous que comme un dépôt. Chose inviolable! (253)

This condemnation of her 'violation' of the father's gift to his daughter is highly charged, of course, in a novel which begins by accusing mother and godfather of exposing Marcelle to the 'viol légal' of her wedding night. Mesnard does, however, persuade her to sell Savenay to the Bishop and to mortgage her other possessions so that they can be repurchased secretly (without even Marcelle knowing).

The narrator's position is made quite explicit in Chapter 6. Jacques and Marcelle have become 'réellement époux malgré l'illégalité de leur union' (as if the 'real' substance of marriage exceeds the law), as time turns their love into 'une tendresse grave et recueillie', and even Marc and Marcelle have grown closer (262). The narrator is deeply critical of the disqualification from marriage faced by adulterous unions such as that of Jacques and Marcelle, and hence of

> la situation de ces trois victimes de l'amour et de l'amitié, ou, pour être plus exact, des lois sociales telles que le dix-neuvième siècle les a comprises et établies, en l'année 1884, c'est-à-dire sept ans environ après l'union de Jacques et de Marcelle. C'est à peine si cette dernière se souvenait d'être nommée, un jour, autrement que madame Lenormand, et l'illégalité dangereuse de sa position ne lui causait plus aucun trouble, dans ce complet oubli d'un passé qui n'existait plus pour elle. (264)

Five years pass after the sale of Savenay, during which time 'ce phénix des amis et des notaires', Mesnard, consolidates the estate for the unsuspecting Marcelle. In March 1886, so poor is Marcelle that she feels compelled to ask Mesnard for help. He replies with hopeful news that the legislature is about to ratify the procedural aspects of the law of 1884:

> La loi sur le divorce, acceptée par les Chambres, vient d'être présentée au Sénat. Selon toute probabilité, elle passera. Vous pourrez donc être libre et retrouver la vie facile et honorée que, selon les gens de cœur, vous n'avez pas cessé de mériter. (270)

But he warns her once more that the law requires its own fictions:

> Mais, pour atteindre ce but, il faudrait agir avec une excessive prudence, et séparer momentanément votre existence de celle de M. Lenormand. Les erreurs passées sont niables ou tout au moins discutables, (ce qui est un en justice,) mais le flagrant délit! ma chère enfant. Songez aux suites qu'aurait une constatation légale.

How, though, can she follow this advice, given that both Jacques and Marc are very ill (the latter due to opium)? On his deathbed, Marc advises her to sacrifice her own love and leave Jacques for the sake of his art. Ironically, then, Mesnard the humanist and Marc the misogynist both encourage separation, but for quite different reasons. Marc accuses her of being 'l'instrument inconscient de ce désastre. La femme est la raison et le complément de la matière en ce qu'elle perpétue l'espèce. En dehors de ce but, elle devient l'entrave' (276). Women, it seems, are to biological production as men are to cultural production (all of which the very authorship of *Adultère et divorce* ironizes). After a trip to Rome with Jacques which fails, she cannot resist the conclusion that 'l'Art est vaincu par la Vie, mais il a dominé l'Amour' (282).

Chapter 10 witnesses the start of Morange's legal assault on Marcelle and her cohabitation with Jacques. The couple return from Rome only for Jacques to learn from the concierge's wife that she and her husband have been compelled by the police to identify Marcelle's portrait. 'C'est pour le divorce, paraît-il,' she notes (283). Jacques, ever the distracted artist, muses to himself hazily: 'Le divorce [...]. La loi a donc passé?' (284). One evening, three policemen pay the couple a surprise visit, but what strikes the reader is the incongruence of the lexis of adultery. Marcelle is sewing, and what the police interrupt is not sex but contentment, hence the stumbling accusation: 'monsieur, je suis le commissaire de police du quartier, et je viens constater le flagrant....,' quickly corrected to 'la situation illégale dans laquelle vous vivez avec madame' (286). This sets into relief the farcical nature of a law which would impede the *régularisation* of such domesticity. Jacques and Marcelle do not flee the banality of coupledom; they embrace it. She is now thirty-two and has been with him for seven years. This is not so much the adultery of *jouissance* as the adultery of *plaisir*, not the moment of sexual explosion but the *longue durée* of satisfaction.

The policemen are accompanied by the grotesque Morange. Even though Jacques asserts his ownership of Marcelle ('elle m'appartient'), the *commissaire* identifies the power of Morange who will try to use this leverage to blackmail Marcelle: 'la loi punit de la prison toute personne convaincue d'adultère. Cette peine, cependant, n'a son effet que si l'époux outragé dépose une plainte. Le fait de la constatation simple ne suffit pas' (286–87). Furious at the apparent loss of Savenay so as to combat his own avarice, Morange demands from la Vertpillère the compromising papers supposedly in his possession. Otherwise Morange will cite adultery, rather than mutual antipathy and ten years of separation, as the grounds for divorce. When la Vertpillère reveals that these papers have been burned, Morange feels free to follow this course of action anyway.

The remainder of the chapter is taken up with Morange's meeting with Maître Guérin, an old school pal and now a brilliant lawyer (and part-time librettist!) who has lost only one case in fifteen years. Morange pretends to be the wounded and deceived husband, who has married a woman whose wealth by no means matched his own; he neglects to mention that he has frittered away his family's resources. In reference to Morange's homosexual experimentation, Guérin expresses surprise that Morange has married at all: 'nous avons donc délaissé Ganymède pour sacrifier à Hébé?' (293). Morange dismisses his 'sottises de collégien, sottises que l'adulte a bientôt oubliées', at which point Guérin professes a liberal attitude, citing the philosopher's dictum that 'en amour, la beauté n'a pas de sexe', which ironically echoes the theme of the androgynous artist. So Morange and Jacques do share this ambivalence (Jacques in art, Morange in sex), which distances them from our heroine. Homosociality thus descends into aestheticism (for in art and sex, beauty is desired), and this alienates Marcelle from her partners.

When Morange explains that Marcelle has been living with Jacques for ten years, Guérin identifies the contradiction in a law which would demonize her behaviour: 'Mais elle a la rage de la fidélité, ton infidèle!' (295). Morange goes on to pervert the truth, accusing Marcelle, Jacques and Marc of forming a *ménage à trois*, and Marcelle of continuing an affair with Georges after getting married. Guérin raises the issue of the dowry which must be returned if there are no children. Although this often impedes divorces, Guérin is sure that a 'millionaire' like Morange will have no difficulty here. He then suggests:

> Faisons d'abord constater l'adultère et entamons un procès sur ce fait. [...] Nous demandons le divorce; je plaide, et nous gagnons. [...] Tu pourras porter plainte; mais je ne le conseille pas. C'est assez malpropre, entre nous, ces noms traînés en correctionnelle, et, en pareil cas, le déshonneur de la femme rejaillit toujours sur le mari. Cette manière d'argumenter n'est bonne que pour les gens qui ne peuvent fournir aux frais d'un procès. (296–97)

At this point Morange admits to his financial ruin, though again he blames Marcelle's self-indulgence. When Morange says that as a former magistrate he will get *assistance judiciaire*, the *avocat* Guérin changes his tune and advises a *plainte* as the quickest and cheapest way forward. Once he has a legal aid *avoué*, Morange may return to see Guérin.

A month after the *commissaire*'s visit, Marcelle receives the 'odieux grimoire' of Morange's *plainte*, heavy with exaggeration and deceit (300). What shocks her most is the way in which the law's engagement with a woman's married life renders her a *femme publique*, with all its connotations: 'tout le monde a pu lire cela'. She wishes to escape the logosphere of France, but Jacques insists they have nothing to fear. Jacques and Marcelle have been asked to appear in a few days' time at the Tribunal civil de la Seine before Tribert, *juge d'instruction*. Mesnard realizes that this might lead to 'une comparution en police correctionnelle et la condamnation publique à la prison' (301). But he remains, in a double sense, philosophical:

> Lutter contre [la justice] et l'insulter, c'est s'exposer à la colère d'une société qui permet des amants à ses filles tant que ceux-là ne leur font pas d'enfants; qui absout la femme mariée introduisant au foyer conjugal ses fils adultérins, et répudie l'amante qui, devenue mère, sans être épouse, a gardé le courage de son amour et de sa maternité. [...] Malheureusement, ces vérités-là sont vieilles comme le monde et constituent l'histoire éternelle des peuples. (301–02)

This is, for Jacques, one of those 'singulières époques pendant lesquelles tout semble se transformer' (303). Mesnard suggests that this potential for radical change be seen as cause for hope, 'la promesse d'une nouvelle existence prête à commencer pour vous deux'. When Marcelle tells la Vertpillère that Morange wants to divorce her, Marcelle smiles at the refusal to recognize modernity in his question 'Le divorce? Qu'est-ce que cela?' (308). She reminds him of a recent divorce of 'un très grand personnage' that was even sanctioned by the Pope. As she observes: 'Certes, après huit années d'absence, il eut été facile d'obtenir une séparation de laquelle le divorce résultait forcément.' She is in fact liberated by the fact that la Vertpillère cannot help her as he has burnt the letters which compromised Morange. The irony is that the ever generous Marcelle concludes by offering this man of God, la Vertpillère, unrequested absolution.

The penultimate chapter of *Adultère et divorce* renarrates from the inside the much-told nineteenth-century tale of the desperate woman (be it the saturated image of the *vitrioleuse* or of the knife-wielding *insensée*). In a haphazardly concocted project, Marcelle plans to demand from Morange a 'désistement', otherwise she will blow his brains out (316). Unfortunately, she doesn't even check whether the rusty old pistol is loaded! When he demands money rather than agreeing to a 'désistement', she draws her pistol, but in a fashion which, we are told, would make most people laugh. She steadies herself, however, and states that ultimately she will become a heroine if she kills him, rather than meekly accepting humiliation, such is public opinion. Under the threat of the pistol he signs the letter of 'désistement' which she dictates and he agrees to appear in court tomorrow to confirm it. Once outside, she accidentally pulls the trigger, but fires a blank. The gun was not loaded. The passers-by take her for a madwoman, but the reader knows better.

As we have seen, *Adultère et divorce* charts, in its very title, the generic displacement from the novel of adultery to the novel of divorce which legal and social changes had afforded. The final chapter takes us through courtroom drama, divorce, and the vistas (both visual and experiential) which await Marcelle and Jacques. Judge Tribert tells Marcelle that

> la loi est formelle sur le délit d'adultère, et [...] elle punit l'épouse coupable et son complice de trois mois d'emprisonnement, au minimum; de deux ans, au maximum. [...] La justice est une et déclare, qu'en aucun cas et sous aucun prétexte, la fidélité conjugale ne doit être violée. (323)

In what might be a cautionary gesture to the female reader, a not unsympathetic if rather stiff Tribert tells Marcelle in his rooms that she should have separated legally from her husband after two years of such abuse. Tribert seems to believe Marcelle's story, although he reminds her that 'aux yeux de la loi [...] l'infamie du mari n'atténue pas la faute de la femme' (324). He suggests that the most equitable course of action would entail Morange dropping his prosecution so that the divorce could quietly go through. Marcelle concludes that there was no need to have gone through yesterday's 'scène tragi-comique' with her blank pistol, as the 'désistement' would have occurred anyway (326). As Tribert and Mesnard predict, the divorce is confirmed, though to Morange's advantage. Marcelle must accept this so as to liberate herself. Once the 'énoncé du jugement' has been rushed through due to Morange's residual influence, Marcelle visits Orleans, but arrives too late as her mother has just died (327). The horizontal and vertical axes of the family do not intersect in satisfactory fashion. Mesnard reveals to Marcelle that he has saved both Savenay and her mother's fortune for her. Marcelle says that she will only move back to Savenay once the 'délai de prescrit' has passed and she has married again. But, in terms worth quoting at length, Mesnard explains the notorious Article 298:

> Si jamais la justice, cette fille du ciel et de la terre, mérita d'être représentée avec un bandeau sur les yeux, ce fut certes lorsqu'elle décréta que, jamais, en aucun cas, l'épouse ou l'époux convaincu d'adultère, ne pourrait épouser son complice, du moment que le nom de celui-ci ayant été prononcé au cours des débats, nul doute ne pourrait être admis sur sa culpabilité. Tel est l'article — 298 — relatif à la loi faite sur le divorce. [...] Ceux qui ont fait cette loi prétendent, qu'en l'établissant ainsi, ils ont sauvegardé le ménage, sinon le mariage, subtilité qui, d'ailleurs, n'est comprise que d'eux-mêmes. (329–30)

Marcelle confirms the illogicality of the infamous article:

> Ainsi [...] je ne puis épouser Jacques, parce que, depuis huit ans, je suis à lui, et, parce que, répugnant à devenir la maîtresse vulgaire qui donne et qui reçoit quelques heures d'amour, sans autre souci que les plaisirs de cet amour même, je me suis livrée tout entière, sacrifiant tout, pour partager les misères et les douleurs de l'homme que j'aime? Je ne puis être sa femme à lui; mais la justice approuverait et consacrerait mon union avec un autre homme. (330)

Mesnard concurs:

> Parfaitement. Et eussiez-vous eu dix ou vingt amants, eussiez-vous vécu comme une courtisane, taxant votre amour, et traînant le nom de votre époux dans les lieux les plus abjects, vous seriez, étant divorcée, absolument libre, de

> vous-même et de choisir parmi tous vos complices celui qui vous agréerait le
> mieux, dès l'instant qu'aucune de vos fautes, devenues des crimes pourtant,
> n'aurait été légalement constatée. (330–31)

All Mesnard can suggest is an elopement to England where Marcelle and Jacques could be married (English law, unlike its French counterpart, allowing adulterous lovers to marry subsequently so as to repair the damage done by divorce to the social fabric). But she refuses such a 'comédie inutile' and asserts that she and Jacques will do without human approval and live together at Savenay.

The novel closes with the couple gazing at the sunset over Marouna's timeless black statue. They imagine that their love is similarly timeless. 'Comme en nos cœurs, rien n'a changé', Marcelle concludes (323). But the narrator intervenes and leaves the reader with a sorry denouement: 'Hélas! ils se trompaient tous deux. Ils s'étaient aimés au printemps et, maintenant, c'était l'automne. Et, lui, songeant à sa gloire avortée, elle, rêvant à sa jeunesse morte, ils échangèrent un baiser, morne et désenchanté comme leurs deux existences.' This sense of limbo seems designed to make the reader ask: what would have made them happy? If they had met earlier, if Marcelle had not been compelled to marry for social *convenance*, if divorce and remarriage had been made easier... Though they are united, they are not one. The weight of the past is not overcome, and regret and fatigue overwhelm them both. Their mutual love has muted Jacques's creative energies, and both types of desire (artistic and romantic) have put them beyond the pale of society. The result of such a carnivalesque *parcours* is indeed another place, but not utopia. Liquid modernity remains a dream.

Finally, we might reflect on Angenot's embrace of the 'insuccès total' experienced by Vautier's novel in that busy year of collective commemoration, 1889. Key to the analysis which runs all the way through this book is a context which we might term socio-sexual, in other words, the ways in which the organization of sexual relations sit with (or unseat) social codes. *Adultère et divorce* is avant-garde in socio-sexual terms, but not in aesthetic terms. Its thematic radicalism seems to have alienated the *bons bourgeois* otherwise attracted to such readerly fiction, whilst its lack of formal ambition offered little appeal to the literary avant-garde. But for Angenot, this melding of thematic radicalism and formal legibility is a badge of honour, characterized by a left-leaning *lisibilité* which dissipates any modernist clouding of the *roman social*. What nags away at any acceptance on our part of this view of art's relationship to the ideological is the sense that perhaps the best aesthetic term to equate with the liquid modern (in which the well-made life plot is subject to radical and barely predictable rewritings) might well be the *scriptible*. In practical terms, however, divorce permeated the Parisian literary world more quickly than most domains, as we shall see in the next chapter.

Notes to Chapter 2

1. For my interpretation of *Bel-Ami*, see chapter 3 of *The Family in Crisis in Late Nineteenth-Century French Fiction*.
2. See Claudie Bernard, *Penser la famille au dix-neuvième siècle, 1789–1870* (Saint-Étienne: Université de Saint-Étienne, 2007); Margaret Cohen, *The Sentimental Education of the Novel* (Princeton, NJ:

Princeton University Press, 1999); Patricia Mainardi, *Husbands, Wives, and Lovers* (New Haven, CT: Yale University Press, 2003); and Allan Pasco, *Revolutionary Love in Eighteenth- and Early Nineteenth-Century France* (Farnham: Ashgate, 2009). My interpretations of subsequent divorce novels are deeply indebted to each of these important studies of earlier French writing.

3. Louvet de Couvray's, *Émilie de Varmont; ou, le divorce nécessaire, et les amours du curé Sévin*, 3 vols (Paris: Bailly & les marchands de nouveautés, 1791), III, 192.

4. Malcolm Cook, 'La Critique de la religion dans le roman révolutionnaire', in *Roman et religion en France (1713–1866)*, ed. by Jacques Wagner (Paris: Champion, 2002), pp. 172–76 (p. 174).

5. John Rivers, *Louvet: Revolutionary & Romance-Writer* (London: Hurst and Blackett, 1910), pp. 46–47.

6. Kathryn Norberg, ' "Love and Patriotism": Gender and Politics in the Life and Work of Louvet de Couvrai', in *Rebel Daughters*, ed. by Sara E. Melzer and Leslie W. Rabine (New York: Oxford University Press, 1992), pp. 38–53 (pp. 49–50).

7. Gustave Flaubert, *L'Éducation sentimentale* (Paris: Garnier Flammarion, 1969), p. 369.

8. For further information on Léo's life and work, see Claire Goldberg Moses, *French Feminism in the 19th Century* (Albany: State University of New York Press, 1984), Chapter 8: 'The Reemergence of Feminist Activism', pp. 173–96, and André Léo, *Écrits politiques* (Paris: Dittmar, 2005).

9. André Léo, *Un Divorce* (Paris: Librairie Internationale, 1866), p. 70. Interpolated references are made to this edition.

10. See entry for 'Grillon' in *Dictionnaire des symboles*, ed. by Jean Chevalier and Alain Gheerbrant (Paris: Robert Laffont, 1982).

11. Marc Angenot, *Le Cru et le Faisandé* (Brussels: Labor, 1986), p. 172. Little is known of Vautier's life. A one-time opera singer, she married Alfred Vigneau, and authored books such as *Monsieur le marquis, histoire d'un prophète* (1886), *Dans la boue* (1892), *Hélène Dalton, roman contemporain* (1893) and *Haine charnelle* (1898).

12. Nicole Ward Jouve, review of *Le Cru et le Faisandé*, French Studies, 41 (1987), 358–59.

13. Claire Vautier, *Adultère et divorce* (Paris: Marpon & Flammarion, 1889), p. 2. Subsequent interpolated references will be made to this edition.

14. By contrast, as we shall see, Marie-Anne de Bovet's *Après le divorce* contrasts the plurality of liberal and radical thought with the powerful homogeneity of Catholicism.

CHAPTER 3

Jealousy before Proust

To the 'Chaste et doux Rédempteur des fragiles humains' who has already forgiven the women taken in adultery, Onézime Seure prays in the fires of 1848:

> Plus tard, de l'avenir créant les mœurs austères,
> Tu nommas le divorce un conflit d'adultères.
> C'est ainsi qu'au berceau de la société,
> Comme un gage divin tu plaças l'unité.[1]

For Paul Bourget, too, divorce and remarriage could not be more than 'a conflict between adulteries', each marriage betrayed by the other. Indeed, conservative opinion either dismissed the morality of divorce out of hand or, in the more interesting terms of, say, Paul Bourget's novel of 1904, *Un divorce*, questioned the validity of the remarriage of a post-virginal woman whose *premier homme* may well be alive and, if children are involved, perhaps still on the scene (a fundamental difference between divorcees and widows, of course). Gabrielle is divorced from Chambault, the father of her son Lucien, and married again, this time to Darras. Bourget reasserts traditional values of exclusive reciprocity which marry an intensely romantic view of love with a conservative vision of family values, both at odds with the burgeoning ambition of erotic self-fulfilment. But the cult of uniqueness depends upon the cherishing of female virginity and a mystification of its loss. Just as Zola's Nana bears the traces of the genetic imprint left on Gervaise by her first lover, Lantier, so Bourget's Gabrielle can never quite escape the influence of that first marriage to Chambault. Darras, like Coupeau, is bound to fail in his bid to suppress the memory of that originary moment, and in that, he is perhaps a quintessentially *fin de siècle* figure, always the second man, always too late.[2] To bring into focus this issue of retrospective jealousy, we will maintain our interest in unknown women and forgotten men: first, Marie-Anne de Bovet's *Après le divorce* of 1908 to which we shall turn shortly; then, at the heart of this chapter, Anatole France's *Le Lys rouge* (1894); and finally, Marcel Prévost's telling notion of the *demi-vierge*.[3]

To understand the context in which *Après le divorce* was published, I shall briefly add to what I have said elsewhere about Bourget's novel, by highlighting how it subsequently engaged both public opinion and the wrath of Naquet. It is worth pointing out that fellow conservatives such as Henry Bordeaux saw in Bourget's vision only a partial, religious critique of divorce, which failed to explore fully its deleterious social ramifications:

Le divorce peut [...] s'envisager de deux manières: au point de vue religieux, et dans ses conséquences sociales. Car il serait erroné de croire que la question du divorce n'est qu'un problème religieux. Le divorce a des adversaires dépourvus de toute croyance dogmatique, notamment Auguste Comte qui, dans son *Cours de philosophie positive*, déclare que pour le mariage il n'y a rien à faire dans l'état social qu'à consolider ce que le catholicisme a si heureusement organisé en consacrant l'indissolubilité fondamentale du mariage.[4]

He goes on to quote Comte:

'L'obligation de conformer sa vie à une insurmontable nécessité, loin d'être nuisible au bonheur de l'homme, en constitue ordinairement, au contraire, l'une des plus indispensables conditions, en préservant l'inconstance de nos vues, et l'hésitation de nos desseins.'

As Bordeaux glosses:

Pour le chef du positivisme, le mariage, une fois contracté, est un fait acquis. Vous êtes pauvre ou riche, beau ou laid, fort ou faible, et force vous est d'accepter l'injustice de la nature, si la nature vous est contraire; votre vie s'arrange en conséquence, il faut l'accepter, se plier à ses nécessités. De même, le mariage indissoluble, en vous imposant l'acceptation, vous obligera à le prendre au mieux. C'est avant d'y entrer qu'il importe de réfléchir et de choisir. Car le mariage indissoluble est la clef de la voûte de la famille, et la société est composée de familles. La famille est l'association-type qu'aucune autre n'a jamais égalée dans l'histoire humaine.

In *Vers l'union libre* Naquet indicates how 'Bourget, dans *Un divorce* a dramatisé l'argument' and cites Lucien's heart-stopping line: 'Tu n'es pas mon père!'[5] The triangulation of desire habitually reserved by fiction for the tale of adultery is now recast by remarriage and 'cette introduction d'un élément étranger', in particular the new husband who is — if we transpose Tony Tanner's terminology — another stranger in the house, perhaps an interloper in the original domestic space, certainly an interpolator in the self-conception of the original family.

In response to Bourget and Cury's dramatization of the novel, Gustave Téry organized a plebiscite of the audience over the course of a fortnight, in the very year Bovet's novel appeared.[6] In a remarkable litmus test of educated opinion, Téry precipitated the connection, key to our entire project, between the law, cultural life and public opinion. By 11 March 1908 this plebiscite gave him the following results:

	Men	Women	Total
For the maintenance of the present law.............................	277	169	446
For divorce by mutual consent...........	748	363	1111
For divorce on the will of one party...	363	222	585
	-----------	-----------	-----------
For divorce in general........................	1388	754	2142
For free union ('l'union libre')..........	980	509	1489
	-----------	-----------	-----------
For the capacity to dissolve marriage in general..	2368	1263	3631
Against divorce................................	1853	1265	3118
	-----------	-----------	-----------

Majority for divorce...........................	515	—	513
Minority for divorce...........................	—	2	—
'Fantaisistes' returns that could be counted against indissolubility	—	—	270
Total majority including this last category...	—	—	783
Total returns.....................................	4221	2258	7019

In *Vers l'union libre*, Naquet addresses Téry's poll on audience responses to Bourget's play.[7] Having apologized for the pages spent in order to 'réfuter les sophismes des indissolubilistes', he uses the poll to assert that there is in fact no question of the public desiring 'le retour à l'indissolubilité' and that the question now is just how far divorce provision can be extended.[8] Rather than pretend that the poll is representative, Naquet claims surprise that such a select audience should produce such enlightened opinion:

> Le public qui va au Vaudeville est généralement un public snob, bourgeois, mondain; et dans le monde il est de bon ton de médire du divorce jusqu'au jour où l'on en profite. Il semble donc que *Un divorce* dût avoir un succès incontesté. Il l'a; mais le succès que le public fait à cette pièce n'est pas précisément celui qu'avaient escompté ses auteurs.

Naquet underlines the majority of 513 in favour of divorce. Even if one discounts Téry's category of 'bulletins fantaisistes', this is 'un milieu où tout était de nature à faire prévoir un résultat contraire'. The gender disparity is explained away by Naquet in the light of Separate Spheres and 'le peu d'habitude qu'ont les femmes de la vie publique'. Stretching a statistical point, Naquet observes that amidst all these women against indissolubility, the numbers who agreed with divorce at the behest of one spouse and with free union were virtually in the same proportion as the number of men who did so. The male vote would have been matched in the female camp by 194 and 524 votes respectively, and the figures were in fact 222 and 509.

Vers l'union libre is quick to satirize the unwitting role in energizing the divorce debate played by Bourget, 'aujourd'hui l'un des hommes qui possèdent au plus haut degré ce genre d'esprit orienté vers le passé'.[9] Naquet aims to infuriate the conservative mainstream by depicting the parasitic relation to their discourse from which social modernizers such as himself and the Margueritte brothers profit:

> Je lui sais gré cependant de sa tentative. Les frères Margueritte avaient fait une vigoureuse campagne en faveur de l'élargissement du divorce. Moi-même, en 1904, j'avais publié un ouvrage, *la Loi du divorce*, dirigé dans le même sens. L'admirable plaidoyer de Paul et Victor Margueritte était tombé sur un public indifférent; leur pièce *le Cœur et la Loi* n'avait eu d'autre succès que ce succès relatif qui tient à la valeur de l'œuvre littéraire, mais qui n'exalte pas l'état de l'opinion, et mon livre, demeuré invendu, avait été une affaire médiocre pour mon éditeur.

Vital in this unwitting dissemination of radical counter-opinion is the press's absorption of the plot concerns of Bourget's novel and play, whereby culture in some sense becomes politics:

Mais M. Bourget, le porte-paroles de la bourgeoisie rétrograde et cléricale, donne au Vaudeville sa pièce *Un Divorce*; et au Sénat M. Bérendeveille invoque la religion, tandis que M. Marcère déplore ses péchés: aussitôt la presse s'émeut, le public sort de son apathie, la question du divorce passionne de nouveau l'opinion comme aux jours qui précédèrent la loi de 1884; et, comme dans une démocratie où, sur les questions de cet ordre tout au moins, la parole étant libre, toute agitation aboutit nécessairement au progrès, il est certain que puisqu'on discute le divorce, le divorce sera élargi.

Naquet sees in the unintended role of the Right a pattern which characterizes the Third Republic: 'Depuis 1871, toutes les campagnes réactionnaires ont profité à la République, au Progrès, à la Liberté.' What the spirit of modernity demands is the ability to solicit visibility amongst the plethora of discourses and debates on which the public might focus. In a set of parodic references to Bourget's titles, Naquet suggests that the colour of one's argument is less significant than the field of discourse (and the force and spirit of History) to which one contributes:

M. Bourget aura servi le progrès malgré lui. C'est une gloire qu'il n'ambitionnait pas sans doute. Mais il se dit psychologue; il pourra peut-être y trouver le sujet d'intéressantes études sur la puissance de l'évolution historique qui, en toutes circonstances, fait tourner à son profit les efforts tentés pour l'enrayer. Au demeurant l'auteur de *l'Étape* aura, à son insu, fait faire une étape nouvelle et peut-être décisive à l'union libre.

More ambivalent than either Naquet or Bourget is Marie-Anne de Bovet's *Après le divorce*.[10] Born in 1855, she married the marquis de Bois-Hébert (a descendant of one of William the Conqueror's knights), but wrote under her maiden name a wide range of material, which is at times hard to pin down ideologically. On the one hand, she attended Juliette Adam's salon and contributed to feminist publications such as *La Fronde*. On the other, she wrote with patriotic fervour during the Dreyfus Affair about the grandeur of the army. This ambivalence is captured by one biographer of the time: 'Bien française est-elle, en effet, par son tempérament intellectuel: l'esprit clair et avisé, hardi en demeurant traditionnaliste'.[11]

The opening section of this four-part novel, dedicated to 'mon cher et grand ami François Coppée', begins and ends with a wedding: first of Jeanne, daughter of the doctor and senator Frédéric Bertereau, and then of our heroine, Élisabeth, his orphaned niece whom he has adopted. Feeling no particular antipathy towards either the general idea of marriage or the particular suit of the wealthy Edmond Lambertier, she is engaged within a few days, and a few sentences later, in 'un tourbillon ne lui laissant pas un instant de tête-à-tête avec son cœur', a society wedding ensues (64). Jeanne's jealous sister, Hélène, suggests that their cousin, Élisabeth, will not be able to tame such a 'noceur fieffé' (62). Indeed, the appearance of *après*, that signifier of subsequence and consequence, in the very title of the novel (thus *before* we read) alerts the least alert of readers to the ironic sense that all will not be well and easy.

The second part of the novel beats us to the punch, however, by declaring in its first sentence that the divorce of Élisabeth and Edmond has been recorded, five years later, 'sur l'impassible registre de l'état civil de la mairie du huitième arrondissement, en marge de l'acte de mariage' (67). The ensuing chapter explains how, in the interim, the wayward and perverse Edmond had returned to his bachelor ways. By forcing her to go riding with him in a horse-drawn drag-cart, Edmond causes her to lose her pregnancy, marking 'la fin du peu qui restait entre eux de vie commune' (74). His concerned mother tries to persuade Élisabeth to try again:

> La mère enseignerait le pardon à l'épouse. Et ainsi se trouverait définitivement écartée l'éventualité d'un divorce, qui exposerait de nouveau au péril de quelque union sans honorabilité ce fils dont, depuis l'âge d'homme, avai[t] été son constant effroi. (75)

Meanwhile, Jeanne is concerned about her own marriage to the wayward Gaston, and the pernicious Hélène suggests that she divorce, arguing that Jeanne would be sure to keep her daughter and that Gaston's professional future seems less than rosy. She hints that it is obvious that Élisabeth only stays with Edmond as he is to inherit, thus showing no awareness of the moral drama which Élisabeth is undergoing. A more enlightened discussion of marriage then follows. Élisabeth claims that it is more than 'intérêt' that keeps a woman in a marriage, which Mme Biscaras mocks with her own gesture towards reason: 'Qu'est-ce qui fait le caractère respectable du mariage? C'est la fidélité réciproque aux engagements librement consentis. Le jour où l'une des deux parties y a failli de façon flagrante l'autre se trouve déliée des siens' (80). The brothers of Hélène and Jeanne then pitch in, Georges arguing that this principle of 'raison' in fact defines love, not marriage, and Marcel (a radical history teacher) arguing that the way to abolish divorce is to abolish marriage. Élisabeth seals the debate, however, with a return to that fundamental conflict between theories of sacrament and of contract which informed the redefinition of marriage after 1789: 'Vous envisagez le mariage comme un simple contrat. Pour nous, vous le savez, il est revêtu de la majesté sacramentelle' (82). In a repeated fictional pattern, Bovet (like other novelists) stresses the gravity of the wife's choice (and not the flippancy). Any ultra-conservative interpretation of Élisabeth's position is clouded by the fact that she too has an investment in the Catholic view of marriage as a sacrament. It is only under the strain of Edmond's ever more public relationship with an actress who sees the chance to marry someone of note, that 'la corde cassa' (83).

Docteur Bertereau warns Élisabeth against the 'demi-mesure' of 'la séparation judiciaire', as Edmond would have the right to convert it into a divorce three years later anyway. 'Plutôt en finir d'un coup, avec dignité,' he advises, thus undermining yet further any association of Élisabeth with glib choice (84). He points out that 'l'Église, en définitive, ne proscrit pas le divorce: elle l'ignore seulement, ou du moins ne le tient que pour une séparation aux effets purement civils, laissant indélibile le sacrement'. The fact, he argues, that her unfortunate marriage would hardly encourage her to 'recommencer l'expérience' should make divorce morally acceptable to her, and indeed it does. So pace Hélène's insinuations, Élisabeth only takes from the marriage the dowry she brought to it: 'mariés sous le régime de la communauté réduite aux acquêts, Élisabeth se trouva retirer profit de la liquidation' (85). Whereas Claire Vautier's heroine is dismayed to return to the parental home after her divorce, as we have seen, here Élisabeth experiences a 'sensation de bien-être moral [...] rentrée sous le toit qui avait abrité son heureuse adolescence' (86). Her mirror even reflects back to her and the reader the momentary fantasy that these past five years are merely 'un mauvais rêve [...] tant l'intacte beauté de ses vingt-six ans avait conservé ce caractère virginal auquel elle devait le meilleur de son charme'. But the manifest reality is that any second husband would not be marrying a virgin (and this is key in the context of retrospective jealousy). In fact, Élisabeth is blind to the plot which she inhabits: 'Et reprenant sa vie au point où elle l'avait laissée, pas un instant ne songea-t-elle que peut-être était-ce seulement une halte sur la route.' She believes she has turned full circle, back to a point of stasis; however, reader, narrator, and in fact her adoptive father too, realize that her narrative journey is not over.

Part II Chapter 2 shows the failure of the Bertereaus to persuade their bachelor nephew, Maurice, to court Élisabeth (whom Mme Bertereau describes as 'veuve', 91). In fact, their mutual attraction has already been suggested in Part I Chapter 3 where they share a sympathetic glance at a dinner party. Most interesting about M. Bertereau's argument on the subject with Maurice is that the latter, like the divorcee he refuses to marry, retains a sense of the sacramental force of marriage. Although the dominant voices of conservative and radical opinion dichotomize the divorce debate in turn-of-the-century France, Bovet suggests that the lived experience of citizens after 1884 is often more ambivalent. Élisabeth accepts divorce in the end, Maurice does not; but both are caught on the spectrum between contract and sacrament, both drawn to one but unable to ignore the pull of the other. When Maurice tells Bertereau that he is jealous of Edmond, Bertereau tells him that he is more in love than he realizes: 'Mais c'est bouder contre soi-même... On en revient' (96). When Maurice complains that her first husband is not dead, the doctor criticizes such 'vanité masculine' which imposes on women the unilinear life plot so as to assert the integrity of male identity: 'Belle thèse passionnelle, mais mauvais sentiment, mon garçon, sentiment égoïste, indigne d'une âme généreuse.' Maurice, though, indulges in what people, in modern-day usage, like to call 'semantics': 'l'obstacle se trouve ailleurs... pas dans le fait du mari, mais dans le fait du divorce.' Maurice insists that he holds Élisabeth in the highest personal regard, but that divorce imposes ideological obstacles (at the point where, in Althusser's language, the ISA of the Catholic Church and the ISA of the Family meet). As the church does not consider Élisabeth to be a widow, they would have to have a civil wedding rather than one in church. When Bertereau bitterly accuses him of thinking of his military career and of hypocritically embracing the tag of 'bon catholique' (which echoes through their conversation), Maurice explains that his shaky faith does not undo the ties of family tradition:

> Bon catholique, non assurément [...]. Mais incroyant pas davantage: seulement mal croyant... imparfaitement croyant, pour mieux dire. [...] Mon père et ma mère ont été mariés chrétiennement et mes grand-parents avant eux, et avant eux, toujours, tous mes obscurs ancêtres... (98)

In a secular confession, Bertereau explains his own regret at having followed this same pattern of passive Catholicism, returning momentarily to the fold in those instants of baptismal and conjugal peripeteia, as so many people still do. His arguments only serve to precipitate theological issues with which Maurice is not intellectually engaged most of the time. Whereas Bertereau has formally rejected all religious belief now, Maurice has not forsaken his credo. The chapter ends, however, with the doctor accusing him of an intellectual wooliness, 'un vague traditionalisme', whose effect is to impede historical change.

Part II closes, as did Part I, with Élisabeth getting married, this time to the lawyer André Rogerin, known for taking on good causes. Once again, the narrative speeds through the process whereby this 'désorbitée' (who has left any predetermined orbit) moves from her 'veuvage légal' to falling in love, as if the process were impervious to ratiocination. And once again, Maurice is supplanted by another eager male. The only bitterness which remains from Élisabeth's first marriage is 'le regret de la maternité', which fills this 'douce créature' with the contrarian energy necessary to work against the narrative grain and look once more for conjugal and maternal satisfaction. And this new narrative track demands the erosion of her fundamental philosophy: 'Que le mariage valût uniquement par le sacrement, c'était chez elle une de ces idées primordiales qu'on porte en dépôt au fond de soi, sans avoir jamais l'occasion ou la fantaisie de la discuter' (118). Experience has made of her religious conscience a 'terrain en jachère', which allows Rogerin's sophisms to succeed with her, so the narrator tells us, where Bertereau's have failed with Maurice (119). In lieu of romantic uniqueness, Rogerin manages to appeal to the sense that they are not abnormal: '"Pourquoi pas moi aussi bien que d'autres?" Elle en avait tant vu de femmes divorcées et remariées, qu'on fréquentait, qu'on choyait, qu'on honorait' (120). Rogerin also displays that ideologically inexact ambivalence and vagueness which Bovet associates with a number of her protagonists. He is not against 'une consécration religieuse', but over the years his spirituality has given way to 'un vague positivisme', and in this he is taken to be typical of 'beaucoup d'hommes de la bourgeoisie lettrée'. As such he accepts, as Maurice could not, the civil path. In the event, the civil ceremony is, mercifully, something of a non-event, not least thanks to the much vaunted anonymity of the modern city: 'Et les choses, au surplus, passent tellement inaperçues en ce grand Paris trépidant...' (121–22). Against the distant plaint of residual faith stands the chorus of hope refound in the final words of Part II of the novel:

> Si son second départ pour le grand voyage de la vie s'attristait chez Élisabeth d'un murmure protestant au fond de sa conscience, sans grande peine elle l'étouffa en s'affirmant qu'elle était bien cette fois en route vers le bonheur. (122–23)

Part III of *Après le divorce* charts the early period of Élisabeth's second marriage, culminating not in a third marriage but in the death of her daughter, Yvonne, who seems to be more healthy, attractive and intellectually precocious than the first child of Élisabeth and Rogerin, Gabriel, but who suffers terminal meningitis. Although we are told in the final sentences of this part of the novel that her spirit is ascending to a more beautiful place, it is hard to resist the gloss that the narrative has imposed on Élisabeth some terrible punishment for her own transgressive story of divorce and remarriage, in the divorce plot's reworking of the logic of the classic adultery plot. Jeanne's problematic marriage to Gaston remains the subject of conversation in Part III, Georges glossing her dilemma thus: 'ou bien lâcher ce vaurien... c'est ce qu'elle pourrait faire de mieux... ou bien faire tête à la situation', but the divorced Élisabeth is more cautious: 'une femme a bien de quoi réfléchir avant de prendre cette grave résolution du divorce' (127–28). Élisabeth may appear

> parfaitement heureuse dans son union avec un galant homme, [...u]ne mélancolie flottait autour d'elle, qui n'était pas de la tristesse, sorte de vapeur dont s'estompaient sa beauté pure et son âme douce, telles ces nuées mauves des crépuscules du Nord. (131)

Not the twilight of the gods, but another Nordic eventide, the secular modernity of those prime turn-of-the-century dramatists of divorce, Ibsen and Strindberg. Rogerin does not probe too deeply and attributes this melancholy to her childhood loss of her parents and the pain of her first marriage, and in this he is not too far wrong, in that Élisabeth's melancholy registers an attachment to the past which means that she cannot simply stride confidently into the future. By contrast with Vautier's distinction between 'les rétrogrades' and 'les avancés', the very breadth of political hue in the wider Bertereau family (in Georges's phrase, 'tous républicains, et pas deux qui soient de même nuance,' 128) informs Rogerin's diagnosis of the weakness of the secular *divorciaire* section of society: 'Se trouve-t-il deux Français dont les opinions s'accordent? [...] Voilà bien ce qui fait au contraire la force de l'Église: elle demeure homogène dans sa doctrine' (135). Rogerin is equally critical of radical dogma (such as Marcel's) and thereby offers an ethos of writing which underpins Bovet's novel as a whole: 'Lorsqu'on écrit, lorsqu'on parle à plume et à langue débridées, c'est facile d'aller loin et de frapper dur. Une fois qu'on a démoli, force est de reconstruire' (137). Human beings, Rogerin suggests, are intellectual sadomasochists, intent on conflict rather than resolution.

The final part of the novel is almost as long as the other three parts put together, and traces Élisabeth's return to Catholicism, her re-encounter with her first husband and mother-in-law, and the resurrection of her second marriage in a wilfully open ending. In this, then, Bovet seems to follow the fictional pattern of Bourget's *Un divorce*, where the remarried heroine is drawn back to the church, only to find a compromise with her new, deeply secular husband. The difference, though, lies in Bovet's equivocation over ideological matters at the end of the novel. For Bourget, such equivocation reflects the crisis of Third Republic family values. Bovet's novel is less keen to position itself in a nineteenth-century tradition that goes all the way back to Bonald.

In the wake of Yvonne's death, Gabriel is sent to stay with a deeply religious friend, Monique Guivarch, who has disapproved of the divorce and remarriage. Élisabeth feels shame at the ease with which she has spent a decade outside the Church. Her husband is dismissive when he learns of this refound faith, explaining family degeneration in terms closer to Zola than to Bourget:

> C'est un phénomène tout scientifique, cette décadence... je dirai même cette déchéance de son sang. [...] Tout cela, te dis-je, était fatal. Oui, les erreurs se paient, s'expient. [...] Mais cela se fait mécaniquement. (218)

After twelve years of marriage, the 'intimité conjugale' of the Rogerins has waned (219). André Rogerin can only hope that 'l'amour de la femme triomphât du deuil de la mère', but his suggestion that they try for another child is met by... a headache (220). In desperation, André visits his old friend, abbé Augustin Aldebert, out at la Villette. This shocking immersion into working-class life outside the city provides this *mondain* novel with an apparent moment of good class conscience (in a manner akin to France's *Le Lys rouge*), where Zola's model of fiction (which is largely unconcerned with the exclusive question of divorce) is accommodated within the upper-middle-class plot. In an attempt to have it both ways (by writing *mondain* fiction and criticizing its exclusivity), Bovet chides the professional and intellectual left (such as Doctor Bertereau and the Biscaras) who have never actually visited such places. Augustin explains that people commit sins all the time, and amongst these are bound to be deadly sins. He chooses not to condemn those who have remarried outside the church but not in open hostility to it:

> Là est bien [...] le vice qui ronge comme une lèpre les sociétés modernes: elles prétendent subordonner tous principes à la satisfaction de l'individu. [...] Vous vous trouvez [...] dans une impasse douloureuse... Il s'agit de vous aider, non pas à en sortir, la porte en étant hermétiquement close, mais à y vivre le moins possible. (251–52)

Overlooking their conversation (literally and figuratively) are copies of a number of pictures by Leonardo, Titian, Rubens, Raphael, and Michelangelo, but most ironically of all, Perugino's *Marriage of the Virgin* (presumably that painting finished in 1504, later confiscated by Napoleon, and now in the Musée des Beaux-Arts in Caen, and one of the inspirations for Raphael's 1504 painting of the same name, in the Pinacoteca di Brera in Milan). For this is the Virgin paradoxically, divinely, with child, the virginity rationalists and secularists could barely accept, and yet which Joseph chooses to accept. One of the scandals of divorce and remarried women in Catholic culture is that once more (but rather differently...) the wedding day and its traditional gift of virginity are uncoupled, in the knowledge that another man (the first husband) walks the earth in full carnal knowledge of the remarrying bride. Overarching this intertextualization of virginity and original sexual experience, at the heart of the divorce issue, is the fact that this image is itself not an original but merely a copy (high culture adulterated in its dissemination to the cultural wastelands of la Villette).

As in the relationship at the centre of Marcelle Tinayre's *La Rebelle* (1905) and the relationship between Lucien and Berthe in Bourget's *Un divorce*, there is a radical version of love which questions marriage itself, here in Marcel's cohabitation with a pretty young Finnish *doctoresse*, Nadèje Elsingborg, schooled in the ideas of German philosophy, Herbert Spencer and Lombroso! Hence Georges's explanation of their cohabitation: 'Parce qu['...] elle est une disciple de Tolstoï... *la Sonate à Kreutzer...* Tu n'as pas lu cela? [...] Le nihilisme de ces régions hyperboréennes englobe toutes institutions sociales, à commencer par la plus bourgeoise, le mariage. Union libre et métaphysique!' (205). Marcel and Nadèje represent the antithesis of the Bourget/Bonald position, whereas Bovet is most concerned with the middle ground of ambivalent belief and necessary compromise through which most people, including characters such as the Rogerins, filter their own experiences and decisions.

The penultimate chapter of the novel sees Mme Lambertier make a surprise visit to Élisabeth and ask her to pardon both mother and her sickening son, Edmond. Her feelings in the carriage are, like the ideology which pervades the novel, intense but not extreme. In visiting Edmond, she deceives her second husband, and even the reader is not allowed access to their encounter. In the narrator's words: 'N'eût-on pas dit une femme coupable sortant de son premier rendez-vous?' (272). In the Catholic logic of Bourget, the second marriage is an adulterous transgression of the first union which can only be properly severed by death (and this is Gabrielle's concern). Here, that logic is reversed, for it is the return visit to the first husband which smacks of adulterous betrayal. But this visit is one of forgiveness not betrayal, and Élisabeth finds absolution in then going to church to pray for the survival of Edmond, the very man whose death would allow her to remarry in the eyes of God. On her return home, she finds herself lying to her second husband for the first time. Precisely by returning to God, she enters a realm of moral ambiguity hitherto unknown to her, her behaviour taking the superficial form of adulterous betrayal.

In the final chapter, the ever malevolent Hélène tells Élisabeth how, at the carnival in Nice, she has bumped into Edmond, 'ton "ex"', 'cette expression d'un goût médiocre étant en usage dans son [Hélène's] milieu, où n'étaient pas rares les femmes divorcées' (280–81). She recounts the miracle of Edmond's return to health (Élisabeth's prayer has worked), and from the other side of the moral mirror, repeats in cattish fashion the point that Edmond's passing would have allowed Elisabeth to 'régularise[r] [s]a situation'. When challenged by André, Hélène defends her position by reference to her own daughter, for whom she is now seeking a husband: 'Dernièrement il avait été question pour Antoinette d'un homme divorcé, à son profit... Cela n'aurait pas été une cause d'hésitation, si sa fortune m'avait paru suffisante' (281–82).

André later presses Élisabeth over Hélène's far from innocent remark that Mme Lambertier was very impressed with Élisabeth's appearance these days. Élisabeth confesses her visit and admits that she offered Edmond absolution, and then argues that André should not care about her prayer for Edmond, if he does not believe in its religious force, to which he replies: 'que cet homme vive ou bien qu'il meure, cela ne m'est de rien, puisque nous nous aimons' (299). In conversation with Augustin, moreover, he admits that there must be more to the force of religion than mere emotion. Rather than ending with an improbable conversion, the door is left open as their conversation ends: 'il n'a pas dit non,' and their meetings will continue: 'Qui sait, en effet?' (302). And at one more of those Bertereau family dinners, André reveals more than a hint of rediscovered faith. In the final words of the novel, even that scrupulous atheist, Doctor Bertereau, must recognize the force of mysticism in the face of the dominant rationality of modernity. Bovet's 'feminist' novel, I would argue, embodies a significant position in the moral ideology of turn-of-the-century France, between patriarchal Catholicism and modernizing feminism. For she sympathizes with the tale of the divorcee (Élisabeth) yet retains a sense of religion's insistent power.

Bourget's and Bovet's accounts of divorce speak to a wider debate at the turn of the century on the subject of retrospective jealousy, and exemplary in this regard is Anatole France's love affair with Mme de Caillavet, and his novel *Le Lys rouge* (1894), on which we will focus in the bulk of this chapter.

The question of jealousy has, of course, received particular attention from psychoanalysis and literature; and the pre-Freudian world of nineteenth-century France helped to define the notion of retrospective jealousy, to which Freud and Proust both speak so eloquently. It is in this context that the divorce debate raises all sorts of problems around the issue of jealousy, in particular male jealousy about women with a past. Bourget's *Un divorce* and, as we shall see in the next chapter, Alphonse Daudet's *Rose et Ninette* are typical of the way in which male authors questioned the possibility of male love surviving the demands of retrospective jealousy. In Thomas Hardy's 1883 novella, *The Romantic Adventures of a Milkmaid*, we learn:

> 'Well,' said Jim [to Margery], with no great concern (for '*la jalousie rétrospective*,' as George Sand calls it, had nearly died out of him), 'however he [the mysterious gentleman] might move 'ee, my love, he'll never come. He swore it to me: and he was a man of his word.'[12]

Certainly Sand (whose long-held notoriety is explained in no small degree by her serial loves) uses the concept, in Chapter 12 of the account of her affair with Musset, *Elle et lui* (1859), to warn against love on the rebound:

> Il faut bien dire [...] que la plus mauvaise circonstance possible pour établir un lien sérieux, c'est de vouloir trop vite posséder une âme qui vient d'être brisée. L'aurore d'une pareille union se présente avec des illusions généreuses; mais la jalousie rétrospective est un mal incurable et engendre des orages que la vieillesse même ne dissipe pas toujours.[13]

Already, though, in *La Cousine Bette* (1847), Balzac too invokes the notion in the context of Crevel's mimetic desire, and thus transposes it from the sexual to the social domain, so as to explain his anachronistic tastes:

> Avez-vous remarqué comme, dans l'enfance, ou dans les commencements de la vie sociale, nous nous créons de nos propres mains un modèle à notre insu, souvent? Ainsi le commis d'une maison de banque rêve, en entrant dans le salon de son patron, de posséder un salon pareil. S'il fait fortune, ce ne sera pas, vingt ans plus tard, le luxe alors à la mode qu'il intronisera chez lui, mais le luxe arriéré qui le fascinait jadis. On ne sait pas toutes les sottises dues à cette jalousie rétrospective, de même qu'on ignore toutes les folies dues à ces rivalités secrètes qui poussent les hommes à imiter le type qu'ils se sont donné, à consumer leurs forces pour être un clair de lune.[14]

Although the influential psychoanalytically inspired reading of Balzac's novel which Fredric Jameson offers necessarily and persuasively draws the social back to the sexual (indeed Freudian) paradigm (note the analogy with 'enfance' here), Balzac himself displaces the habitually sexual language of jealousy so as to read Crevel's social desires as the emblem of the class history of post-revolutionary France. The new man, or parvenu, Crevel, cannot help replicating the style of the old. Given the focus on the second lover in works such as *Le Lys rouge*, it is worth noting Flaubert's subsequently erased use of the term in the *brouillon* vol. 6 folio 44^{v} of *Madame Bovary*. Of its version of Part III Chapter 6, where we witness the rapid

decadence of her affair with Léon (her second lover), Hervé Audouard offers the
following transcription:

> il en était ~~venu~~ à ce point de ~~curiosité froide~~
> *passion*
> où on désire les origines, et où on entrevoit les antécédents
> qui n'est pas de la jalousie rétrospective mais une curiosité scientifique
> un besoin de critiquer[15]

So much for lexical history. What of narrative theory? One of the most significant
accounts in recent decades of jealousy in literature has been Malcolm Bowie's *Freud,
Proust and Lacan*, in particular Chapter 2 on 'Proust, jealousy, knowledge'.[16] He
highlights those hitherto obscured sections of Proust's novel (*Sodome et Gomorrhe*, *La
Prisonnière* and *La Fugitive*) 'in which the narrator discusses at length such "negative"
emotional states as jealousy, distrust or envy' (46). Bowie identifies the paradoxical
connection between the psychologically negative experience of jealousy and the
narratologically positive force of epistemophilia: 'The jealous lover hears, and
heeds, an imperious call to *know*. His privilege is to be summoned to the limits of
what is thinkable, and to risk everything for a glimpse of what lies beyond' (49). In
the context of Albertine's enigmatic sexuality:

> Jealousy [...] is the quest for knowledge untrammelled and unsupported by
> things actually known. It is a continuous journey towards a receding goal,
> an itinerary with no-stopping places and no landmarks; it is an appetite for
> knowledge but knows nothing. (58)

But then:

> Jealousy is an alertness of eye and ear and intellect; it is an experience of manifold
> potentiality; it is a stimulus to the making of fictions; it is a comprehensive way
> of inhabiting space and time. When these things are produced by pain and
> absence they may be called jealousy. But the same things, rediscovered in joy,
> and by joy transformed, may as fittingly be called *knowledge*. (64)

Both lovers and narrators love to know, and in particular love to know about love.
And these positive and negative elements point to what we might term this paradox
of paranoia. In their famous guide to Freudian vocabulary, Laplanche and Pontalis
do not have the space for 'an exposition of a Freudian theory of paranoia'. The
one point they do gloss, however, is that 'paranoia is defined in psychoanalysis,
whatever the variations in its delusional modes, as a defence against homosexuality'.
Pre-Proustian divorce plots defend themselves against homosexuality (but thus in
some sense expose themselves) by exploring homosocial bounds between men. The
second man takes from the first man, but in theory at least he takes that which has
already been yielded by the first, as French law forbad the subsequent marriage of
spouse and lover (by contrast with the reparative model of English law and custom
which encouraged such recuperative marriages).

    The focus of Bowie's analysis of paranoid jealousy is Proust's 'comedy of mis-
applied intellect' in *La Prisonnière*, and in particular the narrator's concern for the
unfathomable quality of Albertine's putative lesbianism. The narrator has phantasies
of omniscience. In Bowie's rendering, 'If only he could travel freely in the time and

space of her hidden deeds [...] he would be omnipresent in Albertine's life' (54–55). And from the kind of masterful *legato* typical of Bowie's prose, his subsequent gloss may remind us of other epistemological issues germane to classic nineteenth-century fiction (Christopher Prendergast's analogy between fictions of adultery and crime, Carlo Ginzburg's conjectural paradigm, and indeed a Foucauldian model of the novel-as-panopticon): 'Surveillance of this kind would produce the state of "total intelligence" that undercover agents no doubt dream about in their moments of rest and recuperation.' Albertine's journey through space and time is not so easily mastered, of course: 'The trouble is always that the beloved has mental processes of her own; to make matters worse, she has a past, and, still worse, she thinks, desires and performs actions when she is not in his company.' Whereas the lesbian theme renders all the more desperate and absurd the scientific aspirations of the narrator, in that it posits another order of desire which the oedipal world cannot decode, the heterosexual divorce and remarriage plot with which we are concerned creates a sense of viable competitiveness, or coherent rivalry, which turns on the notions of repetition and copy in love and threatens the idea of unique romantic love. Is the second man at root little more than another version of the first man, caught in the same structure of relationship? This structural similarity between previous and subsequent heterosexual loves both facilitates and impedes the imaginative capacity of male paranoia; the second man is at once both too similar to and too different from him — or, heaven forbid, those — who precede him. Although novels of the time did not always view the problem of a woman's past from the perspective of the second man, that perspective was afforded by fiction a considerable force. Such jealousy was an emotion which could not simply be wished or washed away by reason.

Now, Bowie is quite right to distinguish Proust from his more banal predecessors, due to 'an epistemological resonance quite different from anything that we could expect from a plain psychological account of jealousy and lying' (52), and *Le Lys rouge* may well be one such account. Still, Bowie concludes his book by appealing for engagement between sociology and psychoanalysis, and I would suggest that the nineteenth-century divorce debate provided a sociologically particular exemplar of a general psychological form. And it is not just that jealousy is a psychological effect of the divorce plot (and the double and serial lives it precipitates). For structurally, jealousy, divorce and memory are all forms of doubleness which, however menacing to the romantic identity politics of the sublime and unique moment, proffer vantage points of reflection and reflexivity. The synthetic potential of double lives (and the doubleness of life) emerges, almost in spite of Empson, in his account of the epiphany of involuntary memory in *Le Temps retrouvé*:

> Sometimes, when you are living in one place you are reminded of living in another place, and this, since you are now apparently living in two places, means that you are outside of time, in the only state of beatitude he can imagine. In any one place (atmosphere, mental climate) life is intolerable; in any two it is an ecstasy. Is it the number two, one is forced to speculate, which is of this encouraging character? Is to live in $n+1$ places necessarily more valuable than to live in n?[17]

And often in a highly literal sense, divorce raises the spectre (and spectrality) of living in $n+1$ places (and finding an afterlife in this life). As Bowie glosses, 'this latecoming joy, which resembles certainty and has the status of proof, is the receding goal of the jealous quest finally bought to a stop' (63).

If one makes inquiries about claret from the Château de Caillavet, one encounters an almost self-parodically French fusion of fine wine, high literary culture and romance:

> Le Château de Caillavet est un grand vin mais c'est aussi un château chargé d'histoire. A la fin du 19ème siècle, Madame de Caillavet accueillait dans ses salons l'élite de la société intellectuelle et mondaine. Elle fût ainsi l'inspiratrice de nombreux écrivains de l'époque: Flaubert, Proust et Anatole France avec qui elle eut une liaison passionnée. Le Château de Caillavet fût en effet le théâtre de cette émouvante histoire d'amour, pleine de rebondissements et de passion entre deux êtres exceptionnels par leur intelligence et leur sensibilité.[18]

Their story is told, or rather translated, by Anatole France's *Le Lys rouge* of 1894. France, like many of the men accounted for in this book, is one of those white-bearded patriarchs who has failed the test of the modernist canon, but without whom Third Republic literary life remains, in truth, incomprehensible. His biological death in 1924 was celebrated by the literary violence of the Surrealist pamphlet *Un cadavre*, which included Aragon's 'Avez-vous giflé un mort?' Readers of this Florentine novel will not be surprised to learn of E. M. Forster's interest in Anatole France's work.[19] Proust himself, of course, was a follower of France and famously consecrated his master in the figure of Bergotte. When the Swedish poet Erik Karlfeldt presented Anatole France for his Nobel Prize in 1921, however, this particular novel by the 'new Voltaire' was singled out for criticism: 'We may reproach him for [...] the hedonistic sentiments, for example, which he describes under the sign of the red lily of Florence, and which are not made for serious minds.' Until the middle of the twentieth century, *Le Lys rouge* was nevertheless ranked amongst the dozen greatest French novels published on the subject of love during the Third Republic.[20] It is, in Pierre Brunel's words, 'un roman de la jalousie comparable aux plus grands.'[21]

The backstory is simple enough, and best recounted in terms of the amorous conveyance of the heroine between men. Thérèse Martin-Belleme, daughter of a wealthy financier, has her marriage arranged with a cold and aloof aristocrat engaged in the world of high politics. Six years on, they lead essentially separate lives, despite keeping up appearances. She takes on a lover, Robert Le Ménil, a sportsman with whom she has a rather uninspiring affair. The plot itself centres on the displacement of this first affair by a second, with the young sculptor Jacques Dechartre, whom she meets at a dinner party in Paris and with whom she begins a liaison during her stay in Fiesole, near Florence, where she stays with an English pre-Raphaelite poet, Miss Vivian Bell (sometimes associated with the English poet Mary Robinson, wife of the Orientalist James Darmester). She is accompanied on the train through France by her loyal friend Madame Marmet and the political radical and writer Choulette (sometimes associated with Verlaine). Despite the vacuity of their passion, Robert refuses to give up Thérèse without a fight ('Qu'est-

ce que vous venez me dire? Une liaison, cela se dénoue. On se prend, on se quitte...
Eh bien, non! vous n'êtes pas une personne qu'on quitte, vous' (144), to which she
later replies, 'Je vois qu'on ne se quitte jamais bien' (149)).

Thérèse maintains an exchange of letters with Robert, even though she has
repudiated his love; and it is this exchange which fuels Jacques's jealousy, not least
when Robert comes in person to Italy. Jacques the aesthete seems naive to the
ethical question of correspondence: 'Il contempla les addresses sans les lire, avec une
admiration sensuelle', looking rather than reading. This theme of correspondence
provides us with an articulation of the triangular, and indeed quadrilateral,
geometry of Thérèse's adultery, which is in a double sense graphic. Husband and
lover (like Charles and Rodolphe) may be correlative terms in the grammar of the
nineteenth-century love plot (just as blasphemy requires law); and Thérèse's sense
that she must reply to Robert seems to reflect the sense of *correspondere* in medieval
Latin as *rendre compte*, or even *payer en retour* (the exchange of love and letters
accorded its market sense too). But both lovers, Robert and Jacques (like Rodolphe
and Léon) can also be viewed in a legal sense as co-respondents (*complices d'adultère*).
Although the adultery plot is inspired by the quest for unique love (the oneness of
two), it habitually degenerates into typological love. The focus of Jacques's obsession
with the epistolary residue of Thérèse's first adultery is her tiny gloved hand (to
which the narrator too habitually returns); it both writes and posts, concealing the
letter in an envelope as it conceals itself in a glove; and the handshake it offers both
is and is not an act of touching.

The novel's story centres on the plot of the failed second affair and Jacques's
ultimate inability to accept Thérèse's past. The 'idée fixe' of his obsessive passion
cannot negotiate the transmission of Thérèse between men as liquid love demands.
In Chapter 21, Thérèse struggles to manage the transmission of confluent love.
Robert's arrival in Florence reminds her, in Bourget's language of the irreparable,
of 'le premier baiser de l'ami, le commencement de l'irréparable amour' (142). She
attempts to break definitively by proposing that the past-in-the-future needs to be
managed carefully. When he refuses to forget, she vainly attempts to recast their
history by claiming falsely that she has been 'légère'. She persists in her bid by tying
friendship to chronology (and an innovative ethics of heterosociality to a confluent
model of amorous time): 'Elle se fit l'illusion qu'elle pouvait peut-être le consoler
d'elle. Amicale et confiante, elle vint s'asseoir près de lui' (146). She implores him:

> Mais gardez-moi un peu d'amitié dans votre colère, un souvenir aigre et doux,
> comme ces temps d'automne, où il y a du soleil et de la bise. [...] Faites-moi
> des adieux comme à une voyageuse qui s'en va on ne sait où [...]. L'avenir est
> toujours inconnu. Il est bien vague, bien obscur devant moi. Que je ne puisse
> dire que j'ai été bonne, simple, franche avec vous, et que vous ne l'avez pas
> oublié. Avec le temps, vous comprendrez, vous pardonnerez. [...] La vie n'est
> pas clémente. On est jetée, poussée, ballottée... (146–47)

Robert meets this heterosocial proposal with violence, trying literally to force
Thérèse's gloved hand to write a letter of repudiation to Jacques, until she declares
her love for Jacques openly. Thérèse's fantasy is that heterosocial and heterosexual
affection (for Robert and Jacques respectively) can run in tandem. Robert believes

(and by that very belief, ensures) that they cannot. Against this heterosocial offer, he warns Thérèse of the 'galanterie' which awaits her: 'L'année prochaine, on dira de vous: "Elle traîne avec tout le monde."' And voices this fear homosocially: 'Cela me contrarie pour votre père, qui est un de mes amis.' Robert's pedestal for Thérèse imposes on love an implacable serial logic: 'elle n'était plus à lui parce qu'elle était à un autre' (150). All of this serves as a prelude to the (re)consummation of the hateful love of Thérèse and Jacques, as Thérèse makes love for the second time with her second lover (the lover being, archetypally, the second man of the virginal bride). Jealousy, France suggests, is implicit in the heterosexual encounter itself: 'Puis, subitement graves, les yeux assombris, les lèvres serrées, en proie à cette colère sacrée, qui fait que l'amour ressemble à la haine, ils se reprenaient, se mêlaient et cherchaient l'abîme' (150–51). Love and art hold this couple in the grip of a conflict over the management of time, hence the dual reference in Jacques's complaint that she has already discovered 'sans lui la beauté des choses'.

By a bitter irony, Miss Bell and one Prince Albertinelli chance upon Thérèse's meeting at the train station with Robert. In fact, she is repudiating his advances once again, but the jealous Albertinelli exposes this tryst before Jacques that very evening. Thérèse tries to persuade Jacques of the virtues of confluent love which liberate the present by repressing the past:

> Le présent est à vous, et vous savez qu'il n'y a que vous, vous seul, toi dedans. Quant à mon passé, si vous savez quel néant c'était, vous seriez content. [...] Les années écoulées sans vous, je ne les ai pas vécues. [...] Il ne s'y trouve rien dont je puisse avoir honte. Avoir regret, c'est autre chose: je regrette de vous avoir connu si tard. (161)

The tragedy of this novel is that Jacques simply cannot rewrite the script of possessive male desire in confluent fashion:

> Il n'y a pas dans le sang, dans la chair d'une femme, cette fureur absurde et généreuse de possession, cet antique instinct dont l'homme s'est fait un droit. [...] La jalousie n'est pour une femme que la blessure de l'amour-propre. Chez l'homme, c'est une torture profonde comme la souffrance morale, continue comme la souffrance physique... (162)

Both he and Thérèse agree that this is absurd; but, in Giddens's terms, their passion is nevertheless imprisoned on the border between romantic and confluent love.

Jacques follows Thérèse back to Paris, as she returns to her husband's side in public life at a time of political turmoil. First it seems that Garain is to form a new government, but then Berthier d'Eyzelles does so. Against this political backdrop and a performance of *Faust* at the opera, Thérèse continues to repel Robert's advances, but gossip, correspondence and unfortunate encounters mark the death-knell of this second adultery (the second second [*sic*] relationship). As in Vautier's *Adultère et divorce*, the *point culminant* is in fact a diminuendo, the embers of love left to burn and die in the ashtray of the emotional life, Thérèse walking out in the final sentence of the novel, 'sentant que tout était fini' (236).

Thérèse's father, Montessuy, entertains beautiful mistresses, whereas her mother has led a cloistered married life back in Joinville. Because he does not associate marriage with love, Montessuy fails to predict that his daughter (whom he takes to be 'une honnête femme') might be unhappy with her husband, Count Charles Martin-Bellème. Within a generation, however, just making do no longer seems acceptable. Her husband's family is associated with the rise of Bonaparte, Charles's grandfather linked in the novel with Joseph Lainé's (1768–1835) somewhat critical report to the Corps législatif of 29 December 1813. Charles's grandfather, a liberal nevertheless appreciated by Bonaparte, is said to have made the trip on New Year's Day to the Tuileries where an enraged Bonaparte called upon the Corps to support him. In a characteristically demagogic moment, Bonaparte clasps the shoulder of Charles's grandfather, leaving him 'tremblant et bègue' (35). Finally dying as a senator under Napoleon III, he continues to feel on his shoulder the Corsican's hand, and bequeaths this 'tremblement héréditaire' to Charles's father. This Napoleonic legacy is introduced to us in Chapter 3, when Thérèse and Jacques meet at a dinner party, where 'la conversation se fixa sur Napoléon plusieurs fois mis au théâtre et nouvellement étudié dans des livres très lus' (38).

Just as France returned to Empire and the name Napoleon, so too does *fin de siècle* fashion return to the figure of Bonaparte. Bonaparte himself took his second chance with Marie-Louise of Austria, disposing of Josephine; it looks, however, as if the nervous young Jacques has missed his opportunity to shine. Thérèse asks him in private conversation later that evening what he thinks of Napoleon. When he quips, 'je n'aime pas la Révolution. Et Napoléon, c'est la Révolution bottée' (43), she chastises him for keeping his wit under a bushel. In the event, he will be given a second chance by Thérèse, but he will not permit her one (or allow himself to be her second second chance).

Once she has planned her escape to Italy, her husband cannot understand why she is not drawn to his counter-offer of a trip eastwards. In a paradox at odds with the supposed autonomy of the male subject, it is he who will suffer most from the geographical separation which dramatizes their affective alienation: 'Ils avaient l'un et l'autre repris leur liberté, mais il n'aimait point être seul. Il ne se sentait lui-même qu'avec sa femme, et toute sa maison montée'. The irony is that she goes to Italy to escape her lover as much as her husband, and her mind wonders to Robert's love nest and a barely recognizable image of herself: 'cette jolie femme [...] à qui un ami donnait des baisers sur la nuque tandis qu'elle tordait ses cheveux devant la psyché, ce n'était pas même une femme qu'elle connût beaucoup ni qu'elle voulût connaître' (60). What she finds in second love (in adultery, and then in the second version of adultery) is the irreducible doubleness of selfhood. Like Mme de Caivallet, Thérèse does not divorce; and the penultimate chapter of the novel suggests that this childless marriage (which seems as sexless as that of George Sand's Indiana) does at least offer the possibility of heterosocial conversation without jealousy, as they discuss the new political situation. Still, in the wake of the scene at the opera, Thérèse must suffer a sleepless night before she can see Jacques again. Conjugal time offers time to kill and time that kills: 'Ce visage et cette voix pâle [of Charles] marquaient pour elle, comme une horloge, les minutes qui passaient une à une, lentement' (224). No sooner does she see him in the morning, however, than she has to return to the side of her husband, who has become a government minister. Rather than sweeping aside the sentimental life, his political success foregrounds the debilitating gap between the public and the private. Like the best Molière cuckolds, he turns out to be less of an unambiguous buffoon than pure farce might desire: 'Il se trouvait devant un secret qu'il ne voulait pas connaître, devant une douleur intime qu'un seul mot pouvait faire éclater. Il en ressentit de l'inquiétude, de la peur et comme une sorte de respect' (231). To return to the language of Donald Rumsfeld, Charles knows what he does not know, and in this he is not a mere victim of domestic ideology (if we define ideology as that which we do not know that we know, in other words, akin to the doxa, which in a double sense goes without saying).

It is one of the fundamental ironies of a novel such as this (like Rod's novels) that political success and personal defeat coincide. It looks in Chapter 31 as if Garain will form the new government. Garain was present at the dinner where Thérèse and Jacques met, when he is presented to the reader as 'l'homme de toutes les améliorations possibles [...] sans rappeler qu'il avait demandé [...] en 1880, la séparation des Églises et de l'Etat', and thus as a partner to the movement which led to the divorce law of 1884 (36). Jacques Dechartre represents a nostalgic critique of Third Republic politicians due to his father's favour under Napoleon III:

> Il fut combattu et injurié par des gens qui voulaient prendre sa place et qui n'avaient pas même, comme lui, au fond de l'âme, l'amour du peuple. Nous les avons vus depuis, au pouvoir. Ciel! qu'ils sont vilains! (178)

Thérèse's husband belongs to this motley crew too, of course. Jacques, it seems, prefers the copy to the original, the third man (like himself) who was in reality the second Napoleonic Emperor. In the chapter which precedes the scene at the opera, it looks as if Garain is to form the new government, but in the event it is Berthier d'Eyzelles who does so (both he and Charles deemed to have betrayed Garain). As the curtain rises on *Faust*, however, we are led to believe that the most influential backroom politician is none other than Thérèse's father, Montessuy. Charles, it seems, even owes his portfolio at *les finances* to his father-in-law, and once in power, feels the full weight of his powerlessness.

In that intimate heterosocial conversation with Thérèse, to which we have alluded above, he confesses: 'Je regardais les choses par le dehors. Vues du dedans, elles changent d'aspect. Et puis je ne suis plus libre' (224). One of the ideological issues which divorce fiction of the Third Republic (and a study such as this) faces is its resolutely supra-proletarian fixation. It is not without reason that Zola (with whom Anatole France only makes late alliance) takes such little interest in the question of divorce over which so much ink was spilt. France negotiates this exclusivity through a self-consciousness which is closer to the clunkiness of the *roman à thèse* or the *roman à clé* than Gide's *mise en abyme*, as we shall see below in the novel's references to reading and literature, and which we see here in Paul Vence's critique of the obsession of both politicians and the people with 'l'illusion du pouvoir' in the face of those universal determinants, hunger, love and death (217). His speech concludes: 'Il était sage, celui qui a dit: "Donnons aux hommes pour témoins et pour juges l'Ironie et la Pitié."' But Madame Martin undercuts such self-capitalizing grandiloquence immediately: 'Mais c'est vous-même qui avez écrit cela. Je vous lis.' The ill-concealed rhyming of Vence and France, and this novelist's self-citation point both outwards, with self-denying self-consciousness, and inwards to the knowingness of a Happy Few who may realize that France is quoting himself here too. This, then, is a way of distancing oneself from the genre of the *mondain* novel of high politics and high society in which one is nevertheless engaged.

At the start of the novel, Thérèse is involved in an affair which leaves her 'sans joie aiguë et sans tristesse profonde' (9). Thérèse's first lover, Robert le Ménil, is frightened of gossip, whereas Thérèse shows less timidity. He may be a sportsman rather than an aesthete (he is said to have introduced the French to football, which is now 'très à la mode' (158)). But he is no hero. Her *de facto* separation from Charles after six years is followed by two years of abstinence (repelling the marquis de Ré), before she yields to Robert. But after three years of the affair, it is clear that their adultery will never be more than platitudinous: 'Il lui rendait la vie, non pas constamment délicieuse, mais très facile, à supporter, et, par moments, agréable' (26). So not so different from her marriage, after all.

The novel, then, charts the ongoing project of Thérèse's desire, and Chapter 2 depicts her dissatisfaction with Robert. In conversation, Paris acts as a screen onto which his banality and her imagination are projected. However patronizing her interest in proletarian life (such as her pleasure in eating chips on a street corner), she can at least proclaim: 'Je n'ai pas un goût, j'ai des goûts' (29). An index of their ideological as well as sentimental difference is her critique of his unthinking religious belief: 'nous ne savons que faire de cette vie si courte, et vous en voulez une autre qui ne finisse pas' (32). These different attitudes to time will be thematized at large in the novel, as Thérèse confronts the problem of making more of a secular life which promises in Hobbesian vein to be 'nasty, brutish and short', if not 'solitary' and 'poor'.

Things come to a head in Chapter 4 once Thérèse has learned by other means that he intends to abandon her for some time by going away on a fox-hunting expedition. She responds by piquing his male paranoia: 'C'est vrai que ce n'est jamais bien prudent de laisser une femme seule' (49), and stresses the influence her father has exerted on her, particularly her pride in his material achievements and her consequent desire not to be taken for a ride: 'Je suis une enfant de parvenu, ou de conquérant, c'est la même chose' (50). When it becomes clear that she could in fact dissuade Robert from going, she declines the opportunity: 'il était trop tard', a refrain, as we shall see, in France's affair with Mme de Caillavet (51). Now separated from Robert, as she is in another fashion separated from Charles, Thérèse walks back home on foot, not shocked to be mistaken for a streetwalker (unlike André Léo's Claire Desfayes). There is a matter-of-factness to her pedestrian reflections on a love now lived through, which facilitates a conspicuously modern desire for sentimental closure: 'C'était une liaison sérieuse. Elle s'était donnée avec la gravité d'une joie nécessaire' (53). Adultery and virtue, she concludes, can coincide: 'Trois ans de ma vie, un honnête homme qui m'aime et que j'aimais, car je l'aimais. [...] Je ne suis pas une femme perdue.' The stereotype of hysterical female transgression appears to be a long way in the distance.

The role of *flâneuse* metaphorizes the alienating gap between her self and her past in a manner which allows her the equanimity to embrace her own future:

> Il lui semblait que l'aventure était arrivée à une autre femme, à une étrangère qu'elle n'aimait pas beaucoup, qu'elle ne comprenait guère. [...] Elle voyait tout comme par une fenêtre, quand on passe dans la rue. (53)

Flippancy allows her to say of Robert's limitations, 'ce n'était pas une faute contre elle, ce n'était rien, c'était tout. C'était la fin', and of their sex life 'la vie n'est pas grand-chose. Et ce qu'on met dedans, ce que c'est peu!' (54). As well as providing access to her own adventures, such flippancy again allows the novel itself to sidestep the accusation that it lacks the gravity of a Naturalist novel (and in so doing, embrace and disarm that accusation). She may now be happy to be alone, but is not alone for long, bumping by chance into Jacques Dechartre. Here we witness the meeting of the aleatory *imprévu* of the modern street and the less random patterns of salon society (or, in other words, of the *urbain* and the *mondain*). They meet by chance, but already know each other. And so the life narrative of serial adultery (rather than the serial monogamy which modern sociologists sometimes take to be the mark of amorous authenticity in our own times) can unfold.

Once in Florence, Thérèse receives in Chapter 12 the reproachful letter she expects from Robert, and burns it: 'Il n'avait pas changé, lui. Il était le même homme qu'avant. Elle n'était plus la même femme' (105). The different selves which generate alienation also generate in Thérèse liquid self-reinvention. But it is precisely the stubbornness of Robert's half-presence which undermines Jacques's feelings for her. Prior to the scene at the opera, which reignites Jacques's jealousy, Robert admits that he has been stalking Thérèse for two days, 'un fantôme vu dans les limbes d'un monde antérieur, dans les ténèbres d'une demi-vie' (207). He explains how he has tried to forget her by taking out to sea for six months a boat with the English name *Rosebud*. And for a moment she almost sympathizes with his lament 'Oh! Si c'était à recommencer!' (208). In the next breathe, he promises to forget the past, if only she will have him back ('je vous pardonne et j'oublie tout', 210), but she knows not to trust such a brittle promise. The next time they will meet will be at the opera. It is alleged that Orson Welles's wilfully enigmatic reference to the word 'rosebud' in *Citizen Kane* (1941) owes less to Anatole France than it does to tycoon William Randolph Hearst's nickname for the clitoris of his mistress, Marion Davies (their relationship thinly veiled in this movie by Hearst's enemy, Kane). As we shall discuss below, the question of women's sexual past is filtered through the floral symbolism attached to the title of France's novel. What value the bud, and the memory of the bud, France asks, in the wake of defloration?

Prior to love is flirtation, that gaze towards other narrative possibilities which opens up negotiations for the transmission of individuals from one relationship to another and thus liquefies love. When Thérèse and Jacques bump into each other in Chapter 4, their first proper conversation concerns the art and women of Italy. This conversation, and chapter, end with him lamenting: 'Les femmes du monde ? Oh! Il y en a de charmantes. Quant à les aimer, c'est toute une affaire', to which she replies, 'Croyez-vous?' before shaking his hand and heading off around the corner (56). At Miss Bell's dinner party, in Chapter 10, he flirts back by complimenting her attire with an informed scrutiny which other straight men seem not to enjoy:

> Elle croyait les hommes capables seulement de sentir l'effet d'une toilette, sans
> en comprendre les détails ingénieux. Quelques-uns, qui avaient l'intelligence
> du chiffon, la déconcertaient par un air efféminé et des goûts équivoques. Elle
> se résignait à ne voir apprécier les élégances de sa mise que par des femmes,
> qui y apportaient un esprit petit, de la malveillance et de l'envie. L'admiration
> artiste et mâle de Dechartre la surprit et lui plut. (96)

When his sexual desire for her blossoms in the next chapter, however, the reader
witnesses the tension between the force of heterosexuality and the fantasy of
heterosociality. His heterosexual desire threatens to close off his heterosocial
openness: 'Il fut presque surpris qu'elle parlât, qu'elle pensât' (102), even though in
his later insistence on the virtues of Dante, he declaims: 'Il faut que vous me preniez
avec mon âme' rather than conquering her 'avec une âme étrangère' (114). At the
start of the next chapter, we see that she requires his sexual love, although her desire
for him is filtered through the beauty of art as well as life: 'C'est par lui, c'est en lui
qu'elle comprenait l'art et la vie' (102). At their first tryst at Lungarno Acciaoli, in
Chapter 16, she promises herself to him on Saturday, but makes him wait. She offers
him friendship but 'la torture de l'idée fixe' of desire compels him to demand an
ideal sexual and artistic fusion: 'Leur existence serait une œuvre d'art belle et cachée.
Ils penseraient, comprendraient, sentiraient ensemble' (122–23). Their reflections are
interrupted by the passage of a night-time funeral procession, 'la Mort importune,
qu'on ne salue pas sur cette terre voluptueuse', and which foregrounds a question
vital to Thérèse's contemplations: what should we do before we die? Even before
their love is consummated, however, they sense the incompleteness of love: 'Est-ce
qu'on possède jamais ce qu'on aime? Est-ce que les baisers, les caresses sont autre
chose que l'effort d'un désespoir délicieux?' (176).

The conversation in the final chapter between 'darling et Dechartre', as Miss
Bell names them, parallels the sleepless night which they have both just undergone,
Jacques almost driven to lunacy. His is not a death-wish, but a desire for untroubled
sleep: 'Il aurait voulu dormir; non pas mourir' (228). In vain, Thérèse explains
the lack of malice in her obfuscation of the truth about her continued contact
with Robert (and thus the contradictory zone of negotiation demanded by the
transmission between confluent loves):

> En mentant, je ne t'ai pas trompé. [...] Je ne savais pas que tu devais venir. Je
> m'ennuyais. [...] Mais si tu savais à quel point cela n'existe plus, n'a jamais existé.
> [...] Pourquoi n'es-tu pas venu plus tôt? (229)

Against the tragedy of tardy love, she asserts the ethics of confluent rebirth: 'Mais
je te parle d'une autre femme. Je n'ai rien de commun avec cette femme-là. Moi,
je n'existe que depuis que je t'ai connu, depuis que j'ai été à toi' (230). Time and
again, she retells him her tale, and time and again, he refuses to accept it: 'Le passé,
l'irréparable passé, elle le lui rendait présent par ses aveux' (233).

Vital to this refusal of reparation is the idealizing logic of the pedestal. She
attempts comparison: 'On voit tous les jours des femmes apporter à leur amant un
passé plus lourd que le mien et se faire aimer, pourtant'; to which he replies: 'Je sais
ce que vous donnez. On ne peut pas vous pardonner, à vous, ce qu'on pardonnerait
à une autre.' She invokes the norm ('je suis comme les autres'), but is condemned

by the ideal ('vous n'êtes pas comme les autres. A vous, on ne peut rien pardonner'). Even her offer of suicide does not suffice.

I would suggest that *Le Lys rouge* remains, in its aesthetic vision, resolutely pre-Proustian and pre-modernist (in spite of its philosophical anticipations of the life politics of liquid modernity, and its foregrounding of thematic concerns which Proust will alchemically transmute). Still, the language of jealousy and betrayal suffuses France's text. At first, amorous jealousy resembles one of the virtues of love. On the train journey to Italy, Thérèse's apparently tame companion, Madame Marmet, explains to her friend's surprise how she had to give up dancing because of her husband's jealousy. Thérèse remembers 'un vieux monsieur timide et absorbé, un peu ridicule', but 'l'excellente veuve' recalls how, when he was fifty-five and she fifty-three, he remained 'jaloux comme au premier jour' (77). And this, it seems, is the novel's model of the faithful marriage. Thérèse compares this to Robert's lack of jealousy. Is this tact, good taste, confidence, or proof of his insufficient love? She does not know and dare not investigate the 'tiroirs de son âme'.

Jacques's jealousy is triggered in Chapter 15 even before their love has been consummated: 'Elle le trouva bizarre d'être jaloux sans en avoir le droit' (120). He rightly presumes that the letter Thérèse posts under the watchful eye of Saint Mark in the church of Orsanmichele is intended for Robert, but he does not understand its content: 'C'était bien clair. Elle avait un amant.' In the chapter which follows the sexual consummation of Jacques and Thérèse, Choulette explains to her the violence of male desire and jealousy by recalling his own unsuccessful flirtation with her: 'En vous voyant sourire, j'ai eu envie de vous tuer. [...] C'est un sentiment très naturel, et que vous avez dû inspirer bien des fois' (134). *La Bête humaine* had been published only four years earlier. When she meets Jacques that afternoon at San Marco, for the first time since their consummation, she is struck by 'la vision brusque de l'irréparable', sex as the experience of the body which cannot be erased. Of course, for Jacques, it is her sexual relationship with Robert which will prove to be, in Bourget's language, irreparable.

It is in the set speeches in Chapter 23 that this conflict comes to the fore. In response to Jacques's paranoid fixation with the 'nom' or the 'idée' of betrayal (160), she offers that model of confluent love and decompartmentalized time we have already met: 'Le présent est à vous' (161). Her regretful fantasy is that he might have been her first lover, not her husband (and first man): 'Je me serais laissé prendre par vous il y a cinq ans, aussi volontiers qu'aujourd'hui.' In a gender-inverted Wagnerian reference, she reminds him of Lohengrin who, France knows, offers his love only on a no-questions-asked basis. Thérèse offers him the future (both her future and the future of modern love), but he cannot escape atavistic masculinity. As in *La Bête humaine*, male sociopathy is in some sense protected from the process of historical change.

In a number of the novels under consideration in this book, heterosexual love becomes the bodily site of an epistemic conflict between an ancient male model (of ancient forces) and a modern female counter-paradigm for love (love reinvented, as Rimbaud beseeches, but in a heterosexual mode). The personal tragedy of living through such historical conflict is only intensified by the self-consciousness of the protagonists. In a striking reworking of Goethe's chemical model of love, Jacques laments: 'Je suis le chimiste qui, étudiant les propriétés de l'acide qu'il a avalé, sait avec quelles bases il se combine et quels sels il forme. Cependant l'acide le brûle et le brûlera jusqu'aux os.' There is no metadiscursive pedestal for the chemists and Pygmalions in the artful science of modern love. Both Jacques and Thérèse are conscious of the 'bêtise publique', or absurdity, of such male possessiveness, which leaves women no inhabitable subject position: 'l'adorer telle que la vie l'a faite et regretter amèrement que la vie, qui l'a tant embellie, l'ait seulement touchée' (163).

In a manner that is so telling in this art novel, this male desire to mould acquires pygmalionesque proportions: 'tu es la matière et moi l'idée, tu es la chose, et moi l'âme, tu es l'argile et moi l'artisan.' Such self-indulgent masculine masochism and pessimism articulate a post-Romantic aesthetic where truth and beauty no longer coincide. In fact, it is this Galetea who shows true artfulness in love: 'dans une sourde volonté de se donner mieux et plus que jamais, elle osa ce qu'elle n'eût pas cru possible d'oser' (164). Such an improbable sexual act might be unspeakable, but it is not *illisible*, encoded as it is in the quasi-pictorial symbolic language of myth and the decorative motifs of the love nest:

> Une ombre chaude enveloppait la chambre. Des rayons d'or, dardés au bord des rideaux, éclairaient le panier de fraises posé sur la table près d'un flacon de vin d'Asti. Au chevet du lit, l'ombre claire de la dame vénétienne souriait de ses lèvres décolorées.

Are Thérèse's lips similarly discoloured? His post-coital melancholy ('je sais maintenant ce que tu donnes') is met by her assertion of the uniqueness of their love (within the narrative series of her life): 'Vous pouvez croire que j'ai été avec un autre ce que je suis avec vous!' (165). 'Perversion' offers an unsuccessful route to authenticity and, in a double sense, originality, as the tearful final words of the chapter proclaim: 'C'est la première fois que j'aime et qu'on m'aime vraiment'. In the penultimate chapter, as she lies awake, she realizes the extent of this jealousy: 'Il était jaloux avec une monstrueuse sensualité. Elle le savait, qu'en lui la jalousie était une torture physique, une plaie avivée, élargie par toutes les tenailles de l'imagination' (225). She may be guilty of a few untruths, but not of sexual betrayal.

The atavistic power of jealousy represents an ancient force which ties Jacques to the past, both personally and paradigmatically, and as such it represents a primary obstacle to the innovative force of confluent love. Quite how such a reform of love might be brought about remains a moot point in the novel. In his discussion with Garain about economic reform, Thérèse's father offers a model of historical change at odds with the interventions of policy and law: 'Dans la société comme dans la nature, les transformations s'opèrent par le dedans' (36). Later, when Thérèse and Jacques meet in San Marco, he recalls their encounter on the streets of Paris, as she walked home, apparently free of Robert. Here, transformation and movement speak to Jacques's aesthetics of beauty: 'Je vous voyais marcher. C'est par les mouvements que les formes parlent' (137). Walking is not, in the other sense of the term, a pedestrian activity. In political terms too, Thérèse refuses the atavistic force of *ancien régime* nostalgia: 'elle ne pensait point que le passé eût jamais été meilleur que le présent' (76). To Choulette she asserts: 'les hommes ont été de tout temps ce qu'ils sont aujourd'hui, égoïstes, violents, avares et sans pitié.' She thereby embraces the future precisely because of universal human qualities.

There were clearly moral dangers for nineteenth-century heroines who embraced over enthusiastically the ethos of confluent love, and France is keen to save Thérèse from such excess. In hindsight, she barely understands why she told her husband that she was leaving to visit Miss Bell in Italy, and in Chapter 6 has to persuade Mme Marmet to accompany her. And France is adept in shifting the dimensions of her decision. Rather than embracing the morally dubious temporal logic of seriality, Thérèse is drawn to the spatial appeal of geometry, 'une agréable symétrie' in leaving Paris as Robert leaves Paris (68). This is a matter of aesthetics rather than 'une petite vengeance'. On the one hand, the break with Robert seems clean enough: 'Tout à coup il était sorti de sa vie.' Yet the chains which hold together a serial life are harder to negotiate: 'Sans que leur liaison fût en rien rompue, il était devenu pour elle un étranger.' It is this undecideability which Jacques cannot accept. All she can array against this is the fantasy of apocalypse, 'la fin du monde', an implausible but irresistible end to things, 'imprévu, nécéssaire'.

This characteristically *fin de siècle* language first appears in Thérèse's daydream at the dinner table with her husband at the start of Chapter 5, when she recalls Robert's announcement of his hunting plans and subsequent departure as 'le tremblement d'un espèce de fin du monde' (57–58). The narrator thus anticipates her conversation, in the next chapter, with M. Lagrange of the Académie des sciences who explains 'avec une sincérité profonde' how the improbable but possible collision of the earth with a comet must be prevented. Unable to muster much enthusiasm for the perpetuation of the planet and the species, she notes of the urgent Lagrange: 'Il aime la vie' (70). The possibilities of confluent love stand opposed to the suicidal impulse of the *Liebestod* voiced at the end of Chapter 9 in Miss Bell's poem 'Lors au pied des rochers...': 'Et souvent ils pleuraient, se sentant trop heureux. / Ils comprirent que vivre était mauvais pour eux' (86). The satisfaction of the lovers' suicide ('ils ne désiraient plus rien') contrasts with Miss Bell's hopeful view of the future: '*Oh! bright king To-Morrow!*' For Choulette, however, waiting represents what Bauman will call liquid fear, rather than liquid hope, in an admixture of the domestic and the infinite which speaks back to the Baudelaire of 'Les Fenêtres': 'Nous avons l'air de gens qui attendent. [...] Vous est-il possible de regarder une porte, [...] ou celle-ci, ou toute autre, sans être saisie d'épouvante et d'horreur à la pensée du visiteur qui peut à tout moment venir?' (89).

And it is the end of waiting which so pleases Jacques when, finally, in Chapter 26, Thérèse visits his home in Paris: 'vous voilà! Le monde peut finir', which reminds her of Lagrange's theories (175). For Thérèse, unlike Jacques, it is the dearth of love which led her to embrace the end of things: 'Quand je ne vous connaissais pas, je m'ennuyais tant!' For her, unlike Jacques, love is not the emblem of end-stopped romanticism, but the reward for refusing death and living on.

In fact, art and love, male possessiveness and liquid female identity meet in an odd union. During the initial idyll of their return to Paris, Thérèse yields to the archetypal mode of feminine submission, defining herself in terms of the male gaze: 'Je m'aime parce que tu m'aimes' (182). With the autofictional force of *style indirect libre*, the narrator asserts the fixity of Jacques's and Anatole France's idealizing male desire: 'On trouve une femme entre mille qu'on ne peut plus quitter, dès qu'on l'a possédée, et qu'on veut toujours, et qu'on veut encore'. When Thérèse fails to recognize herself in the sketch of her which Jacques carries in his pocket, he stresses yet further the appropriative force of male desire: 'Il est probable que tu ne te vois pas tout à fait comme je te vois' (183). But then he gaily cites Paul Vence's idea that 'En ce sens on peut dire qu'une même femme n'a jamais appartenu à deux hommes,' with which Thérèse agrees. Precisely because of the male gaze, it is suggested, women may reinvent themselves anew for their next lover. In his darker moments, though, Jacques can find no better metaphor for the fusions and separations of confluent love than the grains of a winnowing basket, or better still, of coffee in a grinder! He thereby comprehends

> le peu qu'il était, le peu qu'on est dans ce monde, où les êtres, agités comme, dans le van les grains et la balle, sont mêlés et séparés par la secousse du rustre ou du dieu. Encore cette idée du van agricole ou mystique représentait trop bien la mesure et l'ordre pour qu'elle pût s'appliquer exactement à la vie. Il lui semblait que les hommes étaient des grains dans la cuvette d'un moulin à café. (192)

Is such confluent love, the novel asks, particular as well as particulate?

What emerge from the conflict between jealousy and liquidity are rival visions of marital satisfaction. Thérèse's companion, Mme Marmet, enjoys the quiescent memories of the widow who profited from her husband's jealousy throughout their married life, unlike France's heroine. For her, the union outlasts death, *pace* the secular, contractual prescriptions of the Civil Code, advising Thérèse that she must be buried in the same tomb as her husband. To Thérèse's question: 'la femme doit être unie à son mari, même après la mort?', she replies: 'Certainement. [...] Le mariage est pour le temps et pour l'éternité' (154). On the other hand, the cobbler Serafino Stoppini laments the loss of the past: 'J'ai eu une femme, des enfants, je n'en ai plus. J'ai su des choses que je ne sais plus' (116).

So wedded is France's writing to social and political theses that his fiction cannot quite free itself from an 'objective' hierarchy of meaning and embrace fully the 'subjective' interpretative pluralism of the avant-garde literature which was to follow. To Thérèse's analysis of her poetry, Miss Bell remarks: 'Une image poétique doit avoir plusieurs sens. Celui que vous aurez trouvé sera pour vous le sens véritable. Mais il y en a un très clair, my love' (106). The novel itself was written at the behest of France's mistress, and bears the marks of such reflexivity. In a *roman à clé* reading, the novel would be seen to reflect (and reflect upon) the mutual jealousy in the relationship of double adultery between writer and salon hostess, the subsequently divorced Anatole France and the never-to-be-be divorced Mme de Caillavet (née Léontine Lippmann), who lament the melodrama of the *trop tard*. In terms of its fusion of cultural and class capital, this relationship bears comparison with other affairs of the period between men of letters and society hostesses, between Jules Lemaître and Mme de Loynes, Paul Bourget and Mme Cahen d'Anvers, Paul Hervieu and Mme de Pierrebourg, and Maupassant and Mme Lecomte du Noüy. In spite of her unhappy marriage to Arman de Caillavet and a de facto separation,

Léontine bore him a child and they did not divorce. In 1877 France married Valérie Guérin de Sauville under the *régime de la communauté réduite aux acquêts* (the 50,000 franc dowry thus belonging in fact to her). Their relationship was certainly not without its initial happiness and produced a daughter, Suzanne Thibault, even if it was a practical rather than passionate venture. After the success of his early novels, France was invited into the salon world and came to dominate Mme de Caillavet's salon in particular. Their affair began at some point after the holidays in 1887 and before July 1888, and over the next few years she encouraged him to write 'their' novel, though he only relented in the wake of his conjugal rupture. Marie-Claire Bancquart explains how France was immediately 'en proie aux tourments de la jalousie rétrospective', and this theme is certainly evident in the first of his novels to be influenced by her, *Thaïs* (1890), in Paphauce's enmity towards Nicias, the former lover of the eponymous heroine.[22] The love triangle (of heroine and consecutive lovers) which excludes the husband and which France depicts in *Le Lys rouge* in fact conceals Mme de Caillavet's own serial narrative: 'Il a... simplifié la vie amoureuse de Léontine en n'attribuant à Thérèse qu'un seul amant avant Dechartre.'[23] Mme de Caillavet may have got 'her' novel in *Le Lys rouge*, but may also have got more than she bargained for, given the diminuendo on which the novel ends (in Bancquart's phrases, 'histoire d'une passion écrite au moment où la passion s'éteint', 'pour essayer de souffler sur les cendres,' although the relationship was far from over).[24] Tylden-Wright explains how

> she had the manuscript, grudgingly copied out by France, bound in calf, fitted with an enamelled clasp in the form of a red lily, and set in a glass frame in her drawing-room. There it rested, an expression of their love — but also in a way, inevitably, its memorial too.[25]

After incessant arguments France had left the family home on 6 June 1892 in dressing gown and slippers, writing to Valérie in the following terms:

> Je quitte une maison où tout travail comme tout repos m'étaient impossibles. Il m'est infiniment douloureux de quitter en même temps ma fille bien-aimée. J'espère que vous serez moins odieuse pour elle que vous ne l'avez été pour moi. [...] J'aurai l'indulgence de vous oublier. Je ne vous demande que de ne plus penser à moi.[26]

Aware of the legal effect of his rhetoric, France understood that such a departure and such an insulting letter would make divorce quite possible. He sent a messenger from the local hôtel Carnot to collect his clothes and a month later moved into an apartment on the rue de Sontay, where he wrote, although he took most of his meals with Mme de Caillavet. Mme France sued for divorce on grounds of desertion and won her case. On 2 August 1893 the divorce was granted 'à ses torts et à ses griefs' in the following terms:

> Attendu que depuis 1888 Thibaut dit Anatole France a peu à peu délaissé son intérieur. Que les années suivantes ses absences sont devenues de plus en plus fréquentes, se prolongeant parfois pendant plusieurs jours. Qu'il refusait toute explication à sa femme, ne voulant communiquer avec elle que par des billets remis par le domestique. Qu'enfin au mois de juin 1892, il a abandonné définitivement le domicile commun, laissant à sa femme une lettre dans laquelle

il lui annonçait en termes offensants sa résolution bien arrêtée de rompre désormais tout rapport avec elle.[27]

Five days later France repaired to Gyp's residence in Lion-sur-mer, and this would become a way for him to see Suzanne, as Gyp became in due course the intermediary between the divorcees.[28] On 19 August, France began work on the novel that would become *Le Lys rouge*.

Mme de Caillavet consoled him, and their subsequent trip to Italy (including Florence) was, in and of itself, a public declaration: 'No one, most especially her husband, could now remain ignorant of the fact that their destinies were closely linked'.[29] Quite remarkably, mother and lover were accompanying her son, Gaston de Caillavet, on his honeymoon. His bride, Jeanne Pouquet, had been pursued romantically, but in vain, by another of the habitués of the Caillavet salon... a young Marcel Proust (Jeanne is said to have been one of the models for Gilberte). Mme de Caillavet paid for the holiday and took the train from the Gare de Lyon with the young couple. For propriety's sake, France did not board the train before Avignon. What common ground on the subject of marriage was shared by this 'petit couple' and the 'couple illégitime', we can only surmise.[30] Keen to find material for this Florentine novel (which would also be 'her' novel), Mme de Caillavet dragged the group around the city, taking notes as she went (though France seems largely to have ignored them in writing the novel). Jeanne, it seems, was saved from exhaustion only by the fact that France tired as easily as she.

Suzanne, eleven years old, stayed with her mother, visiting France each Sunday at the home of the Comtesse de Martel, who acted as hostess for these meetings permitted by Mme France. Mme France received 350 francs per month, a sum that was 'not over-generous', and kept the house on rue Chalgrin (also in the 16th arrondissement).[31] In fact, he would have poor relations with both mother and daughter, the latter deemed at fault by the court in her divorce from Henri Mollin on 24 May 1905, having married him in December 1901, only to marry again on 28 April 1908, this time out of necessity to Renan's grandson, Michel Psichari, her lover by whom she was pregnant, although their relationship was already in trouble. France disapproved and did not attend the ceremony.[32] They would, however, produce a grandson for Anatole: Lucien Psichari. As the years passed, the dissymmetry between the divorced France and the married Mme de Caillavet seems to have added to their growing distance, and he struck up an affair with Mlle Jeanne Brindeau on his tour to South America in 1909.[33] He broke off the affair, but Mme de Caillavet died on 12 January 1910. Never able to cope domestically, on 17 February he wrote to her second *femme de chambre*, invited her to dinner, and then took her in. On 11 October 1920 (at the age of seventy-six), France himself would get married again, this time to Emma Laprévotte, just four years before his death. In August he had suffered a mild stroke which left him paralyzed for a few days. Without the marriage, as he realized and Carter Jefferson explains, 'Emma would be ignored by any court that probated his will'.[34]

Léon Carias stresses the gravity of the death of Mme de Caillavet, 'celle qui, depuis vingt-cinq ans, était la confidente de ses travaux, de ses joies, de ses peines [...] qui l'aima d'un amour infini et qu'il chérit lui-même si désespérément,' and in this regard he cites France's encoded reference to her death in his limited edition *Poèmes du souvenir*: 'Par elle, tout s'achève et s'harmonise, et ce que nous avons aimé dans la discontinuité et la dispersion qu'est la vie, nous l'aimons plus chèrement dans l'unité, la pureté, la simplicité d'une mémoire fidèle.' It is as if France would apply to the liquid possibilities of experience (and its language of discontinuity and dispersal) the neo-classical aesthetic with which his intellectual career was associated. Carias then cites, though, France's letter of 2 August 1913: 'Je ne la cherche plus à la croisée des chemins. Je sais maintenant qu'elle ne reviendra pas. Et que son retour déjà dérangerait des choses, changerait des destinées.'[35] Carias finds no conflict in this shift from mourning to revivification (in the sense of starting to live and love again): 'Qu'on puisse vivre après avoir perdu un tel lien, c'est un fait qui surprendra seulement ceux qui ont étudié le cœur humain dans les drames romantiques' (147).

In the context of the *roman à clé*, as elsewhere, however, the novel is quick to shed its generic skin (and thus retain a certain liquidity), hence Thérèse's 'ennui' at Mme Marmet

> découvrant sans cesse dans les figures des vieux peintres la ressemblance de quelque personne à elle connue. Le matin, au palais Ricardi, sur les seules fresques de Benozzo Gozzoli, elle avait reconnu M. Garain, M. Lagrange, M. Schmoll, la princesse Seniavine en page et M. Renan à cheval. M. Renan, elle s'effrayait elle-même de le retrouver partout. Elle ramenait toutes les idées à son petit cercle d'académiciens. (87–88)

In this, Mme Marmet is no more insightful than the visitors to the Louvre in Chapter III of *L'Assommoir*. So just as we might be about to attach to *Le Lys rouge* the label of *roman à clé*, the novel retreats from us. To her father's mistress, princesse Seniavine, who asks her in a later scene whether she is enjoying the book she is reading, Thérèse expresses melancholy doubt with the words: 'Nous ne trouvons que nous dans les livres' (200). The further irony is that this comment on the text as mirror is, we are told, a quotation from Anatole France's textual double, the novelist, Paul Vence.

In view of such reflexivity, it is worth observing that the novel is also quite aware of many of the literary contexts it inhabits (even if it cannot know the Forsterian context which might draw readers of *A Room with a View* (1908) to this novel of foreigners' amorous self-discovery in Florence). We can only imagine the seed-planting when that admirer of Anatole France, E. M. Forster, read of the post-consummation kiss between Thérèse and Jacques in San Marco, 'presque au regard de deux Anglaises qui allaient par les corridors, consultant le Baedeker' (137).[36] Indeed, it is worth noting that Henri Matisse uses the very notion of retrospective jealousy to defend the active (rather than passive) engagement of subsequent readers (by analogy with subsequent lovers) with past works of art:

> If the spectator renounces his own quality in order to identify himself with the spiritual quality of those who lived when the work of art was created, he impoverishes himself and disturbs the fullness of his own pleasure — a bit like the man who searches, with retrospective jealousy, the past of the woman he loves.[37]

As we have already seen, the *mondain* novel positions itself vis-à-vis the Naturalist novel by thematizing the act of reading. Only the previous year Zola had finished his *Rougon-Macquart* series. Mme Marmet sets out the party line in the opening pages of the novel by recalling that her husband 'qui avait beaucoup de goût littéraire, avait gardé jusqu'à la fin de ses jours l'horreur du naturalisme' (13). This world is not, however, without avant-garde aspirations. Princesse Seniavine has already reported to her on the previous evening's performance at Mme Meillan's of 'une pièce scandinave' (12), the dramatist (Ibsen or Strindberg?) left delicately unspecific. The gap between this world and that of the Naturalist novel is straddled by the heroine's trans-class curiosity, however patronizing this curiosity might seem. To an appalled Robert, she proposes: 'Nous irons demain, voulez-vous, dans des quartiers lointains, dans ces quartiers bizarres où l'on voit vivre les pauvres gens. J'aime les vieilles rues de misère' (21). His fear of *les classes dangereuses* emblematizes the lovers' incompatibility. Where she will go, he barely dare follow. As Thérèse's train bound for Italy leaves Paris, we catch a glimpse of 'les laideurs de la banlieue, sur cette frange noire qui borde tristement la ville', but of course her train does not stop there (73). Choulette is damning in his condemnation of her aesthetic sensibility: 'vous vous occupez de vaines images, mais moi, je demeure dans la vie et dans la vérité'; but Choulette's ultimate self-regard is subject to a corrosive irony which distances France from his radical politics (82). He too is patronizing in his estimation of the *peuple*, though his aesthetic conclusion brings him closer to Jean Richepin than to Zola: 'Le vers, très simple, violent ou joyeux, était en définitive l'unique langage qui convînt au peuple. La prose ne plaisait qu'aux gens d'une intelligence très subtile' (169).

Before we presume that Paul Vence *is* Anatole France, we should note the ironic potential of his pseudo-Naturalist claim to '**évidence**' as he explains to Thérèse the aesthetics of his new novel about an anarchist sculptor: 'C'était une étude, dans laquelle il s'efforçait d'atteindre à cette vérité formée d'une suite logique de vraisemblances qui, ajoutées les unes aux autres, atteignent à l'évidence' (44). Still, Vence's implicitly Flaubertian view of literature as an imperfect translation between ultimately solitary human beings speaks eloquently to Thérèse's view that 'on s'explique toujours, on ne comprend jamais' (61). Vence laments:

> Qu'est-ce qu'il en fait, le lecteur, de ma page d'écriture? Une suite de faux sens, de contresens, et de non-sens. Lire, entendre, c'est traduire. Il y a de belles traductions, peut-être; il n'y en a pas de fidèles.

This maxim compares translation and female infidelity in the tradition of the *belles infidèles* to which Edmond Jaloux will later contribute with his oft-cited observation that 'les traductions sont comme les femmes: quand elles sont belles, elles ne sont pas fidèles; et quand elles sont fidèles, elles ne sont pas belles.' The subsequent comparison (or translation?) between literature, translation and women sets into ironic relief Thérèse's project of infidelity which aims in vain at a perfect translation of affect between men and women.

This concern for influence and context necessarily informs the novel's sustained reflection on the topic of artistic originality, filtered through the novel's Baedeker-style guide to Florentine painting.[38] Should art too, France asks, be jealous of its own past? The metatextual status of jealousy (in other words, its ability to comment on the art that houses it) disarms any either/or interpretation of art and love in *Le Lys rouge*:

> Because jealousy is figured as watching and interpreting, as telling and silencing, it also acts as a trope for both consuming and creating art and literature.[...] The act of reading and decoding that lies at the very heart of jealousy encapsulates both the creation and the deciphering of texts [...]. Jealousy in literature is not merely a theme but also, and more vitally, a strategy, both readerly and writerly.[39]

The question of artistic originality emerges at the start of the novel in the discussion of the Jewish philologist, Schmoll, of the Académie des inscriptions, whom Thérèse naively places at a dinner party next to the widow of his arch intellectual enemy, Louis Marmet. Vence explains to her how Schmoll, 'un latiniste de grande valeur et, après Mommsen, le premier épigraphiste du monde' (18), ridiculed Marmet's claims to mastery of the Etruscan language. Schmoll accused Marmet of knowing Etruscan too well and not knowing Latin well enough! When one day Marmet refused to shake his hand on the steps of the Institut, Schmoll met the rebuff 'Je ne vous connais pas' with the question: 'Me prenez-vous pour une inscription latine?' (19). Vence even suggests that it was this witticism which killed Marmet. Schmoll, moreover, has just been presented as an unimaginative and proprietorial epigraphist who criticizes Vivian Bell's use in the poem *Yseult la Blonde* of a Latin inscription over which he claims ownership: 'ces mots sont traduits textuellement d'une inscription funéraire que j'ai publiée et illustrée le premier' (17). He explains how she has truncated and denatured the translation he sent her after impressing her with the original at a dinner party. His unscholarly motives are underlined by Thérèse's amusement at his 'galanteries lourdes et rouillées', and this brutal wit himself suffers at the hands of the narrator: 'Ce grand philologue, membre de l'Institut de France, savait toutes les langues, excepté le français' (16). In all events, he fails to distinguish between discovery and invention, confuses publication and authorship, and fails to understand the creative artist's absorption of other texts which Miss Bell recasts for fresh purposes.

Architecture provides a forum for the aesthetic conflict between the impulse to go back to origins and the urge to add further palimpsestic layers to the built environment. In other words, is it possible to be original without going back to a point of origin? Vence explains how Jacques's father, Philippe Dechartre, an architect once favoured under Napoleon III, conflicted with the omnipotent Viollet-le-Duc:

> Ce qu'il [Dechartre] lui [Viollet-le-Duc] reprochait, c'était de vouloir rétablir les édifices dans leur plan primitif, tels qu'ils avaient été ou tels qu'ils avaient dû être à l'origine. Philippe Dechartre voulait, au contraire, qu'on respectât tout ce que les siècles avaient ajouté peu à peu à une église, à une abbaye, à un château. Faire disparaître les anachronismes et ramener un édifice à son unité première, lui semblait une barbarie scientifique aussi redoutable que celle de l'ignorance. (63)

In Dechartre's terms, every addition is its own original. Modern voices are so used to chastising the falseness in Viollet-le-Duc's creations (witness any number of conversations one might have about Carcassonne which are worthy of Flaubert's dictionary) that modern ears may be startled by this association of Viollet-le-Duc with restorative authenticity. It is thus ironic that Dechartre's own son cannot accept the accretion of experience which has formed the palimpsest of Thérèse's love life; and it is certainly possible to see his father's aesthetic as a liquid modern vision of architecture. In language which speaks to the example of Sherlock Holmes in Ginzburg's conjectural paradigm, but dismisses his quest for the original fingerprint, Philippe insists that the detective quest is itself criminal: 'C'est un crime que d'effacer les empreintes successives imprimées dans la pierre par la main et l'âme de nos aïeux.' Rather than mastering the historical process, the 'architecte archéologue' should aim merely to 'soutenir et à consolider les murailles' (63–64).

In art, if not in love, Jacques relinquishes the cult of primacy (and thus of legacy, just as the two are connected in the bio-logic of legitimate reproduction), hence his praise of fifteenth-century artistic apprenticeships in Chapter 10:

> Bienheureux temps [...] où l'on n'avait pas soupçon de cette originalité que nous cherchons si avidement aujourd'hui. L'apprenti tâchait de faire comme le maître. [...] C'était sans le vouloir qu'il se montrait différent des autres. [...] Le désir d'atteindre la postérité [...] ne les troublait pas. Ne connaissant point le passé, ils ne concevaient point l'avenir, et leur rêve n'allait pas au delà de leur vie. (92)

Dechartre's authenticity contrasts with Choulette's feigned indifference to posterity, claiming to write on cigarette paper, but in reality hording every line he has ever written. For him, the past and the future determine the efforts of the present:

> pour que la vie soit grande et pleine, il faut y mettre le passé et l'avenir. Nos œuvres de poésie et d'art, il faut les accomplir en l'honneur des morts, et dans la pensée de ceux qui naîtront. (97)

Still, Dechartre is quick to condemn the fakery in the gallery of his love rival Albertinelli, whispering to Thérèse: 'Cette galerie est un dépôt où les marchands de tableaux du monde entier accrochent le rebut de leurs magasins. Et le prince y vend ce que des juifs n'avaient pu vendre' (108). Of a would-be Michelangelo: 'J'ai vu cette sainte famille chez des marchands de Londres, de Bâle et de Paris. Comme ils n'en ont pas trouvé les vingt-cinq louis qu'elle vaut, ils ont chargé le dernier des Albertinelli d'en demander cinquante mille francs' (109). All that Albertinelli can proffer in return is doubt: 'Je n'affirme pas que celui-ci soit original. Mais il est toujours resté dans la famille, et les vieux inventaires l'attribuent à Michel-Ange. C'est tout ce que je puis dire.' In subsequent retaliation, he will be only too keen to remind Jacques that, in terms of Thérèse's adulterous transgression, he is no original. Amidst all of these debates and intertexts, perhaps it is not a painting, nor a building, but in true Stendhalian fashion, an opera which best dramatizes the tension between an original text and the project of self-reinvention. But the opera does not take place in Italy, nor is it even Italian. For, as we have seen, the culmination of Jacques's struggle with Thérèse's past takes place at the Opéra de Paris during a performance of Gounod's *Faust* (1859, libretto by Jules Barbier and Michel Carré from Carré's play *Faust et Marguerite*, in turn loosely based on

Goethe's *Faust, Part 1*). The many interpretations of the Faustian myth include those which highlight the tension between the original pact with Mephistopheles (the contract from which one cannot escape) and Faust's bid for happiness through self-reinvention and the embrace of fresh experience (which does not turn out to be perpetual, as he had hoped). Faust dreams of liquid modernity but is dragged back to its heavy (theological) version, as are Thérèse and Jacques.

And so to end at the beginning. The origin of the novel's reflection on origins, original sin, innocence and defloration could also be situated at that point of textual origin: the title, where the author names his progeny *Le Lys rouge*. This flower is a symbol of Florence (named at one point 'la ville de la Fleur', 166), which evokes both blossom and blood (or the floral and defloration). The symbol is presented in the opening paragraphs of the novel as a gift to the virgin in Vivian Bell's *Yseult la Blonde*:

> La vierge, en visitant les pommiers du verger,
> Frissonne d'avoir vu venir le messager
> Qui lui présente un lys rouge et tel qu'on désire
> Mourir de son parfum sitôt qu'on le respire. (10)

The connection between the loss of virginity and the death which comes of breathing in the scent of the red lily is echoed later in the lament of the cobbler who, as we have seen above, has lost wife and children. Thérèse's enthusiasm for violets is met with his fatalistic: 'Si la pauvre petite fleurit, elle mourra' (117). As they wonder the backstreets of the city on the very next page, Vivian points out to Thérèse the 'façades sordides où pendaient des loques rouges, quelque joyau de marbre, une Vierge, une fleur de lys' (118). When Jacques buys Thérèse an ice-cream on the streets of Florence, he also provides a little red spoon he has bought from a local antiquary, its handle ending in 'le lys de Florence, au calice émaillé de rouge' (140). He explains that the ice-cream-seller does not provide any implements and that he wanted to save her from the shock of having to 'tirer la langue', however 'joli' this would have looked. The domesticated lily (on a spoon) is intended to save Thérèse from all this phrase's connotations — of appetite, sexual, culinary and economic; and of a Lolita-style erotic provocation. Thérèse is too old for lollypops.

The colour red informs the demise of this second love affair. When, in Chapter 21, a frustrated Robert beats Thérèse, it is he who catches his hand on the pin in her corsage and starts to bleed. With Jacques's jealousy ignited by Chapter 23, she tries to calm him with the observation that she has kept that little red spoon and uses it to stir her tea every morning, so that in some sense he is with her as she awakes (160). At the ensuing scene of some unnamed perversion which Thérèse offers to Jacques (to which we have alluded above), their exhaustion is matched by the image of a rose in a glass, its blossom too heavy, and its leaves falling one by one (164). The flower of innocence is not simply the single bud of virginity, but, in an image fit for this subject matter, a rose of many petals. And in this archly literary use of 'feuille' as petal, France recasts for modern ears Ronsard's comment on the rose in *Les Amours* (1552–56): 'Languissante, elle meurt, feuille à feuille déclose.' Two images of flowers in the novel, one as mortal, the other as self-rejuvenating, animate the tension between the rival paths of love which France explores. When the lovers return to Paris, she writes to him from her conjugal home 'une lettre pleine de ces paroles semblables aux fleurs dans leur perpétuelle nouveauté' and informs him that she has brought with her that little spoon bearing the red lily (171). At the height of their short-lived joy back in Paris, her resplendent image is confirmed in all its floral majesty: 'elle vit dans la glace sa nudité fleurie' (182). As we have seen, Robert's boat *Rosebud* symbolizes his refusal to allow her to flower once again elsewhere and for someone else.

When Thérèse appears in her box at the performance of *Faust*, her angelic white dress is set off by a broach over her left breast in the form of a large ruby lily. By the final act, the lovers are alone in the box with Vivian, and in rather heavy-handed fashion France has Vivian praise the brutal beauty of this love symbol:

> je suis exaltée en pensant que vous portez sur le cœur le lys rouge de Florence. Et monsieur Dechartre, qui a une âme d'artiste, doit être bien content aussi de voir à votre corsage ce gentil joyau. Oh! je voudrais connaître le joaillier qui l'a fait, darling. Ce lys est svelte et souple comme la fleur d'iris. Oh! il est élégant, magnifique et cruel. Avez-vous remarqué, my love, que les beaux joyaux ont un air de magnifique cruauté? (219)

In the terrible ensuing scene where Robert's intervention manages to spoil this second love affair, this time for good, Thérèse is described as 'longue et blanche, au côté la fleur sanglante', whilst on stage the fallen woman Marguerite prepares to rise to heaven (221). Once she has returned to the heterosocial retreat which her marital home has become, her maid cries out when she notices the blood of her mistress on that white dress. Without realizing it, in the heat of the commotion, Thérèse must have caught her hand on the stamens of the red lily. The flower has in some sense been cruel, as Vivian has predicted. Thérèse removes this 'joyau emblématique' and gazes upon this image of the sexuality which she offers to Jacques (222). She fantasizes in vain that she will once more win him over: 'elle le forcerait [...] à voir qu'elle l'aimait, qu'elle était sa chose, son trésor vivant de joie et d'amour' (223).

And so *Le Lys rouge* stares bravely in the direction of liquid modernity, only to turn away as, in Faustian fashion, the pull of the prior arrangement cannot be avoided. As such, I would claim for this novel what Robert Lethbridge calls, in the context of Bancquart's work on France, 'not the celebration of a forgotten genius, but rather the measured rehabilitation of a representative intellectual attitude'.[40] In light of Colette's own serialization of fictional desire, her subsequent treatment of divorce in *La Retraite sentimentale* (1907) and *La Vagabonde* (1910), and her own experience of more than one divorce, it is worth noting that the modern paperback editor of the novel, Pierre Kyria, concludes his introduction by quoting a letter to France from the young, unknown Colette: 'Qu'est-ce que vous croyez qu'a fait Thérèse après? Eh bien! elle n'a plus eu d'autre amant, c'est moi qui vous le dis' (7). Colette herself would not accept such an abruptly end-stopped life of the heart. Indeed, it is worth recalling the greatest of the numerous illusions in the modern utopia dreamt up in Léon Blum's *Du mariage* (1907), namely that jealousy itself might be abolished.

Notes to Chapter 3

1. Seure, *Le Divorce, précédé d'une lettre de Victor Hugo*, p. 12.
2. For my interpretation of *Un divorce*, see the coda to *The Family in Crisis in Late Nineteenth-Century French Fiction*.
3. This chapter is deeply indebted to Masha Belenky, *The Anxiety of Dispossession: Jealousy in Nineteenth-Century French Culture* (Lewisburg, PA: Bucknell University Press, 2008).
4. Appendix to Bordeaux, *Âmes modernes* (Paris: Perrin, 1912), p. 404.
5. Naquet, *Vers l'union libre*, pp. 75–76.
6. Gustave Téry gathered these responses to Bourget and the divorce question in *Les Divorcés peints par eux-mêmes, mille et une confessions* (Paris: Fayard, [n.d.]).
7. Naquet, *Vers l'union libre*, pp. 203–05.
8. In an habitual strategy, Naquet quotes his enemies, here Louis Legrand: 'Il faut bien le reconnaître, le divorce entre chaque jour davantage dans les mœurs. [...] Ce n'est pas un des moindres vices du divorce qu'un pays ne peut plus s'en débarrasser, une fois qu'il l'a inoculé dans sa législation et de là dans ses mœurs. L'exemple de la Belgique est là pour le prouver.' As so often in the French imagination, Belgium incarnates a marginality which is comprehensibly francophone and geographically close but deemed 'un-French' by conservative opinion.
9. Naquet, *Vers l'union libre*, pp. 28–30.
10. Marie-Anne de Bovet, *Après le divorce* (Paris: Lemerre, 1908). Interpolated references will be made to this edition.
11. Henry Rousset, *Les Dauphinoises célèbres* (1908), cited in *Archives biographiques françaises*.
12. Thomas Hardy, *Life's Little Ironies and A Changed Man* (London: Macmillan, 1977), p. 487.
13. George Sand, *Elle et lui* (Neuchâtel: Ides et Calendes, 1963), p. 259.
14. Honoré de Balzac, *La Comédie humaine*, vol. VII (Paris: Gallimard Pléiade, 1977), p. 156.
15. <http://flaubert.univ-rouen.fr/jet/public/trans.php?corpus=bovary&id=4478> [accessed 20 June 2012].
16. Malcolm Bowie, *Freud, Proust and Lacan*, pp. 46–65.
17. William Empson, *Seven Types of Ambiguity* (London: Chatto & Windus, 1953), p. 131.
18. <http://www.vignoblesdecaillavet.com/chateau-caillavet.asp> [accessed 22 November 2007]. This webpage included a picture of the stained glass portraits of this troubled couple.
19. Interpolated references will be made to Anatole France, *Le Lys rouge*, ed. by Pierre Kyria (Paris: Calmann-Lévy, 1983).
20. *Le Figaro littéraire* of spring 1956 surveyed seventeen significant novelists in order to construct this list. See Marie-Claire Bancquart, 'Notice', in Anatole France, *Œuvres*, 3 vols (Paris: Gallimard Pléiade, 1984–91), II, 1217.
21. Pierre Brunel, '*Le Lys rouge* et le monde de l'idylle', in *Anatole France: Humanisme et actualité*, ed. by Marie-Claire Bancquart and Jean Dérens (Paris: Bibliothèque historique de la Ville de Paris, 1994), pp. 23–31 (p. 29).
22. Marie-Claire Bancquart, *Anatole France: Un sceptique passionné* (Paris: Calmann-Lévy, 1984), pp. 148, 156.
23. *Anatole France: Un sceptique passionné*, p. 203. She names her significant other lovers as her husband's cousin, Gassou, and Victor Brochard, the Hellenist philosopher: 'Mme de Caillavet n'en était pas à son premier essai. On disait même qu'elle avait du mal à rompre, et gardait un temps le précédent élu sous le règne d'un autre.' Bancquart, *Anatole France, polémiste* (Paris: Nizet, 1962), p. 51.
24. *Anatole France: Un sceptique passionné*, p. 156; *Anatole France*, p. 56. In this latter book, Bancquart is struck by 'l'insistance du roman sur le caractère éphèmere de l'amour' and his initial desire to call the novel *La Terre des morts* (p. 57). Mme de Caillavet squashed this idea.
25. David Tylden-Wright, *Anatole France* (London: Collins, 1967), p. 165.
26. Quoted in *Anatole France par lui-même*, ed. by Jacques Suffel (Paris: Seuil, 1954), p. 44.
27. Quoted in *Anatole France: Un sceptique passionné*, p. 191.
28. It is worth noting that both Gyp and Mme de Caillavet did their best to help Suzanne deal with her parents' separation, the latter encouraging France in his relationship with his daughter and

often receiving her at home. Gyp herself forayed into this fictional domain with her diptych *Autour du mariage* (1883) and *Autour du divorce* (1886).

29. Reino Virtanen, *Anatole France* (Boston, MA: Twayne, 1968), p. 86.
30. *Anatole France: Un sceptique passionné*, p. 190.
31. Tylden-Wright, p. 159.
32. Bancquart quotes Suzanne's conversation with Michel (as late as November 1905) where she complains of 'encore une fois de plus des plaintes justes ou injustes sur papa et qui me sont aussi pénibles à entendre les unes que les autres! Je vais tâcher d'oublier encore les querelles de maman et de papa qui se passent sur mon pauvre dos innocent' (*Anatole France: Un sceptique passionné*, pp. 294–95).
33. In Bancquart's words, 'Il n'est pas question pour Mme de Caillavet de divorcer; cela ne se fait guère encore dans son monde.' As long as 'les convenances du temps' were obeyed, 'il faut avouer que la société ferme volontiers les yeux' (*Anatole France: Un sceptique passionné*, pp. 50–51).
34. Carter Jefferson, *Anatole France: The Politics of Skepticism* (New Brunswick, NJ: Rutgers University Press, 1965), p. 209.
35. *Les Carnets intimes d'Anatole France*, ed. byLéon Carias (Paris: Émile-Paul frères, 1946), pp. 81, 83, 115.
36. As Yves Hervouet recalls, it was also 'one of Conrad's favourite books, one from which […] he could, late in life, quote by heart' ('Conrad's Debt to French Authors in *Under Western Eyes*', *Conradiana*, 14.2 (1982), 113–25 (p. 113).
37. Quoted in Jack D. Flam, *Matisse on Art* (New York: Phaidon, 1973), p. 135.
38. See Elizabeth Emery's important analysis in 'Art as Passion in Anatole France's *Le Lys rouge*', *Nineteenth-Century French Studies*, 35.3/4 (2007), 641–52, which argues that 'although the love story is the most remarkable aspect of the plot, it is art that steals the show in *Le Lys rouge*' (p. 648). I argue that the discourses on beauty and desire in the novel inform each other.
39. Rosemary Lloyd, *Closer & Closer Apart: Jealousy in Literature* (Ithaca, NY: Cornell University Press, 1995), pp. xi–xii.
40. Robert Lethbridge, review of Anatole France, *Œuvres*: 1 (1984) and Marie-Claire Bancquart, *Un sceptique passionnée* (1984) in *French Studies*, 40 (1986), p. 94.

CHAPTER 4

Famous Fathers and Grumpy Daughters

Although Anatole France describes an exclusive world, the realm of *mondanité* opened onto the public sphere via both politics and cultural life. These realms were explored in divorce novels of the 1890s, one by Alphonse Daudet and two by Édouard Rod, not least because divorce threatened to expose intimacy to the public gaze, in spite of the press restrictions of 1886. In these novels, the father–daughter relationship lends particular acuity to the pain of divorce.

Imagine the scenario, 'un premier chapitre très curieux':[1] a newly divorced father sits alone in his rented bachelor flat, waiting nervously for that first Sunday visit from his two daughters who now live with their mother. This could be the opening cliché of any number of soap operas, made-for-TV movies or mini-series. It says much for the effacement of this cliché's origins that we might be surprised to learn that this is how one of the most successful French novelists of the early Third Republic, Alphonse Daudet (1840–97), begins his short novel, *Rose et Ninette* (1892), which focuses on the fictitious playwright Régis de Fagan's relationship with his eponymous daughters, Rose and Ninette, after his divorce from their mother. The novel looks back on the cause and means of their divorce, and explores through her remarriage and his relationship with Mme Pauline Hulin the deleterious effects of both divorce and separation on parent–child relations.

At first glance the novel may not seem to merit a second one, but various contexts might encourage us to return to this largely forgotten text of this often overlooked writer. First, *Rose et Ninette*, subtitled *Mœurs du jour*, represents Daudet's mature reflection on the fate of family life since the advent of the Loi Naquet. As such, it suggests that far from ending the debate, the new law produced new cases which fuelled yet further argument about the benefits and dangers of a social reform which not only viewed marriage as non-sacramental but also allowed social structures to be eroded on the basis of individual whim. From Daudet's secular view, such social fragmentation was far more perturbing. Indeed, the corollary context in which to read *Rose et Ninette* is the effect of divorce on the literary circle which he inhabited, for the sorry tale of paternal alienation which this novel relates both reflects and anticipates actual divorce cases which were to touch the author profoundly, first the divorce of Adolphe Belot (1829–90), novelist and theatrical collaborator of Alphonse on the dramatization of the latter's *Fromont jeune et Risler aîné* (1874) and *Sapho* (1884), and second the divorce of his own son Léon (1868–1942) and Victor Hugo's granddaughter, Jeanne (1869–1941). As such it is a novel written for a new father, by his own father. Alphonse had his own reasons to depict the tribulations of married life. He and his wife, Mme Julia Daudet (married in 1867), had agreed to co-author a fictionalized autobiography. Once Alphonse had completed seven chapters, Julia censored the project. Daudet would return to the question in Chapter 7, 'Mémoires d'un agent', in *Le Soutien de famille* (1898) where he notes how conjugal behaviour had been changed by the very debate itself: '[Valfon] fouillait les tiroirs de sa femme, comme cela lui arrivait fréquemment depuis que la Chambre s'occupait de la loi Naquet et de la question du divorce.'[2]

Daudet's earlier work was cited explicitly by the pro-divorce lobby. In an early study of his writing published in that key year, 1884, Antoine Arbalat stresses the connection between *divorciaire* arguments and the Montesquievian tradition of the Enlightenment:

> On tirerait d'une multitude de faits, arides à indiquer ici, la plus énergique conclusion en faveur de la nécessité et de l'évolution prochaine d'une morale nouvelle dont la loi du divorce ouvre la première phase. Et cette morale qui doit nécessairement sortir du chaos littéraire et social de la passion, devient la chose du monde la plus naturelle, si l'on admet que toute morale est relative et varie de peuple à peuple, de climat à climat. Question de temps, alors.[3]

As Dobie writes, 'Though [Alphonse] had favoured such legislation when he was young, now his views had changed, and he was primarily concerned with the ill-effects of divorce on the children.'[4] But the Goncourt *Journal* notes a few years later how Edmond and Alphonse discussed

> le divorce, ce tueur du mariage catholique, ce radical *métamorphoseur* de la vieille société, dont il comparait l'action, dans un temps prochain, 'à la blessure au-dessous de la flottaison, dans le flanc d'un navire en train de couler'. (III, 65; 1 October 1887)

Amongst those keen to take advantage of the new law was the Parisian intellectual elite, not least Adolphe Belot who himself drew on the divorce motif in his novel, *Adulter*, of 1885. Edmond de Goncourt's journal entry for 12 July 1891 confirms that 'l'histoire Belot' is the model for *Rose et Ninette*.

If the case of Belot served as a model for Alphonse's novel, the novel itself antici-pated the fate of his own son, Léon, and Jeanne Hugo, the young heroine of that famous collection of poems *L'Art d'être grand-père* (1877). They were engaged in the summer of 1890 and married on 12 January 1891 at the *mairie* of Passy in the 16th arrondissement, the bride's family insisting that there should be no religious ceremony, supposedly 'en hommage au grand-père, Victor', but in apparent fact 'pour d'obscures manœuvres politiciennes dont Lockroy, le beau-père, est un maître subtil'.[5] The Daudets were less than pleased about this decision and the fact that Jeanne's mother opted for *le régime dotal*. The reason for this can be gleaned from Toulouse's *Manuel pratique du mariage*:

> Sous le régime de la communauté le mari est tout, et [...] la femme ne peut disposer de rien sans son consentement, pendant le mariage; mais à sa dissolution, elle a droit à la moitié des biens communs. — Sous le régime dotal, [...] la position de la femme est plus avantageuse [...], puisqu'elle administre ses biens paraphernaux, et qu'elle n'a pas à craindre la perte de ses biens dotaux, qu'elle reprend à la dissolution du mariage.[6]

Long before the Loi Naquet, the *régime dotal* was subject to critique, as in the Goncourts' comment of 11 June 1862:

> Rien de grotesque comme mon cousin Alphonse s'avançant dans le mariage. C'était l'Avarice s'avançant avec gémissement dans les cycles de l'Enfer du Dante. [...] Singulière chose [...] que ce régime dotal! C'est une de ces prodigieuses chinoiseries, comme on en rencontre tant dans la société! Entre les époux, la conjonction est complète. On les met dans le même lit; ils échangent leur sang, mêlent leurs santés et tout, sauf l'argent. Ils n'ont qu'une table de nuit, ils ont deux fortunes. Ils entrent dans la communauté en laissant leurs bourses à la porte. (I: 823)

Julia Daudet seems nevertheless to have been delighted to see her son married off: 'c'est une joie générale dont vous prendrez votre part bientôt. Il y avait pour nous bien des scrupules dans ce mariage mais enfin on s'aimait et notre pauvre garçon arrivait à toutes les souffrances, les jalousies d'un vrai amour.'[7] Lucien Daudet is keen to stress that Alphonse had reservations about the match, even though he had known Jeanne and her mother, Mme Charles Hugo, for a long time, the latter having remarried the radical politician, Édouard Lockroy (1840–1913) in 1877, six years after Charles's death. Lockroy was, however, in the coterie of Naquet. Lucien writes in the tradition of those who caricature Jeanne as a tempestuous beauty, stereotypically the feminine fruit of grand-paternal genius, 'qui de profil ressemble à une jeune Junon de la grande époque grecque, de face aux plus jolis portraits de Nattier, et dont la beauté a quelque chose d'invraisemblable'. And the marriage was from the start passionate but tempestuous. By the autumn of that year Alphonse was committed to writing *Rose et Ninette*, finally dated 31 December 1891, and published in 1892 by Flammarion.

The importance of the divorce question can be seen in a range of interpretations of the novel. Alphonse V. Roche chooses to read against the grain, seeing in its hesitant tone the seeds of what we would call the deconstruction of an anti-divorce thesis (or perhaps of the thesis novel as such): 'The case against divorce [...] is not at all convincing. [...] Evidently, the family has been destroyed and "divorce is not the solution", but keeping the family together in this particular case would not have been one either, with such a partner as Mme de Fagan.'[8] Jean-Paul Clébert points out Daudet's aesthetic (rather than merely ideological) difficulty in absorbing the complications of divorce into the received family plots of the novel genre: 'Il n'en voit pas la fin. Il ne peut s'empêcher de rajouter les scènes à l'intérieur d'autres scènes, mise en abyme, multiplication des miroirs, stéréotypie des personnages qui se dédoublent à l'infini.'[9] Lucien Daudet reasserts the conservatism of the family ideology behind the artfulness of novel writing: 'sans phrases, sans malédictions, ni vitupérations, il prouve que le divorce est une infamie', and Frédéric Mistral puns in praise of this 'beau coup d'épée dans le flanc du Divorce'.[10]

On 5 February 1892 Jeanne gave birth to Charles Daudet, and in Clébert's phrase, a 'ménage apparemment réconcilié' was re-established (242). Textual magic, however, did not work, and the father's tale (Alphonse's and Régis's) failed to immunize the son against the misfortune of divorce. The Daudet–Hugo match was media property from the start and rumours of marital unhappiness offered grist to the mill. On the first page of *Le Matin* on 30 May 1893 we read:

> On parlait depuis plusieurs semaines à mots couverts d'un divorce appelé à
> faire quelque bruit dans le monde des Lettres: aujourd'hui, paraît-il, la chose
> aurait passé du domaine des potins à celui de la réalité. Il s'agit d'un tout récent
> mariage dont la jeune femme porte un nom illustre entre tous et dont le mari,
> fils d'un célèbre romancier, a débuté il n'y a pas bien longtemps en littérature.

In a letter of June that year Alphonse writes to Edmond de Goncourt:

> C'est un infâme mensonge venu de je ne sais où et partagé par *la France* et *le
> Matin*. Mon pauvre Léon a été malade. J'ai empêché qu'il y eût duel mais toute
> mon habileté, je crains bien, et ma tendresse n'empêcheront pas que la chose
> ait lieu quelque jour. Il a tant d'ennemis ce bon et cher garçon qui n'a de haine
> pour personne.[11]

As the marriage deteriorated, Alphonse refused to delude himself: 'Nous sommes
dans le malheur, le malheur provisoire, j'espère bien. J'entends la délivrance de
mon pauvre gars'.[12] Jeanne left the family home in December 1894. By January
1895 the couple were indeed divorced. Léon himself colluded in the creation of
a personal myth which suppressed the memory of his divorce. He is by no means
alone in this regard. One need only think of Georges Clemenceau, whose divorce
of 1892 is hardly highlighted in the hagiographies of the public, political figure
which appeared after World War One. Léon's right-wing affiliations meant that he
later became profoundly embarrassed about his involvement in the use of what was
perceived to be an anti-Catholic law sponsored by a Jewish radical.[13]

Critics have argued about the extent to which Alphonse intended the novel to
be a direct warning to his son, although Alphonse writes: 'A mon cher fils Léon
Daudet au poète et au philosophe je dédie cette page de la vie contemporaine'.[14] The
dedicatory paratext highlights a relationship between father and son which is also a
relationship between writers, and as we shall see, the intertextual resonances which
echo through the novel — to Vigny, Wagner and most ironically of all, Verdi and
Balzac — can be understood as encoding, for a son with ears to hear, the anxious
influence of a worried father. But in a reversal of the value which such writers
might ascribe to purely cultural concerns, the dedication will in hindsight highlight
the dangers in poetry and philosophy distracting his son from the demands of 'la
vie contemporaine'. For Régis de Fagan brings to his dramatic art an acuity which
is absent from his dealings with the real world.

The novel's epigraph which Alphonse borrows from Vigny's *Journal d'un poète*
(published posthumously in 1867 and reissued in 1882 in the Petite Bibliothèque
Charpentier) defuses and disarms the potentially explosive power-play between
father and son:

> Après avoir vu clairement que le travail des livres et la recherche de l'expression
> nous conduisent tous au paradoxe, j'ai résolu de ne sacrifier jamais qu'à la
> conviction et à la vérité, afin que cet élément de sincérité complète et profonde
> dominât dans mes livres et leur donnât le caractère sacré que doit donner la
> présence divine du vrai, ce caractère qui fait venir des larmes sur le bord de nos
> yeux lorsqu'un enfant nous atteste ce qu'il a vu. (299)

Once more the accretions of cultural knowledge (and its resultant paradoxes) are questioned, this time in favour of conviction, truth and sincerity. The figure of such truth is, importantly, the witness of a child which brings us to tears. As such, the figure inverts the parent–child relationship: according to the figure, the child informs and the adult is moved. By this very figure, though, Alphonse reminds his adult son that he, Léon, is still his child.

Let me now offer an apology, for once again, the way in which the divorce topic leads us to the Great Unread — both 'minor' women writers and unfashionable patriarchs — necessarily constrains our critical mode. If these divorce novels nowadays go virtually unread, then any comprehensible interpretation of them must be tethered to sequential storytelling. In other words, there can be no re-reading without at first reading, no running without walking, and no hare without the tortoise.

This short third-person narrative comprises ten chapters, the first setting up the post-divorce situation from the *vaudevilliste*'s perspective. Though this allows Alphonse to channel a dialogue between himself and Léon, to some degree it avoids the narrative difficulty of properly absorbing the children's viewpoint into the thrust of the tale. It is precisely this challenge which Alphonse's acquaintance, Henry James, faces in *What Maisie Knew* (1897), which attempts to recuperate what Andrew Counter has called 'that most foreign and denigrated of all subjectivities: [that of] the little girl'.[15] The latter's library at Lamb House in Rye, England, contains a copy of *Rose et Ninette*. The intertextual and interpersonal network of divorce literature grows when we recall Daudet's friendship with George Meredith, author of those early divorce poems, *Modern Love* (1862). The opening line of Daudet's novel suggests that Régis has been liberated: 'Divorcé depuis quinze jours, et tout à l'ivresse de la fin de sa peine' (299). This 'peine' is, however, immediately replaced by the sobering 'angoisse de l'attente' as he awaits, at the ironically named 37 boulevard Beauséjour in Passy, that first visit of sixteen-year-old Rose and eleven-year-old Nina, announced in a letter which affects him more than any of the letters which this successful playwright has received from female admirers (300).

The children become the conduit through which Régis and his ex-wife — who has done the normal thing, even at that time, and returned to her maiden name, Ravaut — wage 'une guerre de coups d'épingles', a particularly conspicuous version of the battle of the sexes (306). The confusion of the initial encounter reflects the play of continuity and transformation which divorce has created: 'Certainement leur père était toujours leur père [...] mais ce n'était plus le mari de leur mère, et de là un changement qu'elles sentaient' (301). In naturalist style this emotional shift is written onto the material environment. Amidst the new furniture they spot his writing desk whose corners he once had rounded so that they could safely play hide and seek. In the elusive play of the novel he will find it harder to protect them, indeed as he seeks them out recast in their mother's new life in Corsica, it will be he who needs protection. The cautionary tale against entropy is then vented:

> Quel désarroi de toutes leurs idées, en même temps, que des êtres et des choses, jadis unis, dispersés maintenant, comme au lendemain d'un incendie ou d'un naufrage. Et que tout cela est compliqué, effarant pour elles, dans ce manque de jugement qui caractérise et signifie l'extrême jeunesse! (303)

In spite of such prescription, Daudet's skill consists in retaining the sense of ambiguity proper to narrative seduction. Régis perceives the ethical paradox that his ex-wife has suddenly become a good mother 'non dans un aveuglement de tendresse, mais par une basse jalousie, un besoin de taquiner, de torturer son mari', whereas the traditional family dovetails the roles of wife and mother (306).

The suspenseful question of why and how they divorced draws the reader into Chapter 2. Régis offers the husband's viewpoint to the reader via a conversation with his supposedly widowed landlady, Mme Pauline Hulin, whose maternal concern for her own sick son, Maurice, impresses Fagan greatly. Given the analogy, habitual in divorce literature of the time, between two ways of losing a spouse, namely divorce and widowhood, 'une intimité venue de leurs situations pareilles, une sympathie échappant encore à l'analyse s'était nouée entre l'écrivain et sa voisine' (308). Ambroise Janvier and Marcel Ballot's comedy, *Mon Nom!*, premiered on 5 December 1892 at the Théâtre-Moderne, exemplifies the way in which different attitudes towards divorce depended on analogies trawled from the received vocabulary of family life. Is divorce, so the play asks, more like widowhood or more akin to bachelordom? Does it represent loss or liberty?[16] In Daudet's novel, the cause of marital breakdown was the Fagans' different attitudes towards the celebrity which Régis's stage career brought. The coquettish confidante, Pauline, 'une femme de bientôt trente ans', introduces the stage when she states that she would not like to have married a man of the theatre given all the temptations he must surely face (309). As well as encoding a warning to Léon Daudet, this reflects a common association between divorce and the glamorous world of salon society where social and cultural capital overlap (visible in another time and another place in the mythology of Elizabeth Taylor). But Régis offers his own pathologization of a marriage entered nearly twenty years ago when he was merely twenty-eight: 'C'est de ma paresse à sortir, de mes habitudes casanières, que ma femme m'en a surtout voulu. Ce fut son premier grief, le motif initial de la rupture... A qui la faute?' (310). His wife's fault, it seems, lied in her desire to reverse the gendering of those separate spheres of private and public life. She saw marriage as a way of entering her husband's domain, he saw it as a way of retiring from 'ce hideux Tout-Paris' (311).

As the Loi Naquet was a compromise which did not reinstate the radically libertarian aspects of the law of 1792, divorce by mutual consent was not actually possible until the law of 11 July 1975. The problem is that their divorce is in some sense 'un livre sur rien', a plot without narrative foundation. As Fagan says of his ex-wife, 'En réalité, elle manquait comme moi de griefs suprêmes' (317), even though 'ses amies la savaient si malheureuse que, malgré les répugnances de la bonne société parisienne pour le divorce, elles le lui conseillaient toutes' (317). As a result the dramatist and his wife had to stage a scene of *flagrant délit*. 'Il nous faudrait un acte décisif', Régis explains to Pauline (312). In spite of his wife's relationship with La Posterolle, Fagan agrees to play the role of adulterer with an unwitting Amy Férat. In keeping with the sexual double standard which persisted in spite of the legal possibility of citing the adultery of either spouse, Régis thereby saved the honour of his daughters and paved the way for Rose's marriage at the end of the novel: 'Quand c'est l'homme qui est pris en faute, le monde pardonne; quand c'est la femme, il y a un rejaillissement de honte sur la famille. Les enfants en restent touchés, marqués à jamais' (312–13). After all, the adultery of the wife raised the spectre of an illegitimate line. As such, the *vaudevilliste* brings farce to real life: 'Pensez à ce ridicule de gens en instance de divorce, marchant côte à côte, se concertant, combinant leur libération. Moi qui cherche des situations neuves, je crois qu'elle l'était, celle-là!' (313).

This co-authored 'farce indigne' is set up in the hôtel d'Espagne on the avenue de l'Observatoire (314). When the knock on their bedroom door is heard, Amy thinks that it is her husband, thus revealing late in the game that she is in fact married too! Fagan exclaims: 'Ma foi, j'ai passé là quelques mauvaises minutes, à ignorer s'il s'agissait de mon adultère ou du sien.' The cognitive matrix which describes the quadrilateral relations between the two couples is a strange one. Normally adultery presupposes a cognitive order in which the lovers share ultimate knowledge (in more than one sense). The cuckold is the victim of dramatic irony. Amy's deception of her husband is just such a classic deception. However, rather than sharing ultimate knowledge (in any sense), she and her 'lover' deceive each other: she does not tell him about her husband, and he does not tell her that she has been drawn into a legal fiction of adultery. In fact, it is the other conjugal relationship which enjoys true cognitive reciprocity. The Fagans manage 'adultery' without deception, they both know what is going on, although neither M. nor Mme Férat do. This situation could be described as the converse of jealousy. Whereas in jealousy a common desire drives individuals apart ('I want what you want'), here the desire to be apart generates a common purpose ('I don't want you and you don't want me'). Edmond de Goncourt's *Journal* entry for 1 August 1885 offers a persuasive model for the farcical *flagrant délit*:

> Mme Daudet me parlait ce matin du divorce de Belot, de ce divorce combiné, arrangé, machiné, entre la femme et le mari et où le mari s'était fait surprendre par le commissaire de police. On dirait vraiment que de leur vie, de leur vie réelle, ils auraient fabriqué une pièce de théâtre, et cela pour le plaisir, la satisfaction, la récréation de leurs goûts d'intrigues des planches, de leurs natures de *carcassiers*, de leurs imaginations cabotines. Et des épisodes très amusants: les difficultés de trouver des femmes qui veulent bien consentir à recevoir en chemise la visite d'un homme de police; puis les vaines attentes de commissaires qui, malgré la promesse à la femme, retenus ailleurs, ne venaient pas quand Belot les attendait, muni de la particulière à procès-verbal — si bien qu'à la fin, Belot disait à sa femme de prendre mieux ses mesures, parce qu'à son âge, elle lui faisait faire un métier assommant. (II, 1175)

Chapter 3 sets in train the twin narrative tracks which allow Daudet to compare divorce and separation. Post-Fagan, Régis's ex-wife is set to marry the aptly named La Posterolle:

> Non certes qu[e Fagan] fût jaloux de son ancienne femme; mais de ses filles, oh! il l'était, à souffrir autrefois de leur intimité avec ce La Posterolle [...]. Que serait-ce maintenant qu'il habiterait la même maison, avec l'autorité et les privautés d'un beau-père, et bientôt, par la suite des choses, par l'assiduité, la présence réelle et continuelle, plus leur père que lui-même. (320)

Even though 'l'image de la femme n'était plus en lui', her prospective remarriage threatens to undo the assertion made during the children's first visit to boulevard Beauséjour that 'leur père était toujours leur père' (301); and thus once again, liquid modernity challenges the solidity of heavy modernity. When Rose and Ninette start to sulk, it seems that Fagan has the worst of everything and the best of nothing: 'Vraiment, était-ce la peine de divorcer, s'il lui fallait subir les mêmes scènes de ménage, suivies de mutismes dont il connaissait bien l'énervante persistance?' (321). Régis's ex-wife incarnates a genealogy of wives which marginalizes him, for her remarriage will enable her to find suitors for their daughters. In contrast to this tale of divorce and remarriage, the narrative track of separation emerges when, with great *Schadenfreude*, Régis's ex-wife reveals to his shock that he will not be able to marry his confidante, Pauline Hulin, as she is merely separated from her husband and not, as she claims, widowed. All women, Régis concludes, are liars. Moreover, in a reworking of the habitual novelistic tale of the guilty woman's sick son, Maurice's injured knee distracts her from her admirer: 'Comme elle était loin de lui en ce moment, la charmante femme!' (326).

The contrast between the fates of the divorced and the separated is developed in Chapter 4. Pauline Hulin explains to Régis — and the reader — how she finally retaliated against her husband's pathological jealousy by leaving: 'J'ai pardonné quatre ans; [...] mais un soir, [...] le misérable, dans une de ses colères, finissant par douter que notre petit Maurice fût son fils, m'arracha l'enfant des bras et le jeta par terre si violemment...' (332–33). In spite of this accusation of adultery and attack on the son, she will not consider anything more than 'pseudo-veuvage' out of respect for her widowed mother: 'La vieille société parisienne garde une prévention, une défiance de la femme séparée; d'autant que rien n'indique, à moins de recherches spéciales, au profit de qui la séparation a été prononcée' (333). Unfortunately the *président du tribunal* granted him control over the child's education. If the sick Maurice is forced to leave for a *lycée* in 3 months, Pauline says 'j'emporte mon petit et je vais me cacher au bout du monde' (335). Régis suggests that she divorce so that she can remarry. But the theological legacy of her family past controls her behaviour: 'Je crois bien que mon expérience du mariage est faite... d'ailleurs j'ai toute une famille très catholique... ma chère mère appelait le divorce un sacrilège, et moi-même, élevée dans ses idées...' This sacramental view of marriage (and thus critique of divorce as sacrilegious) means that her 'widowhood' mourns her *own* loss of vitality as she gives up the hope of starting again (*répétition* is not merely a professional, theatrical issue in Régis's life; it is also a matter of personal philosophy). Régis chivvies her along: 'Supposez-vous divorcée, Hulin pourrait se remarier, se refaire un intérieur, une famille, et vraisemblablement vous laisserait tranquilles tous les deux' (336). She admits that Régis is intellectually correct but still she cannot bring herself to divorce.

After this voicing of contrary theses, however, Chapter 5 triggers events which will lead to the conclusion that children pose insurmountable problems for those whose marriage has failed. The ex-wife manipulates her children and perverts the common bond of parenthood. To make them jealous of Régis's relationship with Maurice, she quips: 'Vous verrez qu'il adoptera cet enfant et ne laissera à mes pauvres petites que ce qu'il ne pourra pas leur ôter' (339). Their next visit is 'encore un dimanche gâté'. For the first time neither father nor children know how to end the encounter, and they leave early, paving the way for a contravention of the informal agreement that the children would not leave Paris, when their mother's new husband, La Posterolle, is offered the post of *préfet* in Corsica — not leaving France, but leaving the Hexagon.

The most 'romantic' gesture in the novel is the father's secret pursuit of his children to Ajaccio. Ninette chastises him when he arrives unannounced, as hardly anybody there knows that Mme La Posterolle is divorced: 'On croyait maman veuve et nous autres orphelines. [...] Tu penses si le divorce est mal vu!' (352). The irony of this rearranged, or postscripted, past is that her mother has learnt Pauline Hulin's lesson of pseudo-widowhood but applied it to her own narrative of divorce and remarriage. Régis only sees them in the evening and tries to remain incognito, 'inscrit sous un faux nom à l'hôtel de France', like some guilty lover (354). Momentarily — but symbolically — the biological father loses the power of his patronymic. The past, however, refuses to be another country, and Régis is recognized by an old friend.

Fagan tries to leave, but storms force his ship back to port, and his old friend, Rouchouze, lends him the mask of Rigoletto so that he can enjoy Mardi Gras with his daughters, themselves wearing fancy dress. The bloodline extends the intertextual reference whereby Verdi's hero is not only 'à la recherche de sa fille', as Fagan quips, but in this case 'de ses filles' as Rouchouze adds. One does not have to be Bakhtin to see that this Mardi Gras stages offstage the carnivalesque farce of displaced identities and inverted orders. Both the name and the face of the father are concealed, but under this cover the biological link to his daughters is momentarily reasserted, until Mme La Posterolle recognizes him and threatens revenge. Beneath the disguise of the fictional father (Régis), the authorial father (Alphonse Daudet) addresses his own son in a cautionary mode. For the very source — or in Bloomian terms the 'father' — of Verdi's opera is the grandfather of Léon's wife, Victor Hugo, author of *Le Roi s'amuse* (1832). Yet this source play, and the opera which it fathers, could be read yet more acutely not only as a conflict between biological paternity (the enraged jester, Triboulet) and royal paternalism (François Ier, in love with his daughter), but as a warning about overbearing fathers (the victim is the daughter and not, as Triboulet intends, the king). As in his opening epigraph, Daudet senior distances himself from the archetype of the berating father via an ironic cultural reference, a 'coïncidence de théâtre' (372).

Mme La Posterolle gains revenge on her ex-husband by entering the public domain which she so covets and he inhabits. She persuades a Parisian newspaper to print a story about this successful playwright's first display of madness at a ball in Ajaccio. She too can write fictions and fables. When he receives a letter from Rose, Régis is sure that Mme La Posterolle has dictated this text too. The process of turning divorce into literary entertainment is itself fictionalized in Rose's indignation: 'Et puis qu'a-t-on dit à M. La Posterolle, que tu allais faire une comédie avec son mariage et ton divorce? Est-ce croyable?' (383–84). Via Rose, Mme La Posterolle's lie actually plants an intertextually resonant seed in Régis's mind: 'Nom de Dieu! oui, une belle pièce à faire avec son histoire... Une pièce où pleureraient tous les pères, peut-être aussi quelques mamans, et qui s'appellerait: *Le Divorce du père Goriot*' (385). What, Régis and the reader imagine, would this plot look like? This is a question which bespeaks a wider cultural imperative: namely, let us imagine French literature since 1816 — Balzac included — if divorce had been possible. More particularly, readers of Balzac will see a potential analogy for Régis in this cautionary tale for self-sacrificing fathers. Only Rastignac will cry at Goriot's funeral at Père Lachaise. Alphonse himself is caught between the models of Verdi and Balzac, between fathers who are too severe and fathers who yield too easily.

The penultimate chapter parallels the preparations for Rose's own marriage with Régis's dashed attempt to marry Pauline. When he visits Malville, the *président* in the Hulins' separation, the lawyer reassures Régis that she is marrying into a respectable family, the Rémorys. When Régis learns that Pauline's estranged husband has also died, he is ecstatic. A hint of star-crossed love, however, can be gleaned as Malville is singing from the love scene in Act II of Wagner's *Tristan und Isolde*, as Régis arrives. The scene of adulterous love centred on the eponymous heroes' duet 'O sink hernieder, Nacht der Liebe' is interrupted by the angry husband, Mark. Even though Pauline's husband is dead, there is foreboding for Régis in this tale of the first man who returns to interrupt true love.

In Régis's ultimate disappointment at the now widowed Pauline's refusal to marry, it is also tempting to see a modern reworking of the classic French novel of renounced love, *La Princesse de Clèves*, a renunciation which persists even when her husband's death facilitates matters. Régis de Fagan is, however, no duc de Nemours. Meanwhile, the La Posterolles arrive in Paris for the wedding and stay at the ironically named *Family* on the Cours-la-Reine. The twin narrative tracks of father and daughters meet when Rose and Ninette confront Pauline at the bedside of the sick Régis. He turns on his daughters with words which bespeak his own alienation and isolation from the company of women with whom he once formed a family unit: 'Je suis divorcé d'avec ma femme, je le serai aussi d'avec mes enfants' (398). Behind this foreground of convoluted unhappiness, however, Alphonse Daudet does then provide one idealized cameo of conjugal bliss in the vision of the Couverchels, actors 'mariés depuis vingt ans, légendaires sur le boulevard par leur tendresse et leur admiration réciproques' (389): 'on sentait que la mort seule pourrait les découpler. Et c'étaient des comédiens, de ces âmes futiles et vaniteuses [...]. Oui, chez d'humbles cabots, c'est là qu'il trouvait le mariage rêvé, idéal' (390). They resemble some Beckett-like couple, but an unambiguously happy one — bohemians of the boulevard, yet masters of the affective life. Theirs is a secret resistant both to analysis and narrative, a notional place for the heart which Daudet will not extinguish but cannot extrapolate.

Rather than resurrecting happy love, the final chapter of this short novel, provides a corrosive desublimation of that social and literary *point culminant*, the wedding day. This day embodies the ways in which the lives of children throw these ex-spouses back together in spite of their own disinclination. When they meet to agree plans, Régis sees in his 'ex' the 'mauvais génie de son existence,

quelque maléficieux kobold niché dans le fond de cette sombre allée d'arbres' (400).
In a final twist, she tells him how Pauline offered herself to her husband one last
time so as to keep Maurice, only for the husband to commit suicide afterwards. By
hinting at the erotic reciprocity which an experienced woman could fashion even
on such a night, she crushes Régis's dream of remarriage. The Régis/Pauline story
contradicts the proto-liquid liberational rhetoric which accompanied pro-divorce
discourse. Pauline's refusal to accept the possibility of remarriage positions this
couple on the fault line of an epistemic shift between two socio-sexual paradigms.
But as Régis's own case suggests, divorce itself does not resolve the compromises
and contradictions of affiliation and affection. Fagan tells Pauline:

> Comme vous avez raison!... Quel méli-mélo que le divorce, et les bizarres
> combinaisons qu'il amène!... Rose se mariera dans quelques jours, et son
> mariage est tout ce qu'il y a de plus régulier, mais ses parents étant divorcés,
> voici l'étrange spectacle que la noce présentera... (407)

Sombre ceremony risks turning into farce. He, the divorced father, will lead the
bride in front of the remarried mother who now has a name different from their
daughter's even before the ceremony: 'si Paris savait rire encore...' (408).

In fact, neither party can resolve the disappointment of a life lived and lost.
Indeed, in a speech which returns us from narrative to thesis Fagan accepts now
that he has lost his children:

> Mes enfants ne sont plus à moi; cette méchante femme les a accaparées [...]. Ç'a
> été un travail de fourmi, de taret, lentement, par petits coups et jour à jour...
> et dire que jusqu'à la fin de ma vie je suis lié à cette créature, qu'elle ne me
> lâchera jamais! Après le mariage de Rose, nous nous retrouverons au mariage
> de Ninette; plus tard, devenus grands-parents, nous nous rencontrerons à des
> baptêmes. Je l'aurai pour commère, vous verrez, une commère qui apprendra
> à mes petits-enfants à me détester, ainsi qu'elle l'a appris à mes filles... Ah! le
> divorce, ce tranchement du lien, que je célébrais comme une délivrance, vous
> rappelez-vous... dont j'étais si joyeux, si fier..., mais quand on a des enfants, le
> divorce n'est même pas une solution.

The language of weddings and baptisms reflects an institutional idealization of
the family from which parents cannot escape. Tellingly though, Pauline depicts
separation as no better: 'avec des enfants, la séparation ne vaut guère mieux... elle
n'est qu'apparente, fictive... l'enfant reste toujours entre le père et la mère' (408–09).
It is parenthood as a legal and social rather than strictly biological phenomenon
which makes a clean break with the past impossible. Because these parents have
invested in the future by raising children, they cannot create a fresh future for
themselves as romantically and erotically recharged individuals. Children return
these parents to the person with whom they have raised progeny — in Fagan's case
— or to the memory of that person — in Pauline's.

Pauline can only sigh in resigned agreement when Fagan concludes by reasserting
the idealized model, already represented by the Couverchels: 'Oui, l'intégrité
du mariage, tout le bonheur serait là... Se dire en choisissant sa femme: Quand
je mourrai, voici l'épaule où j'appuierai ma tête pour dormir' (409). As another
Wagnerian tune provides background music in the reader's ear, Fagan's idealization

of marriage of course reflects an idealization of womanhood. In the final scene of the novel, this morose couple, Pauline and Fagan, catch sight of the triumphant triumvirate of Mme La Posterolle and daughters:

> Et c'était bien une victime du divorce, ce pauvre homme, regardant ses filles, leur mère, sa vraie famille, s'éloigner à toute vitesse dans ce landau plein de rires et de rubans clairs, tandis qu'il restait au bord du trottoir, incertain et vague dans la nuit presque venue, avec cette femme et cet enfant, dont le grand deuil, qui l'accompagnait mais ne partageait pas, disait assez combien ils étaient, combien ils demeureraient probablement toujours étrangers les uns aux autres. (410)

And so the novel closes. The doubt inherent in 'probablement toujours' serves only to torture this tragic couple inasmuch as it offers a glimpse of hope. Whereas Mme La Posterolle and daughters seem capable of carrying on regardless of the past, Régis and Pauline are too sensitive for the rigorous journey of modern love with its false starts, cancellations, rerouting and new timetables. The reader at the start of the twenty-first century cannot help protesting to the author at the end of the nineteenth that this novel either occludes or avoids the versions and perspectives of Mme La Posterolle and her two daughters. Rare amongst French fictional titles in its use of two female names, the novel is no *Thelma and Louise*. Rose and Ninette are advertised as the mere objects of frustrated paternal affection. Régis, it seems, is left stranded, between two families and between two historical moments. We have seen how the literary world provided one *mondain* context not only for textual representations of divorce but also for its enactment. As we shall see, politics offered another rarefied double context for divorce — as an object of parliamentary debate which returns to haunt the private lives of politicians.

   Édouard Rod (1857–1910) has long since fallen into the gap between, on the one hand, a pedagogical reliance on the novelistic canon and, on the other, the critical excavation of cultural margins. Between the long since canonical and the once marginal, however, there remains a treasure trove of novels which received serious consideration from *fin de siècle* contemporaries both for their literary achievements and social pertinence. The aesthetics of modernism and after have displaced these achievements, and it may well be only via the path of social history, broadly understood, that both these achievements and this pertinence may be recovered. The best example of such a lost son of literary history is Paul Bourget, known of and yet so often not known. Like Bourget, Rod addresses the question of divorce. Such historical concerns which may in general turn on politicized questions of gender and class bring us face to face with literary texts which are supposedly unreadable precisely because their *lisibilité* is so dull, and confront us with a critical problem not dissimilar to that faced by the author of *Madame Bovary*: namely, how to find the interesting at the heart of the banal, and then how to make the apparently boring interesting. In the words of his contemporary Henry Bordeaux, however, 'L'amour moderne, c'est l'amour souffrant qui sait trop bien l'inanité de sa joie, la fragilité du bonheur qu'il apporte [...]. M. Édouard Rod est l'un des plus troublants interprètes de cet amour moderne, si douloureux et si frémissant d'inquiétude.'[17]

   In her analysis of women-authored sentimental social novels from earlier in the century Margaret Cohen offers a fluent defence of a critical interest in 'the great unread'.[18] The scepticism of fellow critics runs thus:

> Isn't it boring reading sentimental novels, both friendly and hostile critics of the project have asked — in other words, wouldn't you really rather be reading Balzac — as if we all agreed that these works were intrinsically uninteresting, even if I could dress them up with critical arguments. The question foregrounds one great problem working on literature *hors d'usage*, which is the continued skepticism concerning its literary value. Attention to forgotten literature is too often treated as antiquarian fussing over texts that deserve to be forgotten.

Her answer follows:

> Working in literature *hors d'usage*, it becomes clear, however, that current obstacles to literary evaluation derive not from the noncanonical but rather from the fact that so little about it is known. Too often, noncanonical texts are fragments of lost solutions or answers to questions we no longer hear.

Édouard Rod's diptych, *La Vie privée de Michel Teissier* (1893) and *La Seconde Vie de Michel Teissier* (1894), previously *hors d'usage*, might now provide one such fragment in the history of family life and its representations.[19] The third-person narrative of *La Vie privée de Michel Teissier* introduces Teissier whose success as a *publiciste* for the newspaper *Ordre* has allowed him to succeed as a right-wing politician, now vice-president of the Chamber of Deputies and about to be made a government minister. His Achilles heel is the force and authenticity of his adulterous desire for a younger woman, Blanche Estève, daughter of his old friend Raoul. The first novel charts his vain attempts to resist this desire, under the tutelage of another boyhood friend, Mondet, whose moral commentary speaks to the reader throughout. Once his wife Suzanne realizes that there is no other solution, she offers Michel a divorce. The first novel ends with the newly-weds, Michel and Blanche, on a train to Rouen from where they hope to find anonymity in England.

Unlike the halfway point of Maupassant's bipartite novel of divorce, *Bel-Ami* (1885) where that other newly married journalist, Georges Duroy, takes the remarried widow, Madeleine Forestier, on her second honeymoon on that same train journey from Paris to Rouen, the divorce motif is not withheld until the end of Rod's tale. Michel Teissier is no widower and though his first wife dies early in the second novel, divorce has already set up a tension between his amorous and paternal roles which will colour the fate of his second marriage, and thereby revisit the concerns of *Rose et Ninette*. His motherless daughters, Annie and Laurence, then invade 'the convenient childlessness' of his second marriage which has settled in Clarens.[20] As fluctuating relations are played out between these three young women who share gender, generation and gerontocrat, the increasingly left-wing Michel is attracted back to the public life of politics in Paris in spite of the risk of courting further scandal. The sins of the father are visited upon his daughter, Annie, whose romantic liaison with Saint-Brun is blocked by the boy's father. During his time teaching at the University of Geneva (1886–93), Rod had fallen in love with Nancy Vuille (who wrote under the name André Gladès). She was one of three daughters of Louis Vuille, the owner of the *Brasserie Saint-Jean*, who, at the time of Rod's professorship, was about to be divorced from his invalid wife. Lerner points out that 'her attachment to Rod was not only a shield against the social repercussions of her parents' divorce and her melancholy home-life, but above all a spiritual communion of intimate and sensitive impressions of life and literature'.[21] It is hard to imagine that Rod did not gauge in Nancy a child's response to divorce. Throughout this second novel, the growing sense that Blanche and Michel's relationship was ill-fated from the start is fuelled by Blanche's fears that she is losing him to Paris, politics and the Left for whom he is to stand for election in Haute-Savoie.

The closing chapter settles scores, yet in ways which leave the future open. Mondet's proliferation of what might be called — in more than one sense — home truths leads to a further rupture, this time of the homosocial variety, with Michel, who turns back to his second wife, Blanche. Michel's letters to her reveal a rediscovered affection in shared guilt: 'Nous avions fait, chérie, une grosse faute: la vie est double, nous l'avons oublié, et nous avions ainsi rompu l'équilibre de ses deux parties' by seeking exile and absolute privacy (SV, 302). He hopes that now he has returned to public life, the 'heures noires' of their marriage will pass — once more the male immersing himself in the public realm rather than coming to terms with the domestic one. But a price is paid, as Annie dies of a lung complaint, and he cannot resist an ethical economy whose principle resembles a fatalistic conservatism: 'il saisissait le lien si ténu, presque invisible, qui faisait de cette enfant morte la martyre de ses désirs atteints, la victime expiatoire, et non peut-être la dernière, de sa chère et belle et douce erreur' (SV, 312). 'Il avait trop aimé son propre bonheur'; eudemonism, it seems, kills. Almost immediately his return to public life is confirmed by a telegram with news of his election victory. This moves Laurence to take up her sister's role by embracing her stepmother and whispering that 'il n'y a que vous qui ayez su l'aimer!' (SV, 313). Michel joins the embrace in a reconfigured family triangle in which gender division reasserts itself: 'il ne devina pas qu[e leurs larmes] venaient d'une même source pour aller se perdre dans un même courant, qu'elles n'étaient qu'un soupir dans la plainte éternelle de celles qui sont les éternelles victimes de notre égoïsme, de nos ambitions et de notre dureté'.

The second novel begins and ends with the death of women from Michel's first family. Indeed, it is almost as if the transformations in the course of women's lives do themselves demand such demise, firstly, of his ageing wife, and secondly, of his daughter who has recently been courted by both Amé and another son of the political classes, Graval. We finish reading with the sense that further mishaps await Blanche (who must herself grow old) and Laurence (who will follow her sister towards fully fledged womanhood). For both merely inhabit the subject positions of the dead women whom the perpetually distracted Teissier has lost. At the end of the first novel, passionate desire drew Michel away from his first family; at the end of the second, political desire draws him away from family quietude back into the uncertainty of public life, back into the hub of narrative that is Paris.

The double nature of life which Michel recalls in the final chapter of the first novel does not merely take the form of the private–public divide highlighted in 'l'homme intime qui doublait l'homme public' (VP, 68), though Rod's description of the politician's divorce does, as will be shown below, allow him to explore public life post-1884 in the light of two notorious actual divorce scandals from England

(to which the newly-wed Michel and Blanche escape). This notion of doubleness —
embedded in the very notion of the couple — reflects both the theme of divorce
(and the quasi-existential questions it raises) and hence the narrative shapes a
divorced life facilitates. To divorce and remarry is to double doubleness, or in some
sense to give up the idea of uniqueness in the very search for the unique elsewhere.
As such, the new legal possibility of divorce after 1884 raised a number of ethical
and philosophical questions described in our Introduction. Most fundamentally,
is it possible to start again? Once Suzanne realizes how Blanche and Michel feel
about each other, but before the need for a divorce has been faced, Mondet warns
Michel that he must recommit himself to his marriage: 'C'est tout à recommencer',
to which Michel quips, 'Je crois plutôt que tout va commencer' (VP, 177). If the
quest for authenticity which can motivate divorce leads to sequential doubleness
(one love after another), then the much fabled private/public division, intrinsic
to bourgeois life but dramatized by the world of politics, demands the parallel
doubleness of hypocrisy. In the same conversation with Mondet, Michel notes how
he experiences politics 'comme en rêve' as 'j'ai si bien appris à me dédoubler, mon
cher, que je vis deux vies; ma vie extérieure [...] et ma vie intérieure: une vie de
moine extatique, de chevalier fervent' (VP, 178–89).

Furthermore, can one redeem the fault of a repudiated marriage by forging
a coherent second life, by committing oneself to a second marriage? There is a
running pun on this notion of secondariness. In the sequence of letters in Chapter
4 of the first novel, Michel recounts to Mondet how his discussions with Suzanne
about what is to be done with their marriage and his passion are controlled by
a civilized tone: 'Nous causions posément, comme des gens qui discutent une
question d'intérêt secondaire' (VP, 131). Though second in sequence, is his passion
for Blanche therefore second in value? In the dedicatory preface to Madame James
Darmester the second novel devoted to a second marriage is anticipated in a
gesture which thereby implies the unitary nature of the diptych: 'Je me réserve de
montrer, dans mon prochain livre, de quelles peines [sa conscience] l'a tourmenté,
secondée d'ailleurs par cette redoutable logique qui veut impitoyablement que le
mal engendre le mal' (VP, vii). Puns are themselves, of course, a type of secondary
meaning in which connotation teases away the fabric of denotation.

Though Michel begins by asserting the linear simplicity of his life ('J'ai lancé
[ma vie] en ligne droite, il faut bien que je continue!' (VP, 23)), he is very soon
discussing with Mondet the bifurcation of the potential plots which await him.
Of all the 'projets insensés' from which he might choose, 'Le divorce était encore
le plus raisonnable... Oui, j'ai rêvé d'enlèvements romantiques, de fuite dans des
pays perdus, de suicide à deux après un mois de bonheur... J'ai songé aussi à la
mort pour moi seul' (VP, 62). He and Blanche dismiss the habitual fate of the
single young woman, unable to accept 'que nous finirons comme tant d'autres, et
qu'elle deviendra tout simplement une maîtresse clandestine, n'est-ce pas?' (VP, 63).
Divorce thus emerges as a potential means of escaping the received plots of social
history and classic fiction.

In other words, the reader is led to inquire whether, by serializing one's desires,
by moving from one passion to another, one can avoid duplicity. Or is a life led

by passions (amorous and political) ultimately a life misled? Is Michel an icon of authenticity or of self-indulgence? These are some of the questions which characterize the philosophical introspection of Rod's diptych, written after his shift — under the influence of Russian novelists, notably Tolstoy — from the naturalism of *Les Allemands à Paris* (1879) and *Palmyre Veulard* (1881) towards the spiritual awareness and resignation of his most famous novel, *Le Sens de la vie* (1889), where he advertises the intersubjective model of neo-Christian pity with which he has been most clearly associated: 'Regarder en soi non pour se connaître ni pour s'aimer, mais pour connaître et aimer les autres'. One of the most perceptive early essays on Rod was written by fellow novelist — and fellow lost son, neither in the canon nor on the margins — Henry Bordeaux who characterizes him as a pessimist in *Âmes modernes*. Bordeaux, though, is typical of critics of post-naturalist fiction who, in their urgency to suggest an intellectual engagement with philosophical and psychological problems beyond the nuts and bolts of naturalism, read novels such as the *Michel Teissier* diptych without actually mentioning the question of divorce, as if Rod's treatment of it were merely a springboard for more profound issues. This critical cult of the *âme supérieure* — which reflects the rise of Idealist thought at the time — conceals the fact that divorce articulated key intellectual positions of the time and staged psychological and philosophical issues in illuminating ways. Bordeaux, though, feels that he is doing Rod a favour by keeping him metaphysical.

Though pessimism of a Schopenhauerian variety led to doubt about the very viability of marriage, Rod's pessimism leaves him pragmatically resigned to the impossibility of building a life on the shifting sands of mere desire. All that remains in the detritus of passion which we call marriage is affection, and to choose affection above all else requires one to practise a humility of which Teissier seems barely capable. More in line with Bourget than Gide, Rod invokes a principle of anti-*disponibilité* where the self is sacrificed to social coherence. This is the lesson of the second novel in the diptych which drags Michel and Blanche back from the sunset of narrative ends into the harsh daylight of a second plot immediately losing its freshness.

At the start of that novel the affectionate kiss seems the only emotional foundation on which to build a life: 'Malgré le temps, malgré l'âge [Michel is now 46], il y avait de l'amour encore, dans ce baiser' (SV, 12). But very soon Teissier's doubts remerge: 'La vie active, avec ses promesses et ses triomphes, vaut-elle qu'on lui sacrifie l'amour?... L'amour, de son côté, mérite-t-il les privations, les regrets, les remords qu'on endure pour lui quand on a trop écouté sa voix?' (SV, 24). The major privation is the absence of his children. He feels so guilty that he cannot even bring himself to take up his paternal visiting rights, but this response is itself ripe for misinterpretation. Should his passion for Blanche have displaced his affection for Suzanne? And as this passion itself transmutes into affection, should he allow it to be threatened by his one unquenchable passion — politics? The irony of this subsidence of passion into affection is that a similar process has already eroded his first marriage. After Suzanne's initial accusation, Michel writes to her in precisely such terms:

> Je ne sais pas pourquoi, après t'avoir aimée comme tu sais, j'ai laissé l'amour
> se transformer peu à peu en une affection solide et tranquille qui me paraissait

> valoir mieux. [...] La plupart des hommes et des femmes acceptent cette
> transformation naturelle, et s'y résignent. Je croyais l'avoir acceptée: je me
> trompais. (VP, 101–02)

In response, Suzanne herself refuses the possibility of a life built on 'affection',
whilst his love is reserved for Blanche. She demands that he choose even if she must
lose out in such a decision.

In the second novel, once Suzanne has died, Mondet lives up to his name with a
worldly wise unwrapping of Michel's false sense of regret:

> Tu ne regrettes rien, tu referais ce que tu as fait, si c'était à recommencer, sans
> plus d'inconscience, quoique avec moins d'illusions. Seulement tu as quarante-
> huit ans, tu as passé l'âge des romans, — et le tien dure encore!... Et même il
> faut qu'il dure. Tu te dois à toi-même, à ta femme, aux autres, de le prolonger
> jusqu'après l'âge. Tu es, comme qui dirait, condamné à l'amour à perpétuité...
> (SV, 86)

The irony is that this language of perpetuity, this notion of marriage as a prison
sentence has already been invoked in the first novel in the conversation which follows
Michel's anti-divorce speech in the Chamber of Deputies (his paradoxical motives
for taking this line are explained below). Mondet believes divorce is necessary and
that before legislative reaction against the law of 1884, it is at least necessary to wait
until its full social effects become visible, but Suzanne defends her husband's quasi-
Bonaldian position: 'Dans son système, tout se tient, la famille, la société, l'Église'
(VP, 10). Because she and Suzanne share the same object of affection, Blanche too
reports with pride on how brilliantly Michel has spoken, even though his revisionist
bill is blocked: 'Vous savez comme il est calme, quand l'orage gronde autour de lui'
(VP, 15). More than a political groupie, Blanche is the love of Teissier's life, but in
spite of her name she will not be able to offer him an emotional *tabula rasa*. At the
end of the evening, Suzanne will spy on their near embrace, the *manqué* expression
of their 'désirs irrésolus' against which they have struggled for a year, 'comme l'orage
dont toute la soirée le bon Mondet avait senti l'électricité dans l'air' (VP, 29). In the
Chamber, as Blanche says, Michel's inner calm confounds the outer commotion;
at home, his outer calm is confounded by inner turbulence. Over dinner Peyraud,
another *publiciste* for the Party, labours the analogy between home and nation so dear
to the Right: 'Pendant vingt ans en France, on a tout démoli, tout renversé. Nous
reconstruirons, voilà tout. Nous sommes entrés dans une maison vermoulue, nous
voulons en faire un édifice solide, dont toutes les parties se soutiennent entre elles'
(VP, 19). This criticism of the triumph of Republicanism sets up a chain between
nation, family and individual, at the end of which an ironic twist is offered by the
love plot of Michel (the individual who claims to represent the nation). Just how
ironic this twist will be is anticipated in Mondet's teasing words offered to Suzanne:
'Vous pouvez être tout à fait tranquille à présent, chère Madame. Si jamais le grand
homme avait quelque velléité de divorcer, — plus moyen, fini, il s'est enchaîné
lui-même' (VP, 20). Nobody laughs. Teissier argues that scandals should not halt a
political career, and cites the cases of Combel and Diel, but Mondet warns him, 'Tu
es condamné à la vertu à perpétuité, mon cher!' (VP, 22). Teissier, however, will
swap one life sentence for another, in both textual and legal senses.

The fictional case of Diel is developed in Chapter VI of *La Vie privée* as the conservatives exploit both the Tonkin Crisis (the metonymic chain extended as the nation adopts its most expansive form as a colonial power) and the situation of the minister for the colonies, Diel, who is involved in a scandalous divorce case following 'une scène de coulisses' recounted in the press (VP, 181–82). Teissier's newspaper, *Ordre*, has not gone for the jugular, by contrast with the tactics he would expect from the left-wing press. Diel survives, and in the first of two analogies with contemporary politics in London, namely the Parnell case, the value of the French division of public and private is affirmed: 'Voilà qui prouve que nous ne sommes pas des Anglais' (VP, 187). The Irish nationalist Charles Stewart Parnell (1846–1891), member of the British Parliament (1875–91) and the leader of the struggle for Irish Home Rule, was ruined by proof of his adultery with Katherine O'Shea, whom he subsequently married. On 24 December 1889 Captain O'Shea filed a petition for divorce, naming Parnell as co-respondent. The suit being defended, the court returned a verdict against Parnell and Katherine O'Shea on 17 November 1890. Parnell married Katherine in June 1891. Rod's attitude towards this reference is manifest in his preface: 'N'a-t-on pas, tout récemment, pour une faute à coup sûr plus vénielle, lapidé un grand homme d'État dont le nom viendra dans ces pages?' (VP, VII). It is particularly ironic that Diel should quip 'tout se sait toujours, tout de suite', when the news emerges at an Elysée palace party that Michel's beloved Blanche is supposedly to marry Graval (VP, 209). The omens for Michel's own secret are less than good. Once the divorce is agreed with Suzanne, Michel tells his fellow party leader about his predicament. De Thornes asks him not to resign: 'En France, ces choses-là ne tuent pas un homme. Nous ne sommes pas des Anglais!' (VP, 266). To reiterate the analogy, 'comme après tout les Français ne sont pas des puritains d'Écosse, vous n'avez pas à redouter le sort d'un Parnell' (VP, 273). Michel, however, prefers exile and 'la solution qui me laissera le moins de remords, avec la possibilité d'un peu de bonheur ou d'oubli' (VP, 271). But Michel is unable to forget either Suzanne, his children or his beloved politics. Nor can he escape into obscurity immediately.

When he leaves home for the Grand-Hôtel before the divorce case begins, the press discovers his whereabouts. Aided by Diel, ironically enough, they connect this divorce with the rupture of the Graval-Blanche engagement. The painful farce of the case is conveyed via letters in which Michel explains how he had to forge 'lettres injurieuses' to provide the court with the necessary 'facts': 'Ils n'ont admis, comme cause de divorce, que des *faits*. Mais qu'est-ce donc que les *faits*, là comme partout? Il n'y a eu aucun *fait* entre nous' (VP, 301). Ironically, it is only this involvement in an actual divorce case which persuades Michel of the need to revise his political opinions and work for a more liberal divorce law: 'Ah! si jamais je reviens aux affaires... Il est vrai que je n'y reviendrai jamais!...' (VP, 302). The further irony is that by the end of the second novel his return to Parisian politics is well under way. His second wedding takes place towards the end of the first novel and is an unglamorous affair, 'badauds' and 'curieux' looking on as they emerge from the town hall, with neither family nor friends present, in a sorry anticipation of the atomization of the modern couple. On the train to Rouen they are joined by a couple of men, one reading to the other M★★★'s charitable article on the Teissier divorce which nevertheless says of Michel, 'Il ne sera jamais heureux!' (VP, 332). On this train going out towards Flaubert territory, the Bouvard-and-Pécuchet-style couple offer a less charitable interpretation of the situation before exiting at Poissy and leaving the newly-weds to their own devices. The latter are, it seems, always either excessively solitary or, as here, insufficiently so. The balance between coupledom and society appears damaged for good. Thus divorce publicizes and dramatizes the fracturing of the adult subject. To have passed through childhood and adolescence is not to have reached a complete state of *Bildung*, in spite of Peyraud's praise of Teissier and 'la belle unité de sa vie' (VP, 20).

In fact public life is not merely the converse of private life. Michel uses his public role to try and direct his private path. Having confessed to Mondet his desperate 'platonic' love for Blanche, he explains how he chose to attack divorce in the Chamber precisely so that he would not be able to follow such a path in his own life without appearing hopelessly hypocritical: 'J'ai brûlé mes vaisseaux [...]. C'est pour me couper la retraite, tout simplement, que j'ai demandé la suppression du divorce' (VP, 59–60). Pitting what we would call parallel doubleness against sequential doubleness, he invokes the spectre of hypocrisy so as to suppress his own amorous authenticity. In the event, though, by going out on such a limb, Michel merely proves to himself how irresistible his unconsummated passion is. Mondet, however, will not allow him to forget his social role, his place in the chain linking individual and nation: 'Tu n'es pas une individualité isolée: tu représentes un groupe social... Tiens! je te dirais presque que tu es l'âme d'un pays' (VP, 61). Though Mondet's rhetoric might sound rather bathetic to the modern ear, the high political plot allows Rod to foreground the issue of social responsibility in a way which extends visibly — rather than merely theoretically — beyond the family realm. How can Michel possibly escape that metonymic chain which conjoins individual, family and society? At moments Michel does echo that wider national discourse which Peyraud and Mondet have highlighted in their very different ways. In a speech in Lyons, he offers 'un tableau magistral de l'histoire de la troisième république', prosecuting its *mentalité*:

> Cet esprit borné qui prend pour la vérité ses manifestations les plus extérieures nie tout ce qui ne tombe pas directement sous les sens. Le génie de la France se desséchait, oscillant entre le grossier matérialisme affiché à l'Hôtel de ville et le naturalisme violent ou le pessimisme découragé des romans à la mode. (VP, 161)

In fact, it is Suzanne who refuses to allow him to live the lie — or rather, not to tell it — and when he protests against her demand that they separate, she claims that his invocation of the children's interests merely conceals his own political motives. Indeed, public life infiltrates the domestic domain like some unwanted but irresistible metaphor. In Michel's words, 'Il me semble que nous sommes deux associés qui ne s'entendent plus, qui ont de sourds motifs de méfiance ou d'antipathie l'un contre l'autre, [...] mais que la communauté des intérêts ou des devoirs retient comme attachés ensemble' (VP, 134). In the terms of this economic metaphor of emotional profit and loss, bankruptcy looms.

As Mondet predicts in the second novel, the passion for active politics will ultimately draw Michel away from sedentary domesticity:

> Une peine très douce au commencement, mais qui devient fastidieuse, avec les années... J'aime, j'aimerais, j'ai aimé, j'aimerai, c'est le verbe charmant, mais un peu monotone, à la longue. [...] Je ne dis pas que ton sentiment soit éteint, non! Il n'est plus le même, pourtant. La passion n'est pas éternelle, pour toi ni personne. [...] Le malheur, c'est que ces idées, ces regrets te hanteront de plus en plus, à mesure que s'amasseront les années, c'est inévitable. Tu n'es pas exclusivement un sentimental, malgré le sacrifice que tu as fait au roman: tu es un actif, aussi [...]. Tu as forgé toi-même les chaînes d'or où tu te débats, mon pauvre ami, et tu n'as plus d'autre lot que de les supporter! (SV, 86–87)

The link between political and sexual appetite is, of course, one which we find over a century later in journalistic accounts of Bill Clinton in the United States, François Mitterrand in France and Jeffrey Archer in the United Kingdom, to name but a handful of such errant male public figures. Mondet, the moral conscience of the novels, has returned to teach Latin at the friends' old *lycée* in Annecy. Though their life is simple, Suzanne sometimes envies his wife who shares him only with their children. He belongs to

> des gens qui ont accepté la vie telle qu'elle est, qui en jouissent, qui ne la gâtent ni par des désirs importuns, ni par des aspirations excessives: tandis qu'il y avait en Michel comme un vide permanent, comme un abîme caché où l'on entendait parfois de sourds grondements. (VP, 7)

The effect seems to be that those who wish to occupy the centre of public life end up, like Teissier, transgressing in their private one, because of 'cette mobilité de sentiment qui lui était particulière' (VP, 155). His proteanism allows him to reinvent himself politically as his opinions migrate from Right to Left in Hugolian fashion. Sentimental reinvention, however, seems more hazardous.

La Seconde Vie de Michel Teissier provides a control experiment in which the peace of their latest bolt-hole, Clarens, associated no doubt with Rousseau, fails to hold this 'touriste sans profession'. After eight years of 'ce monde inactif et ambulant' which might have been all right for the 'Eurotrash' referred to as 'des gens, oisifs de naissance et de goûts', Clarens ends up seeming as tiresome as everywhere else (SV, 2–3). The couple learn that there is little more dangerous than the 'désœuvrement' of fulfilled desires: 'Sans traverser aucun océan, ils s'étaient enfermés dans une île déserte' (SV, 7). Blanche intuits that the dilemma at the heart of this second marriage is an externalization of Michel's inner division between competing drives which address the political and domestic spheres respectively. The persistent passion of politics threatens to submerge the waning passion of married life, and the hint is that Blanche may herself be blanked out, returned to the subject position of the woman she has replaced, the half-abandoned wife of a man whose true mistress is politics. The presence of Anne and, in particular, Laurence in Clarens after Suzanne's death proves highly problematic at first, and the crisis over Laurence's mistreatment of the servant, Candida, allows Michel to voice his desire to return to Paris. Blanche fears that a return to politics will represent a return to Michel's former life, as if his 'abdication complète' had been 'la rançon de leur faute, la garantie de leur fragile bonheur' (SV, 143–44). In his discussion with Mondet who is sceptical about such a return to 'the scene of the crime', Michel cites another case of political and sexual scandal to match Parnell's, that of Sir Charles Dilke. He concludes that 'Parnell a eu grand tort de mourir, qu'il ne faut jamais désespérer, qu'un homme n'est point un vaincu tant qu'il lui reste un souffle de vie et de volonté' (SV, 89).

Sir Charles Dilke (1843–1911), a British statesman and Radical member of Parliament, became a member of the Cabinet in Gladstone's second administration but was ruined at the height of his career when cited in a divorce suit. Disraeli had prophesied that Dilke would one day be prime minister, but in 1885 Dilke was cited as co-respondent in a sensational divorce suit. Virginia Crawford, the twenty-two-year-old wife of a Scottish Liberal lawyer, told her husband that she had been Dilke's mistress since 1882. When the case was heard, in February 1886, there was adjudged to be no evidence against him, although Crawford got his divorce. A press campaign, in which the *Pall Mall Gazette* took the lead, ensured that this was seen as a sufficient victory for Dilke. To try to clear his name totally he got the queen's proctor to reopen the case, and a second hearing took place in July 1886. This went heavily against Dilke. One of his public difficulties was that, although he rebutted Mrs Crawford's allegations, he was forced to admit to having been her mother's lover — thus not quite matching the notorious achievements of the British politician, Alan Clark (1928–99). Six years later, as Rod was preparing the first novel in the diptych, Dilke returned to the House of Commons. He would hold his seat until his death nearly twenty years later. Much of his energy, however, was devoted to gathering evidence that might clear his name. The accumulated evidence showed decisively that much of Mrs Crawford's story was a fabrication; whether there was a substratum of truth remains uncertain.

For Blanche, the silver lining in a return to Paris would be that she might then be allowed the religious ceremony which would reassure her about Michel's commitment to their marriage but which does not appeal to him. This lukewarm male attitude towards religious consecration of the second marriage in some sense anticipates Paul Bourget's *Un divorce* in which the divorcee, Gabrielle, longs for a religious marriage with her second husband, Darras, now that her first husband, Chambault, is — like Suzanne in Rod's novel — dead. Like Teissier, Darras is less than keen, but by the end of the novel a glimmer of hope burns in Gabrielle's heart. Darras's resistance is not merely anti-clerical; he refuses to accept the implication that hitherto Gabrielle has been nothing but his mistress. Whilst Gabrielle's motivation is largely religious, Blanche is more interested in the 'caractère social' (SV, 144) of such a sanction. Blanche also argues that Michel would make things easier for the young lovers, Annie and Saint-Brun, if he agreed to 'enlever ses derniers vestiges d'irrégularité' (SV, 174). By the end, though, she feels that same melancholy. In both cases, the desire to 'regularize' the union seems to be intrinsically linked to women's need for respectability in society rather than their own marital history (Gabrielle is divorced, Blanche is not).

Back in Paris Michel discusses with Peyraud how he might reconstruct his political career and, for reasons quite different to Blanche's, his colleague also suggests that he agree to 'régulariser' their marriage. Peyraud encourages Michel by reference to contemporary history: 'Bah! le passé, qui donc y songera?... Est-ce que la puritaine Angleterre n'a pas rouvert les portes de son Parlement à sir Charles Dilke?' (SV, 159). Peyraud seems to be clutching at straws as he tries to prove that politicians can survive divorce scandals. In 1886, it was decreed that French newspapers could not report divorce cases openly — in that specifically Gallic tradition of trying to safeguard public figures from private revelations. But the coded scandal-mongering of journalists certainly continued. In spite of the revised law, it was clear that divorce was *ipso facto* a making public of private matters and often a voicing of the *interdit* as fault had to be established. Perhaps the greatest French political survivor of divorce during the Third Republic was Georges Clemenceau. In 1869 he married Mary Plummer, who had been a pupil at a finishing school in Stamford, Connecticut, called Miss Aiken's Seminary for Young Ladies, where he had taught French and horse riding. On his return to Paris, his political and amorous adventures developed apace, both visible to the capital's public. Though they separated in 1876, their marriage lasted for over twenty years. In a beautiful emblem of the double standard, as soon as Clemenceau discovered in 1892 that Mary had finally taken a younger lover herself, he flew into a rage and succeeded in getting a divorce within days. As Jack Ellis continues:

> Even this was not enough to appease his anger. His grandson tells us that because French law was in his favor, he had her threatened with imprisonment and finally had her escorted by two policemen to Boulogne-sur-Mer, where she was put aboard a ship bound for Boston. At home he packed her belongings in a trunk and sent them to her sister. He took a hammer and smashed a marble statue of Mary that he had kept in his study, and he destroyed everything else that reminded him of her, including photographs and paintings.[22]

All of this seems a long way from the recollected image of a mature statesman at the Versailles conference at the end of the Great War. Clemenceau himself and his coterie of admiring biographers (Jean Martet, Gustave Geffroy, Léon Daudet, Georges Suarez, and General Jean-Jules-Henri Mordacq) played no small part in bracketing this awkward memory.

Peyraud's cynicism views the path of divorce and remarriage as the way of naïve idealism: 'Votre plus grand tort a peut-être été de prendre votre affaire au tragique... Qu'est-ce qu'une histoire d'amour, dans la vie d'un homme d'État?... Pour ces choses-là, on n'est jamais sévère' (SV, 160). If only Michel had remained within the generic boundaries of the comedy of adultery, he would have had no need to reinvent himself. Divorce, then, is not merely the product of a cynical culture which realizes that marriages do not always work; it is also a reflection of an idealistic strain which privileges hope above experience. Divorce deludes Michel into thinking that true romance is not merely a Bovaryesque fantasy to be simulated in adultery, but an aspiration which divorce might allow him to realize. He does not push Suzanne into the divorce. In fact it depends upon her understanding the degree of his unhappiness. Now that divorce had become possible once more, the affective range of individuals had changed. Hence, a particular form of dissatisfaction was produced by a law which offered the possibility of legitimizing transgressive desires. The pathos of modern love is conveyed bathetically, however, as Michel can only conceive of it in the terms of an ingrained classical model: 'il fallait choisir, ainsi qu'un héros de tragédie, entre le devoir et l'amour: il fallait choisir, et le choix, cette seconde fois, serait irrévocable' (VP, 237). Divorce thus appears to have become a new form of tragedy for the modern age.

In this light, the subsequent critical neglect of Rod seems less than axiomatic. Such oblivion led to him being dubbed Anatole suisse after his death — the model for such oblivion was, of course, Anatole France. In the Baumanesque language of fluid dynamics, these three patriarchs of the French novel — France, Daudet and Rod — are all keen to register the 'drag force' of heavy modernity which resists liquid motion. As we shall see in our final case, Camille Pert's series of Cady novels, it would be a mistake to imagine that French women writers embraced the potential of liquid modernity without ambivalence.

Notes to Chapter 4

1. Edmond and Jules de Goncourt, *Journal*, 3 vols (Paris: Laffont, 1989), III, 607 (12 July 1891).
2. Alphonse Daudet, *Le Soutien de famille* (Paris: Fasquelle, 1898), p. 264.
3. Antoine Albalat, *L'Amour chez Alphonse Daudet* (Paris: Ollendorff, 1884), pp. 275–76.
4. G. Vera Dobie, *Alphonse Daudet* (London: Nelson, 1949), p. 258.
5. Jacques Rouré, *Alphonse Daudet* (Paris: Julliard, 1982), p. 269.
6. Jean-Isaure Toulouse, *Manuel pratique du mariage (contrat de mariage, mariage civil et religieux), du divorce, de la séparation de corps et de la séparation de biens, avec détail et total des frais de chaque matière* (Paris: A. Giard, 1891), pp. 25–26.
7. Mme Daudet's letter to Edmond de Goncourt (1 July 1890) in *Edmond de Goncourt et Alphonse Daudet: Correspondance*, ed. by P. Dufief with A.-S. Dufief (Geneva: Droz, 1996), p. 275.
8. Alphonse V. Roche, *Alphonse Daudet* (Boston, MA: Twayne, 1976), p. 103.
9. Jean-Paul Clébert, *Une famille bien française: Les Daudet, 1840–1940* (Paris: Renaissance, 1988), p. 245.
10. Lucien Daudet, *Vie d'Alphonse Daudet* (Paris: Gallimard, 1941), p. 237; *Histoire d'une amitié: Correspondance inédite entre Alphonse Daudet et Frédéric Mistral (1860–1897)*, ed. by J.-H. Bornecque (Paris: Julliard, 1979), p. 234.
11. *Edmond de Goncourt et Alphonse Daudet: Correspondance*, p. 328.
12. *Edmond de Goncourt et Alphonse Daudet: Correspondance*, p. 366.
13. For anti-Semitic caricatures of Naquet, see Léon Daudet, *Souvenirs des milieux littéraires, politiques, artistiques et médicaux* (Paris: Nouvelle librairie nationale, 1920), pp. 80, 121–22, 195, 265, 278, 457. *Le Partage de l'enfant*, his own novelistic response to his father's cautionary tale, appeared in 1905.
14. Alphonse Daudet, *Rose et Ninette* in *Œuvres complètes*, vol. XI (Paris: Alexandre Houssiaux, 1901), p. 297. Interpolated references will be made to this edition.
15. Andrew Counter, *Inheritance in Nineteenth-Century French Culture* (Oxford: Legenda, 2010), p. 113.
16. See my 'The Name of the Divorcée: Janvier and Ballot's Theatrical Critique, *Mon Nom!* (1892)', *Romance Quarterly*, 49 (2002), 215–27.
17. Bordeaux, *Âmes modernes*, p. 274.
18. Cohen, *The Sentimental Education of the Novel*, pp. 23–25.
19. Édouard Rod, *La Vie privée de Michel Teissier* (Paris: Perrin, 1893) and *La Seconde Vie de Michel Teissier* (Paris: Perrin, 1894). Written between July 1891 and June 1892 *La Vie privée* was the first of Rod's novels to be serialized in Brunetière's *Revue des Deux Mondes*. Subsequent interpolated references will be made to VP and SV.
20. Michael G. Lerner, *Edouard Rod: A Portrait of the Novelist and his Times* (The Hague: Mouton, 1975), p. 122.
21. Lerner, p. 25.

22. Jack Ellis, *The Early Life of Georges Clemenceau, 1841–1893* (Lawrence: The Regents Press of Kansas, 1980), p. 141.

CHAPTER 5

Novel Series and Serial Lives

As the century turned, divorce remained one of the major objects of retrospection in this society's self-analysis. On the one hand, divorce was praised by the likes of the Margueritte brothers, the male feminist authors of *Deux Vies* (1902), as a landmark on the road to modernizing French mores. This vision of modernity is contradicted by a fear of decadence, of which the most influential example was Paul Bourget's *roman à thèse*, *Un divorce*, of 1904, which argues that the fantasy of a starting a genuinely new 'second life' depends upon an unbearable repression, especially if children from the first marriage haunt the wife's subsequent union. Catholic guilt is invoked as a moral and fictional mechanism which triggers the 'return of the repressed' in this tale of renunciation. This conservative view of the unfeasibility of divorce echoes a pattern familiar to the nineteenth century in which women's lives are inscribed in a single movement from virginal girlhood through marriage and motherhood. Contrary to divorce's promise of second — even multiple — life narratives, the primacy of the 'first man' is asserted by Bourget as the widely discussed phenomenon of 'retrospective jealousy' is used to wreck the heroine's attempt to escape into an uncompromised future with her new lover. Contrary to all those narratives of adultery fuelled by the fear of paternal uncertainty, the rights and certainties of biological paternity are asserted in Bourget's novel precisely when the 'social father', the stepfather appears to have usurped the position of the *premier homme*. In blunt terms, the issue seems to be whether men can accept wives with a sexual past, like widows, prostitutes, married lovers.

In this vein, the narrative significance of Marcel Prévost's flirtatious pubescent *demi-vierge* (who enjoyed remarkably widespread currency and controversy in the *fin de siècle*) can now be understood in the light of Adam Phillips's analysis of flirtation as 'a way of acknowledging the contingency of our lives — their sheer unpredictability, how accident-prone we are — without at the same time turning their unpredictability itself into a new kind of masterplot'.[1] In particular men feared those wives with a living past which may return, as in Marcelle Tinayre's *La Rebelle* of 1905 where the 'new man' (in both senses) Noël discovers that he is not as 'new' as he thought.[2] He learns that his soulmate's son was fathered by her ex-lover, Maurice, rather than by her now deceased husband. It is only after seeing a play on this very theme, the appropriately titled *L'Ineffaçable*, and being told by the heroine that Maurice has indeed returned momentarily but to no effect, that he can accept that a woman's past should not undermine her future. The idealism of this ending lies in the belief that women might inhabit a radically different narrative pattern which condones serialized desires and not just single ones, perhaps offering a new definition of the 'honnête femme' in her relation to monogamy. This view was developed before World War I by Léon Blum who advocated pre-marital sexual experience for both men and women.

Divorce displaced the notion of a single sexual relationship sanctioned by the civil contract (and still reclaimed after 1789 by the holy sacrament), and propounded a model of encounters and commitments which were no longer unique and, as the twentieth century opened, might even take a serial form. This shift from linear to serial lives had profound implications for narrative. In the high age of the *roman-fleuve*, the possibilities of serial romance are reflected in serial fiction (exemplified in the inter-war years by the marriages of Cécile and Richard Fauvet, and Joseph and Hélène Pasquier in Georges Duhamel's *Chronique des Pasquier*). Moreover, divorce generates a new kind of literary coherence from lives whose very ruptures invite an episodic treatment of single characters. Camille Pert's tetralogy of *Cady* novels — *La Petite Cady* (1909), *Cady mariée* (1911), *Le Divorce de Cady* (1912) and *Cady remariée* (1926) — begun in the *belle époque* but completed after the First World War, presents a cautionary tale about the dangers of a life whose value is diluted through repetition. Colette's *La Retraite sentimentale* (1907) and *La Vagabonde* (1910) promote a more adventurous model of sexual and affective itinerancy in keeping with Giddens's model of 'confluent love' and indeed the author's own biographical path through divorce (beginning with her divorce from Willy in 1910). In theory at least, serial love facilitated the development of the *femme nouvelle* as an individual who could shed her old self in what Richard Sennett calls the 'Romantic search for self-realization', even though the harsh reality of the sexual double standard led to the ostracism of divorced and separated women throughout this 'long nineteenth century'.[3] Colette's experiments have received ample critical treatment in recent years from critics who, quite reasonably, look back from the present rather than forward from the past. There were, however, other kinds of women's writing which spoke to a more typical, if less avant-garde, feminine ambivalence with regard to divorce. As Jean Anderson, France Grenaudier-Klijn, Elisabeth-Christine Muelsch write of the likes of Madeleine Pelletier and Nelly Roussel, 'ces féministes de la première heure demeurent l'exception.'[4]

One of the myths in and about much popular romance fiction concerns its aspiration to rise above the particular demands of the historical moment. However, Camille Pert's tetralogy of novels about her heroine, Cady, provides a conspicuous and evocative case of the way in which such an easily derided genre may filter romantic idealism through the shifting contexts in which female desires are situated by place and time. As Jennifer Waelti-Walters has shown, there were all too comprehensible economic and institutional reasons why Frenchwomen often chose to write in this supposedly sub-canonical mode in the final decades of the nineteenth century and the first decades of the twentieth.[5] In fact, romance fiction became a privileged space of dialogue between women with the time and means to read, and it was often under its carapace that the shifting narrative potential of French-women's lives was experimented upon during the *fin de siècle* and the *belle époque*.

Though hindsight might teach us to view the apparent advances made in French-women's rights at that time with some scepticism (note the postponed enfranchisement of Frenchwomen), both conservative and progressive contemporaries felt that a woman's lot was indeed in the process of transformation. Camille Pert is significant as she embodies conservative female opinion which viewed with some trepidation the effects of radical liberal thought on the remapping of gender relations. As Jennifer Waelti-Walters and Steven C. Hause point out:

> The feminist movement of the belle époque was not a homogenous, monolithic phenomenon [...]. Catholic women had begun to organize groups that would later become the largest women's organizations in France. Even the most explicitly feminist of the Catholic women's groups [...] had doubts about the republic [...] and the programme of republican feminism.[6]

They cite comtesse Pierre Lecointre as a prime instance of a 'conservative feminist' who attempted to safeguard women's position within the family in the face of rapid social change. It is easy to see how modern academic interests might draw us towards more unambiguously radical figures such as Nelly Roussel whose views may in some senses anticipate subsequent gender theories; but equally it is difficult to see how the history of Frenchwomen during the late nineteenth century and the belle époque can be plausibly reconstructed without the analysis of such conservative feminism. As Waelti-Walters and Hause warn, 'Because she declined to join the feminist organizations of the era [...], little is known about Countess Lecointre's life' (42–43). The ideology of Camille Pert's fiction suggests a similarly conservative approach to the reform of women's situation.

The pen name Camille Pert was the sexually ambivalent pseudonym of one Louise-Hortense Grille de Rougeul née Cyrille (1865–1952), daughter of an *inspecteur général des ponts et chaussées*, born in Lille. For all its romantic excess, her literary output reveals an intense investment in the values of family life as World War I approached. The theme of *Le Bonheur conjugal* was asserted in the novel of that title which appeared in 1905. Three years later she offered a yet more practical manual for the negotiation of modern society, *Le Dernier cri du savoir-vivre, guide pratique de bonne éducation et de parfaite connaissance du monde suivant les usages les plus modernes*. In 1910 her *Mirage de bonheur* appeared in Hachette's *Petite bibliothèque de la famille*.[7]

Pert enjoyed not only a secure family life, but also a certain status within the intellectual culture of her time. She was the only woman to contribute to the four volume *La Femme dans la nature, dans les mœurs, dans la légende, dans la société* (Paris: Bong) directed by Edmond Perrier. She belonged to a literary team which included V. Du Bled, Jules Claretie, Frédéric Loliée, Marcel Prévost and A. Schalck de la Faverie. In the first edition of *Qui êtes-vous?* (1908) she gives her address as 70 boulevard Magenta, Paris, which she shares with her husband Jules, *chef d'escadrons d'artillerie* (who has no separate entry). Both their sons, Serge and Robert, became engineers. As well as writing for various newspapers (*L'Illustration, L'Écho de Paris, Le Journal, Le Matin* and *Le Petit Parisien*) and enjoying cycling and sea fishing, she directed the *Informateur des Gens de Lettres* from 2 rue de Bouloi and belonged to their society. By the 1909–10 edition the family had moved to 85 rue de Turbigo, but by 1924 they had retired to L'Étang-la-Ville in the Seine-et-Oise region. In fact, her responses to the 24 questions sent out to *contemporains* of note were by this time rather less forthcoming. The inclusion by other rather notable public figures not only of an address but also of that elite object of desire, a home telephone number, is testament to the relative innocence of fame in an earlier age.

Cady is a cautionary figure used to warn Pert's readers against the supposed selfishness of modern mothers.[8] The opening novel, *La Petite Cady*, sets out the terms of an unfortunate *éducation* against which her adult life is a mere reaction. She is neglected by a mother who is caught up in the public whirl of her 'career' as a politician's wife and allows her ne'er-do-well servants to raise her daughter abusively. This speaks back to the milieu of Michel Teissier and to the ambitions of Rose and Ninette's mother. Free to develop at unseemly haste, this 'jeune apache' flirts with her father's friends and mixes with desirable undesirables such as the *demi-mondaine*, Paulette, and her son, Georges. The term 'apache' is used to link Cady, the servant class and the *classes dangereuses* who are allowed to misguide our heroine. In the *avant-propos* of *La Petite Cady* Pert voices class suspicion at the expense of gender identification when she complains that modern mothers are unwilling to question the current system of *bonnes* and *domestiques* as things had apparently not been so bad in Paris thirty years ago: 'c'étaient des brutes insignifiantes, grossières comme le sont les paysans mais non pas comme les apaches de Grenelle ou des Buttes-Chaumont' (x). At the very beginning of the novel Cady is described as a 'jeune apache' as she resists the attempts of her future husband, Renaudin, to question her about the attack on her governess, Armande de Lavernière (6). In the flashback which the rest of the novel involves, Armande herself calls her 'un apache' when she learns that Cady is to exploit her parents' absence all day and into the night to visit her friend, the painter Jacques Laumière (151). In *Cady mariée* Cady admits to the jealous Laumière that her eternally returning Georges is 'une manière d'apache' (164). In Chapter 18 she then persuades Georges that their worlds are really not so different. Hers is merely one of snobbish dissimulation behind which even the smartest people may turn out to be 'apaches' too. Gradually, then, this category of ethnic exclusion serves to absorb polite society itself into its definition as the home of the marginal. It is interesting that *Le Petit Robert* dates back only as far as 1902 the origin of this particular use of the term to signify urban delinquency.

The next three novels — *Cady mariée*, *Le Divorce de Cady* and *Cady remariée* — which deal respectively with her marriage to Victor Renaudin (one of her father's friends), their subsequent divorce, and her vengeful second marriage to her one-time enemy Deber, are all haunted by the idealization of her passionate relationship with Georges. Pert actually wrote a volume entitled *Georges à Paris*, so popular was this impish hero. In the *avant-propos* she tries to justify such flippant wartime activity as a response to readers' demands in spite of her current 'indifférence pour les œuvres littéraires'.[9] In different places, she muses publicly on other plans for the series including *Son enfant* and *L'Angoisse de Cady*. We have not found proof that such novels ever appeared.

The tension between the ethos of maternal duty and the ideal of amorous passion is held in unresolved conflict, even at the end of *Cady remariée* when a pall of doubt clouds the heroine's hope that Georges will return from his own *Bildungsroman* to make her his own once and for all. The socialization of ideal desires always remains in the future tense. This is why the series must halt at this point. Bad mothering apparently leaves the heroine sexualized but not socialized, first a child with a precociously womanly sexuality, then a woman with a childlike disparagement for the responsibilities of adult life. Cady is an embodiment of the *femme-enfant*, mythologized in Catulle Mendès's colossal *roman contemporain* of that name (1891). Trapped between innocence and maternity, girlhood and womanhood, she is perhaps best seen now as a teenager in a culture then without the vocabulary yet to bear such a concept. If the subversion of the gendered division of private and public space is seen to be responsible for the crisis of mothering which Pert diagnoses, then the other apparent source of familial discord was the new divorce law which allowed Pert to chart the serialized married life of Cady. In Pert's ultimately conservative view of things, divorce is not an absolute marker of freedom, but merely a means of liberating the devils within the spirit. Here, it allows Cady to break the heart of her devoted first husband, the incongruously named Victor, and to enter a second marriage in an act of mere spite. We do not know whether she will divorce for a second time, but the institution of marriage is clearly eroded under the malign influence of a dysfunctional mother–daughter bond.

Cady's parents enjoy a swish Parisian existence from their base on the quai du Louvre, but the *hamartia* of such high society appears to lie in the collapse of the gendered division between private and public life. In the wake of her socialist husband's political success, Mme Darquet embarks on a full array of social activities which alienate her from her core maternal duties throughout *La Petite Cady* in which the effects of childhood are depicted. She is introduced to the reader as a 'femme de tête' of forty-six years whose lingering beauty is, we are told, somewhat spoilt by a nasty red hair dye (14). Her first husband having died in a duel, her second was selected for his sublime mixture of potential and malleability which was bound to attract such an ambitious *femme de trente ans*. Though his fidelity is uncertain, she is past the games of *galanterie*. The arrival of the new governess, Armande, allows Pert to inform the reader of their domestic details. As 'ils sortent beaucoup et reçoivent souvent', Cady does not often eat with her parents (26). Even the architectural disposition of family life reflects this division of the generations:

> Les chambres exiguës de la nursery, donnant sur une étroite cour intérieure, formaient avec la cuisine et l'office un département distinct, totalement séparé des pièces spacieuses du devant occupés par M. et Mme Darquet. Aucun bruit, aucune odeur désagréable ne s'échappaient du domaine commun où les enfants et la domesticité vivaient à part, pour ainsi dire étrangers à l'autre existence que menaient les époux. (30–31)

The upper-middle-class family is no longer the panopticon it dreams of having once been.

The irony is that the primacy of coupledom over the family, to which Giddens alludes, defines Cady's own relationship with her father, as precocious as her relations with his friends. When he does take her out to the theatre or circus, she does not allow her younger sister, Baby, to attend: 'Ces jours-là, je suis la petite femme de papa, et alors, Baby serait comme notre enfant... Vous ne voyez jamais un mari et une femme emmener leur petit enfant pour se promener avec eux' (27). In spite of the affective deficit in their lives there is a surprising sympathy between Cady and her sister, Baby. We learn that 'ni l'une ni l'autre ne connaissent les câlineries, les chansons, les doux baisers de la mère qui, le soir, endorment les tout petits, dans l'ombre tiède des rideaux tirés. Toutes deux avaient un embarras pour offrir ou réclamer des caresses' (36), but Cady watches over her sister as she falls asleep following her accident with a knife in the kitchen that evening. As Cady passes, one of the servants, the inappropriately named Clémence, asks whether 'le sang ne pisse plus?' (37). Indeed, blood relations no longer carry much weight in this political family whose well-being is sacrificed to a wider set of social imperatives. As the Darquets are busy influencing the politics of the country, they fail to influence their own family life in a benevolent way. The unwitting crime of the political family, as far as the conservative Pert is concerned, is to have reneged on the division of private and public space on which bourgeois culture is seen to rely. Of particular irony is the fact that one of Mme Darquet's chief charity activities involves attending functions of L'Œuvre de l'Enfance abandonnée, charity itself being perceived as an acceptable public form of that eminently feminine virtue of homely sensibility.

Dramatic irony privileges our access to Cady's secrets at the expense of Mme Darquet's dinnertime speech about the need to keep her daughter pure for entry to the marriage market at the age of eighteen. Fiction takes Pert's polite readers to places which they should otherwise not inhabit, including the shock of popular culture when Cady takes her teacher to the public ice rink where they meet up with Cady's cousins, Alice and Marie-Annette, and their teacher, Mme Garnier. Armande, who is shocked by this underhand cross-class subculture of adolescence, is reassured by Mme Garnier that mothers do not even want to know the truth:

> Pour avoir la paix, pour être libres, pour n'avoir ni à combattre, ni à se tracasser, ni à se reprocher leur veulerie, leur égoïsme, leur sottise, leur lâcheté à remplir leurs devoirs de mères! [...] Il en est de même dans tous les intérieurs parisiens... C'est toujours des enfants élevés Dieu sait comment!... (67)

This critique of maternal egotism is amplified in a reference to Molière which proposes that the choice of the cousins' mother, Mme Serveroy, to remain an unremarried widow has nothing to do with maternal self-sacrifice: 'C'est une malade imaginaire... une égoïste dont vous ne trouveriez pas facilement le second numéro!... Tout tourne autour d'elle...' (68). The doctor who attends Baby after her alcoholic English nursemaid has tied her down in a freezing cold bath offers a similar critique. In the narrator's words, 'L'aberration qui fait que tant de mères croient pouvoir, sans inconvénient, se décharger de leurs enfants ne supprime point dans leur cœur une affection dont le principal tort est de ne se manifester que par intervalles' (256). The weakness of blood ties is seen to allow liminal figures such as servants, male friends and unwanted neighbours (such as Georges) to undermine the family. In Molière's plays, it is the father's foibles which are exploited in potentially disastrous ways. In *Le Malade imaginaire* the family core — along the axis of the father and the daughter by first marriage — is threatened by what might, from a nineteenth-century bourgeois perspective, be termed a *para-family*, a set of relations with a second wife and her cronies, notaries, pharmacists and doctors who all acquire access to the core family to which they do not belong by marriage or blood. The happy ending of the comedy is assured by the wise counsel of brother and servant. In Pert's fiction, such cross-class social coherence is a thing of the past. Servants hinder, they do not help. The vanity of mothers, it seems, is still at fault. Molière provides a benchmark of family drama against which the seemingly irretrievable tragedies of the modern French family are measured. Amidst her father's friends after dinner, the flirtatious *femme-enfant* is teased about her savings by her father who calls her 'petite Harpagon' (43). Gender and generation are transformed in a reference which encodes the coquetry of the *demi-vierge* and demystifies the innocence of girlhood. How, Pert implies, can Cady be fathered by a man who gives her the name of the father (but not the *non du père*)?

A politicization of this critique is offered by Paulette's driver, Émile, who escorts Cady on one of the *demi-mondaine*'s visits to a client out in the country. Inspired by drink, he offers Cady one more speech against the absent modern mother which underlines the hypocrisy in imposing one's progeny on a class one despises:

> Si vous seriez à moi [...] vous ne traîneriez pas comme cela dans les jupes d'une Margot et que vous ne feriez votre société des types comme moi pendant des journées!... Je vous respecte, ça va bien, mais il y a des camarades qui n'en feraient pas autant! [...] Qu'est-ce qu'elle fout, votre mère?... Je ne serais pas fâché de le savoir!... Non, vraiment, dites-le moi, où est-elle? [...] Voilà comment sont les bourgeois! Ils méprisent le peuple, ils ne voudraient pas serrer la main d'un prolétaire ni coucher dans son lit, la sueur du travailleur les dégoûte... Et, à côté de ça, ils flanquent leurs enfants à élever ce qu'il y a de moins propre!... Tout cela pour ne pas se donner la peine de les éduquer eux-mêmes. (199–200)

Like Cady, Mme Darquet has her own secrets. Cady finds in one of her mother's drawers some old photographs, including a group picture with a young man who so resembles Cady that she imagines him to be her deceased brother or 'une Cady travestie en homme' (140). When confronted, her mother has to correct her story by explaining that Armand Woechlin committed suicide, aged twenty-three, eleven years ago, and thus one year after Cady was born (and not before, as she initially claimed). To Cady's distress, Mme Darquet throws the pictures onto the fire. The reader is invited to put two and two together and to wonder whether Woechlin is the biological father of an illegitimate Cady, for whom Mme Darquet would not leave her politically advantageous marriage. Post-1884, the very possibility of divorce makes an issue of this lover's refusal to leave her marriage and start again. Is Woechlin, the biological father, trapped by suicide in the transsexual photographic identity of brother and sister? Is he the first victim of his daughter in her role as *femme fatale*? Or is she the victim? Cady, by implication, will be the fallen daughter of this fallen woman.

The subsequent novels will show the reader how this story of neglect leads Cady down the slippery slope. Perhaps the greatest crime of Mme Darquet is to stunt her daughter's own maternal instinct. In *Cady mariée* she tells Georges that she does not want children precisely because she would feel compelled to go through the tiresome task of correcting her own mother's wrongs and devoting herself to her own progeny. The moral of the tale tries to force women into the role of dutiful mother and carer; the reality seems to be, though, that motherhood is something of a lost art. The bad mother, Mme Darquet, thus provides one conservative answer to the forensic question which this and other narratives propose: 'Who is guilty?' Umberto Eco argues that

> people like thrillers not because there are corpses or because there is a final celebratory triumph of order (intellectual, social, legal, and moral) over the disorder of evil. The fact is that the crime novel represents a kind of conjecture, pure and simple. But medical diagnosis, scientific research, metaphysical inquiry are also examples of conjecture. After all, the fundamental question of philosophy (like that of psychoanalysis) is the same as the question of the detective novel: who is guilty?[10]

As we saw in the Introduction, such forensic logic has a particular epistemological function within the 'conjectural paradigm'. The detective model does indeed provide the introductory frame of Cady's tale. Who, everybody asks, has murdered the governess, Mlle Armande Lavernière? Here Cady is an innocent victim who is drawn into a web of deceit, and this will be key in the series' incorporation of the narrative model of detective fiction. Because of the improper nature of class relations, so Pert warns her invited bourgeois reader, the sexual relations in Cady's life take an improper turn, first in the form of a precociously sexualized childhood and adolescence, second in an immature attachment to that regressive object of delinquent desire, Georges, whose continual (if not continuous) presence drags Cady back through the self-refashioning of divorce in the novels which follow *La Petite Cady*. It is noteworthy that young Georges and his mother's lover, Paul, are the burglars responsible for Armande's death: Cady knows this, but the police are clueless.

From the very beginning of *La Petite Cady* that future husband-cum-detective, Renaudin, cannot get to the bottom of Armande's murder as he is transfixed by Cady, 'déjà passionnément flirteuse' (7). It is, it seems, impossible for men to have innocent relations with the young Cady, not least because they do not imagine that they can. When Mme Darquet has the doctor, Trajan, check Cady over after the novel's founding incident, Renaudin cannot help projecting the thought that Trajan is checking her out. One sign of Cady's precocity is her awareness of the sexual subplots around her: it is she who tells Armande that her father is chasing after the governess; it is she who shows her the other servant, Valentin, in an embrace with the florist. For Cady, this is a source of delight as she knows she will be able to use this adult knowledge in the service of her childish desires (blackmailing Valentin so as to receive more ice cream from him!).

As she goes to bed after the 'Le sang ne pisse plus?' episode in Chapter 4, Cady looks in the mirror at this 'étrange et séduisante miniature de femme, à l'inquiétante flamme du regard à la fois innocent et averti; curieuse fleur précoce de civilisation, adorable et troublant petit monstre'. As Cady flirts with all his after-dinner pals, her father notes, in language Colette will echo, 'elle a tous les vices en herbe' (44). Maurice Deber may criticize 'les enfants modern-style', but even this apparently resistant colonial civil servant will yield to her, harassing her through *Le*

Divorce de Cady, only to suffer the punishment of having his desires fulfilled, when the ever-perverse Cady gets married for a second time, this time to Deber, only to torture him by her continued affiliation with Georges. By the end of this chapter, however, Cady is confused: 'Est-ce que je suis une petite fille? [...] Ou presque une petite femme?' (50). Pert invokes the turn-of-the-century debate in France on the dangers for young women of what was then supposed (not least by Marcel Prévost) to be that American pastime of flirting. Whereas romantic sentimentalists such as Cady's cousin, Marie-Annette, dream of marrying their first and unique love, cynical pessimists such as Cady see things differently: 'Elle ne comprenait le flirt ainsi qu'une sorte d'escarmouche rapide et légère, où la femme pique la curiosité de son partenaire, harcèle son désir et s'enfuit tout à coup avec un rire insouciant, l'esprit distrait par un jeu et un but nouveaux' (237).

Pert's novel series suggests an ideologically resonant alignment between, on the one hand, this discourse on the blurring of boundaries between girlhood and womanhood, and on the other, that marker of refashioned sexual mores in the early to middle years of the Third Republic, divorce. Both flirting and divorce brought into ironic relief the naiveté of a feminine script for life which conceived of no possibility other than the irreversible transmission between men of the innocent bride to the groom. The well-made family was so brittle a social institution as almost to invite that most well-made yet over-baked of nineteenth-century literary plots, the tale of wifely adultery. The possibility of flirting before marriage and divorce afterwards, however, dissolved the petrified ideals of girlhood innocence and marital knowingness. Adolescent flirting and divorce revealed that the feminine plot did not involve merely the sudden and ceremonial transmission between two static norms. Whereas widowhood was in theory at least a state of uncoupled sexual knowingness imposed upon the grieving spouse, the divorcee had, to borrow Shakespeare's terms, yet more reasons to be merry, or at least relieved. But both divorce and flirting underlined the fact of feminine sexual life before and after wedlock, and it is the reactionary achievement of Pert's well-crafted fictional series to have absorbed this alignment of divorce and flirting into a causal structure flowing from the crime of bad mothering.

One of the ironies of the final chapters of *La Petite Cady* is that our heroine steals Renaudin, her first husband — whom she will in turn divorce — from a divorcee, Fernande. The latter's mother, Mme Durand de l'Isle, claims that her daughter was beaten by her lawyer-husband, though Fernande refuses to explain their prompt separation, offering merely an enigmatic smile. The dinner ostensibly arranged to celebrate Baby Jeanne's recovery is in fact intended to complete the matchmaking of Renaudin and Fernande, but Fernande and her mother stand no chance against our delightful and infuriating heroine whose protean, even polymorphous, perversity is saturated with relationships of all kinds. As she tells Renaudin: 'toi, tu n'es pas pour les divorcées.[...] Tu épouseras une jeune fille... très jeune... beaucoup plus jeune que toi, avec qui tu seras content de faire le papa. [...] Tu m'épouseras quand je serai sortie de nourrice!... Tu ne penses qu'à ça...' (293). And she is right, for Renaudin subsequently explains that he cannot marry Fernande as 'il paraît qu'elle rossait son premier époux!', besides he prefers 'un corps indemne... à tous points de vue' (307–08). Renaudin perceives the reality of divorce but cannot understand the culture of flirting, and in this way he is not truly liquid modern.

Once Cady's prediction has come true, she diagnoses the desire of her besotted but exasperated new husband: 'Ce que tu aimes en moi, c'est l'inceste [...]. C'est pas de l'inceste pour de vrai inceste, mais c'est de l'inceste imaginatif... parce que tu m'as vue toute petite, et que tu étais comme un papa pour moi... une espèce de papa à la manque, une manière d'être vertueux vicieusement' (*Cady mariée*, 7). The family romance of the *jeune fille* has been merely displaced, not extinguished, so that the promise of yet one more displacement (and yet one more husband) might still be seen to socialize young Cady's yearnings. *Cady mariée* identifies divorce as a trait of a Parisian socio-cultural elite which is peddled by romantic fiction as the focus of *belle époque* glamour. When Paul de Montaux makes a play for Cady, she thwarts his advance by asking of his mistress, 'Est-ce que c'est vrai que Rosine Derval, après avoir divorcé, songe à reprendre son mari pour jouer avec lui au Théâtre-Moderne?' (81). Divorce infiltrates the social vocabulary of hypocrisy by which the narrator caricatures the double-handedness and affective instability of the chic crowd which takes the train down to Hubert Voisin's new venture on the Riviera, the Printemps-Palace: 'Des amants de la veille ou du lendemain, des divorcés effectifs ou latents, des gens qui derrière le dos se traitaient des pires noms, ou qui s'étaient insultés en plein visage, s'accueillaient ce soir avec grâce et sérénité' (271). The novel culminates in the affirmation of the series' sequence which the reader has already learnt: divorce will follow marriage. On the opening night of the Printemps-Palace, at the very end of *Cady mariée*, a jealous Argatte invites Cady to *bostonner* and forces her to admit that it is Georges whom she truly loves.

Le Divorce de Cady explains exactly how she leaves Renaudin, however it does not lead to her union with Georges, but instead to her humiliation of yet one more of her father's friends, Deber, in *Cady remariée*, as if marriage were not a question of socializing her desire to master her father, but of mastering the desires of those with whom her father socialized. Georges is the trigger for Cady's emotional displacements, but not their ultimate goal. He provides the scenario for the *Aufhebung* of conjugal stasis, he allows her to move on but not to move in. He represents a desire that will not hold, not least because he allows her — and Pert's readers — to imagine a form of heterosexuality where paternalism is defused. Others are less mobile, in spite of the availability of divorce. Fernande's marriage to Hubert Voisin has become little more than a truce:

> A ses débuts, Fernande était de moitié dans toutes ses opérations, et dame! elle en sait trop long pour qu'il ne soit pas bien aise de la tenir si elle s'avisait de se rebiffer et d'essayer de lui jouer de sales tours... Comme elle n'a absolument rien à elle, un divorce serait l'écroulement... Elle retomberait dans la sombre dèche où se trouve sa mère, dans laquelle elle a vécu pendant toute sa jeunesse. Et Dieu sait qu'Hubert possède vingt fois ce qu'il faut pour faire prononcer un divorce *de plano...* (*Le Divorce de Cady*, 61–62)

She is one of Georges's lovers, and Cady is embarrassed to think that he drove her at the start of the novel to the brink of suicide — that other route out of unhappy marriage, exemplified by Emma Bovary, and diagnosed by Émile Durkheim's *Le*

Suicide (1897), which explicitly links the phenomenon to divorce. When Renaudin discovers this attempt, he recognizes that she leads 'une existence morale cachée de moi' (74) and he says that he will give her a separation if she says that there is some-one else who has taken his place, but she is too wise to confess Georges's role in her life, knowing that this offer is merely a ploy used to expose her passion. The very possibility of divorce is thus used — this time in vain — to ensnare the adulteress.

She in turn manipulates the possibility of divorce. She asks Laumière whether Renaudin would consider it, but he accuses her of being 'toquée' even to consider marrying Georges: 'tu souffrirais profondément d'être déclassée, disqualifiée' (88). It is fine to flirt with such a world, but not to inhabit it for good. Renaudin is, he says, 'le mari rêvé', as long as his sublime blindness is indulged and preserved (89). Cady suggests that she could marry Laumière who would allow her to take Georges as a lover, but the painter refuses on the grounds of male honour. A pliant lover is seen as 'un vicieux', but a tolerant husband is merely disdained (90). The irony is that when he does subsequently agree to marry her after a divorce, she has decided in the meantime that this plan would no longer work (181–82). He paints her for Renaudin, but when he finally yields to his desire and kisses Cady's breast, Renaudin is there to observe the transgressive kiss.

In the next chapter the reader is treated to a version of that new set scene of post-1884 fiction, the interview in the lawyer's office. Cady asks the young Argatte 'comment faut-il bâcler cela pour que ce soit très vite fini?' (208). When she shows initial reticence, he warns her that 'le divorce, c'est très bien de le réclamer, mais ça ne s'obtient pas comme cela!...', at which point she not only accepts that the divorce will be pronounced against her on the grounds of adultery but embraces this outcome (209). When she explains that she wants a divorce so that she can marry her 'petit gigolo', Georges, the jealous Argatte refuses to help her. She then throws her arms around the lawyer who kisses her, 'bouleversé par une émotion sensuelle qu'il n'aurait pu comparer à aucune de celles éprouvées jusqu'alors', and in triumph she returns to her questions about divorce (213)! This is an emblematic scenario of its kind in which the official is shown to be susceptible to the plot of transgressive desire which it is his job to manage on behalf of the state machine.

This also bears comparison with 'Conciliation', a short story in Marcel Prévost's *Nouvelles lettres de femmes*, in which one Mme Ardeville goes through the process of divorce, only to return within a matter of weeks to her husband, Paul. Meanwhile she has been subject to the sexual attentions of virtually every rank of the legal profession: 'Une femme mariée, pas permis de se laisser baisser la joue. Divorcée, veuve, tout ce qu'on voudra, on est libre. Ma liberté aura été courte, mais je puis me rendre cette justice que j'en ai profité de mon mieux. Maintenant, je connais à fond le barreau, j'ai vu la magistrature assise, debout, dans toutes les attitudes...'.[11] There is, Prévost implies, a promiscuity to the very legal process which makes of the divorcing wife a public woman (with all that this connoted): 'Demander le divorce', she continues in her letter to a friend, 'je m'imaginais, moi, que ce n'était pas plus compliqué que de demander une loge à l'Opéra. Ah! ma chère, ne divorce jamais, va! Tu n'imagines pas tout ce qu'on a inventé pour dégoûter les clients. Il faut un avoué, puis un avocat, puis des juges, un président...' (232–33).

Nevertheless Argatte warns Cady that 'vous en avez pour un an ou dix-huit mois!... On ne divorce pas comme on change de chemise, ce serait trop commode!', to which she replies that it only took her six weeks to get married (215). Only if Renaudin is compliant will Cady have her divorce in less than six months, and he tells her that the 'lieu de réfuge classique' would be her mother's home. Argatte then informs Deber (who loves this woman who hates him back). Cady realizes what Deber's offer of help signals: 'A mesure que le vide se fait autour de moi, vous vous rapprochez' (230). She then questions how his family would respond to such a union: 'Je croyais votre famille passablement cléricale... Est-ce qu'elle vous autoriserait à épouser une femme divorcée?' (231). He explains that their religion is not so rigid as she imagines, even if he has moulded the story of Cady which he has given them: 'Il y a des choses que, dans l'avenir, nous devrons oublier, vous et moi... Donc, nul ne doit les apprendre... J'ai dit aux miens que le désaccord, que les malentendus profonds survenus entre vous et votre mari avaient rendu un divorce nécessaire' (232–33). Finally, she yields to his offer of staying on the Brittany coast with his mother, sisters and elder niece — and thus not quite the maternal refuge Argatte had in mind.

As she wakes up after two months of bronchial sickness, Deber's sister is tending to her. When Cady asks her how this divorce sits with her traditional view of marriage, Denise accepts that 'je suis d'un illogisme qui me stupéfie moi-même!... Je l'ai en horreur, je ne l'admets en aucun cas... Et, cependant, pour vous, il ne me choque aucunement; il me paraît naturel' (254). Cady senses that Deber has not told her the whole story, but as Cady is about to confess, Denise indicates that she would rather not know, preferring to imagine a rupture between Cady past and present. Her sadness inspires in Denise a certain moral relativism: 'avez-vous été vraiment coupable?... ou seulement coquette... imprudente?...' (261). Like her brother, Denise sees the need for wilful forgetfulness. News of the confirmation of the divorce is something of a non-event. The courtroom scene is an absent centre of this particular novel, recounted to Cady, Denise and the reader, but not dramatized in the narrative. Denise is a little shocked at Cady's matter-of-fact receipt of such a paradigmatic shift in her life's pattern. She must attend to practical details and explains to Denise how 'ma dot reprise, mes revenus ne seront pas lourds' (267).

More interesting still is the philosophy of existence with which Cady glosses her divorce, and which draws this book towards its conclusion. She begins by explaining how people react differently to such a failure in their *Lebensplan*: 'pour certains, il faut dix ans pour se consoler, pour d'autres dix mois, et d'autres encore dix jours' (269). Beyond individual needs, however, she asserts the modern subject's project of embracing the disjunction of experience in a process of wilful repression:

> Au fond de moi, il y a encore... il y aura toujours... un tas de choses tristes... Oh! bien plus que vous ne sauriez l'imaginer!... mais la vie a repris en moi... le besoin non pas d'effacer, non pas d'oublier l'ineffaçable, l'irréparable, mais... comment dire?... de poser dessus quelque chose d'hermétique... Mon existence, et celle de beaucoup de gens, je crois, est à compartiments, empilés les uns au-dessus des autres... Ce qu'il y a dans les tiroirs d'en dessous y reste... il n'y a pas de communication avec ceux d'en dessus... il ne faut pas qu'il y en ait. (270)

She then contrasts her own life with Denise's: 'nos vies sont tellement dissemblables!... La vôtre fut si unie... On ne voit pas, en effet, quelles séparations pourraient exister... Ça a coulé, ça coule, ça coulera toujours à peu près pareil... Moi, c'est différent.' Cady is to liquid modernity what Denise is to heavy modernity. Denise cannot believe that Cady wanted a divorce, but Cady asks what she could have done once Renaudin abandoned her: 'selon vous, je devrais demeurer éternellement blessée, pleurante, en deuil de mon bonheur conjugal?' As her botched attempt at suicide showed, 'ne peut pas toujours se suicider celui qui a le plus sincère, le plus fervent désir de mourir... Alors, puisque je dois vivre, je vis!...' (271–72). Her life is to be something more than a life sentence. This is a philosophy for a life of serialized desires, of 'confluent love', whose joy is not to be found in its unity or linearity. There is, Cady will admit, something to be said for Georges's pop psychology which has the sloth of mind to rely upon a received notion of feminine mystique: 'Une femme, c'est tout en compartiments et en contradictions' (*Cady remariée*, 110). But that something ('du vrai') is itself an excess which men cannot retrieve.

In *Cady remariée*, this final yet hardly definitive novel in the series, Cady torments her new husband, Deber, whose aid she has accepted in an act of revenge. By yielding to her enemy's desire, she finds a way of accepting the plot which he has imposed upon her, only to shove it back down his throat. After 'six mois de mariage et d'invraisemblable lutte' which has sapped his self-belief, she remains 'cette femme que la loi lui avait donnée sans qu'il eût pu la posséder entièrement, ni moralement, ni même matériellement' (11). He admits that 'je te tiens, entre mes mains, mais néanmoins tu m'échappes' (15); he owns her but cannot possess her. In spite of the philosophy of the New Woman which she has professed, she cannot herself find happiness. Herein lies the conservatism of Pert's project. In the epistemological terms presented in our Introduction, the human subject is seen to be radically constrained by its origins. Deber cannot escape the fate of Cady's first husband: 'Demeurerait-il à son tour devant elle sans action, sans pouvoir, pareil à ce lamentable premier mari qu'elle avait conduit au désespoir et au divorce, et qui lui inspirait jadis à lui, Maurice Deber, tant de mépris?'(11). He fantasizes that she can in some sense be 'revirginalized':

> C'est justement l'existence d'une âme invraisemblablement vierge qui te conserve impolluée malgré les pires contacts, malgré les boues que tu as traversées, et qui ont laissé intacte cette partie intellectuelle de toi-même dont je veux m'emparer, qu'il me faut... que je conquerrai à la longue... (17)

But so precocious was the *demi-vierge* that it is hard for the reader to recall a time in the narrative when Cady was still innocent.

Cady uses her marriage to Deber to punish the world which denies her the itinerant Georges. She and Georges do escape for an initially idyllic eight days. In the end, though, the past returns to haunt their union, for they are both conjoined and distanced by the jealousy inspired by their respective erotic histories. As they go for a walk up a hill, Georges tells her not to look round at the magnificent view until they have reached the three cypress trees at the top, and Cady confirms that 'évidemment, si on désobéit, on sera changés en pierres comme dans le conte des *Mille et une nuits!*' (149). Their tale, and the tale of those with a past, is presented, however, as a kind of Anti-*A Thousand and One Nights*. Slowly, Georges and Cady kill each other with their stories. They return to Paris and Georges leaves for America, promising to return with the means to take Cady away from the unhappy second marriage she has chosen. Though an air of foreboding clouds the ending, we do not know whether her fear of a 'sort peut-être tragique' will be fulfilled (254). The irresolution which animates the series is conveyed tonally in the play of sadness and exuberance which colours Cady's life and narrative, an irresolution which leaves her in a no-man's (or in another sense everyman's) land between infantile and mature sexuality, between servants and socialites. The conservative reading invited by Pert's fiction fears the loss of such class and gender difference. Given his apparently immature bisexuality, Georges is in the end an amalgam of oppositional terms, a magnet which attracts, absorbs and thereby destroys the differences we might readily associate with his marginal existence. The enigma of our heroine's strange *Bildungsromane* — in the plural — could only be resolved by the return of an unwilling hero socialized in the afterlife of the series and by his own *Bildungsroman*. But this story remains to be written.

Notes to Chapter 5

1. Adam Phillips, *On Flirtation* (London: Faber & Faber, 1995), p. xii.
2. For a particularly adroit account of Tinayre's cultural significance, see Rachel Mesch, 'A Belle Epoque Media Storm: Gender, Celebrity, and the Marcelle Tinayre Affair', *French Historical Studies*, 35 (2012), 93–121.
3. Richard Sennett, *The Fall of Public Man* (Cambridge: Cambridge University Press, 1976), p. 6.
4. *Écrire les hommes*, ed. by Jean Anderson, France Grenaudier-Klijn and Elisabeth-Christine Muelsch (Saint-Denis: Presses Universitaires de Vincennes, 2012), p. 18.
5. See Jennifer Waelti-Walters, *Feminist Novelists of the Belle Epoque: Love as a Lifestyle* (Lincoln: University of Nebraska Press, 1994).
6. *Feminisms of the Belle Epoque: A Historical and Literary Anthology*, ed. by Jennifer Waelti-Walters and Steven C. Hause (Lincoln: University of Nebraska Press, 1994), p. 4.
7. For critics who do address Pert's work, see Rachel Mesch, 'Husbands, Wives and Doctors: Marriage and Medicine in Rachilde, Jane de La Vaudère and Camille Pert', *Dix-Neuf*, 11.1 (2008), 90–104, and Juliette Rogers, *Career Stories: Belle Epoque Novels of Professional Development* (University Park, PA: Penn State Press, 2007).
8. Camille Pert, *La Petite Cady* (Paris: Mignot, 1914); *Cady mariée* (Paris: Mignot, 1913); *Le Divorce de Cady* (Paris: Mignot, 1914); *Cady remariée* (Paris: Albin Michel, 1926). Interpolated references will be made to these editions of the novels.
9. Camille Pert, *Georges à Paris* (Paris: Mignot, [1917]), p. v.
10. Umberto Eco, *Reflections on 'The Name of the Rose'* (London: Secker and Warburg, 1989), p. 54.
11. Marcel Prévost, *Nouvelles Lettres de femmes* (Paris: Lemerre, 1894), p. 228.

CONCLUSION

'Bâtis ta maison toi-même et brûle-la toi-même.'[1]

Joan Scott has written that 'war is the ultimate disorder, the disruption of all previously established relationships [...]; peace thus implies a return to "traditional" gender relationships, the familiar and natural order of families.'[2] Before a brief invitation to look forward in time, my series of close and contextualized readings concludes with a momentary reflection on the seismic jolt to family life imparted by the mass de facto separation of married couples which the Great War produced, exemplified by Élie Dautrin's *L'Absent* (1919). Women-authored fiction usually voiced a patriotic desire for family unity during the war years. Rather than offering a solution to personal incompatibility, divorce was depicted as a residue of the selfish indulgence of 'decadent' pre-war France (see, for example, Mary Floran, *On demande une marraine* (1919), and Delarue-Mardrus, 'The Godmother' — published in translation in 1918 — where the *divorcée* painter Géo sends parcels to soldiers at the front and ends up in correspondence with her ex-husband whom she sets about winning back). The fears of wifely dalliance in the absence of the soldier-husband have been amply documented by historians, not least by Stéphane Audoin-Rouzeau.[3] For other reasons too — including the problem of re-domesticating a brutalized army — the years following the return of soldiers from the war were key in French social history. We can identify a crescendo in the divorce rate (34,800 in 1920 and 31,100 in 1921) for the first time since the immediate aftermath of 1884 (when long-suffering couples swelled the ranks of divorcees in the initial years of the new law). In this way too, the Great War marked an epoch-changing loss of innocence for France.

The widespread sense of marriage in mutation occasioned by the aftermath of World War One produced considerable consternation, emblematized by Henry Bordeaux's fears in *Le Mariage (Hier et aujourd'hui)* (1921). Asked by Henry Simond to write a series of articles on post-war society for *L'Écho de Paris*, he began by writing 'Crise du mariage', which generated an avalanche of letters over the next year. These provide the basis of the 'Enquête sur le mariage et la famille' which forms Part I of the book. At first, the absence caused by war had made the heart grow fonder, but by the end of the war both husbands and wives had changed: 'Le résultat fut que les séparations officieuses ou judiciaires, que les divorces se multiplièrent.'[4] Bordeaux begins by holding women responsible for the welfare of marriage: 'c'est, d'habitude, la femme qui fait les bons ou les mauvais ménages, et peut-être surtout aujourd'hui [...]. C'est à la femme qu'il appartient de mettre de l'ordre dans sa maison, et d'y ajouter de la clarté, de l'agrément, la paix' (22). He even resorts to emotional blackmail of wives, citing a modest and doleful letter from an ex-conscript at some length, and then concluding: 'La femme, qui est avant tout tendresse et pitié, peut-elle y demeurer insensible?' (36). What is more, this 'entreprise d'entente conjugale' exerts a great influence on the next generation: 'la génération des jeunes filles qui, elles, n'ont pas encore trouvé de mari, qui ne sont pas assurées d'en trouver, et dont il convient de s'occuper' (23). After listing wifely grievances, he cites letters from men, including one which contrasts the women of the day, or 'la génération du divorce et de l'infidélité', with those of thirty years previous who gave birth to 'la phalange des soldats de la grande guerre' (32). Good marriages, Bordeaux argues, display feminine quietude: 'les bons ménages n'éprouvent pas le besoin d'appeler l'attention sur eux, ne fréquentent pas les tribunaux, ne font aucun bruit dans le monde' (24–25). The commercial banalization of private sentiment in the public sphere is reflected in the way he dismisses certain letters from his enquiry, such as those from marriage and divorce agencies, e.g. one which advertises itself thus: '*Divorce très rapide, et à forfait, succès certain. Paris-province. Tarif inversement proportionnel à la durée de la procédure: 2000 francs un an; 5000 francs trois mois*' (25). Divorce then is seen to represent a crisis in the horizontal relations within the family tree which upset its vertical unfolding down through the generations.

Of course, the recursive relationship between the experience and the history of family life continues beyond the end of the 'long nineteenth century' and the First World War. Of Gérard Thibault-Laurent's 1938 thesis *La Première Introduction du divorce en France sous la Révolution et l'Empire (1792–1816)*, Ronsin sighs: 'On lira, on citera et on relira Thibault-Laurent sans prendre toujours conscience de la façon dont ce travail de très haute qualité peut être imprégné d'une vision de l'idéal familial que l'on pourrait qualifier de "pré-pétainiste".'[5] The mass de facto separation of couples by dint of the First World War and the experiences of men in the trenches and women in occupied France recast expectations of marriage in the post-war period. Liberalizing reforms in the '20s and '30s were reflected in the 26,300 divorces in 1938. The conservative reaction of the Vichy regime reduced the number to only 14–18,000 divorces per year. The end of the Second World War saw another spurt in the divorce statistics. De facto separation of couples in the service of the nation state led, inexorably it seemed, to de jure divorce (via the judicial mechanisms of the state). In these cases it seemed as if the law served to regularize situations created by the broad brush of history, and in 1946 there were 52,000 divorces in France. Still, it was only later that the taboo on divorce would be lifted. The divorce rate doubled in France between 1970 and the early 1980s. Key in this process was the 1975 law which finally reintroduced divorce by mutual consent. The legal recognition of civil unions without marriage, with the advent of the Pacte civil de solidarité (PACS) in 1999, belongs to this same history of nuance in the law's relationship to matters of the heart.

If the divorce motif is nowadays in danger of becoming a cultural cliché, one literary response is to absorb this narrative turning point into a wider human poetics of beginning, continuing and ending — as in Laurent Mauvignier's novels *Loin d'eux* (1999) and *Apprendre à finir* (2000). If the plot which heads towards divorce might now seem kitsch, the plot which begins with departure (in a sense the most obvious of openings) has asserted its own paradoxical force, in Hanif Kureishi's

Intimacy (1998) and Jean Echenoz's *Je m'en vais* (1999). Both seem wilfully to choose to begin where platitude might end. The former begins: 'It is the saddest night, for I am leaving and not coming back.'[6] The latter begins:

> Je m'en vais, dit Ferrer, je te quitte. Je te laisse tout mais je pars. Et comme les yeux de Suzanne, s'égarant vers le sol, s'arrêtaient sans raison sur une prise électrique, Félix Ferrer abandonna ses clefs sur la console de l'entrée. Puis il boutonna son manteau avant de sortir en refermant doucement la porte du pavillon.[7]

The publicity blurb for this re-edition in the 'Double' series stresses the normative force of divorce in modern culture: 'Ce n'est pas tout de quitter sa femme, encore faut-il aller plus loin. Félix Ferrer part donc faire un tour au pôle Nord.' Escape and discovery are poles apart. If the hope of divorce is that it will separate two futures, it does not separate two pasts. Indeed, to begin the plot at the point of exit serves only to highlight the way in which that past infiltrates those futures. Divorce is not amnesia.

The Anglo-Saxon interest in divorce 'French style' has culminated in Diane Johnson's Gallically named novel, *Le Divorce* (1997), whose American narrator, Isabel, tells the tale of her stepsister Roxy, an ex-pat in Paris.[8] At once testament to an American fascination with Paris and the designer desires of the more cerebrally challenged readers of *Harper's Bazaar*, what appears to be high-class trash is studded with a series of knowing literary references, not least to *Adolphe*. The version of Frenchness we encounter is emblematically schizoid: part Catholic self-sacrifice, at least on the part of the wife; part sexual knowingness (as Roxy says, 'It's Ireland that's priest-ridden, not France. In France they invented the morning-after pill' (24)). The ex-pat, Roxy, is symbolic of the foreignness at the heart of the 'family romance':

> She had wanted her whole life to live in France. I never understood why. Some instinct, some non-fit, had caused her from childhood to disapprove of the land and city of her birth. The way children believe they are changelings and not the children of their parents, so she believed herself displaced, sprung from another race. (20)

Isabel arrives in Paris only to discover that the pregnant Roxy has been abandoned by her French husband, Charles-Henri, for Magda, a Czech sociologist (only those from the land of Kundera, it seems, are more sexually dangerous than the French). The choice facing Roxy is dramatized by the different opinions of her French and American friends:

> The women of the Place Maubert, Tammy de Bretteville and Anne-Chantal Lartigue in particular, agreed with Roxy's take on it. A pattern of infidelity once begun is never abandoned. But they also did not believe that Roxy should divorce. In France you just put up with the way men are. This was also part of Suzanne de Persaud's pitch. '*Le divorce* is always a mistake. [...]' French husbands — like men everywhere — just always philander, she explained. 'Why ruin your life and lose your social position over it?' Roxy condemned this attitude as Victorian, a vestige of a time when women were powerless and lacking in self-respect. 'That is so American,' sighed Suzanne impatiently. 'Think of

the children, their need for a father. Think of the inconveniences of single motherhood.' (62)

The demands as well as the possibilities of serial love are also made clear: 'I have myself been divorced,' Mrs Pace observed, 'and I'm not sure it solves a great deal. Though it does permit you to marry someone else. In my experience the soundest procedure is to have the someone else lined up beforehand' (62–63). The epigraph to Chapter 13 quotes from Hervé Bazin's *Madame Ex* (1975): 'The important thing in the divorce is what follows' (90). Only the American narrator believes in confluent love:

> I was the only one of Roxy's confidantes who wasn't so sure she was wrong. What about love? How can you stay married to someone who loves another better than you? What about the future, perhaps with another mate? She had her whole life in front of her, in the phrase. I tried to slow her down, we all did, but part of me thought she just ought to bag this marriage and get on with her life. (63)

The ultimate irony of the plot trajectory is that there is in the end no divorce, as Magda's husband murders Charles-Henri: 'Only slowly it began to dawn on her that she was a widow and that a widow was something different from a divorcée. That she could have her chest of drawers back from Drouot, and Saint Ursula, there wasn't going to be any divorce' (294). The plot tends asymptotically towards the divorce of which it can finally dispose. Its patron saint is to be found in a painting by Georges de La Tour (or one of his students) of Saint Ursula who 'regards a dark future of proposed matrimony' (32).

Let me conclude then by suggesting that not only does the question of divorce tell us much about the history of both private and national life as France leaves the nineteenth century, but that its possibilities contribute to a reappraisal of narrative forms. For it helps us to construct a fuller vision of turn-of-the-century literary culture by addressing the traditional male 'heavyweights' of classic literary histories such as Marcel Raimond's *La Crise du roman* — be they Daudet, Rod or France — as well as the recent rediscovery of women writers such as Vautier, Bovet, Léo and Pert. This unusual 'double vision' provides the reader with an alternative map of the history of narrative which leads from Flaubert, not so much to the modernism of Gide and Proust, but instead to the fiction of Colette and the string of recent representations of divorce in modern French culture (novels such as Chandernagor's *La première épouse* and films such as *Jules et Jim*, *La Crise* and *La Séparation*). Nevertheless, the fictions of love found and lost which this book treats are perhaps not so far after all from the Gidean ideal of *disponibilité* and Proust's disquisition on the pain of departure in the transition from *La Prisonnière* to *Albertine disparue*. Beyond focused treatments of the motif, divorce is unobtrusively present in literally countless recent plays, novels, films, and television dramas. It is part of the wallpaper of modern life. But wallpaper is not just background. It changes the colour and the light of the very rooms in which we live and love.

Notes to the Conclusion

1. Marcel Schwob, *Le Livre de Monelle* (Paris: Union Générale d'Éditions, 1979 [1894]), p. 43.
2. Joan W. Scott, 'Rewriting History', in *Behind the Lines: Gender and the Two World Wars*, ed. by Margaret Randolph Higonnet, Jane Jenson, Sonya Michel, and Margaret Collins Weitz (New Haven, CT: Yale University Press, 1987), pp. 19–30 (p. 27).
3. Stéphane Audoin-Rouzeau, *L'Enfant de l'ennemi, 1914–1918* (Paris: Aubier, 1995).
4. Henry Bordeaux, *Le Mariage (Hier et aujourd'hui)* (Paris: Flammarion, 1921), p. 21.
5. Ronsin, 'Du divorce et de la séparation de corps en France au XIX siècle', p. 11.
6. Hanif Kureishi, *Intimacy* (London: Faber & Faber, 1998), p. 3.
7. Jean Echenoz, *Je m'en vais* (Paris: Minuit, 2001), p. 7.
8. Diane Johnson, *Le Divorce* (London: Chatto & Windus, 1997).

BIBLIOGRAPHY

ALBALAT, ANTOINE, *L'Amour chez Alphonse Daudet* (Paris: Ollendorff, 1884)

ANDERSON, JEAN, FRANCE GRENAUDIER-KLIJN and ELISABETH-CHRISTINE MUELSCH, eds, *Écrire les hommes* (Saint-Denis: Presses Universitaires de Vincennes, 2012)

ANDRÉ, GINETTE, 'Alfred Naquet, adversaire de l'Empire et défenseur de la République radicale, 1867–1884', 5 vols (unpublished doctoral thesis, Université d'Aix-Marseille, 1972)

ANGENOT, MARC, *Le Cru et le Faisandé* (Brussels: Labor, 1986)

ARMSTRONG, JUDITH, *The Novel of Adultery* (Basingstoke: Macmillan, 1976)

AUDOIN-ROUZEAU, STÉPHANE, *L'Enfant de l'ennemi, 1914–1918* (Paris: Aubier, 1995)

BALZAC, HONORÉ DE, *La Comédie humaine*, vol. VII (Paris: Gallimard Pléiade, 1977)

BANCQUART, MARIE-CLAIRE, *Anatole France: Un sceptique passionné* (Paris: Calmann-Lévy, 1984)

——*Anatole France, polémiste* (Paris: Nizet, 1962)

——and JEAN DÉRENS, eds, *Anatole France: Humanisme et actualité* (Paris: Bibliothèque historique de la Ville de Paris, 1994)

BAQUIAST, PAUL, *Une dynastie de la bourgeoisie républicaine: Les Pelletan* (Paris: L'Harmattan, 1996)

BAUMAN, ZYGMUNT, *Liquid Fear* (Cambridge: Polity, 2006)

——*Liquid Life* (Cambridge: Polity, 2005)

——*Liquid Love* (Cambridge: Polity, 2003)

——*Liquid Modernity* (Cambridge: Polity, 2000)

——*Liquid Times: Living in an Age of Uncertainty* (Cambridge: Polity, 2007)

BEAUMARCHAIS, J.-P., ed., *Dictionnaires des littératures de langue française* (Paris: Bordas, 1994)

BELENKY, MASHA, *The Anxiety of Dispossession: Jealousy in Nineteenth-Century French Culture* (Lewisburg, PA: Bucknell University Press, 2008)

BERNARD, CLAUDIE, *Penser la famille au dix-neuvième siècle, 1789–1870* (Saint-Étienne: Université de Saint-Étienne, 2007)

BERENSON, EDWARD, *The Trial of Madame Caillaux* (Berkeley: University of California Press, 1992)

BIRNBAUM, PIERRE, *Les Fous de la République* (Paris: Fayard, 1993)

BITARD, ADOLPHE, *Dictionnaire général de biographie contemporaine* (Paris: A. Lévy, 1878)

BLACK, MICHAEL, *The Literature of Fidelity* (London: Chatto & Windus, 1975)

BLANCHARD, GEORGES, *De la formation et de la dissolution du mariage romain et du mariage français* (Paris: F. Pichon, 1874)

BLANCHE, ESPRIT-SYLVESTRE, *La Folie doit-elle être considérée comme cause de divorce?* (Paris: Masson, 1882)

BORDEAUX, HENRY, *Âmes modernes* (Paris: Perrin, 1912)

——*Le Mariage (Hier et aujourd'hui)* (Paris: Flammarion, 1921)

BORNECQUE, J.-H., ed., *Histoire d'une amitié: Correspondance inédite entre Alphonse Daudet et Frédéric Mistral (1860–1897)* (Paris: Julliard, 1979)

BOWIE, MALCOLM, *Freud, Proust and Lacan: Theory as Fiction* (Cambridge: Cambridge University Press, 1987)

BOVET, MARIE-ANNE DE, *Après le divorce* (Paris: Lemerre, 1908)

BROOKS, PETER, *Reading for the Plot* (Cambridge, MA: Harvard University Press, 1992)

BRUNEL, PIERRE, 'Le Lys rouge et le monde de l'idylle', in *Anatole France: Humanisme et actualité*, ed. by Marie-Claire Bancquart and Jean Dérens (Paris: Bibliothèque historique de la Ville de Paris, 1994), pp. 23–31

CARIAS, LÉON, ed., *Les Carnets intimes d'Anatole France* (Paris: Émile-Paul frères, 1946)

CARRANCE, ÉVARISTE, *Le Divorce*, monologue en vers (Agen: Librairie du Comité Poétique et de la Revue française, 1884)

CAVILLY, GEORGES DE, *La Séparation de corps et le divorce à l'usage des gens du monde, et la manière de s'en servir: Manuel des époux mal assortis* (Paris: Jouvet, 1882)

CLARÉTIE, JULES, *Les Célébrités contemporaines: Alexandre Dumas fils* (Paris: Quantin, 1883)

CLÉBERT, JEAN-PAUL, *Une famille bien française: Les Daudet, 1840–1940* (Paris: Renaissance, 1988)

Le Code civil, 1804–1904: Livre du centenaire, publ. for La Société d'études législatives (Paris: Arthur Rousseau, 1904)

COHEN, MARGARET, *The Sentimental Education of the Novel* (Princeton, NJ: Princeton University Press, 1999)

COOK, MALCOLM, 'La Critique de la religion dans le roman révolutionnaire', in *Roman et religion en France (1713–1866)*, ed. by Jacques Wagner (Paris: Champion, 2002), pp. 172–76

COUNTER, ANDREW, *Inheritance in Nineteenth-Century French Culture* (Oxford: Legenda, 2010)

COUVRAY, LOUVET DE, *Émilie de Varmont; ou, le divorce nécessaire, et les amours du curé Sévin*, 3 vols (Paris: Bailly & les marchands de nouveautés, 1791)

DALLOZ, DÉSIRÉ, *Jurisprudence générale* (Paris: Bureau de la Jurisprudence Générale, 1890)

——*Répertoire de législation* (Paris: Bureau de la Jurisprudence Générale, 1858)

DAUDET, ALPHONSE, *Rose et Ninette*, in *Œuvres complètes*, vol. XI (Paris: Alexandre Houssiaux, 1901)

——*Le Soutien de famille* (Paris: Fasquelle, 1898)

DAUDET, LÉON, *Souvenirs des milieux littéraires, politiques, artistiques et médicaux* (Paris: Nouvelle librairie nationale, 1920)

DAUDET, LUCIEN, *Vie d'Alphonse Daudet* (Paris: Gallimard, 1941)

DELEUZE, GILLES, and FÉLIX GUATTARI, *Anti-Oedipus*, trans. by Robert Hurley (New York: Viking, 1977)

Dictionnaire biographique du mouvement ouvrier français, vol. XIV (Paris: Les Éditions ouvrières, 1976)

Dictionnaire des symboles, ed. by Jean Chevalier and Alain Gheerbrant (Paris: Robert Laffont, 1982)

DOBIE, G. VERA, *Alphonse Daudet* (London: Nelson, 1949)

DUFIEF, PIERRE, with ANNE-SIMONE DUFIEF, eds, *Edmond de Goncourt et Alphonse Daudet: Correspondance* (Geneva: Droz, 1996)

DUMAS FILS, ALEXANDRE, *La Question du divorce* (Paris: Calmann Lévy, 1880)

DURKHEIM, ÉMILE, *Le Suicide: Étude de sociologie* (Paris: Alcan, 1897)

ECHENOZ, JEAN, *Je m'en vais* (Paris: Minuit, 2001)

ECO, UMBERTO, *Reflections on 'The Name of the Rose'* (London: Secker and Warburg, 1989)

ELIOT, GEORGE, *Middlemarch* (London: Everyman, 1991)

ELLIS, JACK, *The Early Life of Georges Clemenceau, 1841–1893* (Lawrence: The Regents Press of Kansas, 1980)

EMERY, ELIZABETH, 'Art as Passion in Anatole France's Le Lys rouge', *Nineteenth-Century French Studies*, 35.3/4 (2007), 641–52

EMPSON, WILLIAM, *Seven Types of Ambiguity* (London: Chatto & Windus, 1953)

FLAM, JACK D., *Matisse on Art* (New York: Phaidon, 1973)

FLAUBERT, GUSTAVE, *L'Éducation sentimentale* (Paris: Garnier Flammarion, 1969)

FORSTER, E. M., *Aspects of the Novel* (London: Edward Arnold, 1927)

FRANCE, ANATOLE, *Le Lys rouge*, ed. by Pierre Kyria (Paris: Calmann-Lévy, 1983)

——*Œuvres*, 3 vols (Paris: Gallimard Pléiade, 1984–91)

——*Anatole France par lui-même*, ed. by Jacques Suffel (Paris: Seuil, 1954)

GIDDENS, ANTHONY, *Modernity and Self-Identity* (Cambridge: Polity, 1991)

——*The Transformation of Intimacy* (Cambridge: Polity, 1992)

GINZBURG, CARLO, 'Clues: Roots of an Evidential Paradigm', in his *Myths, Emblems, Clues*, trans. by J. and A. C. Tedeschi (London: Hutchinson, 1990), pp. 96–125

GLASSON, ERNEST-DÉSIRÉ, *Le Mariage civil et le divorce dans l'Antiquité et dans les principales législations modernes de l'Europe* (Paris: Pedone-Lauriel, 1880)

GONCOURT, EDMOND and JULES DE, *Journal*, 3 vols (Paris: Laffont, 1989)

La Grande Encyclopédie (Paris: Lamirault, 1885–1902)

GUÉRARD, ALBERT LÉON, *Five Masters of French Romance: Anatole France, Pierre Loti, Paul Bourget, Maurice Barrès, Romain Rolland* (London: T. Fisher Unwin, 1916)

HARRIS, JANICE HUBBARD, *Edwardian Stories of Divorce* (New Brunswick, NJ: Rutgers University Press, 1996)

HARDY, THOMAS, *Life's Little Ironies and A Changed Man* (London: Macmillan, 1977)

HEMMINGS, F. W. J., *Theatre and State in France, 1760–1905* (Cambridge: Cambridge University Press, 1994)

HERVOUET, YVES, 'Conrad's Debt to French Authors in *Under Western Eyes*', *Conradiana*, 14.2 (1982), 113–25

HIGONNET, MARGARET RANDOLPH, JANE JENSON, SONYA MICHEL, and MARGARET COLLINS WEITZ, EDS, *Behind the Lines: Gender and the Two World Wars* (New Haven, CT: Yale University Press, 1987)

HOLMES, DIANA, *French Women's Writing: 1848–1994* (London: Athlone, 1996)

HORNE, ALISTAIR, *The Fall of Paris* (London: Macmillan, 1965)

JEFFERSON, CARTER, *Anatole France: The Politics of Skepticism* (New Brunswick, NJ: Rutgers University Press, 1965)

JOHNSON, DIANE, *Le Divorce* (London: Chatto & Windus, 1997)

KUREISHI, HANIF, *Intimacy* (London: Faber & Faber, 1998)

LECKIE, BARBARA, *Culture and Adultery: The Novel, the Newspaper, and the Law* (Philadelphia: University of Pennsylvania Press, 1999)

LÉO, ANDRÉ, *Un Divorce* (Paris: Librairie Internationale, 1866)

——*Écrits politiques* (Paris: Dittmar, 2005)

LERMINA, JULES, *Dictionnaire universel illustré de la France contemporaine* (Paris: Boulanger, 1884)

LERNER, MICHAEL G., *Edouard Rod: A Portrait of the Novelist and his Times* (The Hague: Mouton, 1975)

LETHBRIDGE, ROBERT, review of Anatole France, *Œuvres*: 1 (1984) and Marie-Claire Bancquart, *Un sceptique passionnée* (1984), in *French Studies*, 40 (1986), 94

LEYDECKER, KARL, *Marriage and Divorce in the Plays of Hermann Sudermann* (Frankfurt am Main: Lang, 1996)

——and NICHOLAS WHITE, eds, *After Intimacy: The Culture of Divorce in the West since 1789* (Oxford: Lang, 2007)

LLOYD, ROSEMARY, *Closer & Closer Apart: Jealousy in Literature* (Ithaca, NY: Cornell University Press, 1995)

LOYSON, CHARLES, *Lettre sur le mariage* (Paris: Sandoz & Fichbacher, 1872)

——*Ni cléricaux ni athées, discours et lettres sur la Troisième République* (Paris: Marpon & Flammarion, 1890)

LUYS, JULES, 'La Folie doit-elle être considérée comme une cause de divorce?', *Encéphale*, June 1882

MacComb, Debra Ann, *Tales of Liberation/Strategies of Containment: Divorce and the Representation of Womanhood in American Fiction, 1880–1920* (New York: Garland, 2000)

McEwan, Ian, *Atonement* (London: Jonathan Cape, 2001)

Mainardi, Patricia, *Husbands, Wives, and Lovers* (New Haven, CT: Yale University Press, 2003)

Mansker, Andrea, *Sex, Honor and Citizenship in Early Third Republic France* (Basingstoke: Palgrave Macmillan, 2011)

Marchant, François, *La Constitution en vaudeville, suivie des droits de l'homme, de la femme, et de plusieurs vaudevilles constitutionnels* (Paris: Chez les libraires royalistes, 1792)

——*La République en vaudeville* (Paris: Chez les marchands de nouveautés, 1793)

Matlock, Jann, *Scenes of Seduction* (New York: Columbia University Press, 1994)

——'The Limits of Reformism: The Novel, Censorship, and the Politics of Adultery in Nineteenth-Century France', in *Cultural Institutions of the Novel*, ed. by Deirdre Lynch and William B. Warner (Durham, NC: Duke University Press, 1996), pp. 335–68

Mesch, Rachel, 'A Belle Epoque Media Storm: Gender, Celebrity, and the Marcelle Tinayre Affair', *French Historical Studies*, 35 (2012), 93–121

——'Husband, Wives and Doctors: Marriage and Medicine in Rachilde, Jane de La Vaudère and Camille Pert', in *State of the Union*, as following, pp. 90–104

——and Masha Belenky, eds, *State of the Union: Marriage in Nineteenth-Century France*, special issue of *Dix-Neuf*, 11.1 (2008)

Mollenhauer, Daniel, *Auf der Suche nach der 'wahren Republik': Die französischen 'radicaux' in der frühen Dritten Republik (1870–1890)* (Bonn: Bouvier, 1997)

Moses, Claire Goldberg, *French Feminism in the 19th Century* (Albany: State University of New York Press, 1984)

Naquet, Alfred, *Autobiographie* (Paris: Sirye, 1939); also pub. by Émile Pillias in *Revue d'histoire politique et constitutionnelle*, 3 (1939), 63–91

——*Cours de philosophie chimique* (Paris: Savy, 1866)

——*Le Divorce*, revised, 'très augmentée' (Paris: Dentu, 1881)

——'Divorce: From a French Point of View', *The North American Review*, 155 (November 1892), 721–30

——*La Loi du divorce* (Paris: Charpentier, 1903)

——*Religion, propriété, famille* (Paris: Chez tous les libraires, 1869)

——*La République radicale* (Paris: Germer Baillière, 1873)

——*Temps futurs, Socialisme, Anarchie* (Paris: Stock, 1900)

——*Vers l'union libre* (Paris: Juven, 1908)

Norberg, Kathryn, '"Love and Patriotism": Gender and Politics in the Life and Work of Louvet de Couvrai', in *Rebel Daughters*, ed. by Sara E. Melzer and Leslie W. Rabine (New York: Oxford University Press, 1992), pp. 38–53

Overton, Bill, *The Novel of Female Adultery* (Basingstoke: Macmillan, 1996)

Pasco, Allan, *Revolutionary Love in Eighteenth- and Early Nineteenth-Century France* (Farnham: Ashgate, 2009)

Pedersen, Jean Elisabeth, *Legislating the French Family: Feminism, Theater and Republican Politics, 1870–1920* (New Brunswick, NJ: Rutgers University Press, 2003)

Pelletan, Eugène, *La Mère* (Paris and Brussels: Pagnerre, Lacroix & Verboeckhoven, 1866)

Pert, Camille, *Cady mariée* (Paris: Mignot, 1913)

——*Cady remariée* (Paris: Albin Michel, 1926)

——*Le Divorce de Cady* (Paris: Mignot, 1914)

——*Georges à Paris* (Paris: Mignot, [1917])

——*La Petite Cady* (Paris: Mignot, 1914)

Phillips, Adam, *On Flirtation* (London: Faber & Faber, 1995)

PHILLIPS, RODERICK, *Divorce in New Zealand: A Social History* (Auckland: Oxford University Press, 1981)

——*Family Breakdown in Late Eighteenth-Century France* (Oxford: Oxford University Press, 1980)

——*Putting Asunder* (Cambridge: Cambridge University Press, 1988)

——*Untying the Knot* (Cambridge: Cambridge University Press, 1991)

PRENDERGAST, CHRISTOPHER, *The Order of Mimesis* (Cambridge: Cambridge University Press, 1986)

PRÉVOST, MARCEL, *Nouvelles Lettres de femmes* (Paris: Lemerre, 1894)

RIFFATERRE, MICHAEL, 'Flaubert's Presuppositions', *Diacritics*, 11 (1981), 2–11

RIVERS, JOHN, *Louvet: Revolutionary & Romance-Writer* (London: Hurst and Blackett, 1910)

ROCHE, ALPHONSE V., *Alphonse Daudet* (Boston, MA: Twayne, 1976)

ROD, ÉDOUARD, *La Seconde Vie de Michel Teissier* (Paris: Perrin, 1894)

——*La Vie privée de Michel Teissier* (Paris: Perrin, 1893)

ROGERS, JULIETTE, *Career Stories: Belle Epoque Novels of Professional Development* (University Park, PA: Penn State Press, 2007)

RONSIN, FRANCIS, *Le Contrat sentimental* (Paris: Aubier, 1990)

——'Du divorce et de la séparation de corps en France au XIX siècle' (unpublished doctoral thesis, Université Paris 7, 1988)

——*Les Divorciaires* (Paris: Aubier, 1992)

ROURÉ, JACQUES, *Alphonse Daudet* (Paris: Julliard, 1982)

SAND, GEORGE, *Elle et lui* (Neuchâtel: Ides et Calendes, 1963)

SCHWOB, MARCEL, *Le Livre de Monelle* (Paris: Union Générale d'Éditions, 1979 [1894])

SCOTT, JOAN W., 'Rewriting History', in *Behind the Lines: Gender and the Two World Wars*, ed. by Margaret Randolph Higonnet, Jane Jenson, Sonya Michel, and Margaret Collins Weitz (New Haven, CT: Yale University Press, 1987), pp. 19–30

SEGAL, NAOMI, *The Adulteress's Child* (Cambridge: Polity, 1992)

SENNETT, RICHARD, *The Corrosion of Character* (New York: Norton, 1998)

——*The Fall of Public Man* (Cambridge: Cambridge University Press, 1976)

SEURE, ONÉZIME, *Le Divorce, précédé d'une lettre de Victor Hugo* (Paris: Chaumerot, 1848)

SICARD, PAUL, *Du divorce en droit romain: De la séparation de corps en droit français* (Paris, 1876)

SINCLAIR, ALISON, *The Deceived Husband* (Oxford: Oxford University Press, 1993)

STACEY, JUDITH, *Brave New Families* (New York: Basic Books, 1990)

STONE, LAWRENCE, *The Family, Sex and Marriage in England, 1500–1800* (London: Weidenfeld and Nicolson, 1977)

——*Road to Divorce* (Oxford: Oxford University Press, 1990)

TAILHADE, LAURENT, *Quelques fantômes de jadis* (Paris: Messein, 1913)

TANNER, TONY, *Adultery in the Novel* (Baltimore, MD: Johns Hopkins University Press, 1979)

TÉRY, GUSTAVE, *Les Divorcés peints par eux-mêmes, mille et une confessions* (Paris: Fayard, [n.d.])

TOULOUSE, JEAN-ISAURE, *Manuel pratique du mariage (contrat de mariage, mariage civil et religieux), du divorce, de la séparation de corps et de la séparation de biens, avec détail et total des frais de chaque matière* (Paris: A. Giard, 1891)

TYLDEN-WRIGHT, DAVID, *Anatole France* (London: Collins, 1967)

VALLÈS, JULES, *L'Insurgé* (Paris: Charpentier, 1908)

VAUTIER, CLAIRE, *Adultère et divorce* (Paris: Marpon & Flammarion, 1889)

VÉRON, LOUIS-DÉSIRÉ, *Mémoires d'un bourgeois de Paris*, 6 vols (Paris: Gabriel de Gonet, 1853–55)

VIRTANEN, REINO, *Anatole France* (Boston, MA: Twayne, 1968)

VOLTAIRE, 'Zadig', in *Romans et contes* (Paris: Garnier, 1953)

WAELTI-WALTERS, JENNIFER, *Feminist Novelists of the Belle Epoque: Love as a Lifestyle* (Lincoln: University of Nebraska Press, 1994)

——and STEVEN C. HAUSE, eds, *Feminisms of the Belle Epoque: A Historical and Literary Anthology* (Lincoln: University of Nebraska Press, 1994)

WALLERSTEIN, JUDITH, and SANDRA BLAKESLEE, *Second Chances* (London: Bantam, 1989)

WARD JOUVE, NICOLE, review of *Le Cru et le Faisandé*, *French Studies*, 41 (1987), 358–59

WHITE, CLAIRE, 'Rewriting Work and Leisure in Émile Zola's *Travail*', *Dix-Neuf*, 13 (2009), 55–70

WHITE, NICHOLAS, *The Family in Crisis in Late Nineteenth-Century French Fiction* (Cambridge: Cambridge University Press, 1999)

——'The Name of the Divorcée: Janvier and Ballot's Theatrical Critique, *Mon Nom!* (1892)', *Romance Quarterly*, 49 (2002), 215–27

——and NAOMI SEGAL, eds, *Scarlet Letters: Fictions of Adultery from Antiquity to the 1990s* (Basingstoke: Macmillan, 1997)

INDEX

abandonment (and absence) 25–26, 30, 57, 63, 66
Acollas, Émile 40, 48–49, 56
Adam, Juliette 109
Adorno, Theodor 15
adultery 25, 29, 30, 31, 32, 33, 34, 37, 47, 56, 57, 58, 60, 64, 65, 66, 67, 68, 75
adultery in fiction 1, 3–4, 8, 10, 14, 19, 77, 85–86
d'Alensson, Jean, 55
Allou, Édouard 62
Althusser, Louis 111
André, Ginette 25, 29, 37, 38, 42, 82 n. 67
Angenot, Marc 92–93, 104
Antonini, Paul 49
Aragon, Louis, 'Avez-vous giflé un mort?' 119
Arbalat, Antoine 142
Archer, Jeffrey 160
architecture 135–36
Aristotle and *anagnorisis* 10
Auclert, Hubertine, *La Citoyenne* 55
Audebrand, Philibert 48
Audouard, Olympe, *Le Papillon* 55
Audouin-Rouzeau, Stéphane 179
Augier, Émile 52, 77
    Madame Caverlet 51
Austen, Jane 85
L'Avenir des femmes 43, 45, 54, 64

bachelordom 146
Balzac, Honoré de 61, 144
    Le Colonel Chabert 63
    La Maison du chat-qui-pelote 86
    La Paix du ménage 86
    Vautrin 10
Bancquart, Marie-Claire 131, 139 nn. 23 & 24, 140 nn. 32 & 33
Baquiast, Paul 37
Barnes, Julian, *Before She Met Me* 22
Barthes, Roland 10, 45
Batbie, Anselme 63
Baudelaire, Charles 129
Baudrillart, Henri 51
Bauman, Zygmunt 2, 10, 13, 15–22, 25
    Liquid Fear 21
    Liquid Life 21–22
    Liquid Love 18–22
    Liquid Modernity 2, 9–10, 15–19, 95, 104, 163
    Liquid Times 21
Bazin, Hervé, *Madame Ex* 182

Beaumarchais, Pierre-Augustin Caron de, *L'autre Tartuffe ou la mère coupable*28
Beck, Ulrich 22–23
Belenky, Masha 139 n. 3
Belle Epoque 9
Belot, Adolphe 141, 142
Bérenger, René 64
Berenson, Edward 32
Bernard, Claudie 104–05 n.1
Berry, Georges 50
Bertillon, Jacques 70–72, 83 n. 106
bigamy 6, 8, 62, 63, 69, 86
Bildungsroman 86, 159, 168–69, 178
Blanc, Louis 43, 45, 51, 57
    Essai sur le divorce 34
Blanche, Esprit-Sylvestre 63
Blanqui, Louis Auguste 40
Blum, Léon, *Du mariage* 138, 166
Bonald, Louis de 1, 32, 49, 72
Bonneau, L. 49
Bonnechose, Cardinal de 39
Bordeaux, Henry 106, 179–80
Boulangism 46, 61, 72
Bourdieu, Pierre, *précarité* 18
Bourget, Paul 20, 73, 106–09, 161, 165
Bovet, Marie-Anne de 5
    Après le divorce 105 n. 14, 106–07
Bowie, Malcolm 6–7, 9, 15, 22, 117–19
Brindeau, Jeanne 132
Brisson, Henri 56, 67
Brunetière, Ferdinand 163 n. 19
Duc de Broglie 43
Brooks, Peter 71
Brouillet, André, *Une leçon clinique à la Salpêtrière* 39
Brunel, Pierre 119
Butler, Judith 2
Byron, Lord, 'Lara' 96

Caillavet, née Léontine Lippmann, Mme de 139 n. 24
Calvino, Italo, *Invisible Cities* 21
Cappelle-Lafarge, Marie 35
Carias, Léon 132–33
caricature 27, 35–37, 41, 50, 59, 83 n. 83
Carrance, Évarance 62
Cavell, Stanley 16
Cavilly, Georges de (pseud. of Georges Vibert), *La Séparation de corps et le divorce à l'usage des gens du monde et la manière de s'en servir* 60–61

Cazot, Jules 38
Cerfvol, *Le cri d'un honnête homme* 49, 72
Cham 52, 82 n. 81
Champagne, Comtesse de 61
Chandernagor, Françoise *La première épouse* 182
Charcot, Jean-Martin 39
Le Charivari 35–37, 49–50, 52, 82 n. 81
Cherbuliez, Victor 52
children 5, 13–14, 18, 20, 23, 26, 27, 30, 31, 36, 39–40,
    57, 58, 69–70, 74, 78, 92, 101, 112, 122, 141–53,
    156, 159–60, 165, 169, 171–72, 181–82
Chirac, Jacques 18
Chouteau, Henri 40, 41
church *vs.* secular republic 2, 4, 48–51, 63–64, 67, 68,
    74, 78, 94, 96, 105 n.14, 110–11, 113–15, 144, 165
Clarétie, Jules, *Les Célébrités contemporaines* 51
Clark, Alan 161
Clébert, Jean-Paul 143
Clémenceau, Georges 40, 144, 162
Clinton, Bill 160
Cohen, Margaret 77, 88, 104–05 n.1
Colette, Sidonie-Gabrielle 138, 166, 172
Combemale, Estelle 39–40, 73
commodification of love 17–21
Comte, Auguste 14, 38, 107
Conrad, 140 n. 36
Constans, Jean 45, 56
Constant, Benjamin 86, 181
contract *vs.* sacrament 33, 56, 68, 78–79, 96, 110–11,
    130, 141, 148, 166
Cook, Malcolm 87
Coppée, François 109
Counter, Andrew 145
Couvray, Louvet de, *Émilie de Varmont* 86–87
Crawford, Virginia 161
Crémieux, Adolphe 34, 55
La Crise 182
Cuvier, Georges 7

Dante Alghieri 126, 143
Darmester, James 119
Daudet, Alphonse 20, 163
    Rose et Ninette 5, 81–82 n. 46, 116, 141–52
    Le Soutien de famille 142
Daudet, Charles 143
Daudet, Julia 142–43
Daudet, Léon 144, 146, 163 n.13
Daudet, Lucien 143
Dautrin, Élie, *L'Absent* 179
death 3, 8, 11, 19–22, 57, 68, 71–72, 86, 95–97, 100,
    112, 129–30, 137, 150, 154
Delarue-Mardrus, Lucie 179
Delescluze, Charles 41
Deleuze, Gilles and Félix Guattari 15
Delpech, C., *La Femme* 55
La Démocratie du Midi 42, 82 n. 54
Diderot, Denis 15, 68

Didon, Père Henri 49, 52
Dilke, Sir Charles 161–62
divorce:
    in Alsace-Lorraine 57
    Article 298: 31, 64–65, 70, 103–04
    in Belgium 57, 139 n. 8
    the Commune 1, 37
    in England 31, 70, 75, 104, 154, 158, 161
    the Enlightenment 22, 68, 142
    the First World War 1, 63, 79–80, 179–80
    the French Revolution 1, 5, 25–29, 37, 67, 68, 72,
        74, 75, 83 n. 96, 86–87
    in Italy 70
    the July Monarchy 32–33
    and literature 2–6, 67, 76–77, 80
    the Napoleonic Code 1, 29–32, 37, 63, 76–79, 86
    in Portugal 70
    and the Restoration 1, 32, 62–63, 83 n. 96
    the 1848 Revolution 33–37, 67, 87–88
    scientific analogy 25, 39
    the Second Empire 1, 37, 87–92
    in Spain 70
    in Slavic countries 70
    in Switzerland 88–92
    the Third Republic 1, 37, 42–80
Dobie, G. Vera, 142
dowry 35, 86, 101, 110, 131
doxa 3, 31, 48, 49, 59, 123
Dreyfus Affair 2, 49, 79, 109
Drouet, Arsène 44
Duhamel, Georges, *Chronique des Pasquier* 166
Dumas *fils*, Alexandre 2, 50–51, 76–77
Durkheim, Émile 14–15, 70–72, 174–75

Eastenders 19–20
Echenoz, Jean, *Je m'en vais* 181
L'Écho de Paris 179
Eco, Umberto 172
L'Égalité 38, 46
Eliot, George, *Middlemarch* 3–4
Ellis, Jack 162
Emery, Elizabeth 140 n. 38
Épailly, Commandant 55
epistemology 2, 6–9, 22, 117–19, 172, 177
existentialism 2

Faguet, Émile 72
Fargeot, Nicolas-Julien 28
feminism 1, 33–37, 45, 49, 54–55, 85–86, 88, 90, 94–95,
    98, 109, 115 165–67
Ferry, Jules 52
Féval, Paul, *Pas de divorce!* 2, 50, 82 n. 77
Fiaux, Louis 48
Le Figaro 39, 52–54, 73, 76
Flaubert, Gustave 1, 134, 136, 159, 182
    Bouvard et Pécuchet 45
    L'Éducation sentimentale 87–89

Madame Bovary 3, 10, 33, 89, 94, 116–17, 152, 174
flirtation 4–5, 125–27, 165, 168, 171–75
Floran, Mary, *On demande une marraine* 179
Forster, E.M. 23 n. 5, 119, 133
Foucault, Michel 13–14
Fouques dit Desfontaine, François-George 28
Fourier, Charles 34
France, Anatole 5, 163
    Le Lys rouge 9, 106, 116, 119–40
    Poèmes du souvenir 133
    Thaïs 131
Freppel, Bishop of Angers 59, 63–64, 83 n. 95
Freud, Sigmund 6–7, 9–10, 17, 39, 116–17
Frollo, Jean 51

Le Gaulois 50, 52
La Gazette des femmes 45, 55
La Gazette du Midi 44
Gambetta, Léon 42–45, 47, 51, 52
Gide, André 95, 156, 182
Giddens, Anthony 2, 10–18, 20, 22, 24 n. 16, 30, 36,
    89, 121, 166, 169
    confluent love 15–18, 20, 30, 76, 120, 121, 126–30,
      166, 177, 182
    Modernity and Self-Identity 10–13
    the 'pure relationship' 11–15, 17–18, 20, 22
    The Transformation of Intimacy 13–15, 22
Gilbert-Martin, Charles 59
Ginzburg, Carlo 6–10, 15, 22, 24 n. 13, 69, 73, 118, 136
Girardin, Émile de 51, 83 n. 88
Girondon, Père 50
Glasson, Eugène-Désiré 49, 68–70, 83 n. 97
Goethe, Johann Wolfgang von
    Elective Affinities 4, 19, 39, 96, 128
    Werther 71
Goncourt, Edmond and Jules de 142–44, 147
Gounod, Charles, *Faust*, 123, 136–38
La Grande Encyclopédie 68–70, 83 n. 97
Grévy, Jules 43, 45, 47, 51
Guérard, Albert Léon 80
Guerre, Martin 63
Guesde, Jules 46
Gyp 66, 132, 139–40 n. 28

Habermas, Jürgen 17
Hause, Steven C. 167
d'Héricourt, Jenny, *La Femme affranchie* 37
heteronormativity 32, 58, 88, 90, 95, 181
heterosocial bonds 89–91, 97, 120–23, 126, 138
Hirsch, Alphonse 67
Hogan, Phil 21
Hollande, François 18
Holmes, Sherlock 6–7, 136
homosocial bonds 8, 44, 88–90, 98, 101, 117, 121, 154
Horkheimer, Max 15
Horne, Alistair 81 n. 29
Hugues, Clovis 38

Hugo, Alice 81–82 n. 46
Hugo, Jeanne 81–82 n.46, 141–44
Hugo, Victor 33–34, 51, 81–82 n. 46, 149
Huxley, Thomas 7

Ibsen, Henrik 113, 134
l'Ille, Dupont de 28
incompatibilité d'humeur 25, 26, 30, 65, 66, 71, 78
inheritance 26, 39, 63, 78, 95–96
injures graves 29, 30, 64–68, 71
Ionesco, Eugène 93

Jaloux, Edmond 134
James, Henry, *What Maisie Knew* 145
Janvier, Ambroise, and Marcel Ballot, *Mon Nom!* 146
jealousy 5, 9, 62, 90, 106–40, 147–48, 165, 177
Jefferson, Carter 132
La Jeune Garde 83 n. 83, 83 n. 88
Johnson, Diane, *Le Divorce* 181–82
Josephine de Beauharnais 29, 86, 122
Jospin, Lionel 18
Jules et Jim 182

Karlfeldt, Erik 119
Kauffmann, P. 60, 83 n. 89
Koppe, Louise, *La Femme dans la famille et dans la société* 55
Kureishi, Hanif, *Intimacy* 180–81
Kyria, Pierre 138

Lafayette, Madame de, *La Princesse de Clèves* 4, 150
Lafond de Saint-Mûr, Baron 62
Laguerre, Georges 73
Lainé, Joseph 122
Laisant, Alfred 73
Laprévotte, Emma 132
Larousse, Pierre, *Grand Dictionnaire Universel* 40
Lasch, Christopher 13
lawyers 55, 61, 66, 75, 83 n.82, 101, 112, 150, 173, 175
Laya, Alexandre 47
Lecointre, Comtesse Pierre 167
Ledru-Rollin 43
Léger, François-Pierre-Auguste, *L'Homme sans façon* 29
Legouvé, Ernest 34, 51
Legrand, Louis 49, 56, 139 n.8
Léo, André 5, 105 n. 8
    Un divorce 85, 88–92, 124
Lerebours-Pigeonnière, Paul 78–79
Lerner, Michael G. 153–54
Lethbridge, Robert 138
Lloyd, Rosemary 135
Lockroy, Édouard 40, 42, 81–82 n. 46, 142–43
Lofez, Ph. 49
Loi Naquet 1–2, 46, 61–67, 75, 141–43, 146
    reforms of 1886: 2, 67, 68–69, 162
Loquet, Charles 45
Louis-Philippe 34
Loyson, Charles 49

Lurat, Abel 39
Luys, Jules 63

McEwan, Ian, *Atonement* 4
madness 25, 35, 63, 149
Mainardi, Patricia 104–05 n.1
Mallarmé, Stéphane 55
Mansker, Andrea 83 n. 100
manuals 66, 167
Marchant, François 27–28
Margueritte brothers 108, 165
Marie-Louise of Austria 86, 122
marriage 2–5, 14, 32, 35, 37, 41, 48, 86, 93–100, 106,
    109–15, 119, 121–22, 124, 127, 130, 132, 141,
    143–44, 146, 148, 150, 152–57, 160–62, 165, 166,
    168–71, 173–74, 176–80
Martin-Feuillée, Félix 62
Martin, Olivier, *La Crise du mariage* 72
Le Matin 144
Matisse, Henri 133
Matlock, Jann 33, 35, 81 n. 24
Maupassant, Guy de 58, 62, 85, 130
    Bel-Ami 86, 153
Mauvignier, Laurent 180
Maynard, Alphonse 48
Mendès, Catulle 169
Mère Duchêne 34–35
Meredith, Georges, *Modern Love* 145
Mesch, Rachel 23 n.1, 178 nn. 2 & 7
Méssac, Régis 24 n. 13
Michelet, Jules 37
Miller, D. A. 73
Millet, Albert 56
mimesis 88, 93
Mistral, Frédéric 143
Mitterrand, François 160
Molière 3, 123, 170–71
Mollenhauer, Daniel 37, 46
Mollin, Henri 132
money 3, 27, 30, 31, 61, 69, 75, 99, 102
Moniquet, Abbé Paulin 50
Montesquieu, Baron de 57, 142
Moreau, Georges 81 n. 33
Morizot-Thibault, Charles 75–76
Morelli, Giovanni 6–7
Mossé, Armand 54
motherhood 4, 26, 34, 36, 41, 58, 94, 102, 112, 168–
    73, 176, 182
Musil, Robert, *Der Mann ohne Eigenschaften* 19, 22
mutual consent 25, 29, 30–32, 44, 59, 62, 63, 65–66,
    68, 70, 72, 75–76, 79, 107, 146, 180

Napoleon Bonaparte 1, 17, 29–32, 40, 76–77, 86, 122
Napoleon III: 18, 34, 38, 41, 43, 86, 88, 93, 122–23,
    135
Naquet, Alfred 1–2, 25, 28, 29, 32, 37–84, 106, 109,
    141, 143, 163 n.13

Autobiographie 39–41, 46, 53–54, 61–62, 63–64, 72,
    79, 81 n. 33, 82 n.60, 83 n. 95
Cours de philosophie chimique 39
Le Divorce 25, 47, 51, 55–59, 82 n.60
'Divorce: From a French Point of View' 66–67, 72–73
La Loi du divorce 73, 75, 108
Questions constitutionnelles 61
Religion, propriété, famille 40–41, 44
La République radicale 43
Vers l'union libre 73–74, 107–08, 139 n.8
Naquet, Eliacin 38
Naquet, Paméla, née Vidal 37–38
Naquet, Semé-David 37–38
narrative 1–6, 9–12, 14, 16, 18, 21–22, 25, 26, 35, 48,
    57, 58, 60, 62, 68, 69, 71, 85–87, 90–97, 104, 108–
    09, 111, 112, 114, 117–20, 125, 128, 131, 140 n.38,
    145–51, 153–57, 159, 165–66, 172–73, 175–82
'New men' and 'new women' 5, 165, 177
Norberg, Kathryn 87
Nus and Belot, *Miss Multon* 51

Pacte civil de solidarité (PACS) 180
Pall Mall Gazette 161
Panama Scandal 72
para-family 170–71
paranoia 9–10, 85, 117–18, 124, 127
Parnell, Charles Stewart 158, 161
Pasco, Allan 104–05 n.2
paternity 1, 10, 31, 41, 49, 72, 141, 149, 152–53, 156,
    165, 174
Pedersen, Jean Elisabeth 82 n. 80
Pelletan, Eugène, *La Mère* 37
Pelletier, Madeleine 166
Pert, Camille, *Cady* novels 5, 20, 163, 165–78
Le Petit, Alfred 50
Phillips, Adam 165
Phillips, Roderick 2, 23 n. 9, 26
Pillias, Émile 72, 79, 81 n. 33
Pin, Elzéar 61
Plummer, Mary 162
politics 152–63
Poujade, Cyprien 42, 73
Prendergast, Christopher 9–10, 73, 118
Prévost, Augustin 28
Prévost, Marcel, 5, 74, 106, 165, 173, 175
private and public lives 2, 12, 17, 18–19, 29, 30, 34–35,
    46, 48, 52, 58, 68–69, 70–71, 83 n. 82, 91, 96, 98,
    122–23, 146, 152–63, 169–70, 180
property 40–41, 46, 75
prostitution 33–34, 41, 75–76, 91, 124, 165
Proudhon, Pierre-Joseph 10, 36, 38
Proust, Marcel 9, 116–19, 127
Psichari, Lucien 132
Psichari, Michel 132

Raimond, Marcel 182
Le Rappel 41, 52

reconciliation 68, 69
Reclus, Élisée 73–74
régimes matrimoniaux 30, 39, 64, 98, 99, 110, 131,
    142–43
Rénier, Émile 44
Le Réveil 41
Revue des Deux Mondes 51, 163 n. 19
reflexivity 10–12, 14, 22, 89, 118
remarriage to first spouse 31, 64
Renault, Léon 48, 59
revanchisme 58
La Révolution 45, 46
Richepin, Jean 134
Richer, Léon 43, 54, 64, 83 n. 96
Riffaterre, Michael 10
Rimbaud, Arthur 127
Rivers, John 87
Robinson, Mary 119
Roche, Alphonse V. 143
Rod, Édouard, the *Michel Teissier* diptych 5, 141,
    152–63, 168
Rogers, Juliette 178 n. 7
roman à clé 123, 130, 133
roman à thèse 123, 165
roman-fleuve 166
Ronsard, *Les Amours*, 137
Ronsin, Francis 23 n. 2, 28, 29, 32–33, 40–41, 43, 45,
    46, 48–51, 55, 59, 67, 74, 80, 83 n. 106, 180
Rouré, Jacques 142
Rousseau, Jean-Jacques 28, 43, 68, 96, 160
Roussel, Nelly 166–67
Royal, Ségolène 18
Rumsfeld, Donald 123

salon society 9, 53–54, 109, 114, 119, 124–25, 130–32,
    134, 146, 152
Sand, George 77, 86, 88, 116, 122
Sarkozy, Nicolas 18
Scheurer-Kestner, August 40
Schoemaeker, Florimond 49
Schwob, Marcel 179
Scott, Joan 179
second marriages 3–6, 8, 17, 26, 31–32, 52, 57, 58, 70,
    104, 106, 111, 112–13, 115, 118, 153–58, 160–61,
    165, 168–69, 173
Sennett, Richard 13, 15, 166
separation 6, 26, 30, 31–32, 35, 37, 57, 58, 60, 61–63,
    65–67, 70, 73, 74, 87, 93, 95, 96, 100–02, 110, 124,
    130, 139–40 n. 28, 141, 147, 148, 150–51, 173, 175,
    177–80
Sercambi of Lucca, Giovanni 9
serendipity 9
serial relationships 4–6, 8, 19, 27, 28, 36, 54–55, 69,
    116, 118, 121, 125, 129, 131, 155, 165–78, 182
servants 69, 160, 168, 170–72, 178
Seure, Onézime, 'Le Divorce' 5, 27, 33–34, 106
sévices 25, 29–30, 35, 64–65, 67–68, 71

Simon, Jules 43, 62
Siquoir, Odile 73
Smith, Adam 15
Société des amis du divorce 55
sociology 2, 9–23, 71–72
song 25–29
Sorel, Albert 76–77
Stacey, Judith 13
Stack, Frédéric 73
Staël, Mme de 86
Stendhal 14, 136
    Le Rouge et le Noir 3
Strindberg, August 113, 134
Sue, Eugène, *Les Mystères de Paris* 33

Tailhade, Laurent 67, 81–82 n. 46
Tanner, Tony 10, 85, 107
Taylor, Elizabeth 146
Le Temps 44, 45, 51, 79
Téry, Gustave 107, 139 n. 6
Thibault, Suzanne 131
Thibault-Laurent, Gérard 180
Thiers, Adolphe 43, 47
A Thousand and One Nights 177–78
Tinayre, Marcelle 5
    La Rebelle 114, 165–66
Tolstoy, Leo, *Anna Karenina* 3, 156
Toulouse, Jean-Isaure 142
Tracy, Destutt de 14
Trierweiler, Valérie 18
Tristan, Flora 33, 97
Tylden-Wright, David 131

union libre 40, 55–57, 73–74, 76, 78, 79, 83 n. 88,
    107–09, 114

Vallès, Jules, *L'Insurgé* 41
Vautier, Claire 5, 61, 83 n. 96, 105 n. 11
    Adultère et divorce 85, 92–104, 110, 113, 121
Vaux, Clothilde de 14
venereal disease 65
Verdi, Giuseppe 144, 149–50
Verlaine, Paul 119
Véron, Louis-Désiré 37
Vidieu, Abbé, *Famille et divorce* 50
Vigny, Alfred de 144
    Chatterton 83 n. 89
Viollet-le-Duc, Eugène Emmanuel 135–36
violence 25, 60, 65, 67, 68, 75, 93–95, 120, 127
virginity 4–5, 58, 61, 65, 93–95, 106, 111, 114, 121, 137,
    165, 171, 177
La Voix des femmes 34
Voltaire 50, 24 n. 13, 119
    Zadig 7–8
Le Voltaire 47, 50, 62
Vuille, Louis 153–54
Vuille, Nancy 153–54

Waelti-Walters, Jennifer 166, 167
Wagner, Richard 127, 144, 150, 151
Wallerstein, Judith and Sandra Blakeslee, *Second
    Chances* 11
Walpole, Horace 9
Ward Jouve, Nicole 92–93
Weber, Eugen 56
wedding 3–5, 19–20, 35, 61, 69–70, 88, 93–94, 99, 109,
    111, 114, 142, 150–51
Welles, Orson, *Citizen Kane* 125
White, Claire 19
widows and widowers 4–5, 8, 26, 27, 33, 35, 57, 58,
    63–64, 71, 73, 86, 95, 98, 106, 111, 130, 146,
    148–50, 153, 165, 170, 173, 175, 182

Wittmann, Blanche 39

Zola, Émile 40, 58, 62, 73, 81 n. 44, 85, 113–14, 123,
    134
    L'Assommoir 106
    La Bête humaine 127
    Au Bonheur des dames 19, 85
    Germinal 46
    La Conquête de Plassans 54
    Pot-Bouille 19, 46
    Thérèse Raquin 25